UNDERSTANDING THE
POLITICAL
WORLD

UNDERSTANDING THE POLITICAL WORLD

AN INTRODUCTION TO ▋POLITICAL SCIENCE▋

JAMES N. DANZIGER

University of California, Irvine

Longman
New York & London

Understanding the Political World:
An Introduction to Political Science

Longman, 95 Church Street, White Plains, N.Y. 10601

Associated companies:
Longman Group Ltd., London
Longman Cheshire Pty., Melbourne
Longman Paul Pty., Auckland
Copp Clark Pitman, Toronto

Photos: p. 3, © League of Women Voters; p. 12, Frost Publishing Group, Ltd.; p. 21 ©
Pamela Price, The Picture Cube; p. 25, © A. Tannenbaum, U.N.; p. 42 © UPI/
Bettmann Newsphotos; p. 50, © Wide World Photos; p. 63, © Rebecca Naden, The
Image Works; p. 74, © Wide World Photos; p. 81, © Joto du Monale, The Picture
Cube; p. 94, © UPI/Bettmann Newsphotos; pp. 104, 111, © Wide World Photos; p. 127,
© UPI/Bettmann Newsphotos; p. 141, © George Tooker, courtesy of The Metropolitan
Museum of Art; p. 149, © UPI/Bettmann Newsphotos; pp. 175, 187, © Wide World
Photos; pp. 192, 208, © UPI/Bettmann Newsphotos; p. 210, © Standard Oil Co.; p. 220,
General Motors; p. 230, © Wide World Photos; p. 235, © The Bettmann Archives; p.
251, © Carol T. Powers, the White House; p. 257, © U.N.; p. 274, the British Tourist
Authority; p. 293, © UPI/Bettmann Newsphotos; p. 302, © Don Rutledge, The Picture
Cube; p. 318, Reuters/Bettmann Newsphotos; p. 334, © Sawliven, U.N.; p. 354, ©
Wide World Photos; p. 373, © Reuters/Bettmann Newsphotos.

Senior editor: David J. Estrin
Production editor: Marie-Josée A. Schorp
Text design adaptation: Renée Kilbride Edelman
Cover design: Renée Kilbride Edelman
Text art: Art Directions
Photo research: Helena Frost Associates, Ltd.
Production supervisor: Kathleen M. Ryan

Library of Congress Cataloging-in-Publication Data

Danziger, James N.
    Understanding the political world: an introduction to political
science/James N. Danziger.
        p. cm.

    Includes bibliographical references.
    ISBN 0-582-29025-2
    1. Political science. I. Title.
JA66.D36   1991
320—dc20   90-35583
                                                CIP

ABCDEFGHIJ-DO-99 98 97 96 95 94 93 92 91 90

To Nicholas and Vanessa

Contents

PART THREE

Political Systems   79

PART FIVE

Preface

The aim of this book is revealed by its title: It is meant to help you understand the political world. It assumes that you are interested in politics. It does not assume that you have substantial knowledge about politics or political science or that you know the difference between politics and political science. I hope that when you complete the book (especially in conjunction with instruction about politics from a teacher), you will feel that you have increased your knowledge about the contemporary political world.

The study of politics is full of fascinating questions. First are the questions concerned with *what is:* Who exercises political power and for what purposes? Why do people accept political authority? How do value conflicts occur and how are they resolved? What causes individuals and groups to act politically? A second set of questions is concerned with *what ought to be:* Who should exercise political power and for what purposes? Why should people accept political authority? How should value conflicts be resolved? Why should individuals and groups act politically? There are very sharp disagreements about answers to both these descriptive (what is) and normative (what ought to be) questions. In addition, the study of politics provokes a third set of questions regarding what we can actually know about the political world. Here there are major disagreements about the appropriate methods for describing and understanding politics.

Although this book cannot resolve the underlying disputes, it offers you the basis for making sense out of politics at all three levels. As author, I make some basic assumptions: that you can think systematically about politics and make general statements about how politics works; that you will learn more about politics by considering the politics of many different places; that every observer of politics (certainly including you and me) has biases, only some of which can be understood; that you need a variety of sources of ideas and information before you can make informed and sensible decisions about the value disagreements that pervade politics; and that this book is one such source that can be helpful to you. My efforts will be successful to the extent that *you* ultimately judge my assumptions to be correct (especially the last one).

There are many sources of ideas and information that constitute the basis of *my* understanding about politics. Broadly, you should know that I was born in and have been educated primarily in the United States. I have studied and/or lived and/or spent significant periods in North America, Western Europe, Eastern Europe, Asia, and Africa. The people and events I experienced in these places have certainly influenced my perceptions about politics. I also want to acknowledge the impact of the teachers who introduced me to political science, especially Professor Emeritus Heinz Eulau. More direct contributions to this book have come from my colleagues in political science, upon whose research I have drawn extensively, and from the many students with whom I have interacted. Explicit guidance and advice regarding the writing of this book have come from several valuable sources: my thoughtful editors at Longman, Irv Rockwood and David Estrin, and my production editor, Marie-Josée Schorp; Stephen Douglas, Peggy DuBose, Marcus Ethridge, Bertil Hanson, Richard Moore, Joseph Pika, Daniel Sabia, Jr., John Wahlke, and David Weaver, who offered intelligent, critical reviews of the book; and friends and students who have provided specific material for the book, including Lesley Danziger, Frank Faye, Inger Feeley, Joakim Gustavsson, Matt Shugart, Darren Smith, and David Stein. I have relied on these many sources, at times extensively, and I am grateful for their help. Yet this book, and especially the roads not taken and the missteps remaining, are my responsibility.

If you find yourself growing frustrated with the treatment of politics at any point in this book, I would say: Reader, be merciful! The study of politics is incredibly complex. Gather bits of understanding where you can find them.

UNDERSTANDING THE
POLITICAL
WORLD

PART ONE

On Knowing the
Political World

CHAPTER 1

Politics and Knowledge

In a democracy, men are more likely to vote than women.
The United States is the most peaceful, least warlike nation in modern history.
Every revolution begins as a movement of liberation but ends as a tyranny.

Each of us encounters many statements about the political world every day. When you are confronted with such a statement, you might

Ignore it
Accept that it is correct
Reject it
Try to assess it more carefully

If you decide to assess it, you would probably ask questions like these: Are the facts accurate? Is it consistent with other things I know about politics? Are the explanations and/or conclusions persuasive? Does it influence any political actions I might take?

When you begin to ask these assessment questions, and especially when you try to answer them, you are doing political analysis. At its core, *political analysis* is the attempt to describe (i.e., to answer the *what* questions) and then to explain (to answer the *why* and *how* questions regarding) political phenomena. A major objective of this book is to enhance your ability to do such political analysis.

Suppose a group of people is instructed to give each of the three statements above a "truth score," ranging from 100 percent (absolutely true) to 0 percent (absolutely false). Do you think that anyone would give all three statements 100 percent? 0 percent? What truth score would *you* give these statements?

> *Stop for a moment. I encourage you to reflect on these questions for 20–30 seconds, rather than to rush ahead in order to complete your reading. Questions like these appear throughout this book. Your responses to these brief "reflections" should help you to clarify your own thinking on the subject being discussed. As novelist E. M. Forster said: "How do I know what I think until I see what I say?"*

So, what do you think? What truth scores do you give these three statements? Did you give every statement a score of either 100 percent or 0 percent? If not, what does this suggest about absolute truth in politics? Do you expect that most other people would report scores very close to your own? Why?

It is reasonable to assume that few people, if any, believe that all the things they hear about politics are absolutely accurate and true. One reason to be suspicious of such statements is that the basic subject being addressed is politics. Statements about politics usually reflect the values and interests of the source of the statement. Can you guess what type of person made each of the three statements to which you gave truth scores?

The first statement was made by political scientists Lester Milbrath and M. L. Goel (1977:116) in a book summarizing the research on political participation. The second was made by Ronald Reagan, president of the United States from 1981 to 1989, during his nomination acceptance speech to the Republican party in 1984. And the third was made by Italian novelist Ignazio Silone (1937). Does your knowledge of who made the statements alter your truth score in any case? Which one(s)? Why?

There are many sources of statements about politics—family, friends, television, books, newspapers, teachers, politicians. Such sources can provide information about politics; but information can be unclear, contradictory, or wrong. You are surrounded by competing claims regarding the political world. How are you to decide what you do know about politics?

Political science is one way of attempting to establish such knowledge. As you will discover in reading this book, *political science* is a body of techniques, concepts, and approaches whose objective is to increase the accuracy of our understandings about the political world. You will learn how some political scientists try to think clearly and systematically about political phenomena in order to describe "political reality" and explain how politics works. And you will be introduced to some of the findings about politics that have emerged from the work of political scientists and other social scientists.

ON POLITICS

Obviously, the subject matter of political science is politics. But it is not obvious how to define the limits of politics as a subject for study. In the United States, for example, more than 40 percent of the national wealth is controlled and distributed by various levels of government. Governments in the United States decide how to spend all this wealth—on items ranging from nuclear weapons to preschool education to loans to small farmers. In addition, these governments establish many rules that set limits on our behavior, from banning the use of certain words on television to regulating how people may invest their money to limiting a woman's right to have an abortion. Moreover, politics includes the procedures through which governments, groups, and individuals determine the nature of all these activities. All such actions and decisions by governments are part of politics. And in most countries, governments' activities are far more extensive than in the United States. Clearly, politics covers a vast terrain of human life.

Among the common definitions of *politics* are these:

Politics is the exercise of power.
Politics is the public allocation of things that are valued.
Politics is the resolution of conflict.
Politics is the competition among individuals and groups pursuing their interests.
Politics is the determination of who gets what, when and how.

This book treats all these as acceptable definitions. All reflect the central notion that politics is about power, interests, and values. There is also an implicit notion that politics is associated with those aspects of life that have public significance. In contrast, other aspects of life are private, and beyond the domain of politics. We shall see that the size and nature of the public and private areas vary greatly across different countries. But the area that is subject to politics is very large in all contemporary societies.

TYPES OF POLITICAL KNOWLEDGE

People differ greatly in their understandings about the nature of politics, the uses of political power, and the distribution of benefits. Their understandings are composed of three general types of political knowledge: (1) descriptions of political facts, (2) explanations of how and why politics occurs as it does, and (3) prescriptions of what should happen in the political world.

Description

Many bits of political knowledge focus on *what* questions, which require a descriptive response based on one or more "facts." In your study of politics, you will encounter relatively straightforward political facts such as these:

> The name of the chancellor of West Germany in 1990: Helmut Kohl
> The number of states in Nigeria: 19
> The tax rate paid by citizens to receive health care in Australia: 1.3 percent

But on many questions about the political world, knowledge is subject to dispute. On some questions, it is difficult to get precise information. Suppose you want to know the number of countries with operational nuclear weapons. Most experts agree that five countries have atomic bombs (the United States, the Soviet Union, Britain, France, and China). But there are about a dozen other countries (including India, Israel, Pakistan, and South Africa) that might have the materials and technology to produce nuclear weapons, but do not provide information about their nuclear capabilities. Thus there is disagreement, even among experts, regarding which countries belong to the "nuclear club." On some questions, description requires the assessment of complicated and controversial issues about political power, interests, and values. Thus it is difficult to reach agreement about the facts. Examples:

> Does every revolution end in a tyranny?
> Do nonwhites and whites in the United States enjoy equal treatment before the law?

BOX 1.1

Where in the World Is It?

The previous description briefly referred to twelve countries on five continents. Do you have a clear sense of where they are? Do you care?

There will be detailed discussions of many countries in this book. Knowing the location of a country and its geographic relation to certain other countries is sometimes extremely important to understand its political choices and actions. When such discussions occur, you are strongly encouraged to consider the country's location. This is why there are world maps on the inside covers of this book.

Several recent studies have shown that American students are more ignorant of world geography than students in most other countries. Help change that.

Explanation

Many questions about politics are even more difficult to answer, because they ask *why* something happens and require political knowledge in the form of explanation. For example, suppose you wanted to establish why the Iran-Iraq War (1980–1988) occurred. Here are some alternative explanations for this lengthy and deadly war:

> Historical ethnic animosity between Persian Iranians and Arabic Iraqis
> Religious conflict between Shi'ite Muslims (controlling Iran) and Sunni Muslims (controlling Iraq)
> Iraq's forceful demand that Iran return control of the entire Shatt-al-Arab waterway, in violation of both a 1975 treaty and international law
> A strategy by leaders in Iraq and Iran to divert their populations' attention from serious internal economic and political problems
> Political manipulation by leaders in other Arab states who feared that the late Ayatollah Khomeini's Islamic fundamentalism might spread to their states if not stopped in Iran

Why is one in eight families "poor" in the wealthy United States? What causes a country (e.g., Argentina, Israel) to have inflation of more than 1000 percent in a single year? Why does revolutionary violence overthrow the government in one country (e.g., Nicaragua) and not in another (e.g., El Salvador)? These are examples of the many questions about politics that require explanation, not mere descriptive facts. Such questions can be among the most fascinating in politics; but adequate explanation is often difficult because patterns of cause and effect can be extraordinarily complex.

Prescription

Statements about politics often include claims or assumptions that certain choices and actions are more desirable than others. These represent a third form of political knowledge, prescriptions regarding what *should* occur and what *should* be done. Prescription deals with *normative* political knowledge—answers to questions about what ought to be, not merely description and explanation of what is.

What should be the government's role in the provision of health care (e.g., doctors, hospitals, medication)? Some possible prescriptive responses:

> The government should take no action that interferes with the private provision of health care.
> The government should only regulate health care providers to prevent dangerous practices.
> The government should establish policies that encourage competition among many private health care providers.
> The government should provide free health care, but only for the very poor.
> The government should subsidize health care for all citizens based on their ability to pay.
> The government should provide free health care to all citizens, paid generally from tax revenues.

Which response is most appropriate? Your normative political knowledge is usually based on value judgments, which are informed by descriptive and explanatory knowledge. That is, it depends upon your understanding about certain facts (e.g., What is the level of health of different individuals in a particular society? What is the quality of health care provided to those individuals?), your knowledge about why certain outcomes occur (e.g., What causes unequal health and health care? What are the effects of a government subsidy for health care on cost, on quality of care, and on taxes?), and, most importantly, on certain value judgments (e.g., Is unequal health care bad? How much profit should doctors be allowed to make? Should government have a direct role in the health care system?).

SOURCES OF POLITICAL KNOWLEDGE

Each individual's political knowledge is a unique combination of descriptive facts, explanations, and prescriptions about politics. What are the sources of our political knowledge? This section describes three important sources that are widely used as a basis of knowledge about the political world: (1) authority, (2) personal thought, and (3) science.

The discussion below suggests that reliance on authority or on personal thought has a key shortcoming: Neither provides a clear method for resolving disagreements about what is true. Different people accept different sources of authority and different interpretations of what an authority means. And reasonable men and women can disagree on the knowledge that emerges from their own modes of personal thought.

Thus a third source of knowledge, the method of science, has emerged as an attempt to devise a better approach for establishing knowledge that can be agreed upon by many people. Political science applies the scientific method as a means to clarify our knowledge about the political world. Political science provides a language for talking about politics and it provides a set of methods for analyzing political phenomena. The discussion of alternative sources of political knowledge begins with a description of the method of authority.

Authority

The method of authority involves the appeal to any document, tradition, or person that is believed to possess the controlling explanation regarding a particular issue. Knowledge about politics can be based on three kinds of authority sources: (1) a specific authority, (2) a general authority, or (3) "everyone."

Specific Authority Sources.   A particular individual (but few others) might place great confidence in the knowledge about politics derived from a specific authority source—a parent, or a teacher, or a friend, or a famous person. Those who are young and those who are minimally interested in politics are especially likely to rely on specific authorities for much of their political knowledge. Chapters 2 and 3 will argue that specific authority sources can powerfully influence some important political beliefs of most individuals. Can you think of a significant piece of your political knowledge that is derived primarily from a parent, an influential teacher, or a public figure you admire?

General Authority Sources.   A general authority source is one that has substantial influence on a large proportion of people in a society. Examples include constitutions, revered leaders, widely respected media or books, and religious teachings. General authorities are especially evident as a basis for normative political knowledge (see Box 1.2 on the role of women in politics).

"Everyone" as Authority.   Sometimes we are convinced that something is true because it is a strongly held belief of many other people. If virtually every sensible person you know agrees on a fact about politics, there is little reason for you to disagree or challenge the fact. One reason to place confidence in strongly held beliefs of many people is the assumption that it is unlikely so many people will be incorrect. Such knowledge has stood the "test of time," since it could have been challenged and repudiated in the marketplace of ideas.

BOX 1.2

General Authorities and Normative Knowledge:
The Role of Women in Politics

General authorities are particularly powerful in providing *normative* knowledge. Normative claims indicate what *should* be, which may or may not be the same as what is. Example: What is the role of women in a political system? For many people, this is a normative question (i.e., it is about what the role of women *should* be) and they look to an authority source to provide the answer.

In the United States, the crucial source of authority for such questions is the Constitution. The U.S. Constitution does not mention women. For nearly 150 years, this was interpreted to mean that women should be excluded from any political role, even from voting. Finally, political pressure resulted in a formal change in the source of authority, with the Nineteenth Amendment in 1920, which added language to the Constitution granting women voting rights (and, implicitly, all political rights exercised by men).

In Iran, like the United States, the key source of authority on women's political rights is a document. In Iran, it is a religious document, the Koran, which proscribes women from active involvement in the political process. Under the political regime of Shah Reza Pahlavi (1941–1979), women were encouraged to participate fully in politics, despite the content of the Koran. But the fundamentalist regime of the Ayatollah Khomeini (1979–1989) restored the very limited political role of women specified in the Koran, although some Muslim women are active in political demonstrations.

In contemporary China, it has been the authoritative pronouncements of a person, Mao Zedong (who ruled from 1949 to 1976), that established the political rights of women. Prior to the revolution of 1949, the role of women in China was defined by the religious traditions of Confucianism. Most women were essentially the property of men, and they had few political rights. As part of Chairman Mao's efforts to fundamentally change Confucian tradition, he granted women full equality under the law and women were encouraged to participate actively in all aspects of political life.

There are fundamental problems with the method of authority as a way of knowing. This should be most obvious with specific authorities. You might think that your parent or best teacher or favorite celebrity has a clear grasp of important political issues. But few of the other 5 billion people in the world have any confidence in this source of your political knowledge.

And, although "everyone knows that X is true," there is no guarantee that everyone is correct. Even "Honest Abe" Lincoln acknowledged that you can fool all of the people some of the time. Indeed, a political belief that is widely held might be particularly immune to careful assessment. Experiments in psychology have revealed the extent to which an individual's beliefs can be altered by the beliefs of others. For example, if several respondents (collaborating with the experimenter) all give identical wrong answers, this can persuade the subject that what she knows is wrong, even when it is correct.

Moreover, "everyone" (i.e., the reference group to whom we look for information and knowledge) usually consists of a limited set of people whose judgments we trust and whose cultural background we share. In such cases, we exclude individuals who might disagree with what "everyone knows."

> "Political terrorism is bad"—Does everyone living under an oppressive political regime believe this?
> "The United States is a democracy"—Do most Albanians believe this?

It is common for citizens in most political systems to believe that the citizens of rival political systems have been brainwashed, and that they have beliefs *we* know are incorrect. Is it not likely that beliefs strongly held by most of us are equally suspect to them?

There are even problems with general authorities. Sometimes, as when listing the countries with nuclear weapons or explaining the Iran-Iraq War, even the most competent general authorities might not have access to crucial information or might disagree about how to interpret the facts. And sometimes, even when a people accepts a single authority, there can be ambiguities and problems of interpretation. Consider the normative issue of the political role of women:

> In the United States, all branches of the national government continually interpret and apply the rather limited framework outlined in the Constitution. The strong political agitation for an "equal rights"-amendment indicates that many people feel that the Constitution, even with the Nineteenth Amendment, still fails to ensure women of political rights equivalent to those enjoyed by men.
> In Iran, some people, especially middle-class women in urban areas, still support the increased women's rights granted by the shah between 1962 and 1979. While the ayatollah's authority, based on his interpretation of the Koran, has been generally effective in reducing the political role of women, some women still do demonstrate, and many vote. And in Pakistan, also governed by the same underlying authority (the Koran and Shari'a law), the current head of government is a woman, Benazir Bhutto.

In China, some people in rural areas never accepted the changes Mao introduced regarding women's roles in political and social life, preferring to retain the traditional Confucian patterns. The Chinese leadership since Mao's death has continued to support his view on the equality of women in politics. But the leadership has explicitly rejected Mao's views on many other subjects, especially on economic matters.

In short, it is common, and perhaps inevitable, for authority sources to offer inconsistent or conflicting knowledge claims about the political world. The overall problem with all appeals to authority as a source of knowledge is that it is extremely difficult to differentiate between alternative authority sources or even to establish widespread agreement on precisely what political knowledge a particular authority source provides.

Personal Thought

Have you ever insisted that some fact is correct because it seemed so "obvious" to you? It is possible to feel confident that you know something on the basis of your own personal thoughts, feelings, or experiences. This second source of knowledge does not rely upon outside authorities; rather, it assumes that the individual can use her own powers of thought to determine what she knows about the political world. Such knowledge can be based on rationality or intuition, grounded in personal experience.

Rationality.   An individual can rely on her own rational thought as a means for deciding that something is correct. Political knowledge can be established by the application of right reason or by the discovery of *a priori* truths. To a large extent, the reliance on rationality assumes that certain propositions are self-evident to all reasonable men and women. For example, the Preamble to the American Declaration of Independence claims that there are "self-evident" truths—that all men are created equal and that they have inalienable rights to life, liberty, and the pursuit of happiness.

Intuition.   A second form of personal thought is intuition. Here, one's knowledge is based on feeling, on a sense of understanding or empathy, rather than on reason. You have probably had experiences where you are convinced that something is correct because it *feels* right. For example, the key slogan of 1964 Republican presidential candidate Barry Goldwater was an explicit appeal to intuition: "In your heart, you know he's right!"

A major problem with personal thought as a source of knowledge is that there is no method to resolve differences of opinion among individuals. It is unlikely that others always agree with what you think is obvious. The problem with intuition should be apparent. There is no reason to assume that different people will share the same intuitive feelings regarding what is true. Goldwater's poor electoral showing (he received 39 percent of the vote) suggests that many people decided (intuitively?) that he was not right, or perhaps they decided (rationally?) that he was too far right, ideologically.

Even rational thought will not necessarily enable people to agree on political facts. Consider the key knowledge claim cited above: "We hold these truths to be self-evident, that all men are created equal." This seems a clear appeal to rationality, to a political fact that is self-evident to all thinking individuals. But what exactly does this claim mean? Do all men have equal physical or mental traits at birth? Do they grow up with equal opportunities? Are they equal before the law, regardless of the quality of legal help they can purchase? Are all women created equal, too? Many legal and political struggles in the United States during the two centuries since this "self-evident" truth was proclaimed have concerned

precisely what equal rights *are* assured in the American political system, with particular concern for issues of race, gender, and age.

The Method of Science

Science uses explicit methods which attempt to insure that different people can agree regarding what they know. The goal of any science is to describe and explain—to answer the questions *what, why,* and *how.* There are four essential characteristics of the scientific method:

1. Science entails a *search for regularities* in the relationships among phenomena.
2. Science is *empirical* in the sense that it is concerned with phenomena that can be observed, or at least measured.
3. Science is *cumulative,* because it tentatively accepts previously established knowledge on a subject as the foundation for further knowledge development. One can challenge existing knowledge, but does not have to reestablish the knowledge base every time.
4. The method of science is *testable.* Its practitioners, "scientists," specify the assumptions, data, analytic techniques, and inference patterns that support their knowledge claims. Other scientists can evaluate all aspects of the claim and can repeat the analysis to insure that everyone reaches the same conclusion.

Most political scientists attempt to use the scientific method to establish shared knowledge about the political world. The following section provides a brief example of how this method might be applied to one of the knowledge claims at the beginning of the chapter: that in a democracy, men are more likely to vote than women.

Gender and Voting: Applying the Scientific Method to Politics. Is it true that men are more likely to vote than women in a democracy? Let us briefly consider how you might analyze this claim by means of the scientific method (see Box 1.3.):

BOX 1.3

Using the Appendix

Our analysis of gender and voting is typical of one form of political analysis employed by political scientists. As you read through it, ask yourself whether you think this is a functional or relational analysis, whether you understand how to interpret Table 1.1, and whether you know the kinds of data that would strengthen the analysis (see p. 381). If you understand these terms and feel confident in answering such questions, you have a strong analytic basis for discussions later in the book. If you feel that you could use a bit more background on such issues, you should read the appendix before you continue. There you will find explanations of the four major analytic approaches in political analysis, the types of empirical data that are employed, and the means of reaching conclusions using such data. Even those readers with some analytic background will find the appendix helpful as a review and as a means of checking their understanding.

1. As you begin to undertake your own analysis, you would want to *examine the existing evidence. Here:* It would be sensible to look in books and journals for relevant research on voting by political scientists or other social scientists (e.g., *Political Behavior of the American Electorate,* by Flanigan and Zingale [1983]; *The Politics of the Gender Gap,* edited by Carol Mueller [1986]).

2. With the background of existing research, you would attempt to *state the issue* you are examining in a precise manner. *Here:* The knowledge claim is already stated in the form of a hypothesis (i.e., a proposition about a political fact): In a democracy, men are more likely to vote than women.

3. Next, it is necessary to *"operationalize" key concepts.* This means that you would specify exactly what each concept means and how it might be measured. Defining political concepts like *democracy* can be extremely difficult (as you will see in Chapter 6). *Here:* Let us tentatively propose that a political democracy is "a state with periodic elections in which most adult citizens are allowed to vote in order to select among genuine alternative candidates for public office." And the probability of voting is operationalized as "the percentage of those eligible to vote who actually do vote on a major political office."

4. Next, you would develop a strategy to *gather appropriate data.* Your evidence should be *valid* (i.e., it should measure what it is supposed to measure) and *reliable* (i.e., it should be accurate). You would also need to decide what specific cases you are going to analyze. In this example, you would choose one or more democracies and certain specific elections for which you are going to gather data. You might gather the relevant data from books or reports, or you might need to go out "into the field" to measure phenomena yourself. *Here:* Let's select the United States as our democracy, the presidential election as our vote on a major political office, and 1976 and 1988 as the elections for which we actually gather data. Do you think these are reasonable choices with which to assess the question? The appropriate data are displayed in Table 1.1.

5. Then you would *analyze the evidence* in order to determine the extent to which the data seem to support the knowledge claim. *Here:* According to the 1976 data in Table 1.1, men do vote at a significantly higher rate than women do (77 percent versus 67 percent).

6. Now you need to *decide what, if any, inferences can be made about the issue* on the basis of your evidence. *Here:* This is where your analytic skills must be especially rich. You must consider whether your evidence is sufficient and whether you have analyzed the evidence correctly.
Is this evidence sufficient? Can you have confidence in a generalization about gender and voting based on only one election? This is a serious problem. To deal with this concern, you need to return to step 4 and gather data for more elections. As an indication of how serious the problem might be, consider the data in Table

TABLE 1.1. Participation of Eligible Voters in the U.S. Presidential Election, by Gender

	1976		1988	
	Men	**Women**	**Men**	**Women**
Voted	77%	67%	56%	58%
Did not vote	23%	33%	44%	42%

1.1 for the 1988 presidential election. The turnout rate for men and women is very similar in the 1988 election, and women actually had a slightly higher turnout rate than men.

This should undermine your confidence in a generalization based only on the 1976 data. It is clear that you need to gather data from a number of elections. If you did, you would find that men voted at a higher rate in U.S. presidential elections from the year women gained voting rights until 1976; but in 1980, 1984, and 1988, women have voted at a higher rate than men. One of the reasons why politics is fascinating is that things do change (sometimes, quite rapidly); but this makes generalizations more difficult and requires the analyst to pay more attention to *longitudinal* patterns (that is, patterns over time). Moreover, if you wanted to establish a really broad generalization about gender and voting, you would need voting data from several democracies, not just the United States.

Have you analyzed the evidence correctly? If you find that there is no clear pattern between gender and voting in recent U.S. presidential elections, you might decide to change your research question somewhat. For example, you might attempt to identify the factors that seem to affect voting rates among men and women. Many other explanatory factors might seem relevant: Age, ethnicity, education, party identification, attitudes on key policy issues, and so on. By analyzing the relationships among various factors, you might gain a clearer understanding about the importance of gender in explaining varying rates of turnout. As an example of the kinds of subtle relationships that exist among different explanatory factors, the appendix reconsiders the 1976 data. The analysis reveals that the apparent relation between gender and voting in the 1976 data is virtually eliminated when the voter's education level is considered.

7. Ideally, the final stage of your analysis is to *offer a tentative conclusion* regarding the issue. Defensible conclusions in analyses of politics often require extensive data, thorough analysis, and consideration of several alternative explanations. Sometimes the phenomena are so complicated or the evidence is so mixed that no generalization is possible. *Here:* the data seem too contradictory to support any clear generalization about gender and voting. Rather, more data and more thoughtful analysis are required. If anything, this brief analysis seems to support the conclusion that, in recent U.S. elections at least, men are not more likely to vote than women.

In this example of political analysis, as in any scientific study, your conclusion, as well as your concepts, data, and methods, are subject to scrutiny and challenge by others. Your conclusion is presumed to be correct until there is compelling criticism and/or contrary evidence that undermines it. Because many knowledge claims about politics concern complex phenomena, it is often difficult to establish with precision what we do know, even when the scientific method is used. At least, the scientific method helps people to identify more clearly the issues on which they agree or disagree regarding political facts. More broadly, it can enable us to identify regularities and ultimately to develop generalizations about politics.

POLITICAL "SCIENCE"?

Critiques of Political "Science"

Not everyone agrees that it is appropriate and desirable to apply the scientific method to politics. Indeed, as we shall see below, four different kinds of criticisms have been aimed at political science.

It Lacks a Paradigm.   The first criticism argues that political science is not "scientific," in comparison to "real" sciences. Stimulated especially by Thomas Kuhn's (1970) book *The Structure of Scientific Revolutions*, there has been much discussion during the last 20 years regarding whether fields like political science have a paradigm. A *paradigm* is a framework that gives organization and direction to a given area of scientific investigation. A paradigmatic science has four key elements:

1. *Concepts* provide an answer to the *what* question, Of what is reality composed? A concept—the name given to some phenomena—can be quite specific, like "Iran-Iraq War"; but concepts usually designate more general categories, like "war."
2. A *theory* is a set of systematically related generalizations. A theory answers *why* and *how* questions, providing explanations and predictions about the linkages between certain concepts, given specified conditions. The most general form of a theory states: If A, then B (under conditions C, D . . .). For example: If a male, then there is a certain probability of voting (under particular conditions of occupation, age, political democracy . . .).
3. *Rules of interpretation* indicate the kinds of observations and procedures that will establish whether the explanations and predictions posited by the theory are right or wrong. These "how to" rules (i.e., how to operationalize and measure concepts, how to analyze and interpret data) describe the scientific method.
4. The *identification of puzzles* indicates the issues or questions that are worth solving (and that can be solved) by those who work within that paradigm.

Judged by Kuhn's standards for a paradigm, social science disciplines (e.g., political science, sociology, economics, and anthropology) are usually classified as *pre-paradigmatic*. This is because researchers in a discipline like political science have not agreed upon a single set of concepts, theories, and rules of interpretation. Rather, researchers use different approaches, which compete to become *the* dominant paradigm. Supposedly, the natural sciences (e.g., physics, chemistry) and the applied sciences (e.g., engineering) have more fully achieved the characteristics of a paradigm.

As you will discover throughout this book, political science *is* pre-paradigmatic. There are many different methods used in political science; there is disagreement on the puzzles and problems that ought to be solved; there is little consensus on what theories or generalizations have been proven; and there is even great difficulty in operationalizing key concepts, like power or democracy.

Its Subject Matter Defies Generalization.   A second criticism is the assertion that it is impossible to develop a science of politics because of the subject matter. In this view, the political world is far too complex and unpredictable for systematic generalizations. Politics is based on the actions and interactions of many individuals, groups, and even countries. Politics occurs in the midst of many changing conditions that can influence those actions. The range of variation in what people might do and in what conditions exist is so vast that clear "if A, then B" statements about politics are impossible. Thus it is not surprising that political analysts cannot precisely explain the causes of war, or why women vote differently than men, or what effect laws banning private handguns will have on crime rates.

Its "Scientists" Cannot Be Objective.   A third criticism is that the analysis of politics cannot be objective in the way assumed by the scientific method. The issues chosen for study and the manner in which variables are defined, measured, and analyzed are all powerfully influenced by the analyst's social reality (i.e., by her culture, ideas, life experiences, etc.). In this view, no one (whether Sunni Muslim or agnostic, rural Nigerian or cosmopolitan Parisian, international lawyer or migrant farmworker) can be totally objective and unbiased in the way she tries to analyze political phenomena (e.g., the causes of the Iran-Iraq War; the relationship between revolution and tyranny).

Its Practice Diverts Attention from Normative Questions.   A fourth criticism faults the scientific method itself, because the method of science diverts attention from the crucial normative questions of politics. Since the time of Aristotle (384–322 B.C.), classical political theorists have insisted that the ultimate aim of political analysis is to discover "the highest good attainable by action." In this view, political analysis is a noble endeavor because it helps determine what government should do in order that valued goals (e.g., social order, a good life, a just society) can be achieved.

In contrast, many of those who use the methods of contemporary political science do not assume that these methods can identify universal principles of political good or can answer normative questions. For example, the influential German social scientist Max Weber (1864–1920) argued that the scientific method is useful for describing and categorizing political and social reality. But, Weber claimed, the scientific method cannot provide answers to fundamental normative questions about what social goals and ends should be valued and about what means are appropriate to achieve those goals. Weber (1958a:152–153) approvingly quoted Russian novelist Leo Tolstoi's assertion that science can provide no answer to the essential question, ''What shall we do, and how shall we arrange our lives?'' Therefore, argues this fourth group of critics, political science becomes an arid enterprise if the scientific method discourages attempts to address essential questions about political values and political good (Strauss 1959; Wolin 1960).

Political Science as a Means of Understanding the Political World

These four sets of criticisms of a science of politics are important and you should assess them throughout this book. In general, this book will make the case that, despite the complexity of politics, generalizations are possible—each political phenomenon is not *sui generis,* a unique thing. If political ''science'' means the attempt to apply the scientific method in order to better understand the political world, it is desirable to attempt such systematic and analytic thinking. And if we are to share *any* knowledge about the political world, we need methods to reach some interpersonal agreement about political facts. Although political science does not fulfill the requirements of a paradigm, it does enable us to develop better concepts, improved methods, and sound generalizations. This makes the study of the political world an exciting intellectual challenge.

In addition, this book assumes that understanding politics is extremely important. As Austrian philosopher Karl Popper (1963:227) suggests, ''we must not expect too much from reason; argument rarely settles a [political] question, although it is the only means for learning—not to see clearly, but to see more clearly than before.'' In the face of fundamental value conflicts and the potential for massive political violence between individuals, groups, and nations, political knowledge might reduce our misunderstandings and misconceptions. Thus it can be the grounds for greater tolerance and wiser value judgments about political good. And enhancing *what* we know about politics should make us more effective in knowing *how* to behave politically—as voters, political activists, and political decision makers. This makes the study of the political world of crucial importance to the creation of humane social life.

Ultimately it is up to you, as you read this book, to decide what can be known about politics and whether you think that political ''science'' is feasible.

PART TWO

Political Behavior

CHAPTER 2

Political Behavior: Beliefs and Actions

It is 5:15 in the morning. Unable to sleep, you take a quiet walk in a local park. As you pass some trees, you are surprised to see someone else. A young woman is sitting by herself, burning a red, white, and blue piece of cloth with a familiar pattern of stars and stripes. What would you do in this situation?

Assuming that you are an American, many reactions are possible. You are likely to recognize that the cloth is an American flag. You might feel anxiety, confusion, curiosity, or even anger. You might turn away abruptly and walk on as if you had noticed nothing, you might cast a disapproving look as you walk by, or you might stop and ask the person what she is doing. Your conversation might lead to a thoughtful political discussion, an angry confrontation, or even violence. You might feel sympathy with her action and offer verbal or actual support. Or you might decide to report the incident to law enforcement authorities.

Your responses to this incident offer interesting evidence about your reactions to the political world. Some of your responses might involve beliefs and others might involve actions. This combination of your political beliefs and actions is the essence of the domain of political science called *political behavior* or *micropolitics*. It is called *micro*politics because the key object of study is the smallest political unit—the individual as a thinker and actor in the political world. Micropolitics can also include study of the political beliefs and actions of small groups, such as families, committees, and juries.

Part 2 of this book explores themes in the study of micropolitics. This chapter focuses on political behavior at the individual level. Initially, it examines political beliefs, developing a taxonomy of an individual's orientations to the political world. It then describes the configuration of orientations held by a given individual, a cluster called a *political belief system*. Similarly, examination of political actions begins with a classification of types of such behavior. Finally, it describes attempts to characterize the dominant patterns of political behavior of an entire society—its *political culture*. Chapter 3 will offer alternative explanations for the particular political beliefs and actions of individuals. Chapter 4 will analyze the behavior of those individuals who are extremely active in politics.

POLITICAL BELIEFS

Some of your reactions to the incident described above might involve your *knowledge* about the political world: for example, what the piece of colored cloth is and the legality of burning it. Other reactions might involve your *feelings:* for example, embarrassment or indifference. And some reactions might engage your powers of *assessment:* for example, an attempt to determine the reasons for the action you have observed. These different reactions typify the three types of orientations that constitute our political beliefs. The following paragraphs describe these cognitive, affective, and evaluative orientations.

A person's *cognitive orientations* include what he believes are political "facts." Such facts might be correct and accurate or they might be totally wrong. (Recall our discussion of "truth scores" in Chapter 1.) A person might know many things about the politics of his own locality, region, and nation, and some things about the broader political world. This knowledge might include such facts as the names of political leaders; the policies supported by particular politicians, political groups, or nations; events in political history; the features of constitutions; or the procedures and actions of a governmental agency.

Affective orientations include any feelings or emotions evoked in a person by political phenomena. For example, what (if any) feelings are stimulated in you when

You see your national flag?

You hear statements critical of your nation's political system?

You learn of "aggressive" actions by your nation's political opponents?

You are faced with the option of voting in an election?

You are present at a political demonstration supporting a policy of which you disapprove?

The nature and intensity of your feelings in these kinds of situations are instances of your affective orientations.

Finally, an *evaluative orientation* involves your synthesis of facts and feelings into a judgment about some political phenomena. If you become aware that your government has proposed a policy that restricts the right of a woman to have an abortion, many different thoughts might be stimulated—your knowledge about the constitutional rights of an individual to freedom of action and of the state to limit those rights; your religious, moral, or scientific beliefs about the status of a fetus; your personal knowledge of the experiences of people who have been involved in decisions about abortions; your gut-level responses to spokespersons for and against the proposed policy. In short, your judgment about a political issue, such as the state's policy on abortion, can be grounded in many different kinds of cognitive and affective orientations that are combined into an evaluation. Ultimately, many of the political attitudes that you would identify as your "fundamental beliefs" are likely to be evaluative orientations.

There are several stages in building our conceptual understanding of political beliefs. If we want to understand one individual's political orientations, we might begin by identifying one or a few specific beliefs held by that person. Does the person know the name of the nation's chief executive? How does the person feel when he hears that his state's governor has vetoed a bill to increase expenditure on health care for poor people? What is the person's opinion on a proposal to reduce the number of nuclear weapons stockpiled by his nation? (Some political analysts distinguish between opinions, attitudes, and beliefs, with each successive category being a more stable, general, and deeply held orientation. In this discussion, this distinction will not be made, although the emphasis is on orientations that are general and relatively stable.)

A similar analytic strategy enables us to report what many individuals think about a specific issue. When the attitudes of many people are aggregated and summarized, they are reported as the most commonly available data about peoples' political orientations, "public opinion polls." For example, do West German adults oppose the placement of NATO (North Atlantic Treaty Organization) nuclear missiles within their borders? Virtually every day, the media and other sources provide data on the percentage of citizens who hold a certain opinion about such political issues (at least in nations where the state allows its citizens to express "public opinions"—until recently we have known far more about what West Germans think than about what East Germans think).

BELIEF SYSTEMS

Beyond the identification of specific beliefs of individuals, other interesting analyses can focus on the array of political beliefs held by an individual. The concept of *belief system* is often used to refer to the configuration of an individual's political orientations across political issues. A related concept used by political psychologists is an individual's *opinion schema*. This is a network of cognitive, affective, and evaluative orientations that serves as a basic framework that guides a person as he processes political information in order to establish an opinion on a particular subject (Hastie 1986).

To examine any component of an individual's belief system, a series of questions can be asked:

1. What is the *content* of the belief(s)—the subject and the nature of the belief(s)?
2. What is the *salience* of the belief(s)—the importance or significance attached to the belief(s) by the individual?
3. What is the level of *complexity* of the belief(s)?
4. What is the *consistency* of the belief(s) with other belief(s) held by the individual?
5. Do(es) the belief(s) *motivate* the individual to undertake any political action?

There has been some empirical research on the nature of belief systems, with a particular emphasis on the belief systems of the political elite or the "mass public"—that is, of ordinary people in the society. The most intensive, analytical research has focussed on belief systems in the United States, and this work has been particularly influenced by the analyses of Phillip Converse (1964). In general, Converse argues that a belief system has two levels of information. One level includes relatively simple and straightforward facts or ideas, such as the notion that there is racial segregation in South Africa. The second level is "constraint knowledge," in which there is a more complex understanding of the dynamics that link ideas, such as the notion that the nuclear arms race increases the instabil-

A beach in South Africa. Only white persons are allowed on that beach.

ity of the international political system. In this example, the constraint knowledge includes some conception of why or how political phenomena affect each other.

Belief Systems among Mass Publics

On the basis of his own empirical analyses of (American) individuals' belief systems, Converse (1964) concludes that there are important and predictable differences between the elite and the mass public in the nature and structure of their belief systems. As you might expect, the belief systems of individuals in the mass public are more simple and narrow and they include far less constraint knowledge than those of members of the elite. Within the mass public, Converse distinguishes five gradations in the level of conceptualization in people's belief system. Only about 15 percent of the mass public have substantial constraint knowledge in their belief system. And almost half of the U.S. public is characterized by the two lowest gradations—extremely simplistic political beliefs or "political ignorance."

While there has been continuing debate regarding the precise nature of political belief systems among mass publics (Nie and Anderson 1974; Bishop et al. 1978; Rosenberg 1988), most researchers agree on certain generalizations about the citizens of Western democracies (e.g., the United States, Canada, the Western European and Scandinavian countries). Like nearly every generalization about politics, the six generalizations below are broadly accurate for "most people," but are subject to many qualifications and some exceptions.

1. Political issues have low salience in relation to other concerns in people's lives. Although Aristotle termed the citizen *homo politicus,* or "political man," most people do not locate political issues in the center of their interest and attention space.
2. People tend to focus attention on concrete issues rather than more abstract concerns.
3. Interest and knowledge are greater on immediate, short-range issues than on longer-term ones.
4. While there is relative stability in people's fundamental beliefs, there can be considerable volatility in their short-term political opinions, which tend to shift when subjected to modest changes in political information. This volatility might be due to limited interest or due to the sheer difficulty of trying to understand complicated political questions.
5. There can be significant inconsistencies across political beliefs, in the sense that people can hold contradictory positions. (For example, an American might express support for the First Amendment right to free speech, but deny the right of a Communist to speak at a public meeting or the right of the Ku Klux Klan to hold a public rally.)
6. The content of beliefs is often inaccurate. (In a recent survey, for example, half the Americans did not know how many U.S. senators serve their state and less than one in six knew who William Rehnquist is. You, of course, know the correct answers . . . don't you?)

Recently, the basic approach and findings of Converse and others have been subjected to an interesting critique (Rosenberg 1988). The critique argues that we should first study and understand *how* people think, not merely ask questions about their specific beliefs and then look for a pattern in their responses. In this view, each individual develops one of several different structured ways of thinking about the world. This structure evolves from a developmental learning process and is influenced by the person's social experiences. If the analyst can identify an individual's structure of thinking, then the person's political attitudes will be generally consistent and coherent within this structure. This is an intriguing alternative way to analyze the political beliefs of the mass public that could change our unflattering picture of most people's belief systems, but there is not as yet much empirical support for it.

Belief Systems among Elites

The belief systems held by members of the political elite are particularly important, because the members of the elite are presumed to have a major role in politics. The kinds of beliefs held by some political leaders is a central theme in Chapter 4. But it might be instructive at this point to provide one example of an analysis of belief systems among a political elite, by James Rosenau and Ole Holsti.

Rosenau and Holsti (1986) characterize three alternative belief systems that, at the time of their study, were held by different members of the elite in the United States responsible for formulating foreign policy (e.g., the president, the secretary of state, the national security advisor, key members of the congressional committees on foreign relations, the Joint Chiefs of Staff):

1. According to the *cold war internationalist* belief system, the international system is bipolar and dominated by the deep conflict between the Soviet bloc (the Soviet Union and its allies in Eastern Europe) and the Western bloc (the United States and its allies, primarily in Western Europe). The primary war danger comes from military inferiority, and Western bloc foreign policy must emphasize military strength to combat Soviet bloc expansionism. The economically less developed countries (mainly in Africa, Asia, Central and South America) are a key target of Soviet aggression and subversion and should be provided with security assistance.

2. From the *post–cold war internationalist* perspective, the international system is complex and interdependent. Although there are some conflicts of interest between the Western bloc and the Soviet bloc, the most dangerous problems emerge from the huge inequalities between these relatively wealthy states and the many poor states among the less developed countries. The primary danger of war is the irrational arms race and overly hostile relations between the Soviet bloc and the Western bloc, who might misperceive each other's actions and slide into an unwanted war. Western bloc foreign policy should emphasize stable and noncombative relations with the Soviet bloc and greater sensitivity to defusing conflicts in the less developed countries.

3. The *"semi-isolationist"* view is that the international system is multipolar and complex. There are few, if any, genuine conflicts between the Soviet bloc and the Western bloc. The overexpansion of military capability is both dangerous and a misuse of vital national resources. The most serious problems in Western bloc states are domestic problems, such as inflation, unemployment, and crime, which threaten the pursuit of prosperity and stability. The primary danger of war is from U.S. and Soviet meddling in volatile less developed countries. Thus it is essential for Western bloc states to stabilize relations with the Soviet bloc, limit military expenditure, and reduce commitments in the less developed countries, in order to free energy and resources to deal with domestic issues.

These three characterizations of foreign policy are ideal types. An *ideal type* is a pure form of a concept, idealized to reveal the concept's essential features. While some individuals might adhere rather closely to one of these perspectives, the views of states, and the foreign policy actions that the states take, are based on complex combinations of these views. Each belief system is based on different assumptions about the nature of the international political environment, the source of the major threats to national security, and the most appropriate kinds of policy responses. One interesting empirical question is whether most or all individual members of the foreign policy elite have beliefs that fit clearly into one of the three belief systems. A second question is whether individuals can change from one belief system to another over time. Third, do most key decision makers share the same belief system? Fourth, if the foreign policy elite is dominated by a group that agrees on one of these belief systems, can the actual foreign policies of the state be predicted according to this framework? Little empirical work has yet been done to answer these kinds of questions raised by Rosenau and Holsti's characterization or by other scholars' hypotheses about the nature of belief systems among political elites in different countries.

POLITICAL CULTURE

Some analysts attempt to identify broadly shared patterns of political orientations that characterize a large group of individuals. The objective is to develop generalizations about the political culture of the group. *Political culture* is normally defined as the configuration of a particular people's political orientations—that is, as the belief system of many individuals. For this reason, it is not precisely a topic in micropolitics; but political culture is examined here because it is embedded in individual-level analyses. (Although some research on political culture includes not only beliefs but also patterns of political action, this discussion will emphasize political beliefs.)

It has been most common to study the political cultures of nation-states or of a major (ethnic or religious) community within a nation-state. The composition of the group that is studied depends on the interests of the researcher. It might be the people of a geographic community (e.g., Londoners, English, British, Europeans) or of a community of shared identity (e.g., Sikhs in the Indian state of Punjab, Sikhs in the Indian subcontinent, all Sikhs in the world) or of a community of shared meaning (e.g., French Canadians, all French-speaking peoples).

National Character Studies

A traditional approach that attempts to capture the essence of a people's political culture is "national character" studies. When the Beach Boys wish all the ladies could be "California girls," this is meant to conjure up the image of a tanned, athletic, easy-going young woman who is not too cerebral. And when someone is described as being "so French," you might think of him as being urbane, romantic, and volatile.

At one level, we recognize immediately that such characterizations are stereotypes that do not fit the majority of individual subjects. Yet most of us, including people in the political world, use these kinds of labels (at least occasionally) as a shorthand method of describing groups or nations. Indeed, Franklin Delano Roosevelt (U.S. president from 1933 to 1945) revealed some belief in the notion when he observed that "the all-important factor in national greatness is national character."

Some political analysts have tried to specify the national character of certain countries and then to predict or explain their political behavior on the basis of such characteristics. Typically, these studies have not claimed that everyone fits the national character profile, but that it is accurate for the politically relevant strata. Thus the top ruling group in Britain has been defined in terms of English national character—control of emotions, a sense of propriety, a belief in class and national superiority, and reliance on "old boy" connections. This national character has supposedly been nurtured by a shared upper/upper-middle class background and training at a public school (in Britain, this actually means an elite private school) followed by Oxford or Cambridge. While there are exceptions to this background (Prime Minister Margaret Thatcher is a notable exception in terms of class and early education, as well as gender), these features do still characterize the orientations and behavior of the great majority of the British political elite in Parliament and in the higher civil service. (Interestingly, the description of the English national character fits Margaret Thatcher quite well, despite her differences in background.)

In another study, Michael Maccoby (1967) describes the 15–25 percent of Mexican males who he terms "macho" or "supermacho" types. These men are described as aggressive and authoritarian, with a desire to dominate and a veneration of the very powerful. According to Maccoby, this characteristic type among Mexican males is composed of ready recruits for any violent, fascist political movement. While some colorful and entertaining national character studies have been done, they are now generally dismissed as caricatures with little capacity to account for the complex actual political behaviors associated with a nation-state.

Survey Research

There is, however, a more systematic and scientifically acceptable method for establishing the nature of a political culture—the use of survey research. This involves taking a carefully selected sample of the population and then asking each person a series of questions that aim to tap individual political beliefs and actions. The researcher then aggregates the individuals' responses, searching for patterns or configurations that profile the political culture of the sample and, by inference, that characterize the political culture of the population from which the sample is taken.

The most famous study of this type is the first major one, *The Civic Culture*, by Gabriel Almond and Sidney Verba (1963). Lengthy interviews were conducted with a large sample of citizens in each of five countries. The data were then aggregated and analyzed in a diversity of ways to provide rich descriptions of each country's political culture. Numerous comparisons between the five political cultures were also presented. Because *The Civic Culture* is a landmark in survey research on political culture, revealing both virtues and shortcomings in such analyses, it is detailed in Box 2.1.

BOX 2.1

Using Survey Research to Characterize
Political Culture: *The Civic Culture*

Political scientists Gabriel Almond and Sidney Verba (1963) selected five countries for the first large-scale, comparative study of political culture using survey research techniques. The countries studied were Italy, Mexico, the United Kingdom, the United States, and West Germany. There is no important theory-based reason why these countries rather than others were selected. In each nation, a sample of about 1,000 respondents was interviewed regarding many aspects of their individual political beliefs and actions. Some sample questions were

If you explained your point of view to the officials (bureaucrats), what effect do you think it would have? Would they give your point of view serious consideration, would they pay only a little attention, or would they ignore what you had to say?

Can you identify the national leaders of the principal parties (in your country)?

Suppose a regulation were being considered by your local government that you considered very unjust or harmful. What do you think you could do?

Do you ever get angry at some of the things that go on during election campaigns?

How would you feel if your son or daughter married a supporter of the (opposition) political party? Would you be pleased, would you be displeased, or would it make no difference?

How often do you talk about public affairs to other people?

Thinking about the national government, about how much effect do you think its activities, the laws passed, and so on, have on your day-to-day life?

Almond and Verba postulated a taxonomy of three "ideal-type" political cultures, as represented in Table 2.1. Each successive ideal-type political culture involves more extensive involvement between individuals and the political order. In fact, only one of the five countries in *The Civic Culture* was actually classified explicitly as one of the three ideal types—the United States was termed a "participant" political culture. Italy was "alienated," Mexico was "alienated but aspiring," Germany had "political detachment and subject competence," and the United Kingdom was a "deferential civic culture."

The methodology of the *The Civic Culture* research has been subjected to impor-

TABLE 2.1. Ideal-Type Political Cultures

	Orientations toward			
Political Culture Type	Political System	Political Outputs	Political Inputs	Self as Political Participant
Parochial	0	0	0	0
Subject	+	+	0	0
Participant	+	+	+	+

NOTE: 0 means little or no explicit orientation; + means positive orientation.
SOURCE: Adapted from Almond and Verba 1963.

BOX 2.1 *continued*

tant criticisms. For example, in Mexico only urban citizens were interviewed, a clearly inadequate basis for generalizing about the Mexican political culture. The findings are very time-specific, with many responses quite contingent upon the nation's political context at that moment. In more recent research, political analysts have particularly challenged whether the observations are still valid, given political evolution in these countries (see, e.g., articles by Conradt, Abramowitz, and Cornelius and Craig, in Almond and Verba 1980). In addition, some major inferences seem problematical. For instance, a major reason why Italy was classified as an alienated political culture was that citizens, when asked what things in Italy gave them great pride, talked about art and culture rather than the political system. In itself, relatively greater pride in culture does not reveal alienation from the political order.

Perhaps the most serious fault with *The Civic Culture* was the ideological biases revealed by Almond and Verba in their celebration of the British political culture. They found desirable its combination of positive citizen attitudes toward the outputs they received from the political system and limited desire to be highly active as participants in political processes. Almond and Verba revealed their uneasiness with the highly participant political culture they found in the United States, because they were uncertain whether a democratic political system has the capacity to handle very high levels of participation and demands from its citizenry. We shall explore this point again when we examine the analytic notion of demands and supports for the political system in Chapter 5. Carole Pateman (1980) has argued persuasively that Almond and Verba's entire conception of democratic participation is quite limited and it emphasizes passive rather than active citizen involvement in government.

In a major reconsideration of the study in 1980, Verba (1980) acknowledges some of these problems. He particularly notes the dependence of attitudes on immediate political events, and the existence of quite varied subcultures within a nation, based on class, ethnicity, region, or generation. Despite its shortcomings, *The Civic Culture* is a path-breaking attempt to undertake a systematic, empirical, and comparative study of political cultures and it has influenced virtually all the subsequent work on this subject.

The bulk of survey research on political culture has attempted to improve upon our understanding of the political orientations of citizens in "democratic" societies. One major study found widespread similiarities in the social and political concerns among citizens across nation-states. Personal desires for a happy family life, a decent standard of living, and good health were most important, and political concerns centered in fears about war and political instability (Cantril, 1965). In research on Western societies, Ron Inglehart (1977, 1989; see also Dalton 1988) suggests that the central sociopolitical values held by citizens have recently changed for many, especially the younger generations. Inglehart concludes that the older adults emphasize "materialist" values for strong defense, order maintenance, and economic growth. In contrast, many young adults stress "postmaterialist" values for a more aesthetically satisfying environment, for freedom of expression, and for more personal power in social and political life. One study found that the proportion of citizens with postmaterialist values in the United Kingdom, United States, and West Germany has nearly doubled between 1970 and 1984, and was between 16 and 20 percent of the population in each country (Dalton 1988:84–85).

The extensive empirical research on political culture, as it has become more precise in its methods and more cautious about cultural biases, has revealed the considerable variability within political cultures across individuals, between groups, and over time. Chapter 4 will examine some of the factors that might account for differences in the political beliefs of individuals within a society. But it is also evident from the survey research that many societies do have a political culture—a general configuration of political beliefs that distinguishes them from certain other societies.

INDIVIDUAL POLITICAL ACTIONS

We have been considering the nature of people's political beliefs. Ultimately, the more important issues regarding the individual in politics are concerned with what people *do* politically, not merely what they think. In the flag-burning incident, for example, the most relevant question from the perspective of the political world is, What did you *do* when you saw the woman? In this section, we examine the prominent modes of actual political behavior of individuals.

Broadly, *political participation* is the term that can be applied to all of the political actions by individuals. The explicit objective of most political participation is to influence the actions and/or selection of political rulers (Nelson 1987:104). What is the range of behaviors that a person might undertake in the political world? At one extreme, there are people who are obsessed with politics, see political implications in most of life's actions, are constantly involved in political discussion and action, and want to make political decisions for others. At the other extreme, there are people who have absolutely no interest in politics, pay no attention to political phenomena, and engage in no politically relevant actions. (Notice that in some instances, such as not voting in an election, not doing anything politically can also be classified as a type of political participation.) Between these extremes, a particular person might engage in many modes of political behavior, such as voting, reading about politics, contributing money to political candidates and causes, attending political rallies, and so on.

Modes of Political Activity

Table 2.2 provides a listing of some modes of individual political action, with specific examples of action in each mode. Broadly, the modes are ranked on the basis of the effort or costs required to perform that type of political action. And the examples within each mode are ranked according to the frequency with which Americans tend to perform them (see Milbrath and Goel 1977:17–20). Some of the most extensive empirical and cross-national analyses of political participation, by Sidney Verba and his colleagues (Verba and Nie 1972, 1975; Verba, Nie, and

TABLE 2.2. Modes of Political Action

Actor-Type	Characteristic Actions
Revolutionaries	Undertake political violence against the political order
Protestors	Riot Engage in civil disobedience Join in public protest demonstrations Attend protest meetings Refuse to obey unjust laws Protest verbally if government does something morally wrong
Partisan activists	Candidate for/hold public office Contribute money to party, candidate, issue Attend meetings, rallies Actively work for party, candidate, issue Persuade others how to vote Join and support party
Community activists	Active in community organization Form group to work in local problems Contact officials on social issues Work with others on local problems
Communicators	Write letters to media Send support or protest messages to political leaders Engage in political discussions Keep informed about politics
Contact specialists	Contact local, state, or national officials on particularized problems
Voters	Vote regularly in elections
Supporters and patriots	Show patriotism by flying flag, attending public parades, etc. Express love of country Pay all taxes
Inactives	No voting, no other political activity No patriotic inputs

SOURCE: Most categories adapted from Milbrath and Goel 1977, Figure 1.1.

Kim 1978) have emphasized four broad categories of political participation: (1) voting (see Table 2.3); (2) campaign activities; (3) personalized contacts; and (4) communal activities (see Table 2.4 on page 36).

There have been two important changes in the recent empirical studies of political participation. First, there has been an increasing recognition of the significant level of "unconventional" political action, such as demonstrations, protest, and rioting, in both democratic and nondemocratic countries. Verba and his colleagues gathered data only on conventional forms of political action. Analysts are now more likely to include unconventional modes of political action in their research. This is reflected in Table 2.2 by the "revolutionaries" and "protestors" categories. We shall have more to say about these actors in Chapters 4 and 12.

Second, it has become clear that political action should not be treated as a single dimension. Most early studies of political participation assumed that political actions were hierarchical—that is, a person who performs a more difficult act,

TABLE 2.3. Voting Participation in Selected States: Percent of Adults Voting in National Election

Country	Percent	Year
Albania	100	1982
North Korea	100	1982
Bulgaria	99	1982
Cameroon	99	1978
East Germany	93	1990
Australia	89	1987
Austria	87	1986
Senegal	85	1982
Sweden	85	1988
Italy	85	1987
West Germany	84	1987
Honduras	83	1981
Ivory Coast	80	1980
Tunisia	80	1981
Costa Rica	75	1982
Great Britain	75	1987
Japan	73	1990
Spain	69	1986
Hungary	64	1990
Peru	62	1980
Bangladesh	56	1981
United States	50	1988
Switzerland	46	1987
Thailand	40	1979
Nigeria	36	1979

SOURCE: Delury 1983; Lineberry, Edwards, and Wattenberg forthcoming.

such as communal contacting, will also perform all less difficult acts, such as voting. But the richer empirical studies have indicated that there are different dimensions of political participation. Thus a person high (or low) on one mode of political action is not necessarily high (or low) on another. While there is some overlap, the campaign activists, communal activists, and those making personalized contacts are not necessarily the same people, and many people specialize in one or another mode. And protestors might not engage in any of the other activities, or they might engage in all of them (Barnes and Kaase 1979; Milbrath and Goel 1977:10–24; Nelson 1987:124; Verba and Nie 1975).

Political Participation Studies

Once categories of political action are established, a basic research question is how many people participate in each category, both within and across various national political contexts. In studying participation, Lester Milbrath (1965) argues that only a small proportion of the population are "gladiators," those people who are active in the most demanding forms of political action such as protest and partisan political work. In his own study of the United States in the early 1960s, Milbrath found that only about 5 percent of the adults were gladiators and more than half the adults were observers or "apathetics."

One of the most extensive studies of political action in the United States is aptly called *Participation in America*. In this book, Sidney Verba and Norman Nie (1972) find that among American adults, about 25 percent are "apathetics" (inactives), about 40 percent are "voting specialists" (a positive way of classifying people for whom voting is the most active form of political behavior), and only about 5 percent are very active in politics. This last group is comparable to Milbrath's notion of "gladiators"—people who are candidates for office or highly involved partisan workers/campaigners (although Verba and Nie did not determine whether people engaged in protest activity).

Some empirical data compare levels of participation across many countries. The most reliable comparative data measure voting in national elections. Table 2.3 provides these data for selected countries. The most striking observation about these figures is the huge variation in voting level, ranging from a reported 100 percent to only 36 percent.

Notice that the very highest voter turnout occurs in countries where one would not interpret the vote as a meaningful action to choose political leaders. This alerts us to a general problem in cross-national analyses of micropolitical data—the same action or belief might have a quite different meaning or significance in different settings. In some of the nations listed (e.g., Australia, Austria, Costa Rica, Hungary, Nigeria, the United States), the act of voting seems consistent with the Western democratic notion of voting—that is, an individual is participating in the selection of political leaders from among competing candidates. In other states, (e.g., Albania, Bulgaria, Cameroon, North Korea), voting is primarily a symbolic act that is supposed to express support for the existing political leadership and there is no real choice among competing candidates. Still other states (e.g., Tunisia, Thailand) are in an intermediate category where there is limited choice among candidates, but the vote has little actual impact on the designation of those who exercise political power. There also are countries (e.g., Chad, Laos, Saudi Arabia) in which the populations are not allowed to vote at all.

It is even more difficult to do cross-national comparisons between modes of individual political participation other than voting. Even more than voting, the same act of political participation can vary in meaning in different political and cultural environments. For example, the significance and potential personal risk of a public political protest is far greater for a person in North Korea than in South Korea, and greater in both countries than for somebody in Denmark.

Nevertheless, some major empirical, cross-national studies have been conducted. Data from Verba, Nie, and Kim's (1971; 1978) ambitious study of seven varied political systems are displayed in Table 2.4. This study, and a more recent

TABLE 2.4. Levels of Political Action in Seven Nation-States

Political Action	Percent Who Perform Act Regularly						
	Austria	India	Japan	Netherlands	Nigeria	U.S.A.	Yugoslavia
Voting							
In national election	85	48	93	77	56	63	82
In local election	93	42	—	—	—	47	—
Campaign Activities							
Attend political meetings	27	14	50	9	—	19	45
Work for political party	10	6	25	10	—	25	45
Member of political organization	28	5	4	13	—	8	15
Personalized Contacts							
With local official	15	12	7	38	2	6	20
With extralocal official	10	6	3	10	1	6	—
Communal Activities							
Active in organization trying to solve community problems	9	7	11	15	34	32	39
Contacted local officials as part of group action	5	4	11	6	2	13	11

NOTE: — = data not gathered.
SOURCE: Verba and Nie 1975:24–25.

comparative study of "Western democracies" (France, Great Britain, the United States, and West Germany) by Russell Dalton (1988), are widely cited in discussions of comparative political participation.

The data in Table 2.4 are consistent with the most prominent finding in virtually all empirical studies of participation in democracies, that is, most people do not regularly engage in high levels of political action. As shown in the above voter turnout data, voting is the most widespread political act, with between 50 percent and 95 percent of the eligible adults casting ballots in various countries. Between one-half and two-thirds of the citizens in Dalton's study report that they have signed petitions (Dalton, 1988:47). The seven-nation study indicates relatively high levels of campaign activities among the Yugoslavs and Japanese, although less than 1 in 4 is involved in an equivalent level of partisan activities in the other countries studied. Except for Yugoslavia, a Communist country with a rather different notion of party involvement than other nations in Table 2.3, three-quarters of the citizens in other countries do not work for a political party. Similarly, Dalton found that as few as 1 in 10 citizens engaged in partisan activities in the four Western democracies he studied (see Table 2.5). And except for the Dutch, less than 1 in 6 (Austrians) to fewer than 1 in 50 (Nigerians) personally contacts a local political official on a regular basis.

A second broad finding is that some citizens are willing to engage in unconventional modes of political participation. Cross-national research by Barnes and his associates (Barnes and Kaase 1979) of citizens in the Western democracies of Austria, the Netherlands, the United Kingdom, the United States, and West Germany and the major study by Dalton (1988) have examined less conventional forms of political action, including some forms of protest behavior. Selected data from Dalton's study are reported in Table 2.5.

Between one-fourth and one-half of the respondents in different countries indicated that they have participated in lawful demonstrations against government policy, or at least are willing to do so (Barnes and Kaase 1979). According to Dalton (1988:65) the proportion of adults who actually did participate in such demonstrations during a specific year (1981) was 1 in 10 in the United States and

TABLE 2.5. Level of Less Conventional Political Action in Selected Western Nation-States, 1981

Mode of Political Action	Percent of Citizens Reporting Action			
	France	Great Britain	United States	West Germany
Join in a boycott	11	7	14	7
Participate in a demonstration	26	10	12	14
Participate in an unofficial strike	10	7	3	2
Occupy a building	7	2	2	1

SOURCE: Dalton (1988:Table 4.1)

Britain, about 1 in 7 in West Germany, and about 1 in 4 in France. Barnes et al. report that as many as one-third of the Dutch citizens (under age 50) were willing to engage in civil disobedience (e.g., blocking traffic, strike), although the proportions were considerably lower in most other democratic countries in the study. The Barnes and Kaase study found that very few citizens were prepared to participate in violent protests against people or property. And in Dalton's study, only the French reported significant levels of participation in unofficial strikes or the occupation of buildings.

These cross-national differences underscore the third broad observation based on these empirical participation studies. There is substantial variation, from country to country, in the proportion of citizens who have undertaken various forms of conventional and unconventional political action. In the Verba, Nie, and Kim (1971; 1978) analyses using the data from Table 2.4, the differences in rates of activity (from highest to lowest) between nations is typically a ratio of 4:1 (except for voting).

Table 2.4 is indicative of the interesting differences in participation from country to country. For example, communal activities are relatively high in Nigeria, the United States, and Yugoslavia and relatively low in Western European and Asian countries. Table 2.5 provides examples of the comparably high levels of crossnational differences reflected in data on unconventional political behavior between the Barnes and Kaase and the Dalton studies.

In democratic countries, about which we have the most systematic empirical data, the evidence generally supports the conclusion that most individuals employ the conventional modes of voting and contacting public (elected or appointed) officials as the key means of achieving political objectives. But data revealing a notable level of unconventional participatory modes involving protest or political violence have increased recognition that individuals' choices of political action might not conform to the democratic model. It is also clear that many individuals continue to rely on nongovernmental channels to achieve objectives that might be reached by contacting public officials (Nelson 1987:117).

Although systematic, comparative data on less democratic countries are few, it seems that the reliance on nongovernmental channels and the incidence of unconventional political behavior are greater (and also vary more substantially) there than in democratic systems. In some less democratic countries, state repression deters the great majority of citizens from participation and there has been a pattern of "departicipation" in recent decades, as the political leadership has weakened or eliminated the mechanisms that enabled citizens to engage in political actions (Nelson 1987:116–120). In others, unsatisfactory political or economic conditions have led to an explosion of protest behavior and political violence against the regime. Such political behavior can manifest itself in strikes, violent demonstrations, insurrections, and revolutionary action.

Now that you have considered these empirical studies, you should be more capable of undertaking your own study. Box 2.2 suggests how you might try to use the concepts and methods of micropolitical analysis to assess such questions.

BOX 2.2

Measuring Students' Political Behavior:
An Example of Micropolitical Analysis

As an example of how to undertake micropolitical analysis, let's consider the political participation of American college students. Do you consider yourself an active participant in the political world? How many of the behaviors in Table 2.2 have you engaged in during the last three years? How might you assess whether most college students are politically active? Using the methods of survey research, you might begin to analyze your own or others' political activity level. Here are the key steps.

1. Conceptualizing Variables. Our objective is to describe and explain college students' political participation. The first task of such an analysis is conceptualization. This entails the development of a set of concepts which clarify and elaborate on the basic idea(s) that you wish to analyze. Table 2.2 provides one useful framework for conceptualizing various modes of political participation (e.g., voting, rioting, contacting officials, and so on).

2. Operationalizing Variables. Once you have decided which modes of participation you will study, you need to specify them more carefully so that you will be able to delimit those instances where the activities have actually occurred. This is called the operationalization of variables. You indicate in detail how key concepts are identified and measured in actual research settings. Operationalization of variables must be done with care and often is more complicated than it initially seems. For example, in operationalizing the concept of voting, do you want to distinguish between voting in national elections and in local elections, as Verba and Nie did? Do you want to determine the proportion of elections in which the individual voted? Do you want to distinguish between those who are and are not registered to vote? Notice that many such questions merit consideration when you attempt to operationalize a major political variable. You must make these decisions before you gather data, or you will not get all the information necessary for your analysis.

3. Data Collection. Once you have defined your operational indicators, the next activity is to collect data. This entails the identification of the *population* (the set of subjects) you wish to study, and the development of a strategy to gather empirical data that measure your key variables for all or some sample of this population. Assume that the population for your study is the students at your college (notice that this is an extremely limited sample for generalizations about all college students).

Typically, it is not feasible to gather data for everyone in the group about whom the analyst wishes to generalize, and so a procedure is developed to *sample* a subset of the group. This can be done by gathering data for anyone who is willing to respond, by selecting people at random, or by devising a more sophisticated sampling strategy that ensures adequate representation of certain key characteristics among those studied (e.g., age, gender, ethnicity, socioeconomic class, region, etc.). This last strategy for sampling is normally used by professional public opinion pollsters and by political scientists. The idea is to gather data from a subset that reflects the most interesting characteristics of the larger population.

In your study, you might not have the time to gather data for all the students at your college (and certainly not "all college students in America"). So you might

BOX **2.2** *continued*

randomly select 1 out of every 50 students in the student directory to serve as your sample. It would be simpler to study the students in your political science class; but, for the purpose of analyzing the political behavior of college students, why is a study of your political science class likely to be more biased than a study from the sample from the student directory?

The next problem is deciding how to collect data about each student's actual political behavior. Since you cannot observe the behavior of all students, you would probably have to settle for asking them to report their own political activity, based on some form of personal interview or questionnaire. To elicit accurate responses about the political actions you are interested in studying, you need an approach that encourages the respondent to answer honestly, with careful wording of questions and precise recording of individuals' responses.

4. Data Analysis: Creating Variables. Once you have gathered the data, you must organize them in the forms that enable you to manipulate the data in various ways to answer your analytic questions. You can merely do analysis based on each student's response to each question. But often, the analyst wants to categorize or summarize the specific responses into broader variables.

For example, you might create a taxonomy of types of participants, based on the student's set of political activities or frequency of activities. For example, you could use the nine modes of behavior listed in Table 2.1, and could count the number of different modes in which a person had done something (during a specified time period). By this technique, each student would have a "political action score" ranging from 0 to 9. But you might decide that such a scoring system provides too little differentiation, because it gives equal value to types of political activity that are quite different in terms of effort and political importance. Thus a more sensitive measure might give a different *weight* to each political action, on the basis of its relative significance—for example, 10 points for serving as a public official, 3 points for contributing money, 2 points for voting, and so on. By summing such weighted scores for each subject of study, you could create an *index* which measures each subject's overall political activity more precisely.

Even more refinements could be added by the inclusion of additional data, such as the frequency with which each activity is undertaken. Most contemporary political analyses attempt to develop these more complex variables, because such measures allow for rich findings and generalizations.

Notice that virtually all of the decisions in the analysis, and especially those about measurement and variable creation, are made by you—the individual political analyst. There are no fixed rules regarding these decisions, although they are not arbitrary. The analyst must attempt to make decisions that are reasonable, in terms of the analytic issues being considered, and defensible, since others might question these decisions, in the spirit of the scientific method.

5. Data Analysis: Description and Explanation. With your data and variables, you now can *describe* the political behaviors of college students in your study. Some of the questions you might examine include:

What are the most frequent political behaviors that the students undertake?

How frequently do the students discuss politics?

BOX 2.2 *continued*

What percentage are politically apathetic?

What percentage have participated in political rallies?

As you will find in Chapters 4 and 5, political analysts are rarely satisfied with answers to these kinds of descriptive questions. Whenever possible, they also attempt to generate more *explanatory* (correlational or causal) statements that search for general patterns among the behaviors or indicate the conditions which seem to cause certain types of political behavior to occur. To do this in your study, you might gather such additional data about your respondents as their personal traits, background experiences, and political beliefs. Then you might be able to offer tentative answers to such questions as:

Do students who discuss politics more also have higher grade point averages?

Are older students more politically active?

Is political protest more common among social science majors than among science majors?

Is partisan activism correlated with parents' income level?

Is ethnicity associated with interest in politics?

You can see that there are many fascinating questions that you can examine as you become a more insightful political analyst. It would be even more interesting to examine these questions across different cultures: for example, what are the similarities and differences in the political behavior of students in China, France, Mexico, Kenya, Poland, and the United States? As political scientists gather more extensive databases and use more refined analytic techniques, they can begin to develop stronger generalizations about the nature and causes of political beliefs and actions.

LOOKING AHEAD

Chapter 2 has begun our exploration of micropolitics. It has emphasized descriptive data and taxonomic theories that focus on the political beliefs and actions of individual citizens. In general, the approaches presented in this chapter attempt to summarize broad patterns of micropolitical behavior by individuals who share some common characteristics (e.g., sense of community, national identity, citizenry within a state). The ultimate objectives of micropolitical analysis, however, require us to move beyond description and to develop explanations of political beliefs and actions. The next two chapters offer various insights regarding the explanations that have emerged in the study of that political behavior. Chapter 3 will suggest some reasons for between-individual, as well as between-nation, differences in political behavior. And Chapter 4 will focus in depth on the political behavior of the ''gladiators''—the especially interesting subset of the population who are extremely active politically.

CHAPTER 3

Influences on Belief and Action

In Chapter 2 we considered the nature of people's political beliefs and political actions. Some of the most interesting questions in political analysis concern the *why* questions—why do individuals hold particular political beliefs and engage in certain political actions? Figure 3.1 indicates four broad types of explanatory factors that might account for individual political behavior: (1) environmental context, (2) agents of political socialization, (3) personal traits, and (4) personality. This chapter considers these four types of influences on political beliefs and actions.

THE ENVIRONMENT

In a major election, it is reported that 100 percent of the adults in North Korea vote, while only about 50 percent of the adults in the United States vote. What best accounts for this difference? In North Korea, voting is an obligatory act, a required gesture of support for the current political leadership rather than a genuine selection among candidates—indeed, there is no choice. Virtually everyone votes, because a comrade who does not vote risks unwanted scrutiny by Communist party authorities. In the United States, voting has always been a voluntary act and there are no sanctions for nonvoting. Thus the citizen decides whether her sense of civic responsibility or her desire to affect the outcomes on ballot choices merits the effort of going to vote. Box 3.1 suggests some reasons why citizens might not vote.

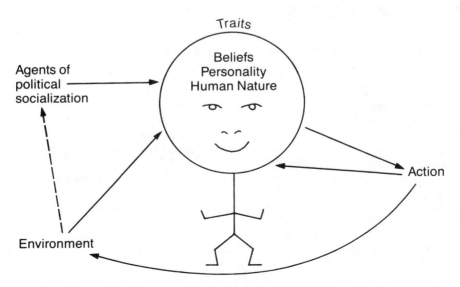

Figure 3.1. A Framework for Explaining Individual Political Behavior

BOX 3.1

Are You Too Smart to Vote?

Everyone knows that you ought to vote in a democracy, so that you can affect the choice of policies and political leaders. But a sensible argument can be made that if you are truly rational, you won't vote.

Many formal theories in political science (see the appendix) are grounded in the approach called "rational choice theory." This theory assumes that political actors are rational and calculating. They can establish the costs and benefits of each outcome to themselves and they can select the most rational strategy to maximize the benefits relative to the costs. If you have studied microeconomics, you might recognize that this description is rather like the "economic man," another version of this rational actor.

From a rational choice perspective, you would be rather foolish to vote in a presidential election. The costs associated with voting are, at least, the time and energy you expend to register, to get to the polling place, to cast your ballot, and to get to the next place you are going. You could also consider the time and energy spent trying to understand which candidates will establish certain policies and to calculate the benefits to you of each likely policy.

Even if you cannot think of things you would rather do with all that time and energy, the benefits side of the calculation is more daunting. Assume that you are smart enough to decide which candidate will actually enact policies that benefit you. As a rational actor, you still must ask: what is the chance that my vote will make a difference? In U.S. national elections, 90 million votes are cast for the presidency. The probability that there will be such a tie that one vote (yours or anybody else's) will determine the outcome, is infinitesimally small—certainly less than one in a trillion. So, what's the point?

This is what rational choice theorists call the "paradox of participation" (Riker and Ordeshook 1973). Since their theory assumes rational behavior, they need to explain why 90 million folks are behaving irrationally. (Of course, they could point to the equal number of people who do not vote or suggest that at least half of the population *is* rational).

One argument is that your vote matters as part of the set of votes from a larger group which shares your interests. If all of your group acted rationally, the loss of the total set of votes might be large enough to affect the outcome of the election. Also, if you have interests related to an election where few votes are cast, the rationality of voting does increase somewhat.

A second kind of argument is that most people are not rational calculators. They make many decisions in their lives (e.g., whether to marry, whether to enroll in a class, whether to drive very fast) without any clear idea of the precise costs and benefits of their choices to them.

A third explanation is that voting is primarily an expression of citizenship, social solidarity, and political communication. In this view, a person might vote because she loves her country and its democratic tradition, or because she wants to be a small part of a large voice saying yes or no to political leaders, or because she wants approval from her peers. In short, the decision to vote can be based on some elements of self-interest and/or civic commitment. But if you are very rational and very selfish, voting should probably be rather low on your agenda.

The example of voting in North Korea and the United States is suggestive of how a person's *environment*—the term applied to denote the broad context in which an individual lives—can powerfully influence her political behavior. In its most comprehensive form, the environment includes literally everything outside the individual herself. It obviously includes political elements (e.g., governmental procedures, public policies, specific political events and actors); but it also includes elements of the social and cultural system (e.g., religious foundations, attitudes toward differences in such traits as ethnicity, gender, class), elements of the economic order (e.g., level of economic prosperity and economic development), and the physical features of the environment (e.g., topography, natural resources). For some analytic questions, it might also be important to distinguish between the environment as measured "objectively" by the analyst, and the environment perceived "subjectively" by the individual who is attempting to understand and act in the political world.

For any particular political belief or action, there are various possible effects from an environmental stimulus. An element of the environment might activate or repress or transform or clarify an individual's political behavior. Since most of the numerous elements of the environment are likely to have little or no effect at any given moment, the task of the political analyst is to identify those few environmental elements that do have especially significant effects on an individual's political belief or action, and to explain how these effects occur.

Since the environmental context is, at least in theory, of enormous scope, it might be helpful to provide a few examples of how an aspect of the environment might affect political behavior. First, let us take two examples regarding the *political environment:*

1. *Effects on political discussion.* In China under Chairman Mao, the Communist party required every person to discuss political issues with colleagues for a few minutes each workday. Individuals were encouraged to relate politics to every aspect of their public and private lives. In Uganda, the political leadership tends to punish dissent with such severity that most citizens view any public political discussion as potentially hazardous to their health, and thus to be avoided.
2. *Effects on information about politics.* In Bolivia, information about politics is so limited that a villager might not be sure whether the most recent government coup has been successful and who the current political leaders are. In the United States, the politically interested citizen has access each day to hundreds of hours of television, radio, and reading materials regarding worldwide political events.

Second, the broader *social, economic, and cultural environment* can have more indirect, but no less powerful, influences on an individual's political behavior than the political environment. If the dominant religion in the cultural environment has traditionally relegated women to a secondary role, as in Iran's adherence to the Shari'a laws of Islam, it is likely that women's involvement in politics will be quite low. If the social environment has an undercurrent of racism, as in the United Kingdom, this will affect many aspects of the political behavior of both the majority and minority racial groups.

The impact of the environment on political behavior is sometimes quite hard to predict. If poverty is widespread in an economic system, will this influence the probability of political rebellion? On the one hand, such poverty might produce a frustrated population who will be responsive to a revolutionary movement promising future prosperity; on the other hand, the people might be too concerned about basic survival to have the time or energy to engage in political action. It should be evident from these examples that there are many aspects of the environment that might influence political beliefs and actions. The analyst must be sensitive to possible environmental effects when attempting to provide an adequate explanation for a particular political behavior.

AGENTS OF POLITICAL SOCIALIZATION

Each person has a complex blend of political beliefs—of cognitive, affective, and evaluative orientations regarding political phenomena. (Recall that these three kinds of orientations were defined in Chapter 2.) Even individuals who exist in the same environment can hold very different political beliefs. Political socialization research attempts to explain how such differences in political beliefs can occur.

Political socialization can be defined as the processes through which an individual acquires her orientations toward the political world. An interest in how this process works is of obvious importance not only to political analysts but also to those who wish to influence people's political beliefs and actions, especially political leaders. Plato (c. 428–347 B.C.) observed that society's most important function is civic training, the instruction of citizens regarding the nature of their sociopolitical order and of their proper roles in that order. The appropriate content and style of such political socialization is subject to debate and disagreement, since one vision of proper civic training might be viewed by other people as indoctrination and brainwashing.

Among political scientists, the emphasis in political socialization research has been on analysis of the *agents* of political socialization—the major sources of political training and indoctrination. The key concerns have been to identify these agents and to explain the processes through which they affect individuals' political orientations. There has been considerably less attention, and very limited empirical success, in linking the activities of specific agents of socialization to individuals' actual political actions. In this section we discuss some of the most important agents of political socialization: the family, the schools, peers, media and culture, and events.

The Family

The family is the first, and often the most powerful and lasting, agent of political socialization. The political orientations of most individuals are deeply influenced by behaviors and beliefs experienced in the family environment. Before individuals are capable of making judgments for themselves, perceptions about the political world have been absorbed from overheard conversations within the family. For example, most 7-year-old children in the United States already identify with one political party and have affective orientations toward both (Niemi 1974).

Even the pattern of interactions between parents and children can have political implications. If the family is very hierarchical, with the father or mother ruling with an iron hand, preventing discussion and using strong sanctions for disobedience, the children might assume that this is the appropriate pattern of authority relations in the society. If the family tends to discuss issues before it determines rules or decisions, the children might feel more strongly that they have the right to participate actively in decisions, even in the political world. (See Box 3.2.)

The Schools

From the perspective of the political authorities, the schools can be the state's most valuable agent for political socialization. The schools offer the opportunity for sustained and highly controlled contact with youth while they are at a highly

BOX 3.2

A Family Problem

Political leaders can perceive the family as a major obstacle to the political behavior they hope to inculcate in their population. A dramatic example is Mao Zedong, who came to power in China in 1949. He was deeply opposed to the traditional loyalties taught by Confucianism, which stressed obedience to the kinship unit, to elders, and to males. These were in fundamental conflict with the Maoist ethic, based on loyalty to the society as a whole and the equality of all people, regardless of age or sex. Mao identified the family, the cornerstone of Confucian training and socialization, as a "citadel of oppression" and he experimented with attempts to eliminate the nuclear family. When these proved unsuccessful, he mounted a campaign stressing that the family must "revolutionize" itself by shedding its entrenched Confucian thinking and behavior. Because Chairman Mao recognized that exhortations to the family were unlikely to alter dramatically the patterns of political socialization within the family, he relied heavily on other agents of socialization, such as the schools and the peer group, to counter the influence of the family.

In addition, Mao also attempted to alter the environmental context within which the family operated, as another means of shifting the nature of the family's socializing "messages." For example, he introduced governmental policies that undercut traditional Confucian values. Prior to the Revolution, and in line with Confucianism, the wife was legally the property of her husband and he could exploit or dispose of her as he wished. But the Marriage Law of 1950 gave a woman equal rights within the family structure to take legal recourse against bodily harm by her husband, to initiate a divorce, or to own property. In the two generations since the Revolution, the state has intervened in many aspects of family life. Such policies are aimed at altering political action and also at transforming the manner in which individuals understand the relationships between themselves, their family, their community, and their political society.

impressionable age when many political beliefs can still be molded. Apart from the family, the classroom is the most evident microcosm of society that young people experience. The teacher is the authority figure, who rewards thinking and behavior that conform to what is deemed desirable by the society and who withholds rewards from or sanctions those who fail to conform. In most societies, students are taught to accept the authority of the teacher, to supress their own desires, to value the symbolic rewards offered by the education system, and to interact with their peers in the manner approved by the school system. Moreover, in every school system there are rituals that support the political system. These might include songs, chants, or activities that express allegiance to political leaders or symbols.

Also important in shaping the student's understandings of the political world is the content of the curriculum in school. The educational authorities can control what subjects are taught, what the textbooks contain, and even what the teachers say and do. An extreme form of this central control over education was achieved during the French Fourth Republic (1946–1958). It was said that the minister of education in Paris could look at his watch and specify exactly what chapter in what textbook the children of a certain age were studying at that moment, all over France.

. Every textbook and every lesson in school is selective and thus contains biases regarding what is emphasized, what is ignored, and how meaning and value are established. Sometimes the level of indoctrination seems extreme, especially to those unsympathetic with the message. Here are three examples. As you read them, attempt to guess who or what subject is being discussed and the country in which they have been used.

Men are superior to women because God has made one superior to the other, and men spend their wealth to maintain the women.

Our forefathers believed, and we still believe today, that God himself made the diversity of peoples on earth. . . . Inter-racial residence and inter-marriage are not only a disgrace, but also forbidden by law. It is, however, not only the skin of the Betas that differs from the Alphas. The Beta stands on a much higher plane of civilization and is more developed. Betas must so live, learn and work that we shall not sink to the cultural level of the Alphas. Only thus can the government of our country remain in the hands of the Betas.

Imperialism knows no other type of relations between States except domination and subjugation, the oppression of the weak by the strong. It bases international relations on abuse and threat, on violence and arbitrariness. Between January 3 and June 10, 1961, Gamma military airplanes violated Delta airspace 3 times in the months of January, 15 in February, 17 in March, 9 in April, 8 in May, and 10 in June. What was the average monthly number of violations of Delta airspace by Gamma military airplanes?

Were you able to identify likely settings for these educational offerings? The first one is a chant by Moroccan 7-year-olds (substitute "Allah" for "God"; personal observation by the author, in Marrakesh). The next one is an excerpt from a South African textbook on race relations (substitute "whites" for "Betas" and "nonwhites" for "Alphas"; Thompson 1966:100). And the third one is the "new math" for Cuban children (substitute "Cuban" for "Delta" and "North American" for "Gamma"; Fagen 1964:68).

These somewhat extreme examples reflect the manner in which the political authorities can influence the content of educational materials in order to buttress the view of the political world most aligned with their own interests. While subject matter in the schools of most nations is less openly political than these examples, the school system of every nation presents materials that are supportive of that nation's politics and dominant cultural norms.

Have you noticed something odd about the use of the pronouns *he* and *she* in this book? To counter the male dominance in the language of most American textbooks, I have alternated feminine and masculine pronouns in odd and even chapters. If you were conscious of the "strange" use of gender references in Chapter 1 and in this chapter, it is indicative of the subtle way in which your cultural norms are reinforced by language and education.

Peer Groups

Although most people absorb a large proportion of their political socialization by the time they leave the educational system, learning never stops entirely (see Box 3.3). As the importance of parents diminishes and after formal schooling ends, peer groups become an increasingly significant influence on many individuals' political socialization. *Peer group* is a general term that includes friends and acquaintances, neighbors, and colleagues at the workplace or in clubs and organizations.

The section on "Everyone" as Authority in Chapter 1 suggests the attraction of bringing one's views into closer conformity with relevant peer groups. In general, a person is more likely to be accepted by her peers if her beliefs and actions are consistent with those in the group. And it is possible that there is a more subtle tendency for a person to be influenced by what "people like me" think. There is evidence that a person's social context (i.e., her peer groups) does modify political behavior (Agnew 1987; Eulau 1980; Johnston 1985; for contrary evidence, see Dunleavy and Husbands 1985).

China used the peer group as a major mechanism for political socialization under Mao Zedong. Small groups on collective farms, in factories, and in other

BOX 3.3

Persistence versus Change
in Political Socialization

The initial political socialization research emphasized the overwhelming importance of early socialization, from the family and from early educational experiences. According to this *lifelong persistence* interpretation, there is little change in the political behavior of most people after adolescence. However, this view was challenged by

BOX 3.3 *continued*

evidence that political learning and attitude change do continue throughout adult life. This second interpretation emphasizes *lifelong openness* to further socialization, asserting that there is continual response to agents of socialization and only minimal lasting effects of early socialization. The idea that a person's political views can continue to change even during adult life is captured in the European saying that anyone who is not a Communist at 20 has no heart and anyone who is still a Communist at 40 has no head.

The current interpretation is essentially a compromise between these two extremes, the *life cycle* interpretation. In this view, persistence is the rule for political attitudes and behaviors that are learned early. But political orientations can change as the result of the agents of political socialization, especially peer groups, and as the result of the individual's personal/social changes, especially at certain key points of development such as young adulthood (Jennings and Niemi 1981).

It is rare for a person to undergo a dramatic transformation in her political thinking, but it does happen. The story below recounts such a change.

Who's That Girl?

A widely publicized instance of several political transformations in one person involved a 19-year-old American college student. She had been raised in an extremely wealthy family, enjoying all the privileges of the upper class, and was a quiet, even dull, young woman. She had no apparent political views other than those of her conservative, Republican background. Suddenly, one evening in February 1974, she

BOX 3.3 *continued*

was kidnapped by a radical group, locked in a closet for 55 days, and subjected to extensive physical and mental abuse and indoctrination.

In her next public appearance—robbing a bank—she had become Tania, revolutionary sister in the Symbionese Liberation Army. Tape recordings were circulated in which she denounced the "fascist ruling class" and "capitalist pigs," including her own parents, and called for a people's revolution. After a lengthy effort, law enforcement officials captured her, jailed her again, and subjected her to another round of political indoctrination. Finally, she appeared in court in 1976, subdued and generally apolitical. She was convicted of bank robbery and served 23 months (of a seven-year sentence) in federal prison. President Carter commuted her sentence in February 1979. By this time, she had (again?) fallen in love with one of her jailors. She married him, and now lives an apolitical life, a suburban society matron, complete with service to social causes such as children with acquired immune deficiency syndrome (AIDS) and Alzheimer's disease.

That girl is Patti Hearst. Her story received enormous media coverage, perhaps because many people were fascinated with this incredible tale of political transformations. Many argued about the "true story" and which, if any, of Patti Hearst's beliefs were authentic. (She tells her own story in *Every Secret Thing* [1982], and a movie based on her experiences was released in 1988.) Yet, we can never fully know what another person really thinks; and in many instances it is hard for us to be sure even of what we think ourselves. Most of us suspect what George Orwell (1949/1967) emphasized in his ominous novel *1984*—that under certain conditions of physical or psychological torture, we can be made to think that we believe anything, even that we love Big Brother.

workplaces were not only required to discuss their political beliefs and actions, they were also supposed to monitor everyone's political behavior. If an individual's views or actions strayed from the "mass line," the group applied various types of persuasion and pressure to help the individual recognize and rectify her errors and return to the proper political position. If this failed, more aggressive forms of peer pressure, including public ridicule (and ultimately, imprisonment), were employed to force the individual to conform.

Media and Culture

Very few of us directly experience the great majority of political phenomena about which we claim knowledge. For most adults, the media, especially television, radio, and the press, become the major source of political information, and thus can be crucial agents of political socialization for either stability or change. These information sources really do *mediate* between the individual and most political reality, selecting both the subjects and the content about which information will be provided. Newspapers, radio, and, increasingly, television, are crucial sources of political information in most societies. It is particularly the case in more modern societies that most people are extremely dependent on the media to provide them with information and interpretations of political phenomena. In the United States, the average 18-year-old has spent more hours in front of the television than in school. While most of this programming is not explicitly political, it does contain subtle information that influences how the viewer thinks about politics and society.

By their selective presentations, the media suggest what to think about, if not what to think. Each evening, Walter Cronkite, then judged the most trusted man in America, would finish his television news broadcast by saying, "And that's the way it is." This is an extraordinary claim, given the many things that have not been reported and the bias that is inevitably associated with every story. The former director of Tass, the Soviet news agency, was somewhat more open when he observed that "news is merely agitation by means of facts." While this acknowledges the manipulative nature of the media, even this statement implies that the media are offering us "facts."

Like textbooks, the media are not neutral; someone has made selections regarding subjects and content. It is revealing to determine who has made those choices about what political phenomena to cover and how the media will report on them. In some nation-states, the major media are owned by members of the wealthy, dominant class, and there is persuasive evidence that their biases are reflected broadly in the content of those media (for the example of Great Britain, see Glasgow University Media Group 1976, 1980, 1984). And in most nation-states, the primary media are controlled by the government. Radio and television stations are either regulated by or, in many countries, operated by an administrative agency of the government.

With the exception of a handful of societies deeply committed to freedom of expression, governments impose major restrictions on the rights of media to communicate political information. It has been estimated that governments in more than 85 percent of the nations of the world practice substantial censorship of their media (Gastil 1988). Such restrictions can be extreme. In Romania, for example, prior to the 1989 revolution the government and the Communist party owned and operated all media. It was even illegal for a citizen to have a mimeograph machine, because this might be used to reproduce newsheets and pamphlets containing information contrary to that in the state-controlled media.

Culture offers an interesting alternative to the media and to other agents of political socialization. Culture can, like the media, be extensively controlled by the dominant political order in a society. In this fashion, it can also be used to reinforce the state's view of the political world. During the Cultural Revolution in China, all traditional plays and operas were banned, and these and other forms of culture were dominated by highly politicized works. Some Communist states, like Cuba, generally insist that culture meets the standards of "socialist realism," which means that no art, theatre, or cinema is to be produced that is abstract or, most importantly, that fails to celebrate the virtues of socialism.

However, culture need not reinforce the dominant order. Culture can inform and criticize subtly, by means of metaphor and symbol, in ways less likely to be interpreted as a direct challenge to the established authorities. This is especially true in societies where there is considerable censorship of the media and state control of most sources of public information. Even during the Communist regimes in East Germany and Poland, for example, there was extensive fiction, cinema, poetry, theatre, art, and music whose political content suggested alternatives to the state's views. Culture can also be subversive, in the sense that it can openly attack mainstream values in the society or advocate opposing values. For example, popular countercultural music by such people as John Lennon, Joan Baez, and Country Joe and the Fish became anthems among those protesting American involvement in the Vietnam War. While most contemporary Anglo-American music has little explicit political content, it can be found in songs by such performers as Sting, U-2, Bruce Springsteen, the now "dead" Dead Kennedys, and some rap music.

Events

The general effects of the environment on political beliefs and action have been discussed above. While the context of everyday life has slow, evolutionary effects on a person's political behavior, a particular event can act as a sudden and powerful agent of political socialization. For example, many leaders of the interest groups lobbying for handgun control in the United States are individuals who, although previously not active in politics, have been mobilized into political action by the trauma of a handgun-related death of a loved one. Another example of this phenomenon will introduce Chapter 9.

Many such dramatic events might transform an individual's political behavior: An aggressive action by another nation-state can convert a person's appraisal of that nation from indifference to hostility; a moving speech by a political leader can inspire feelings of loyalty or support; disclosure of a politician's personal improprieties can undermine her popularity. While individuals usually absorb events into their existing belief system, extraordinary events add a certain element of unpredictability to political beliefs and actions.

The general flow of events during an entire period can influence the political orientations of many people, especially those who "come of political age" during the period. For example, the combined impacts of such events as American military involvement in Vietnam and Southeast Asia, the "hippie" culture, and the Nixon presidency seem to have had strong effects on the political understandings of many Americans who were reaching adulthood during the late 1960s. In Europe, many of those who experienced the rise of fascism in the 1930s developed intense feelings about Germany and Germans, about extreme political movements, and about the dangers of attempting to compromise with an aggressor nation.

PERSONAL TRAITS

Suppose you have been challenged to predict how a particular person voted in the 1988 American presidential election, but you cannot know anything about the person's political beliefs or actions. Would you accept the challenge? If so, what data would you find most useful?

To predict a person's vote for Bush or Dukakis (or non-vote or vote for an-other candidate), you might seek information about that person's political social-ization or environmental context. But if you were familiar with the research on voting behavior, you would probably make your prediction on the basis of certain "objective" personal traits of the individual. These traits, sometimes called *de-mographic characteristics,* include age, education, gender, ethnicity, income, so-cial class, and occupation. What would be your predictions for the people profiled in Table 3.1? How confident are you in your predictions? Would you have been more confident in predicting the 1984 election (Reagan versus Mondale)?

None of the characteristics in Table 3.1 is a certain predictor of vote; but some do seem associated with a vote choice. And where key personal traits seem consistent in direction, you might have greater confidence in a correct prediction. What underlying dynamic might link personal traits with political behavior?

Personal traits can be thought of as filters that influence the manner in which the environment and the agents of political socialization affect an individual's po-litical behavior. For example, the relevance of the environmental factor of ethnic racism will have very different effects on the political beliefs and behaviors of a white South African and on those of a black South African. Similarly, the current impact of parents as an agent of political socialization is likely to be greater for a person of 18 than for one of 68. Personal traits are filters in the sense that they shape the nature and significance of the environment and agents of political social-ization as factors influencing the political behavior of a given individual.

Table 3.1 (like the example of correlational analysis in the appendix) explores the relationship between voting and personal traits. In your predictions in Table 3.1, you were probably guided by some assumptions about the propensity of cer-tain types of people to vote for a particular political party or a specific candidate

TABLE 3.1. Predicting Voting Behavior in the 1988 U.S. Presidential Election

	Person 1	Person 2	Person 3	Person 4
Demographic Characteristics				
Age	65	35	20	45
Education	High school	M.B.A	11th grade	Ph.D.
Ethnicity	Black	Caucasian	Hispanic	Asian-American
Sex	Female	Male	Male	Female
Annual income	$8,000	$65,000	$22,000	$48,000
Occupation	Retired	Middle manager	Marine	College teacher
Vote Prediction				
Did not vote	_____	_____	_____	_____
Dukakis (D)	_____	_____	_____	_____
Bush (R)	_____	_____	_____	_____
Other	_____	_____	_____	_____
Confidence Level (0–100 percent)	_____	_____	_____	_____

or to abstain. With actual data from a large number of people, you could empirically validate your predictions.

Table 3.2 provides actual data for addressing the same question in a different context. The case study is the French presidential election of 1981. Do personal traits seem associated with a tendency to vote for the candidate of the left, François Mitterrand, or the candidate of the right, Valéry Giscard d'Estaing (who had won the previous election against Mitterrand in 1974)?

What is particularly striking about these data is that most indicators in the table are differentially associated with the two candidates. For example, men clearly preferred Mitterrand, although there was only a modest preference for Giscard among women. Candidate preferences also differ quite substantially across profession of household head, age, and religion. This table is another example of correlational analysis. While there are clear associations between variables, we cannot conclude that any personal trait actually caused a person to vote for Mitterrand or Giscard.

TABLE 3.2. Voting Choices in the 1981 French Presidential Elections, by Personal Traits

	Mitterrand	Giscard
Total	52%	48%
Sex		
Male	56	44
Female	49	51
Age		
18–24	63	37
25–34	63	37
35–49	51	49
50–64	47	53
65 and over	40	60
Profession, Head of Household		
Farmers, agricultural workers	33	67
Shopkeepers, craftsmen	40	60
Executives, professionals, businessmen	38	62
White-collar employees	58	42
Workers	67	33
Nonemployed	45	55
Education		
Elementary	51	49
Secondary	50	50
Technical or commercial	58	42
Higher education	50	50
Religion		
Regular church-goer	20	80
Occasional church-goer	40	60
Never goes to church	61	39
Without any religion	88	12

SOURCE: Ehrman 2d ed. 1982, Table 8.

Indeed, so many traits are associated with voting choice that we cannot determine which of these personal traits are the most powerful predictors of candidate choice without statistical analysis (such as regression analysis, a statistical technique that identifies how much variance in the dependent variable—vote choice, in this case—can be attributed to each subject's level on various independent variables). Nonetheless, Table 3.2 certainly does provide reasonable support for our assumption that personal traits can be very strongly associated with political behavior—in this case, voting choice.

Much of the empirical research on political behavior attempts to establish and clarify the relationships between personal traits and specific political beliefs and/or actions. The political action that has been most extensively studied is the act of voting. Of particular interest to researchers (and to politicians) have been studies indicating who is more likely to vote and what factors seem to explain the particular voting choice.

While global generalizations are always difficult, there is some consistency in the empirical research on the personal traits of those who do vote (in political systems where there are genuine voting choices). In general, a higher probability that an individual will vote is related to such personal traits as membership in organizations with interests in politics (e.g., political parties, unions), higher education, higher income, higher social class, greater age, and gender (male). Incidence of voting is also associated with the individual's political beliefs, especially a strong identification with a party, a greater sense of personal capacity to influence the political world ("political efficacy"), and better understanding of the available political choices.

The research findings on other modes of political behavior are less extensive and less consistent. As in the taxonomies of participation, the cross-national work by Verba and his colleagues (Verba and Nie 1972; Verba, Nie, and Kim 1978) is among the most influential in identifying the individual traits correlated with each mode of political action. Participation in campaign activities is especially linked with higher education, higher income, and gender (males). Socioeconomic traits are also most strongly correlated with the likelihood that an individual engages in communal activities, and identification with a particular social group (religious, ethnic, or linguistic) can be extremely important if there are political cleavages associated with these group differences. Individual contacting is least clearly related to personal traits, and some research suggests that its use depends more upon whether the individual has more attractive public or private means to gain her objective. Our analysis of political activists in Chapter 4 presents additional empirical findings regarding the traits associated with those at the highest levels of political participation.

POLITICAL "PERSONALITY"

The three types of explanatory factors discussed to this point are either outside the individual (the environment and the agents of political socialization) or are surface traits. However, some political analysts insist that an adequate explanation of political behavior requires explication of the "political personality"—the psychological dynamics *inside* the individual.

Personality

Personality can be broadly defined as the propensities within an individual to act a certain way, given a particular context. If someone is usually cheerful or aggressive or thoughtful under a variety of circumstances, this style of behaving could be termed a personality trait of the individual. And the cluster of basic personality traits that dominate an individual's attitudes and behavior is what most people mean when they talk about someone's personality "type."

The political personality approach assumes that knowledge of the relevant personality traits will enable the analyst to understand and explain political attitudes and behavior. In its descriptive modes, certain personality traits are identified, and their effects on political beliefs or actions are specified. In its more analytic modes, there is an attempt to delve deeper, explaining the needs, drives, or experiences embedded in the individual's psyche that result in beliefs and actions.

A classic example of this mode of political personality research is the famous study by Adorno and his colleagues, *The Authoritarian Personality* (1950). In the aftermath of the horrors of German Nazism and anti-Semitism during World War II, these scholars attempted to analyze people who become supporters of rigid, ideological political movements and/or who are deeply prejudiced.

On the basis of many types of psychological testing of individuals, the researchers characterized a personality syndrome they termed *authoritarianism*. Initially, they defined the personality traits of those with this syndrome:

Authoritarians are extremely conventional in their attitudes and morality.
They are particularly hostile toward minorities or those with unorthodox lifestyles.
Their world is organized on the principle of hierarchy—they offer obedience to those they judge to be of high status and they attempt to dominate those perceived to be below them in the sociopolitical order.

The Adorno group was particularly interested in moving beyond description to answer the *why* question, What produces an authoritarian personality? While the answers of the Adorno group are complex, their basic explanation involves a psychological dynamic called *externalization*. Like most of us, the people who become authoritarians experience aggressive impulses and strong sexual drives during childhood; but these people had authoritarian parents who suppressed their opportunities to express these impulses and drives. Thus, as adults they become authoritarian personalities because they project this pent-up hostility onto groups that they judge to be inferior to themselves, such as minorities and other unconventional types. At the same time, their love/fear of the authoritarian parent leads them to venerate those who exercise great power and authority in the society.

There have been many criticisms of the methods and findings of the Adorno group. Some research (Rokeach 1960; McCloskey and Chong 1985) has suggested that authoritarianism can be found among people who support extremist politics of either the right or the left. Adolf Hitler seems to have believed this. He instructed Nazi party officials to immediately accept into membership anyone who had previously been a Communist, the archenemies of the Nazis. Presumably, Hitler assumed that these people, who were called "Beefsteak Nazis" (brown on the outside, red on the inside), would redirect their vigorous political support from one ideological extreme to the other. But most studies have reinforced the basic notion in *The Authoritarian Personality* that the syndrome is fundamentally associated with a psychological and political conservatism.

Human Nature

Some of those who offer a psychological explanation for political behavior argue for a more generalized conception grounded in human nature—in innate motivation and invariant drives shared by all people. At some time, most of us have engaged in a discussion about the possibility of a utopian society. Typically, someone takes the position that a benign utopia is not possible because humans are imperfect—that men and women are intrinsically greedy or individualist or violent. The person making such an argument is linking the performance of the political system and the political behavior of individuals with notions about innate (and possibly universal) human nature.

Some political psychologists confront this issue, asking whether there are innate human motivations that affect individual political behavior. They assume that such human nature is prior to nurture (i.e., the learned behavior emerging from socialization) and is only marginally altered by particular personal traits. Given the obvious difficulty of studying political behavior independent of socialization and personal traits, the applications of this perspective to political behavior have been modest and quite derivative. In most cases, general psychological theories have been loosely related to politically relevant behavior.

A notable example of this approach is the attempt to develop a political component for humanistic psychologist Abraham Maslow's ideas about a "hierarchy of human needs." In *Motivation and Personality* (1954; see also Maslow 1968), Maslow argues that humans have a hierarchy of innate needs that are fulfilled in a developmental pattern. First, there are basic physiological needs, such as those for food, water, and sleep. Next are safety needs, involving protection from physical danger. Next up the hierarchy are the needs for love and belonging, for the desire to be accepted into and cared about by some human group. The fourth level of need is for self-esteem, for a sense of one's own self-worth and value. Finally, the ultimate level of need fulfillment is self-actualization, in which one's skills and talents are developed fully and one acts in a positive fashion to create a desirable state of personal and interpersonal life.

The obvious question is, How do Maslow's five levels of innate human needs translate into insightful observations about political behavior? For those who have attempted to apply Maslow's views to the study of politics, the answer is that all of these needs can be related to individuals' political goals and values, and thus to belief and action.

For example, Thomas Hobbes's (1588–1679) ideas about the state of nature and the social contract can be linked to the notion of meeting both physiological and safety needs. In Hobbes's (1651/1958) well-known conception, the continual fear and danger of violent death in the state of nature led human life to be "solitary, poor, nasty, brutish and short." Thus all individuals agree to abide by a social contract, which is an explicit attempt to create a state that is empowered to enforce the safety needs of all. The state's authority also insures the operation of a political economy that organizes the production and exchange of such basic commodities as food and shelter.

Political phenomena can also serve the need for love and belonging defined by Maslow. Although politics is not the only source, or even the primary source of such affiliations, the world of politics does offer groups to which one can belong and form strong emotional attachments. As Goethe observed, "If you cannot be a whole, join a whole." There are many individuals who fix intense loyalty on political groups or symbols, such as political parties, flags, political causes. It can be argued that a person with an intense need for love and belonging that is not met through other social structures (such as family and friendship networks) might gravitate to extremist political groups of the right or left, and might follow the political exhortations of that group with fanatical energy. (This is akin to Maccoby's arguments about Mexican "supermachos" described in Chapter 2.)

It might even be that maintenance of a democratic political order requires that a substantial proportion of its citizens operate at the level Maslow terms self-esteem. Because these individuals have sufficient confidence in themselves, they do not interpret every political issue as one on which they must prove themselves and they are able to tolerate defeat. And because they have self-respect, they are able to accept both successes and failures in their political participation and to adapt to the political decisions that emerge from that process.

Interestingly, it is less clear whether a political order can maintain its stability with a high proportion of self-actualizers. These people might tend to be visionaries (e.g., utopians and revolutionaries) who are deeply committed to achieving a political world that matches their ideals. Their active efforts to use the political process to achieve their vision of an ideal sociopolitical system might strain the capabilities of the political order to maintain its control. Some might object to this interpretation, arguing that the truly self-actualized person is also so high on self-esteem that her efforts would be moderated and she would not subject the political order to extreme stress.

The issues regarding human nature and political behavior are fascinating ones. Are there fundamental elements of human nature that cannot be significantly altered by socialization and institutions? Some theorists make extraordinary claims about the extent to which all human behavior is based on essential biological/genetic foundations (see, e.g., the sociobiology approach of Edward Wilson [1978]).

In dramatic contrast, a fundamental tenet of Marxist theory is that nothing is intrinsic about human nature (although this is not always the view of Marx himself, whose early writings do suggest basic human needs and patterns of development). It is assumed that people's social behavior, if not their basic nature, can be shaped via proper socialization and enlightened institutions. Such shaping into a humane cooperative society is the theme of behavioral psychologist B. F. Skinner's novel *Walden Two* (1948). But the power and danger of such pervasive socialization in shaping political society is a central theme in Aldous Huxley's classic novel *Brave New World* (1932).

In general, one claim underpinning the human nature approach seems reasonable—we are not merely the product of our environment. But the crucial issue relevant to understanding politics concerns the extent to which individual personality and human nature cause political behavior. In the late-night college dormitory debates about the impossibility of a utopian society or the inevitability of conflict and war, the issues often boil down to one's view of the malleability of human nature. Are there innate characteristics of human nature so deterministic that they are subject to only minor modifications from particular patterns of political socialization and from specific political environments? Empirical social science has not yet provided clear answers to these questions about nature and nurture and politics.

CONCLUDING OBSERVATIONS

Our exploration of micropolitical analysis has continued with a consideration of primary explanations for individuals' political beliefs and political actions. The research and theories that have attempted to answer the *why* questions regarding political behavior emphasize four types of explanatory factors: environmental context, agents of political socialization, personal traits, and personality. The basic assumption is that some combination of these factors influences the kinds of political stimuli to which an individual is exposed, the manner in which she interprets these stimuli, and the kinds of responses to the stimuli that occur. In general, each of these types of explanations is helpful in accounting for some micropolitical behavior, although no single type seems to offer a complete explanation for all behaviors.

The *environment* presents the individual with stimuli and opportunities and also with obstacles to certain political beliefs and actions. While an individual can ignore or misperceive these broad environmental constraints, they do constitute a framework that guides, and to some extent determines, political behavior. In most micropolitical research, the analyst can (and should) identify those major features of the environment that might affect the probability that an individual will manifest certain political beliefs or actions.

In a similar manner, an individual's *personal traits,* such as age, gender, social class, education, and so on, can have a powerful cumulative influence in several ways. First, they can influence the kinds of political phenomena to which the individual is exposed. Second, they can influence the expectations that others have regarding how she ought to think and act politically. The empirical evidence is often quite clear (as were the data on voting in the French presidential election) that certain personal traits (in a given environmental context) are significantly correlated with particular political beliefs and political actions. Thus personal traits, rather like the environment, can be understood as a set of forces that influence the nature and intensity of, but do not determine, individual political behavior.

The inadequacy of either the environment or personal traits as a complete explanation for most individual political behavior is reflected in the fact that individuals with comparable personal traits and/or who operate in a similar environmental context do not necessarily manifest identical political beliefs or political actions. For example, of two intelligent 19-year-old Chicanas at the same university, one might be deeply involved in Democratic party politics and the other might be politically inactive. While the environment and an individual's personal traits might not provide a total explanation, a strong case can be made that these factors do tend to set the boundaries within which much political behavior occurs.

The attempt to build an empirically validated causal theory regarding the effects of *political socialization* is extremely promising, although it entails major challenges. The analysis must specify exactly how the mix of different agents of political socialization and different information have been internalized by the individual, which agents and which information have had the most powerful effects regarding a particular political belief, and then how political beliefs are converted into political action.

A major analytic shortcoming with most of the empirical research on political socialization is that it has been difficult to identify precisely which agents have had which specific effects on a person's political orientations. In most instances, researchers lack the methodologies and the data-gathering instruments to measure how the messages of various agents of political socialization are being absorbed by individuals. Rather, they must attempt to infer what socialization agents have been important, by asking individuals to recall the major sources of their own political beliefs.

The socialization process typically occurs over a long period of time, and most people experience a complex pattern of different inputs from the agents of political socialization, especially during childhood and adolescence. There can be considerable time lags between exposure to some agent's information and the absorption of the content into one's political beliefs. Information can be transmitted or received imperfectly, and information from different agents can be inconsistent. All of these factors increase the difficulty in identifying the precise source(s) of a particular belief.

An even more serious problem in the study of the agents of political socialization has been the difficulty in demonstrating empirically that there is a clear causal linkage between a specific agent of socialization, a particular belief, and then a politically relevant behavior. The discussions in Chapters 2 and 3 reveal that the political orientations of each individual are a complex pattern of sometimes reinforcing, sometimes contradictory cognitive, affective, and evaluative orientations, and they are only a small portion of the individual's *Weltanschauung* (the German word meaning "worldview"). Thus it can be extraordinarily difficult to establish causality between specific components from this complex socialization pattern and what a person does politically.

Despite these empirical difficulties, the study of political socialization has been quite useful in increasing our understanding of the major forces that influence how individuals learn about the political world and evaluate political phenomena. In their attempt to utilize the agents of political socialization, political regimes clearly affirm their own belief that these socialization processes can create and preserve popular support for the existing political order.

Our discussion has provided examples in which the agents of socialization have been used with particular skill in nations attempting to transform the political orientations of their population and to create a new political consciousness. And research suggests that where the agents of political socialization are ineffective or where they provide contradictory messages to the individual, that person's political behavior will tend toward apathy or, in a few cases, to total activism (the politically energized "gladiator"). While the precise linkages between agents of political socialization, political beliefs, and political behavior have not yet been empirically verified, this area of inquiry is a fascinating and important one for political scientists.

The explanation of micropolitical behavior by reference to *personality* is perhaps the most intriguing of the four sets of factors. It is also the explanation of political behavior that has been least fully explored by means of social scientific inquiry. To some extent, personality-based explanations use some of the same evidence as the other approaches. For example, this approach might explain political personality in terms of the relation of the child to the parents, as would an explanation based on the family as an agent of political socialization. Thus personality is difficult to isolate from the forces of nurture—the environment, the personal traits, and the political socialization and learning—that intervene between human nature and political behavior and that shape personality. To a large extent, the work from a psychological perspective differs from the other approaches less in the evidence it examines than in the psychoanalytic framework within which the evidence is interpreted.

The subjects of such psychologically oriented inquiry have also been somewhat limited. The political behavior of ordinary men and women has been subject to little analysis based explicitly on personality-based approaches. The studies that have examined general personality traits in relation to mass politics have tended to be the broad and overly simplified characterizations of "national character" or "modal personality," like those described in Chapter 2. While some of the work has examined ideological extremists, like the authoritarian personalities, most of it has focussed upon the extraordinary political actors, especially top leaders. Since the political behavior of such groups is the topic of Chapter 4, our appraisal of this explanatory perspective is best deferred until the end of that discussion.

CHAPTER 4

Political Activists:
The Gladiators

Prime Minister Margaret Thatcher of the United Kingdom and Prime Minister Benazir Bhutto of Pakistan

He thrives on adversity, even at the White House. He needs to feel challenged, admired, put upon, despised, loved; he needs to feel cornered so he can out-perform everyone, almost as though he enjoys overcoming adversity and showing off his brilliance and subtlety.

—*Alan Elms,* Personality and Politics

One can sense, even from this brief description, that this is a person who thrills in the "action" associated with the political world. Who is this man? Could it be John Kennedy? Jimmy Carter? Henry Kissinger? Ronald Reagan? Richard Nixon? You might feel that this description could fit any of these people, all of whom are among the small number of people intensively involved in politics. One of the most fascinating aspects of micropolitics is the analysis of individuals like the one described above, who is Henry Kissinger. This chapter considers the question, What makes these political activists tick?

The "gladiators" are the true political activists—individuals who actively attempt to shape the political world in which they live. They circulate petitions rather than merely signing them; they get out the voters on election day rather than merely voting; they enthusiastically advocate political ideologies rather than merely listening to them; they take to the streets to demonstrate their displeasure with government rather than merely grumbling about it; they might even hold public office. Comparative data in Chapter 2 suggested that only as many as 20 percent and sometimes as few as 1 percent of the adults in a political society are gladiators.

What do we know about these people? Are some people more likely to become gladiators than others? What motivates them to engage in politics at such an intense level? This chapter summarizes the basic insights that have emerged regarding political gladiators. Given their interesting nature, our systematic knowledge about them is quite modest. Using the several broad explanations of political behavior developed in Chapter 3, this chapter suggests what seems to influence and motivate these political men and women. The discussion treats three types of gladiators: (1) political "foot soldiers"; (2) extremist-activists; and (3) top political leaders.

EXPLAINING POLITICAL ACTIVISM

Chapter 3 offered broad explanations for why ordinary people think and act as they do in the political world. The explanations were necessarily general, because the focus was usually on patterns of political behavior among large collectivities, such as "those French who vote for Mitterrand." However, in research on the few people who tend to be highly active in politics, analysts have sometimes been able to gather detailed data on specific individuals and thus to provide explanations at greater levels of depth.

This research on political activists, which is sometimes called *political personality studies,* has generally relied on the same explanatory variables described in Chapter 3. First, political activism, like all forms of political behavior, is contingent upon the *environment* within which it occurs. Second, the *agents of political socialization* might exercise important formative or continuing influence over the beliefs and actions of political activists. Third, one can identify those *personal traits* of the individual that are related to activism. Fourth, the analyst can specify elements of the individual's *personality and psychological drives* that might produce political activism. Each of these four types of explanatory variables is employed below, to the extent it has been emphasized in accounting for the political behavior of "foot soldiers," extremist-activists, or top leaders.

"FOOT SOLDIERS"

In terms of the political-activists-as-gladiators metaphor, the "foot soldiers" are those activists who do the basic work of politics. These individuals link the government and the top political leadership to the masses. These are the people who might raise money for candidates or political issues, work in the local offices of political leaders, communicate the views of top leaders to the citizens, or voice their opinions to political leaders on a frequent basis. In most nation-states, these activists are members of political parties, although party membership is not necessarily synonymous with political activism.

It is very important to emphasize that any explanation of the foot soldiers is highly contingent upon the environment in which they are operating. The examples in Chapter 3, which indicate how the political, social, cultural, and economic environments can stimulate or prevent political behavior, are even more salient for the potential actions of political activists. In a fundamentalist Islamic state where religious laws discourage or forbid political participation by women, such laws will particularly constrain women from roles of high political activism. And in a Communist state that uses the party and various party organizations to draw the population into political life, many activist political roles will be fostered by the state.

The effects of the environment on political activism is particularly evident in nation-states when there is a major change in the nature of the political order. During periods when democratic processes are expanded, there is usually a considerable increase in the political activity of the population, stimulating not only voting but also the recruitment of foot soldiers who join political groups and incorporate politics into their daily lives. However, major political transformations in these states can also result in periods when most political activity is either discouraged or suppressed ("departicipation"). Examples of these shifting contexts which altered the level of political activism include Greece (from the military junta to an elected government in 1974), Iran (from Shah Reza Pahlavi to Ayatollah Khomeini in 1979), Nigeria (from an elected government to a military junta in 1983), South Africa (the inclusion of "coloureds" into the electorate in 1984), and

Poland (the legalization of opposition parties in the election of 1989). The political context can also change without a clear change in leadership or policy. This is a particularly ambiguous situation since the environment can provide confusing signals regarding the level and forms of political activism that are acceptable. The explosion of democratic demands and then the violent repression of the activists in China in 1989 is a dramatic recent example of shifting political behavior in such an environment.

Overall, it is quite difficult to generalize about the level of activism or the nature of political activists in most states without defining a time- and place-specific political environment. The empirical research on political "foot soldiers" primarily describes how many activists engage in certain activities in a particular environment and specifies the personal traits that are most common among such activists. And most of the research on the traits of "foot soldiers" examines activists in developed political systems. The following paragraphs suggest the considerable variations in the numbers and personal traits of political activists in the more developed countries.

In Britain and France, for example, about 1 out of 5 adults is a party member, but only 1 in 20 is a political activist. In West Germany, less than 1 in 20 of the adults is even a party member, and fewer than 1 in 100 is an activist. In Britain, the activists are a relatively representative cross section of the adult population in terms of class, occupation, and gender; but in France, the activists are a cross section only of the men, with few women activists. And in West Germany, political activism is primarily the domain of the educated upper-middle class (Bishop and Mezaros 1980:153–172).

Prior to the recent changes in the Soviet Union, about 1 out of 10 adults has been a member of the Communist party, and most party members have been quite active in the political process, in the sense of guiding and monitoring the political life of the society. When leaders in other party organizations are included, as many as one-fifth of the adults in the Soviet Union have been involved in political activism. These activists are broadly representative of the occupational and class composition of the society and, to a lesser extent, of gender and education levels (Bishop and Mezaros 1980:172–176). This very high level and breadth of political activism is common in the industrialized states of Eastern Europe. One of the many interesting questions associated with the sweeping political changes in Eastern Europe is whether the activists will increasingly come from a more narrow range of the population, as has been the case in Western Europe.

Although systematic knowledge about the socialization and personalities of foot soldiers is fragmented, the research does suggest broad similarities in the political beliefs of these individuals. The major study by Verba, Nie, and Kim (1978) found quite consistent political beliefs among the political activists in Austria, India, Japan, and the United States (the Nigerian sample was not analyzed in this manner). Not surprisingly, there is a very substantial statistical association in all four countries, and particularly in Austria, between being a foot soldier (called a "campaigner" by Verba et al.) and having a strong psychological involvement in politics. This means that foot soldiers have an avowed interest in politics and frequently discuss politics and public affairs (Verba, Nie, and Kim

1978:44–45, Table 15). To a far lesser (but still statistically significant) degree, foot soldiers identify more strongly with a political party than do other adults. Finally, there is a slight correlation between this type of political activism and the individual's belief that he can contribute to the general welfare of his community by his actions.

EXTREMIST-ACTIVISTS

If foot soldiers are those political activists who work inside the system, the extremist-activists are outsiders whose ideal political world requires a dramatic shift in the nature of the existing system. Extremism is a subjective and also a relative concept, since a person is politically extreme only in comparison to some standard position, typically the broad center of the existing political order.

The extremist-activist typically engages in extensive political action, from organizing grass-roots movements to guerrilla warfare. For many, the classic extremist is a revolutionary—a person who desires to overthrow the existing political order by violence and to replace it with a quite different one (see Chapter 12). Contemporary examples range from organized groups like the Sendero Luminoso in Peru to individuals involved in spontaneous rioting against apartheid in South Africa. The label *political extremist* can also be applied to other "radicals" whose beliefs locate them on the margins of the existing system, even when they have no explicit goal of changing the system by force. Examples range from neo-Nazi activists in France to antinuclear activists in West Germany. Political analysts have always been interested in revolutionaries. In recent decades, they have also turned considerable attention to radicals of the right and the left, primarily those in such democracies as Britain, France, the United States, and West Germany.

Personal Characteristics

The most common method of studying extremist-activists has been the attempt to specify the personal characteristics that typify a particular type of activist. One group of activists who have been intensively studied are the blacks who engaged in political violence in the urban areas of the United States and Britain during the 1960s and 1970s. Some analysts claimed that these people were "riffraff" who were, in the words of one scholar, "rioting mainly for fun and profit" (Banfield 1974, Chap. 9). Such a viewpoint mixes conceptions of their personal characteristics (unemployed, undereducated, young males) with notions regarding their personality (limited time horizon, propensity for violence, minimal ego strength).

However, rigorous empirical analyses seemed to undermine this viewpoint. The rioters were predominantly male and relatively young, but they were similar to the average male in their community on such personal characteristics as education, income level, and occupation. From this perspective, the political activists were not distinguished in terms of personal characteristics, and thus other types of explanatory factors seem necessary to explain why these particular individuals expressed their politics "in the streets." Inconclusive data suggest that many of these activists explained their own activism with sociopolitical rationales, particularly unhappiness regarding employment opportunities and mistreatment by the police (Feagin and Hahn 1973; Sears and McConahey 1973).

Another group of extensively studied American extremist-activists is the college and university students in the late 1960s, who were protesting U.S. involvement in Southeast Asia and, more broadly, social injustice in Western democracies. Studies developed a profile of the most common traits of student activists. Analyses of California college students, for example, found that political activism tends to be more common among those majoring in the social sciences or the humanities, less common among those majoring in business, engineering, or the natural sciences. Activists tend to be lower-division more than upper-division students and to live on their own rather than in dorms or at home. Activists are more likely to have Jewish or no religious tradition and not to attend church, while nonactivists tend to be Catholics or Protestants and to attend church at least occasionally (Smith, Haan, and Block 1970).

Do you think that the activists of the early 1990s are different from those in the 1960s? This suggests many interesting questions for comparative analysis. Is there continuity in the types of issues on which there is activism? (E.g., have there been changes in importance attached to such issues as nuclear weapons, superpower intervention in Africa, Asia, and Latin America, and environmental degradation?) Are the characteristics of the activists similar? (E.g., are the activists mainly young or are they possibly a resurgence of the radicals from the 1960s?) Are their tactics comparable? (E.g., are they less violent?) Are the radicals in traditionally communist systems like China and Poland similar to each other and to those in Western democracies?

Political Socialization

Studies of the political socialization of young political activists indicate that they have been raised in families that tend to be more educated and wealthier than the families of those who are not activist-extremists. Many of them have been socialized in families where the political orientations are more extreme (i.e., more liberal or more conservative) than in average homes. Rather than reacting against the extremism of their families, they tend to extend their families' political views.

This pattern of socialization is particularly evident among those who take up leftist politics. These political activists report a relatively high level of family conflict; but the families are more open to impulse and individuality, and are more humanistic in values than other families (Smith, Haan, and Block 1970). The main disagreements seem to be on extent to which children are more activist than their parents rather than on the intergenerational consistency in the direction of fundamental political beliefs. There is some empirical support for Kenneth Keniston's (1973) "red diaper" theory—that the children of very liberal or left-wing parents engage in political actions to support ideas their parents have only talked about (see also Jennings and Niemi 1981; Wood 1974; Sampson 1967; Feuer 1969; Middleton and Putney 1963).

Personality Approaches

Some political analysts attempt to explain political activism of extremists at a more fundamental level, referring to a person's personality, basic psychic drives and needs, and/or psychological life history. In this perspective, activist political behavior is seen as a response to an individual's psychological makeup. In the mode of *social adjustment,* an individual attempts to gain acceptance from significant others (such as parents or peer groups) by expressing certain beliefs or taking certain actions. As an example, psychic needs, such as the need for love and belonging (recall the discussion of Maslow's hierarchy in Chapter 3), might cause the individual to conform in his political behaviors to the group norms of some extremist political group that offers him membership.

Another mode of responding is *externalization,* in which a person projects onto the political world unresolved problems or unmet needs in his personal life. Harold Lasswell (1960), one of the intellectual fathers of behavioral political science, argued that the activist political personality is motivated primarily by the drive to overcome failure in the fulfillment of private needs. In his symbolic notation

$$p > d > r = P.$$

That is, a person's private needs *(p)* are displaced onto public objects *(d)* and rationalized in terms of the public interest *(r)* and the result is "political man or woman" *(P)*. Lasswell offers a somewhat pathological view of political behavior, since the strong drive for power of the active political personality is essentially a substitution for a low sense of self-esteem.

In their more psychoanalytic forms, these kinds of explanations have been applied mainly to top political leaders, as we shall see in the next section of this chapter. However psychological, personality-based approaches have also been used to account for the behavior of political radicals. The following paragraphs summarize empirical findings representative of this research. Much of the research has examined student radicals. As a student who has experience with other students, what do you hypothesize about the student radicals? Are student extremists different from other students in their intelligence or idealism or independence? Are student radicals of the left different from student radicals of the right?

Generally, the research suggests that student radicals *are* different from their nonradical peers. In terms of personality, the American student radicals tend to be more intelligent, creative, idealistic, and independent than the nonradicals. And among British and French students, the radical (left) activists exhibit "highly principled moral reasoning," in which their political behavior is justified in terms of a logical and consistent belief system and abstract notions about social justice (O'Connor 1978). Although these admirable characteristics are often attributed to leftist radicals, there is evidence that they apply to all political radicals, whether their political orientation is left or right (Kerpelman 1972; see also Smith, Haan, and Block 1970:274–278). Empirical studies identify some student radicals with substantial personality disorders of the type hypothesized by Lasswell (1960). But the political behavior of most student radicals seems better explained either as an outcome of the process of social adjustment or as a move toward self-actualization through participation in politics to pursue important ideals.

POLITICAL LEADERS

The most extensive, and perhaps the most intriguing, research on political personality has studied top political leaders. This chapter began with a glimpse into the political personality of Henry Kissinger, who has been variously described as brilliant and/or pathological. Many of us are fascinated with the ultimate political gladiators—top political leaders, such as Fidel Castro, Winston Churchill, Adolf Hitler, Mao Zedong, and Richard Nixon. Can political personality analysis increase our understanding of why these and other top political leaders behave as they do?

Personality Approaches

An illuminating and well-known application of the personality approach to the analysis of top political leaders is James David Barber's study, *Presidential Character* (1977). For Barber, there are two critical dimensions (characteristics) relevant for understanding the political personality. One dimension is "energy to task," which refers to the level of energy with which an individual approaches his work and responsibilities—Barber's categories are "active" and "passive." The second dimension measures the individual's "affect to work," that is, the person's feelings about his work—the categories are "positive" and "negative." As displayed in Table 4.1, these two dimensions are employed by Barber to generate four political personality types, which are then used to taxonomize American presidents. Barber does not name these types, except to call them "active-positives," "active-negatives," and so on.

Most of Barber's attention is focussed on the active-negative and the active-

TABLE 4.1. Barber's Presidential Personality Types

		Affect to Work	
		Positive	*Negative*
Energy to Task	*Active*	F. D. Roosevelt Harry Truman John Kennedy Jimmy Carter	Woodrow Wilson Lyndon Johnson Richard Nixon
	Passive	James Madison Warren Harding Ronald Reagan	George Washington Dwight Eisenhower

positive presidents. The active-negatives are hard workers who find little intrinsic reward in the strenuous efforts that they associate with their job. Because they have a high need for personal achievement and because they lack self-esteem and personal identity, they tend to enter politics in order to fulfill personal needs (hence this group does seem to fit Lasswell's [1960] formulation). They believe that politics, and life generally, are often determined by fate and luck, rather than by personal action. Thus politics becomes an arena for power manipulation and personal reward, not for the accomplishment of major goals. Barber's major examples of active-negative presidents are Woodrow Wilson and Richard Nixon.

In contrast, the active-positive presidents derive great pleasure out of their work and believe that they can achieve their goals. They are detached and spontaneous in their interpersonal dealings and are open to experience. They have considerable confidence in their own adequacy as individuals. Thus they exercise political power in order to serve others and to fulfill their ideals, not to externalize unmet needs for self-esteem. For Barber, Franklin D. Roosevelt, John F. Kennedy and Jimmy Carter were active-positive presidents.

Barber (1988) classifies Ronald Reagan as a passive-positive president. Barber observes that although Reagan greatly enjoyed being president, he was very willing to let others take initiatives and grapple with the complexities of the issues that faced the government. Barber observes that Reagan "presented himself to the American people as informed, decisive, in charge—and from the accounts of his advisers he is the opposite of those things." Barber's evidence of passivity is the series of books by Reagan's former aides (e.g., by Chief of Staff Donald Regan, Deputy Chief of Staff Michael Deaver, and Press Secretary Larry Speakes). These books revealed the extent to which those other than the passive president (including themselves, Nancy Reagan, and perhaps even astrologers!) helped determine major policies and also day-to-day decisions about White House operations.

For Barber, key personality traits define each of the four types of political personality. But what is the source of these traits? Barber argues that these traits can be traced back to three components of personal development and socialization. The first component is *character,* which involves one's orientation to life, and especially one's sense of self-esteem, and which emerges during childhood. The second component is *worldview,* which includes one's political belief system and broad assumptions about human nature, morality, and so on, and is developed primarily during adolescence. The third component is *style,* which, in the political arena, entails the usual way that one performs political roles, and which is mainly established during young adulthood. In a sense, these three components are akin to personality, beliefs, and action-experiences.

Barber acknowledges that political personality is not deterministic in a strict sense. Political behavior is also contingent upon the environmental context. In explaining presidential behavior, this context includes both the relevant distribution of political power on the specific issue and also the expectations of other actors. Critics of Barber argue that he does not place much emphasis on either element of the environmental context in his discussions of presidential behavior in specific situations, and that he relies almost exclusively on his overly simplistic notions of political personality (Gianos 1982:61–64). Some also argue that Barber does not make a persuasive case that energy to task and affect to work are the two best dimensions for developing a taxonomy of political personality types.

Although Barber's analysis can be faulted, do you think such a specification of a political leader's central personality traits can inform voter choice, as Barber hoped? Can it enhance our understanding of the leader's behavior in a given political situation? Many political analysts assume this, although there is very limited empirical validation of this assumption.

Psychoanalytic Approaches

Traditionally, our formal knowledge about top political leaders came from relatively straightforward reports of biography and journalism. Recent analyses of the political personality of top leaders often take a more explicitly psychoanalytic perspective. Much of the work in this tradition, which is termed *psychobiography* or *psychohistory,* is greatly influenced by Freudian and neo-Freudian assumptions. This work attempts to illuminate those key developmental experiences that shape the individual's personality, and hence behavior. Attention is typically directed to issues such as the relationship of the young child to the mother and the father, patterns of toilet training, development of social and sexual identity, and the means used for resolving early interpersonal dilemmas.

Harold Lasswell (1960) was among the first to apply a psychoanalytic perspective to the study of political leaders. Lasswell's conception (presented in the previous section), that political personality is essentially a projection (externalization) of unmet private needs, was developed explicitly to explain the "psychopathology" of top political leaders. The evidence with which Lasswell supported his arguments was interviews with politicians and psychiatric case histories of individuals he defined as highly political. Some more recent analyses, such as Barber's active-negatives and some psychobiographies of top political leaders, support Lasswell's conception. However, the most systematic empirical evidence suggests that the majority of political leaders are actually higher on self-esteem and psychological well-being than the average adult and thus do not fit Lasswell's characterization (Sniderman 1975).

Among the best known and most influential work in this psychohistorical tradition are studies by Erik Erikson. In *Childhood and Society* (1950), Erikson examines societies such as the Hopi Indians and Sioux Indians. He identifies what he believes to be the crucial elements of child rearing and early socialization that determine the cultural style of such societies. And in his psychobiographies of single individuals, *Young Man Luther* (1958) and *Gandhi's Truth* (1969), he applies Freudian concepts to indicate how a particular individual (in these books, Martin Luther and Mohandas Gandhi) experiences and responds to the key developmental challenges in the period from infancy to the end of adolescence. For Erikson, understanding basic psychological drives enables the researcher to derive insights about the development of an individual's sense of personal identity and to assess the individual's behavioral responses to key decisions.

The psychobiographical approach has most frequently been applied to individual major political leaders (Freud and Bullitt 1967; George and George 1964; Mazlish 1973; Wolfenstein 1967). Consider, for example, these "facts" about a boy later to become a major political figure. His father emphasized strenuous effort to achieve goals and total obedience to those in authority, and he ranted about corrupt politicians. His mother was a devout Quaker, opposed to war and teaching stringent control over emotions. The boy was so worried about identification with femininity and women's work that he closed himself in the kitchen and drew the blinds when he was obliged to wash the dishes. He was an effective but ruthless debater in school, often demolishing not only the arguments of the opponent, but also attacking the opponent's personality as well. He lacked athletic ability, but he chose to go out for the "tough and manly" sport of football in college. He rarely played and was given a football letter in his senior year, essentially as a reward for serving as a human tackling dummy for four seasons.

Or consider these beliefs about great political leadership, articulated by the man himself, at the end of his political career:

> "In evaluating a leader, the key question about his behavioral traits is not whether they are attractive or unattractive, but whether they are useful. Guile, vanity, dissembling—in other circumstances these might be unattractive habits, but to the leader they can be essential. He needs guile in order to hold together the shifting coalitions of often bitterly opposed interest groups. . . . He needs a certain measure of vanity in order to create the right kind of public impression. He sometimes has to dissemble in order to prevail on crucial issues." And about Abraham Lincoln, he said, "Toward that end [preserving the Union] he broke laws, he violated the Constitution, he usurped arbitrary power, he trampled individual liberties. His justification was necessity." (Nixon 1982)

Who is our mystery man? Some piece of this characterization might have led you to identify him: Richard Milhous Nixon, U.S. president from 1969 to 1974. This material is gleaned from the psychobiographies of Nixon and from his own writings (Nixon 1982). Nixon has been subjected to as much psychoanalytic study as any political figure in history. The small amount of information in the two paragraphs above is clearly inadequate to account for Nixon's complex political behavior, from his aggressive role on the House Un-American Activities Committee in the 1950s, to his running war with the press, from his political flexibility on the China initiative, to his disastrous inflexibility during the Watergate scandal. However, is it possible that major insight into Nixon's political personality and political behavior might be possible, if one had extensive data of the type in the two previous paragraphs?

This last question is at the heart of the disagreement about the value of such political personality studies. It seems likely that even if you knew many such "facts," you would find it difficult to predict the political behavior of the individual. However, if you knew that the subject of your study was Richard M. Nixon, you might be quite effective at using hindsight knowledge of his actual political behavior to link his actions to particular psychological observations. In essence, all such psychobiographies, of Nixon and other political leaders, attempt to pro-

vide information about the leader's political personality and to explain how such information helps us make better sense of how and especially why the leader acts as he or she does.

BOX 4.1

Psychoanalyzing Burmese Political Leaders

Lucian Pye (1962) has made an interesting application of the psychohistorical approach to explain the behavior of the top political leaders of a nation and, indirectly, to account for an entire political culture. Few studies are such ambitious efforts to explain the entire set of gladiators in a political society. Pye, a political scientist influenced by the work of Freud and especially by its applications to cultural analysis by Erik Erikson, undertook a major study of Burma, one of the largest countries in Southeast Asia (about the size of Texas), with a population of about 20 million. Pye was attempting to answer the general question, Why do transitional societies have such difficulties creating an effective modern state system?

Given Pye's theoretical orientation, he assumed that political culture can be understood as political personality writ large—that is, that Burmese political culture has been shaped by the political personalities of the set of individuals in key political roles. In turn, the political personalities of these individuals can be explained in terms

BOX **4.1** *continued*

of two factors: (1) their understandings of the political history of their society, and (2) their individual life histories, emphasizing their childhood development of a sense of personal identity.

Regarding the political history of their society, Pye argues that the development of an identity as a modern nation state in Burma has been profoundly affected by its political leaders' colonial experiences under the British. Pye observes that the Burmese leaders found themselves captivated by the British, whose political style and institutions they attempted to copy. But this capture by a foreign culture has left the Burmese uncertain about the authenticity and value of the hybrid culture that has emerged.

Pye's Freudian analysis of the childhood development of Burmese political leaders led him to argue that the Burmese adult has no confidence about the world of social relationships. For Pye, these sets of understandings can be traced primarily to the patterns of child rearing practiced by Burmese mothers, who tease, love, reward, and ignore in a way that baffles the child. Thus the individual comes to believe that the behavior of others is unpredictable and is not based on trust and cooperation, and that there is no linkage between one's own behavior and rewards. One must appear cooperative, but only to lull others so that one can destroy them before one is destroyed by them.

From the perspective of building a modern political order, these understandings are devastating. There is no sense of a coherent national culture and identity that deserves the support and loyalty of the citizenry, or even of the leaders. In Pye's view, such a national identity must be an anchor point for a stable, modern nation-state. And the political leaders' own political personalities make it virtually impossible for them to create and sustain the kinds of stable, interpersonal relationships necessary for effective bureaucratic organization and for political cooperation among opposing factions.

In the case of Burma, the failure to create a strong modern state and tolerate political opposition is clear. In 1962, the democratic government was overthrown by a military coup. The military leaders (who later resigned to become "civilian" rulers) have ruled continually since that point. Burma is a repressive, one-party state, and the few attempts to promote a more democratic politics have been brutally suppressed. In September 1988, military officers seized power again after public demonstrations in support of more liberal politics. The attempt to create a national identity and to escape the shadow of colonial influence was still evident in June 1989. The new military leadership announced that the name of the country would be changed to the Union of Myanmar, the Burmese word for their own country, replacing the British colonials' word *Burma,* which connotes one particular ethnic group.

Unlike Pye's analysis in Box 4.1, most studies in the psychoanalytic research tradition have the modest goal of accounting for the behavior of one or a few particular political activists. But there is continuing disagreement over the possibility of providing valid theories or even sound empirical observations or using this approach. In one of the most comprehensive assessments of the "personality and politics" research, Fred Greenstein (1969) offers two critical criteria for evaluating the utility of personality-based explanations: (1) Are the individual's actions likely to have substantial impact on the political phenomena being explained? (2) Would different individuals act differently under similar circumstances? Clearly, as the individual's political role is more substantial and as his actions are more unique, political personality approaches have increased potential for enhancing our understanding of politics (Gianos 1982:53).

WHAT MAKES THE POLITICAL GLADIATOR RUN?

We began this chapter by asking whether it is possible to understand what makes political activists run. Within any environment, the political gladiators, and especially the extremist-activists and the top leaders, are not just plain folks. It is clear that some features of their external and/or internal political world distinguish them. The evidence in this chapter suggests that knowledge of the environmental context, political socialization, personal characteristics, and personality of political activists can each provide insights regarding their political behavior.

In general, the focus on gladiators entails a far more intensive examination of individual political actors than did the study of political beliefs and actions of the "mass public" discussed in Chapters 2 and 3. This more detailed and individualistic approach facilitates more accurate linkages between explanatory variables and the political behavior of gladiators. However, the same shortcomings identified in Chapter 3 are also present in the analysis of gladiators. It remains extremely difficult to provide unambiguous empirical evidence that one feature of the environment or one agent of socialization or one aspect of personality is the direct cause of some political behavior.

In fact, these explanatory factors are almost always employed in an inference structure where it is impossible to judge among competing explanations. That is, these analyses can rarely prove that one particular characteristic or one agent of political socialization is almost always *the* basic causal factor accounting for a gladiator's political activism. And a general theory of political activism is even more problematic, since this would require a compelling case that a certain pattern of interaction among explanatory elements is the necessary and sufficient cause of certain political behaviors by one type of activists.

This is a serious weakness for causal analysis using any of these different explanatory approaches. And the problems are most substantial for the "deeper" explanations based on personality and psychoanalytic approaches, because such studies are often presented as a total explanation of the political behavior and attitudes of an adult, especially of a political activist. Studies of political personality can be interesting and entertaining reading. And supporters of personality-based approaches might be correct that in-depth analysis of the unique political personality and motivation of the gladiator is the most fruitful method of understanding extraordinary political actors.

But this research invariably entails selective reporting of "facts" and very subjective interpretation of an individual's psyche. For critics, such an approach provides a deeply flawed, reductionist explanation, attempting to account for complex actions by a few psychological mechanisms whose existence and significance are unproven. And the basic data that serve as evidence of childhood development and psychological characteristics are usually derived from very indirect methods and bold inferences.

The goal of fully understanding political gladiators entails fascinating questions. The focus on the single political actor has analytic advantages, since data gathering and analysis can be precise and intensive. The challenge of single-actor research, however, is the effort to move beyond idiosyncratic explanations that are too deeply entrenched in the specific case. When we study large aggregates, such as all French voters or all students registered to vote, it is rather easy to ignore the unique aspects of each individual, and to focus on broad explanatory factors. But when particular individuals are studied in detail, especially those who have a dramatic impact on their countries' politics, it is extremely difficult to avoid the tendency to explain their political behavior in terms of its uniqueness. Ultimately, a central objective of political theorizing is to replace proper names by abstract concepts. There are few domains of political analysis where this challenge is greater or more exciting than in the study of political gladiators.

PART THREE

Political Systems

CHAPTER 5

States and Nations

Examining the political beliefs and actions of individual people, as we did in Chapters 2–4, is only one of the levels at which the political world can be analyzed. In this chapter, we increase the scale of our subject unit considerably, focusing on large collectivities of individuals. These collectivities are referred to by such terms as *countries, nations, states,* or *nation-states.* In this chapter, we initially examine and distinguish two crucial concepts, *state* and *nation.* In the last section, a major analytic concept used by political scientists, the *political system,* is discussed.

THE STATE

Anthropological evidence suggests that early social organization among humans was probably based on small living groups of family or kin. Human groupings formed for reasons not unlike those suggested by Maslow (1954)—to increase the capacity with which the physiological, safety, love, and belonging needs of people could be met (see Chapter 3). As groupings became larger, tribes or bands were formed on the basis of more extensive kinship ties. It might be argued that the first ''state'' had emerged when a multiplicity of such tribes were combined under some leadership structure and some pattern of organization. By this definition, there have been states since ancient times, in the sense that a state exists when there are distinctive leadership roles, rules for social interaction, and a set of organizational arrangements to identify and serve collective needs.

A Legal Definition

However, the social scientific concept of the state is a relatively modern one, based on the legal notion that the state is ''a territorially bound sovereign entity.'' (See Box 5.1.) The idea of sovereignty emerged in the sixteenth and seventeenth centuries. In current interpretations, *sovereignty* is the premise that each state has complete authority and is the ultimate source of law within its own boundaries. Sovereignty is the key element in the legal concept of the state. It is a basic assumption of international politics, and is reflected in a fundamental principle of the United Nations, the sovereign equality of all member states. This means that, before the law, Chad is equal to China, Sri Lanka is equal to the Soviet Union. While sovereignty has legal standing and moral force in international law, the reality of international politics is that a state's sovereign rights depend ultimately on sufficient power to enforce the state's position. Thus it is not likely that, when major national interests are at stake, China will yield to Chad merely on the basis of Chad's ''sovereign rights.''

Associated with the idea of sovereignty is the doctrine of *territorial integrity.* This holds that a state has the right to resist and reject any aggression, invasion, or intervention within its territorial boundaries. As with the more general notion of sovereignty, a state's protection of its territorial integrity depends on the state's capacity and political power.

It might seem there are many relatively clear examples where a state's terri-

BOX 5.1

The Concept of the State

The concept *state* is among the most extensively used words in political science, and it has various meanings. A source of confusion for American students is that they are accustomed to thinking of a state as one of the 50 units of subnational government in the United States, such as Illinois or Alabama. This is one appropriate meaning of the concept. However, in the general language of political science, *state* usually refers to the organizational units and individuals that perform the political functions for a national territorial entity, such as France or Indonesia or Nigeria. In this chapter, and in this book, the term *state* will usually denote the highest governmental level within the society.

You should also be aware that the language of political science often treats the state as though it were a single actor. For example, consider the statement just above in the discussion of sovereignty that "a state has the right to resist . . . any aggression. . . ." In reality, the state is composed of many individuals who behave as individuals, but whose combined behaviors are characterized as if they were performed by a single actor. In this book, there are other collectivities, such as the group, the political party, the army, and the bureaucracy, all of which are complex aggregates discussed as though they operate as a single actor.

torial integrity is violated, such as the invasion of France by the German army in 1940. But there is often considerable disagreement and dispute over claimed violations of territorial integrity. First, territorial integrity is a fuzzy concept when there is a dispute over boundaries. For example, both Canada and the United States claim that certain fishing waters are within their territorial boundaries and each state attempts to exclude the other's commercial fishing fleets from its territorial waters. In this case, the dispute has been settled by adjudication. But border disputes can also become a cause of violence between states, as when Iran and Iraq each claimed certain land along their mutual border, precipitating a war in 1980.

Disputes over legitimate rulers are a second underlying problem with claims that territorial integrity has been violated. For example, in 1979 a Marxist government came to power in Afghanistan by military means. Since then, Afghan *mujahideen* (Islamic religious warriors) have waged war against this Marxist leadership, which they refuse to accept. The Soviet Union, which assisted the original political takeover by the Marxists, has provided substantial military forces to maintain the government against the Islamic "counterrevolutionaries," withdrawing its own troops only in February 1989. But the struggle over control of the state within Afghanistan continues. Given this situation, consider the following questions:

Were states (such as the United States) correct in claiming that Afghan sovereignty was violated by the military support that the Soviets provided to the Marxist revolution?

Can the current Afghan government properly protest that its sovereignty has been violated by outside states (such as the United States) that provide military equipment to the *mujahideen?*

Clearly, answers to such questions depend upon one's interpretation of how sovereign power is established and maintained. Similar claims regarding violation of sovereignty are made by almost every state experiencing substantial political violence generated by internal or external forces.

A Structural-Functional Definition

A state can be defined in terms of its essential structures and functions, rather than by its legal standing. In this view, the state is the *organized institutional machinery* for making and carrying out political decisions and for enforcing the laws and rules of the government. This definition first emphasizes the many organizational *structures* that operate as "the government." And secondly, it identifies the key *functions* that the state performs.

For the great political sociologist Max Weber (1864–1920), the one function that distinguishes the state from all other organizations is its monopoly on the legitimate use of force and coercion in the society. That is, only the state has the right to use violence to enforce the laws and decisions of the society.

The "state-centered" definitions of the state offer a more expansive conception of the state's functions. In this view, the essential functions of the state are to maintain order and to compete with other actual or potential states (Skocpol 1979:30). The state is an autonomous actor, composed of public officials making decisions. The state has goals, broadly understood as the "national interest," that it attempts to achieve against resistance from both domestic and international actors (Krasner 1978:10). The particular way in which a state's structures are configured has crucial effects—on the content of the public officials' policy preferences, on determining whose preferences will be adopted as those of the state, and on the state's effectiveness in implementing those policy preferences in the society (Nordlinger 1987:370).

A widely used approach emphasizing the structures and functions of the state is based on the work of Gabriel Almond and his colleagues (see, e.g., Almond 1960). Their conceptual framework asks two central questions:

1. What functions must be performed if the state is to persist?
2. What structures perform these necessary functions within a given state?

Chapter 12 provides a recent elaboration of this basic structural-functional approach, called *capabilities analysis*. In the earlier, classical version of this approach, Almond identified seven "requisite functions"—that is, functions that must be performed by every state:

1. *Interest articulation* is the low-level communication, by citizens and groups, of what they need or want from the state.

2. *Interest aggregation* is the transformation of all these political needs and wants into a smaller number of coherent alternatives.
3. *Political socialization* is, as outlined in Chapter 3, the processes through which individuals acquire their cognitive, affective, and evaluative orientations toward the political world.
4. *Political communication* is the mechanism by which political information is transmitted.
5. *Rule making* is the process by which the state establishes policy decisions and value allocations.
6. *Rule application* is the implementation of such policy decisions.
7. *Rule adjudication* is the interpretation and resolution of disagreements regarding what the policies mean and how they should be implemented.

Given these functions, analyses using Almond's approach have primarily attempted to identify the particular structures within a state that are most significant in the performance of each function and to describe how the structures contribute to performing each function. While it might seem obvious at first glance that a certain structure always performs a particular function, more reflection (and later chapters) will suggest that the actual situation can be quite complex. For example, it is not simply the case that Congress performs the rule-making function in the United States. Many policy decisions are made by the president, by the cabinet departments, by the bureaucracy, by the courts as they both interpret and reshape laws, by structures at the local levels of government, and by the citizens through electoral initiatives.

In most contemporary states, virtually every political function is performed by a variety of political structures. Thus the central questions in structural-functional research address the characteristic processes of each structure and the subtle interrelationships among structures as they contribute to a given function. These questions are especially germane in comparative research, where the analyst attempts to specify how the structure-function patterns vary between states.

The Domain of State Action

One other way of characterizing the state is to define its appropriate domain of action. When we examine "appropriate" rather than "actual" state action, the central question is normative, rather than descriptive or analytic. A normative question asks how something *should* be, rather than how it is (recall Chapter 1). Many of the most fascinating and fundamental issues in the political world have normative components. Political scientists attempt to distinguish the normative elements of their discussion from the descriptive-analytic elements. But, as Chapter 1 observed, there are always subtle normative judgments organizing the manner in which every political question is examined.

There is a fundamental, unresolved debate in everyday political discussion, as well as in political theory, regarding how extensive the state's role in society should be. Everyone agrees that the boundaries of state activity should be limited to *res publica,* a Latin phrase meaning "things of the people." But what "things" should be included? And how expansive should the state's involvement with these things be?

In contemporary political thought, there are at least three broad views regarding the appropriate domain of state action, each providing a different conception of *res publica*. And each society has its own perspective on how to define the specific elements associated with each of the three broad views. To illustrate the kinds of elements associated with each of the three views, we shall use the one with which most of you are familiar, the American perspective.

The Conservative View of the State.   In the conservative view, the range of *res publica* should be minimal. The state must have the military or political power to defend the society (and its sovereignty) against external aggression. But within the society, there is great confidence in the dynamics of the free market to motivate and coordinate human action. If left alone, the people will produce a relatively efficient and functional social and economic order. Thus the state should be mainly a night watchman, a low-profile policeman who insures the basic safety of every individual. The state might need to control a few dangerous or unscrupulous individuals or groups who might do serious harm to others. And the state might need to provide a small amount of benefits to a few helpless or hapless individuals who would die without that assistance. But to a large extent, the state can be benign and passive. Jefferson's slogan which captures the conservative view is, "That state governs best which governs least." In its extreme form, this view is usually termed *libertarianism,* which advocates the reduction of *res publica,* and hence of the domain of appropriate state action, to almost nothing.

The Liberal View of the State.   In the liberal view, there are two crucial reasons why the state must intervene actively in the free market relations between individuals and groups. First, there are many powerful or ruthless groups whose actions are extremely harmful to others, to the proper functioning of market forces, or to the society in general. Negative effects of such scale and magnitude can be prevented only by strong state action. Second, there are major inequities in the society—the market leaves many people to suffer from severe economic and social disadvantages. Thus the liberal state is quite active, taking an expansive view of *res publica*. The state is regulatory—constraining the actions of individuals and groups that might harm the public interest. And the liberal state is redistributive—intervening in social and economic processes to insure that all citizens receive a humane level of goods and services. In the contemporary political world, such a liberal state is often termed a *welfare state,* reflecting its commitment to act positively in implementing public policies that enhance the quality of life and well-being of all citizens in the society.

The Radical View of the State.   There are many variations among radical views of the state, and it is possible to define radicalism in terms of ideologies of either the right or the left. Here, the more common definition of radicalism, that of the left, is employed. This left–radical view defines a state in terms of the groups that it primarily serves. Every state is seen essentially as a set of structures whose main purpose is to preserve and expand the interests of the dominant class in the society. Many contemporary states, which are characterized by deep inequalities, are coercive mechanisms to protect the dominant class. In the words of Soviet revolutionary leader and theorist V. I. Lenin (1870–1924), such a state is "a body of armed men, weapons, and prisons." Radicals generally support the fundamental goal of equality of political, economic, and social resources in the society. Thus they contend that a state that preserves huge inequalities must be overthrown, and that its overthrow usually requires revolutionary political violence.

In the ideal society after the revolution, there will be justice for all, based on economic, social, and political egalitarianism. If the state does still exist, it will be the agent of all the people, organizing and distributing the resources of the society for the common good. Thus the domain of *res publica* becomes very large, since all major resources and most individual and group action must be controlled by the state in order to serve society. Some radicals assume the state will ultimately be eliminated (in Marx's words, the state will "wither away"); but even in this view, organizational structures would remain to administer policy. The extreme radical conception, in which the state disappears, is labelled *anarchism*. This does not mean a situation of chaos and disorder; rather it is a stateless society where individuals and groups organize spontaneously to create a sociopolitical order in which all people participate and all benefit from commonly produced goods and services.

Other Views of the State.   It should be noted that these are the three dominant Western political views of the state. There are also conceptions that do not emphasize a unique political "state." For example, in some societies dominated by all-encompassing religions, there is no political state that is independent of the religious order. In fundamentalist Islamic regimes, Shari'a law, the law of Islam, establishes a religious state that defines all aspects of social life, including such issues as the content of *res publica*. And in historical terms, there have been many societies that had no conception of a distinct political order. For instance, there were no specifically political structures in most precolonial African societies. Rather, the rules governing the society were based on tradition, as interpreted by community leaders (such as tribal elders or religious authorities).

THE NATION

The concept of the nation has a psychological and emotional basis, rather than a legal or functional basis (like the state). A *nation* is defined by a deeply shared fundamental identification and/or attitude among a set of people. Different factors might constitute the basis of such identification: shared descent (belief in a common kinship and/or history), shared culture, shared geographic space, shared religion, shared language, or shared economic order. The nation is a community of understanding, of communication, of trust (Connor 1987).

Most people feel some identity with a variety of different reference groups or communities. For example, you might identify with various groups, such as a religion, a local community, an ethnic group, a social club, a sports team. In the usage here, what distinguishes a nation from other reference groups is that the nation is a major group, beyond the family group, with whom the individual identifies very powerfully. It is an essential division between "us" and "them." The strength of a person's primary national identity depends on the relative importance she places on various identities and the extent to which the most important identities reinforce her basic conception of "us" versus "them."

A fundamental challenge to many governments is to create and maintain a viable nation-state. Ideally, a *nation-state* has a citizenry whose primary national identity is coterminous with the territorial boundaries of the state. There are a few modern states where common geography, history, culture, ethnicity, and language have all combined to result in a strong sense of shared nationality among nearly the all citizens governed by the state. Japan is an example of such a homogeneous nation-state. Minimally, a nation-state needs citizens who are willing to cooperate with each other in political and social life, despite opposing national identities.

The problem is that many, perhaps most, states do include groups whose fundamental identities are associated with different nations. There are obvious problems for the stability of the state if these different groups are in conflict with each other (Horowitz 1985). There can also be problems if a group's allegiance to its nation reduces, rather than reinforces, its allegiance to the state. The two examples in Box 5.2, the British Isles and the Indian subcontinent, illustrate the kinds of differences between state and nation that exist in many contemporary societies.

BOX 5.2

State and Nations

The British Isles

The United Kingdom is typically viewed as one of the longest-lived and most homogeneous political systems in the world. However, it is also a complex amalgamation of different nations. Among the earliest peoples in the more than 1,000 islands in the area were the Celts, religious tribal groups who inhabited the central areas in the main islands. Later, waves of other ethnic groups begin to invade the islands by sea and to drive these original natives to the peripheral areas of the islands. The Roman legions of Caesar arrived in the first century B.C. and established political control over a network of many towns, calling this part of the Roman Empire *Britannia*. The Angles and Saxons invaded from North Central Europe in the fifth century and were leaders in forging, from the disparate feudal states, the first kingdom in the islands. In the eleventh century, there were two invasions, first by King Canute and the Danes and then by William the Conqueror, from Norman France. The British still celebrate the Norman Conquest in 1066 as the last time a "foreign" army stepped onto British soil.

BOX **5.2** *continued*

Each of these groups brought its own culture and traditions. Slowly, these different nations were assimilated into one society with a broadly common identification. But this blending into a single nation has never been total. The original Celts most strongly resisted assimilation, with many of their tribes being driven to the hinterlands of the British Isles, where they continued to speak Gaelic and follow their own traditions and culture. The central and southeastern part of the islands was dominated by the English, who emerged primarily from the Angle, Saxon, and Norman French groups. Although the English, Welsh, and Scots were different nations, distinguished by language, ethnicity, and religion, the English used a combination of diplomacy and military action to bring some of these other groups into a common state (a "united kingdom"). The southwestern region, Wales, was officially joined to England in 1284 and the northern region, Scotland, came into the union in 1707.

The greatest resistance to union came primarily from the Gaelic peoples who inhabited the largest separate island to the west, Ireland. These peoples had a quite different national identity, based on language, culture, and religion. From the seventeenth through the early twentieth century, there was continual conflict in Ireland. To pacify the native Irish (Catholic and Gaelic-speaking), the English crown used its military power and it induced many Scots (Protestant and English-speaking) to move to Ireland, by giving them the best land. In response, the native Irish used violence in the attempt to free themselves from control by the English and the settlers. Those groups, in turn, used violence and state power to protect their position.

After centuries of struggle, native Irish pressured the British government to grant some autonomy to part of Ireland in 1921. Only in 1949 did a second, fully independent state, the Republic of Ireland, officially emerge in the British Isles. This new state included about three-fourths of the territory of the island of Ireland. The citizens and territory of the remaining one-fourth of Ireland, called Northern Ireland, remained part of the British state. Some groups, like the Irish Republican Army, have continued a violent struggle to unify the entire island and the whole Irish nation in this single state. While some describe the struggle in Northern Ireland as simply a religious one between Catholics and Protestants, it is, rather, a far more complex struggle among nations.

The actual name of the British state gives some indication of its blending of nations: The United Kingdom (a unification of the English, the Welsh, and the Scots) of Great Britain and Northern Ireland (the inhabitants of Ireland who did not join the Republic). The primary national identity of more than two-thirds of the "British" is not British, but rather English, Welsh, Scots, or Ulster/Irish. There is also about 5 percent of the population who, as nonwhites from Afro-Caribbean or Asian descent, are least fully integrated into the British nation.

In general, the United Kingdom is a good example of a place where different nations have combined into a single state, which, by most accounts, is a relatively successful and stable nation-state. Linguistic domination is now substantial, religious differences are not crucial, and ethnic and cultural distinctions are diminishing. Nonetheless, the differences in national identity are still evident in the United Kingdom. There are recurrent protests by nonwhite groups (especially those of Asian or Afro-Caribbean heritage) regarding discrimination; there is periodic political pressure for greater local political control in Wales and Scotland; and, in particular, there are continuing violent disputes in Northern Ireland regarding what nation and what state should enjoy the loyalty of its citizens.

BOX 5.2 *continued*

The Indian Subcontinent

The problem of discontinuities between nations and states is often most severe in states that have gained independence in the last 40 years. The Indian subcontinent reflects the problems that these postcolonial areas have experienced. The vast Indian subcontinent was a feudal society divided into many small kingdoms ruled by princes (*maharajahs*). From the sixteenth century, the riches of India were pursued, and often exploited, by many traders, including the British, Dutch, French, and Arabs. The states from which these traders came began to struggle for dominance over the Indian trade, and the British finally gained hegemony in the eighteenth century after defeating the French. From that time until 1947, the Indian subcontinent was the major jewel in the British imperial crown, treated as a single territory under colonial rule.

After a lengthy and often violent campaign of political and social action by Indian nationalists, the British relented and granted the subcontinent independence in 1947. However, despite the desires of the British and the efforts of some Indian leaders such as Mohandas Gandhi, the subcontinent was deeply split, on the basis of religion, between Hindus and Muslims. Since it seemed impossible to fashion a single state out of these two nations, two states were formed: India, which was predominantly (82 percent) Hindu; and Pakistan, which was predominantly (90 percent) Muslim.

The situation was further complicated by the concentration of Muslims in two geographically distinct areas in the northeast and northwest regions of the subcontinent. As a consequence, Pakistan was composed of two parts, separated by more than 1,500 miles of rival India's territory. Many Hindus in Pakistan and Muslims in India were forced to leave their homelands and migrate to the new state based on their own religion. The hostility and bloodshed associated with the partition resulted in 1 million deaths. There have been periodic violent boundary conflicts ever since.

While the major religious difference on the Indian subcontinent was generally resolved by this partition, many other nationality problems remained. Within Pakistan, for example, there was a long-standing animosity between two major ethnic groups, the Punjabis and the Bengalis. When the Bengalis, dominant in East Pakistan, were victorious in a national election, the Punjabi-dominated West Pakistan attempted to reassert political power through their control of the military. When the Bengalis attempted to form their own independent nation-state (with some support from India), a terrible civil war resulted. After hundreds of thousands of deaths due to war and starvation, the Bengalis of East Pakistan were successful in the civil war and created a new nation-state, Bangladesh.

And while India is dominated by Hindus, major nation-based cleavages continue to plague the state. These cleavages create tremendous barriers to forging a single identity as a nation-state among the peoples of India. There are 13 official languages and the "national" languages, Hindi and English, are understood by only about one-third of the population. In all, there are about 1,650 different dialects in India, most of which are mutually incomprehensible. And there are at least five major religious groupings in India: Hindu, Muslim, Sikh, Christian, and Buddhist. Most of the non-Hindu groups are regionally concentrated, enhancing their identity as religion-based nations.

Recent political unrest in India has been most prevalent among the Sikhs. The Sikhs have a very strong identity as a religious community and an ethnic group. They

BOX 5.2 *continued*

are concentrated in the northwest part of India called the Punjab, and they perceive themselves to be discriminated against politically by the Hindus. The Sikhs demand greater political autonomy and, since the early 1980s, some have insisted on an independent nation-state in the Punjab. The best known of the continuing series of violent confrontations between the Sikhs and the Hindu majority in India was the assassination of Indian Prime Minister Indira Gandhi in 1984. This was done by several Sikhs among her private guard and the act was justified as a retaliation for the storming of the Golden Temple, the Sikhs' most holy shrine, by Gandhi's army. In sum, the many strong cleavages in India, based on religion, language, ethnicity, and region, expose the state to persistent pressure and instability.

This problem of multiple nations within a single state is endemic in the contemporary world. For most of the nation-states that have gained independence since 1945, territorial boundaries were based on the arbitrary administrative decisions of colonial powers. Thus in most of Africa and Asia, states were formed with boundaries that were not sensitive to nationality differences in the areas. Many of these states have experienced traumatic nationality conflicts. There are reports every day of such struggles as those by the Kurds in Iraq, the Eritreans in Ethiopia, the Tamils in Sri Lanka, the Ibos in Nigeria, and so on. And even in the more established states, there are frequent explosions (sometimes, literal ones) of nation-based cleavages. Recent examples include the activities of the Quebequois in Canada, the Basques in Spain, the Irish Catholics in Northern Ireland, and the Armenians, Estonians, Latvians, and Lithuanians in the Soviet Union. The attempt to create and maintain viable nation-states where there are conflicts between nation and state is a recurring theme that influences many of the topics we examine in this book.

THE POLITICAL SYSTEM

While concepts like state and nation are extremely useful, political scientists have sought an additional, more general and analytic concept to describe the structures and dynamics of organized politics at all levels. Many political scientists use some version of the concept of the *political system,* developed in the work of David Easton (1953, 1965). Easton was searching for an analytical concept that would facilitate the development of a general theory of politics. He found the basis for such a concept in the notion of general systems theory from biology.

Systems in General

The essential concept is the idea of a *system,* which is a group of components that exist in a characteristic structural relationship to each other and that interact on the basis of regular patterns. Because the components are interdependent, change in one component will have some effect on other components. Such change can cause minor or even major alterations in the manner in which the total system functions. In a mechanical analogy, an automobile engine can be viewed as a system, as a set of components interacting in a regular way. If one spark plug is dirty, the performance of the automobile-as-system will be substantially altered, and if the spark plug is removed, the system might not work at all.

The same interdependency of components is evident in human systems, such as families, sports teams, factories, or bureaucracies. The components of human systems—people in roles—are more likely to vary in the range of their actions than are the components of most mechanical systems. This means that the performance of human systems tends to be far more variable and less predictable than mechanical systems. Human systems function relatively smoothly as long as most of the components (the people) interact within a tolerable range of expected action. For high performance, some human systems, like a symphony orchestra or a drill team, require far more rigid adherence to predictable roles than others, like a jazz combo or a basketball team. People's capacity to adapt and improvise means that human systems can sometimes adapt effectively to unexpected circumstances. But human variability can also result in system performance that is unexpected, with negative or even disastrous effects.

The Political System Defined

For Easton, the political system is a system of behavior, and it is defined by its distinctive activities, *the authoritative allocation of values for a society*. This definition is central to the idea of a political system, as it is used in this book and in many political analyses. Thus it is appropriate to examine each aspect of the definition in greater detail.

"Values."   *Values* are those things that have significance and importance to people. We can discuss values in terms of the idealized abstractions that inspire or justify much political action: liberty, equality, freedom, justice. Or values can be defined more specifically: they can be material goods, such as a decent house or road system; they can be services, such as quality health care or protection from crime; they can be conditions, such as security from national enemies or clean air; they can be symbolic goods, such as status. As well as positive values, there are negative values, such as coercion or imprisonment, polluted water, epidemic disease, and so on.

By definition, values tend to be scarce resources—either there is an insufficient amount of a given value to satisfy everyone or the enjoyment of one value by some requires a loss of value to others. To use an example from the previous paragraph, there is no political system where all citizens have housing that they would consider adequate. Some would view their housing as too small, or too expensive, or in the wrong location, or lacking in sufficient luxuries. Even if a state could provide everyone with identical housing, some would be dissatisfied because they want better housing or because they object to the use of their taxes or work to subsidize the housing of others. A vast arsenal of nuclear weapons in one's state may make one individual feel quite secure, while it makes another individual extremely insecure. One person might favor large expenditures on missile systems while another would prefer to spend the resources on housing and a third might prefer lower taxes to expenditure on either weapons or housing. Every value distribution entails trade-offs between different values as well as some inequality in the distribution of benefits and burdens. Thus there are always disagreements, competition, and even violent conflict over whose values will be served and whose will not.

"Allocation." Pierre Mendes-France, distinguished premier of the French Fourth Republic, observed that "to govern is to make choices." *Allocation* refers to this choice making—to the process by which decisions and actions are taken to grant values to some and deny values to others. One useful definition of politics is that it is the processes though which competition and conflict over values are resolved by choice making. Value allocations occur at each moment when decisions are made to alter or even to sustain the existing distribution of values.

"Authoritative." Value allocations are taken as *authoritative* when the decisions are accepted as binding by people affected by the decisions. One of the most fascinating questions in political analysis is, Why do people accept the authority of the political system to allocate values in a manner that is not to their direct advantage? Why do people accept the imposition of taxes, policies, and laws that they judge to be undesirable to themselves? The discussion in Box 5.3 suggests some of the reasons why the authority of the state is accepted.

BOX 5.3

Why Do People Accept Authority?

There are many answers to the question of why people accept the authority of the state. In the classic definitions, authority is voluntaristic. Authority is based on a subjective belief in the *legitimacy* of the state: A person willingly accepts the decisions of the state because it is "the right thing to do." The individual's judgment that the state's authority is legitimate might be grounded in one or more of the following phenomena (see Weber 1958a:295–301):

1. *Law.* The individual believes that the laws of the state are rationally established, purposeful, and enacted with formal correctness by appropriate public actors, and thus compliance with those laws is proper behavior.

2. *Tradition.* The individual is influenced by a long-standing habit among most people in the society to accept patterns of authoritative action.

3. *Charisma.* The individual is persuaded by a dynamic leader whose personal qualities are so extraordinary that she captures their trust and unquestioning support. (Among the examples of twentieth-century charismatic political leaders are Adolf Hitler, Mao Zedong, and the Ayatollah Khomeini.)

4. *Social contract.* Most broadly, classical political theorists such as Thomas Hobbes (1588–1679) and John Locke (1632–1704) suggest that acceptance of the state's authority is due to a "social contract" in which each individual sacrifices certain personal values to a state whose actions insure that social order will replace the violent state of nature.

5. *Socialization.* The effective efforts of the agents of political socialization might convince (indoctrinate?) the individual that the state has authority

BOX 5.3 *continued*

to make decisions and that obedience is proper, without relying specifically on any of these other sources of authority.

In many contemporary states, explanations of the acceptance of the state's authority by most citizens are often based on a more explicit assessment of material incentives or sanctions:

6. *Individual utility.* The individual is satisfied with the array of values that the state provides specifically to her, or with the broad values provided to all citizens, such as economic growth or social stability, to which she attaches great importance (Linz 1978:16–23).

7. *Fear of sanction.* The individual might fear the negative values, such as deprivation of valued benefits, coercion, imprisonment, or even death, that the state might render on her if she were to challenge the state's authority. With sanctions, the line between authority and power exercise might have been crossed.

The debate over the legitimacy of the state's authority is a perpetual one. A fascinating cultural expression of the authority debate is Greek dramatist Sophocles' (496–406 B.C. 1967:144) classic play *Antigone.* Antigone violates a rule promulgated by Creon, who is not only her uncle (and potential father-in-law), but also the king. In defense of social order, Creon argues, "He whom the State appoints must be obeyed to the smallest matter, be it right or wrong . . . There is no more deadly peril than disobedience." In a similar way, contemporary political analyst Samuel Huntington (1968:7–8) observes, "The primary problem is not liberty but the creation of legitimate public order. Men may, of course have order without liberty, but they cannot have liberty without order."

Ultimately, Antigone decides to do what seems morally correct to her, and she breaks the law. Thus Antigone represents the other side of the debate, which is characterized by eloquent defenders of the individual's right and even the obligation to resist the state's authority, when she believes the state to be wrong. In "Civil Disobedience," American philosopher Henry David Thoreau (1817–1862) writes, "If [the law of the state] is of such a nature that it requires you to be the agent of injustice to another, then, I say, break the law. Let your life be a counter friction to stop the machine. What I have to do is to see, at any rate, that I do not lend myself to the wrong which I condemn" (Thoreau 1849/1966:92).

In some cases, the objective of resistance to authority is social change. Mohandas Gandhi's essential strategy in resisting British rule in India was *satyagraha,* repeated episodes of (generally) nonviolent resistance to a system of laws and authority that Gandhi judged to be immoral. Gandhi's approach was applied by the civil rights movement in the United States during the 1960s, in order to protest laws that failed to prevent discrimination on the basis of race. In other cases, the resistance to established authority is more aggressive, and the objective is establishment of a new political order. Marx and Engels, in the famous *Communist Manifesto* (1848/1978:500), conclude, "In short, the Communists everywhere support every revolutionary movement against the existing social and political order of things. . . . They openly declare that their ends can be attained only by the forcible overthrow of all existing social conditions. Let the ruling classes tremble at a Communist revolution. The proletarians have nothing to lose but their chains. They have a world to win. Working men of all countries, unite!"

BOX 5.3 *continued*

Jawaharlal Nehru (left) and Mahatma Gandhi (right)

"For a Society."   The final element in Easton's definition of the political system is meant to solve the difficult analytic problem of defining the boundaries of the political world. Easton limits the domain of the political system to those areas where values are being allocated "for a society"—that is, to those values where the state must act to protect and serve the public's interests. Recall the notion of *res publica* or "things of the people." The political system, in establishing the range of value allocations included in *res publica,* also sets the boundaries of its own domain of action.

Every political system defines its boundaries of legitimate action differently. This is a crucial point reflected in the contrasting views of the role of the state discussed earlier in this chapter. We shall see throughout this book, and especially in Part Five, that some political systems allocate values in virtually every aspect of their citizen's lives, while other systems intervene minimally. One political system might provide a total health care delivery system to all citizens, with no direct charges for doctors, hospitals, or treatment, while another system subsidizes only hospitalization for the very poor. One political system might require daily religious instruction in school while another system forbids even the general discussion of religious philosophies.

It should be noted that Easton's definition seems to cover only political systems at the level of the nation-state. The idea of a political system for an entire society serves the purposes of this book well, since the book primarily discusses entire nation-states. But analytically, a political system could exist at any level, even one that does not have ultimate authority. This concept could certainly apply to subnational political systems (including such American examples as states, counties, and municipalities). And it could also apply to a supranational system that encompasses more than one nation-state (for example, the European Communities.) Perhaps a more generalized definition of the political system might describe it in terms of "the authoritative allocation of values *for a collectivity*."

Conceptualization of the Political System

Easton's conceptualization of the political system, characterized in Figure 5.1, is based on the idea of an "input-output system" within a broader environment. This means that, within an environment, the system receives certain phenomena as inputs, does some processing of those inputs, and then generates outputs back into the environment. Each of the elements in Figure 5.1 can be specified more fully.

Environment.   The *environment* is the name given to all those activities that are not included within the state's activity domain of *res publica*. Thus it encompasses all those physical and social domains where the authoritative allocation of values for the society is *not* the dominant activity. Do not think of the environment as a separate physical area, because it is often the case that the political system operates in the same physical environment as other subsystems like the economic environment and the social environment. The activities in the "intrasocietal" environment are occurring in the same spatial area as are the activities being performed by the political system. The environment is vast, because it includes not only all the activities within the society, but also an "extrasocietal" environment, which includes virtually every activity in the world that is external to the territory of the state.

Clearly, only a few aspects of this enormous environment are considered in any particular analysis of a political system. What is important about the concept of the environment is the idea that any aspect of the environment might affect the

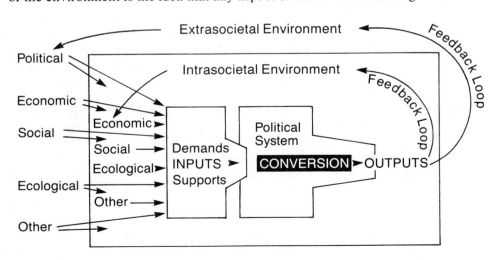

Figure 5.1. Conceptualization of the Political System. SOURCE: Based on Easton 1965:31.

political system. That is, the environment provides opportunities and obstacles, resources and constraints that are relevant to the functioning of the political system.

For example, there might be a shortage of fossil fuels within the state (i.e., in the intrasocietal ecological system). This "input" might provoke the political system to take some action (policy decision) to insure more fuel for its citizens and its economy. Among the various policies the political system might adopt are these:

1. Stimulate additional fuel production within the society by subsidies for exploration
2. Reduce fuel consumption by a very high fuel use tax
3. Encourage innovative alternatives by supporting research and development of synfuels
4. Obtain fuel resources from outside the state by using military force to capture some other state's fuel resources

Can you think of other feasible policy responses to this problem in the political system's environment?

Demands and Supports.   Among the inputs from the environment, the most direct inputs to the political system are demands and supports. *Demands* are wants or desires for particular value allocations. Demands might come from individuals, groups, or systems that are either within or outside the society. When a citizen prefers lower taxes, or more expenditure on health care, or greater regulation of corporations, or a freeze on nuclear weapons construction, these preferences become demands to the political system when they are communicated directly by the citizen or by other actors such as spokespersons, interest groups, or political parties. (This corresponds, in functional language, to interest articulation and political communication.)

Supports are actions by individuals or groups that indicate either favorable or unfavorable orientations toward the political system. These actions can be directed toward individual *actors* in the political system (e.g., George Bush, Fidel Castro), toward elements of the *regime* (e.g., the prime minister, the Supreme Court, the municipal council), or toward a broad *political community* (e.g., the Sikhs, the national flag, Francophones [all peoples speaking French], the Third World, the World of Islam). Support can be positive, as, for example, when an individual pays taxes, serves in the state's military, salutes the flag, or votes. But there can also be negative support, in the sense of actions that criticize or oppose the political system. Examples of negative support are refusing to pay taxes, avoiding military service, burning the flag, or defacing the ballot.

Conversion.   At the heart of the political system framework is the conversion process—the process by which political actors assess demands and supports within the context of the relevant environmental forces, and then determine what values will be allocated to whom. In Easton's own discussions, the conversion process is treated a bit like a "black box," in the sense that little detail is provided about how decisions are made.

But many analysts have been especially interested in studying how the political system actually does make policy decisions and allocate resources, whether or not they use Easton's systems model. The most widely proposed general explanations of the decision process are the *class approach,* the *elite approach,* and the *group approach.* In each, certain groups in society (the dominant class, the small ruling elite, or a diversity of private groups) exercise their power and influence. The state's decision makers respond to these societal pressures, implementing the most powerful pressures as public policy. Each of these three approaches will be explained in detail in Chapter 10, and thus will not be described at this point.

There are other, specific analytic descriptions of the dynamics of the political decision-making system in addition to the class, group, and elite approaches. Here are brief sketches of several of these alternatives:

In the *state-centered* approach, the major public decision makers act autonomously from the diversity of groups in the society. They define a national interest, and they then formulate and implement policies to achieve this national interest, regardless of contrary views from subunits in the government or from groups in the society (Krasner 1978).

In the *rational process* approach, decision makers calculate the expected utility (the net benefits minus the net costs) for each alternative decision. They select the action with the most favorable benefit-cost calculus.

In the *incremental* approach, choices are typically marginal changes from existing policies. In this view, decision makers lack the cognitive capacity and the comprehensive information that would enable them to calculate utilities rationally. Also, the balance of political forces has resulted in the current policy compromise. For these reasons, it is more sensible and more politically prudent to make periodic small changes that readjust policy toward their broad goals.

The *bureaucratic politics* approach emphasizes that a decision maker's particular role in the organization greatly influences the way she structures the issue, the information she receives, and the choices she makes. Decision makers are loyal to their own subunit and its perspective, rather than to the organization as a whole. Decisions are compromises based on bargains blending the agendas and values of the different subunits involved in the process (Allison 1971).

The *organizational process* approach assumes that an organization develops certain routinized, standard operating procedures. These determine the flows of information, the formulation of alternatives, the patterns of interaction, and the criteria for choice. Thus the established routines for making decisions are more important than the views of particular actors (Cyert and March 1963).

Outputs.   Once political decisions have been made, they become outputs of the political system. Some analysts find it useful to distinguish *outputs,* which are the decisions and the implementation process, from the *outcomes,* which are the impacts of those decisions. Some outputs are visible and obvious, as when the political system authorizes the development of a new missile system, spends the money with which the missiles are built, and points them toward its enemies. But it is sometimes quite difficult to identify decisions (outputs), since decisions might involve subtle actions, secret policies, or even "nondecisions" that perpetuate the existing value distribution or bury issues. For example, if some people demand government subsidies for small farmers and the government does nothing, there has been an allocation decision, even though no visible policy action can be identified. A policy might also be implemented in a multiplicity of ways for different people, making it difficult to specify exactly what the policy output is. For example, the state might have a law that an individual cannot kill another person; yet the state does not mete out identical punishment to all those who do kill.

Policy outcomes are another very interesting subject for inquiry. Ultimately, it is the impacts of the political system's policy choices that really affect people's lives. The essential question is, What difference did that policy choice (that value allocation) make? How does the implemented policy affect people's health, welfare, security, knowledge, self-worth? How does it influence their life, liberty, and pursuit of happiness? Even more than in the analysis of outputs, it can be extremely difficult to identify with precision the overall effects of a policy and its effects on particular individuals and groups.

Feedback.   The final component in the systems approach is the "feedback loop." It is assumed that outputs might have impact on aspects of the environment and thus will affect the next round of demands and supports reaching the political system. *Feedback* is the term applied to the dynamics through which information about the changing nature of the political system and its environment are monitored by the system. Political actors are supposed to monitor this information, because changes in the environment, in inputs, and in the political system might require the political actors to revise the value allocations they have previously made. In Figure 5.1, feedback is characterized as a loop to emphasize that there is continuous, evolving interdependency among components in the system.

System Persistence

For Easton, the underlying question is, How does a political system persist in a world of change? The political system is embedded within a complex and changing environment. The political decision makers must maintain a delicate balance of forces: The environments must be prevented from constraining or overwhelming the political system and must be exploited for the resources and opportunities that they present; political actors must be sensitive and accurate in their perceptions of the effects of all other components in the system; demands must be managed so that they are not irreconcilable and so that they do not overload the resources available; positive support must be nurtured and negative support discouraged or suppressed through some mix of value allocations that maintain the loyalty or acquiescence of the citizens. In short, the conversion process must operate with political skill and political will.

What happens if there is insufficient political skill or political will? The pressures on the decision makers might overwhelm their capacity to respond effectively. If the political system's performance is poor, there is likely to be a reduction in the quality of the citizens' life, more problems from the internal and external environment, loss of support for the political system, and a rise in disorder.

At any point, it is possible that there will be changes in the political system: (1) The *authorities* who hold political positions might be replaced, by election, by political pressure, or by violence; or (2) the *regime* might change, through the implementation of new governing structures or procedures or through significant alterations in the pattern of value allocations. If these changes in the regime are massive and fundamental, it is even possible for a political system to "die." While Easton and others have never fully specified the necessary conditions for the death of a political system, they would involve sudden and major transformations in the nature of the conversion process and/or the configuration of value allocations. The discussion of Cambodia in Box 5.4 describes a rapid series of major changes, some of which might be considered deaths of the political system.

BOX 5.4

"Death" of a Political System: Cambodia

The idea that a political system might die can be best grasped by examining Cambodia, a state that has recently undergone several major transformations in a short time span.

The Cambodia of 1962 *(Cambodia I)* was a small, beautiful state in Indochina that had been granted its independence by France in 1953. It has been said that the most important activities in the lives of the Cambodians were to dance, make love, and watch the grass grow. They were ruled under a rather authoritarian political system by Prince Norodom Sihanouk, a hereditary leader who attempted to balance the forces of the left and the right within Cambodia and to maintain Cambodia on a course as a neutral state.

However, in the late 1960s Norodom Sihanouk was unable to prevent Cambodia from being drawn into the increasingly widespread and intense war in neighboring Vietnam, especially because of the underlying power struggle in the area, between the Soviet Union, the United States, and China. Some Vietcong (the guerrillas attempting to overthrow the South Vietnamese state) took sanctuary in Cambodia; but Sihanouk insisted that Cambodian sovereignty prevented the United States and South Vietnamese armies from invading Cambodia to attack these Vietcong. Sihanouk also attempted to direct international attention to the "secret bombing" raids in Cambodia conducted by the American military but denied by the American political leadership.

Because of Sihanouk's resistance to their military objectives, the Americans supported (and perhaps directed) a March 1970 coup in which the leaders in the Cambodian army overthrew Sihanouk and replaced him with General Lon Nol, a rightist dictator who was generally viewed as a puppet of the United States. Under the Lon Nol government *(Cambodia II)*, there were dramatic changes in the political structure and foreign policy of the nation-state, and there were also considerable

BOX 5.4 *continued*

changes in domestic policy. This political system was maintained by the United States from 1970 to 1975. In turn, the Cambodian government and military assisted the U.S. military in fighting the Communist insurgents. There was escalation of the guerrilla war by Cambodian Communists (the Khmer Rouge) against the Lon Nol government and extensive fighting in Cambodia by the military forces of the United States, South Vietnam, the Vietcong, Cambodia, and the Khmer Rouge.

With the collapse of the U.S. military effort in Southeast Asia, Lon Nol's government was among the casualties. Thus the Khmer Rouge came to power in April 1975 and created yet another political system, renaming the state Kampuchea. Under the Communist regime of Pol Pot, Kampuchea *(Cambodia III)* experienced one of the most dramatic shifts in a political system during the twentieth century. The new government immediately relocated everyone from urban areas into the countryside, organized the entire population into collective farms that were really forced labor camps, and implemented a massive reeducation (indoctrination) program. In a brutal reign of terror, about one-third of the population of 7 million was either killed or died during a total restructuring of the society.

For the Vietnamese, this time of disruption was an ideal moment to invade and conquer the Cambodians. This invasion was mainly prompted by the centuries-old animosity between the Vietnamese, on the one hand, and the Cambodians and their Chinese allies on the other. The successful invasion of Cambodia by the Vietnamese army resulted in the installation of a Vietnamese puppet government under President Heng Samrin (a dissident Khmer Rouge) in January 1979. Thus Kampuchea and Pol Pot's barbaric policies were eliminated and a new political system *(Cambodia IV)* was born. In 1989, the Vietnamese withdrew their military forces from Cambodia. Cambodian groups loyal to the current political system under Premier Hun Sen, to the Khmer Rouge, to Norodom Sihanouk, and to the rightist Cambodians (as well as external governments such as Vietnam, China, and the United States) are engaged in complex negotiations and guerrilla wars in an attempt to establish the nature of the potential *Cambodia V*.

In summary, the political system of Cambodia has undergone dramatic changes during a 20-year period. Minimally, three regimes failed to persist. And it seems reasonable to argue that there was at least one "death" of a political system, with the fundamental transformations associated with the replacement of Lon Nol by Pol Pot. And the elimination of the Pol Pot government by the Vietnamese might also be classified as a death and rebirth of the political system, since much of the coercive and massive restructuring of Cambodian society was undone (although not the commitment to communist collectivism).

Can you think of other examples of the death of political systems since you became aware of politics? During the last dozen or so years, the list might include the shift from Shah Reza Pahlavi to Ayatollah Khomeini in Iran (1979), from Somoza to the Sandinistas in Nicaragua (1979), from white-dominated Rhodesia to black-dominated Zimbabwe (1980), the granting of independence to former colonial territories such as Antigua and Barbuda (1981), and the overthrow of the Marxist leaders by the United States in the military invasion of Grenada (1983). In the twentieth century, more than 200 political systems have died.

There are also many examples of regime change, where a political system has undergone a considerable change in leadership, in political processes, or in value allocations, but has not been transformed to such an extent that it is appropriate to talk of the "death" of a political system. Examples of substantial but not fundamental change might include the shift from Mao Zedong to the "revisionist" leadership of Deng Xiaopeng in China (1976), the change from civilian to military rule in Nigeria (1982), the change from military to civilian rule in Uruguay (1984), the shift from President Ferdinand Marcos to President Corazon Aquino in the Philippines (1986), and the electoral defeat of Sandinista leader Daniel Ortega by Violeta Chamorro for the Nicaraguan presidency (1990).

Since 1988, there have been substantial changes in most political systems of Eastern Europe (Czechoslovakia, East Germany, Hungary, Poland, and Romania). The changes in this set of relatively similar systems (discussed more fully in Chapter 15) offer researchers an interesting opportunity to clarify the analytic difference between regime change and the death or birth of a political system. A unification of East Germany and West Germany certainly constitutes the death of the former's political system. In other East European states, the establishment of free elections, a multiparty system, and a less state-dominated political economy seem to be transformational changes. One central question in these states will be: How much of the old political system remains, either because of human and organizational resistance to change or because the basic patterns of a society usually cannot be altered rapidly? Whether political systems "die" is a matter of debate; but there is no question that dramatic changes occasionally occur within many political systems.

The Utility of the Political Systems Approach

There is disagreement among political scientists about the utility of the political systems approach. Some political scientists think it is an overused and seriously flawed conceptual framework. It has important shortcomings as a potential paradigm for political analysis. Crucial concepts are defined in several different ways, and there have never been clear operational measures developed for these concepts. Moreover, the linkages between the concepts (the theoretical element) have never been specified with much greater precision than are indicated in Figure 5.1. And the approach has provided few concrete predictions or hypotheses that are subject to rigorous empirical measurement and testing. Given these shortcomings, critics dismiss the political systems approach as a nontheoretical and nonempirical abstraction that does little to advance a science of politics.

Few political scientists expect that the political systems approach will fulfill the early hope that it might become the paradigm of political science. But it has been quite influential as a *metaphor*—as a conceptual framework that describes how the political system operates and that suggests key variables and their linkages. It encourages the analyst to think of politics in terms of political actors, structures, and processes that constitute a system that is dynamic and adaptive as it constantly interacts with its environment(s). The political system is open, in the sense that the environment and inputs generate forces that affect the system and to which it must respond. And the political system is itself an active force, since its actions are aimed at modifying and shaping its environment and inputs by means of a constant flow of outputs. Many political scientists use this conceptualization of the political system, either consciously or subconsciously, when they attempt to explain the dynamic processes of politics.

THREE MAJOR CONCEPTS: A REPRISE

This chapter has focussed on three major concepts that characterize large political entities. *State* is a concept that emphasizes the legal standing of these governmental entities, the necessary functions that they perform, and the organizational structures through which they take action. The discussion of three alternative views of the appropriate domain of state activities reveals the considerable range of differences in defining *res publica,* "things of the people."

Nation is a concept indicating a mental state characterized by a sense of shared identity among a set of people, distinguishing "us" from "them" in the sociopolitical world. The widespread problem of disjunction between state and nation within the nation-state was revealed by the examples of the British Isles and the Indian subcontinent.

Finally, the notion of the *political system* attempts to provide political scientists with the basic analytic concept for building a general theory of political entities. It specifies the crucial components in a dynamic and adaptive system whose essential function is the authoritative allocation of values for its society. We shall continue to use the idea of the political system in the next chapter, where we examine different ways to classify and describe national political systems.

CHAPTER 6

Political Institutions I:
Classifying Systems

President Corazon Aquino of the Philippines

We know that all national political systems are not identical. But are all political systems different? A basic task in political analysis is to determine whether there are some criteria by which political systems can be classified. Consider the 20 nation-states listed below. Do you make any distinctions among these political systems? Does your distinction enable you to place each of the 20 into one category but no other categories? Would other people agree with your classification?

Some Nation-States

United States	Iraq	Egypt
Libya	Kenya	El Salvador
Yugoslavia	Poland	Nigeria
Cuba	Italy	Saudi Arabia
Philippines	Thailand	Laos
South Africa	Venezuela	United Kingdom
China	Soviet Union	

In this chapter and Chapter 7, we examine a variety of distinctions among different political systems. These distinctions can be understood as variations on the theme of political institutions, because they all consider the institutional arrangements through which politics is organized. For example, this chapter will discuss such descriptive concepts as *democracy, totalitarian regime, federation,* and *cabinet system.* Chapter 7 will continue this discussion, emphasizing such major institutional structures as *legislatures, executives,* and *administrations.* All of these topics will be useful both in the sense that they provide *analytic information* about specific taxonomies that are used in the study of political systems (for more information on taxonomies, see the appendix) and also in the broader sense that they provide *descriptive information* about the basic differences among actual political systems.

BROAD TAXONOMIES

How satisfied are you with the categories in your initial attempt to classify the political systems listed above? To the extent you have distinguished the political systems by means of criteria that are *inclusive* (include all cases), *mutually exclusive* (each case fits in only one category), and *consistent* (others could apply the same criteria and make the same classifications), you have developed an adequate taxonomic scheme. Whether your classificatory system is useful is another matter, and this depends on whether it provides a meaningful ordering of the cases.

Taxonomic theory (as discussed in the appendix) is often the first stage in political analysis because it provides an initial grouping of the cases, facilitating comparative analysis and theory building. The appendix provides one example of taxonomic theory, Aristotle's classification of political systems into six types, on the basis of two criteria: (1) how many rule (Aristotle's division was one, a few, and many); and (2) in whose interest they rule (self-interest or interest of all).

There are a number of ways in which the political systems in our list of nation-states might be taxonomized. For example, they could be ordered on the basis of a geographic dimension, such as those in the North Atlantic region, those in Eastern Europe, in the Middle East and North Africa, in Sub-Saharan Africa, in Latin America, in South and East Asia, and in Oceania. Or they could be ordered on the basis of a religious dimension, such as predominantly Christian, Muslim, Eastern, Asian, secular, traditional indigeneous, or mixed. An economic dimension might include categories for subsistence agriculture, nomadic, industrial, and postindustrial economies. Table 6.1 categorizes the 20 political systems in a few possible taxonomies. As you attempt to apply any of these classificatory schemes, you will notice that some states are difficult to classify. This is one of the challenges with such taxonomies: The attempt to apply a taxonomy can reveal ambiguities in the classificatory scheme. But it also can reveal interesting similarities and differences among the cases.

Beyond the meaningful ordering of data, a taxonomy is especially valuable if it facilitates the development of theoretical generalizations. There are many hypotheses that might be generated and tested using the kinds of taxonomies suggested above. For example, one could posit that predominantly Muslim states will be more active in war than will states where most of the population follows "Eastern" religions. The rationale for this hypothesis is that Islam celebrates the virtue of *jihad* (holy war) against infidels, while such religions as Hinduism, Buddhism, and Taoism emphasize passivity. To test this hypothesis, a sample of Muslim and Eastern-religion states would be selected and empirical data for a certain time period would be gathered, based on a careful and precise operational definition of "active in war" (a variable that might be measured by such data as number of wars, days at war, number of casualties, proportion of population who are combatants, number of combatants). This hypothesis is representative of the kind of intriguing ideas that can be tested when political systems are classified on the basis of nonpolitical dimensions.

For a political analyst, as for most other observers of politics, the most widely used taxonomies involve more explicitly political dimensions. Political scientists have proposed a variety of different classificatory schemes for political systems. For example, Roy Macridis (1986) distinguishes democratic regimes (pure and cryptomilitary), totalitarian regimes (communist and noncommunist), authoritarian regimes (dynastic, single-party, and military), and unclassifiable regimes. Other widely used political classifications are democracies and dictatorships; Free World, Communist World, and nonaligned states; federal systems and unitary systems; and so on. A common political-economic dimension distinguishes the "First World," "Second World," "Third World," and, perhaps, the "Fourth World."

No taxonomy is employed in all analyses, because each taxonomy emphasizes different aspects of the political world. Choice of a taxonomy depends upon the interests of the political analyst. In Chapter 8, for example, the political economy categories will be explored in detail. In this chapter, we examine in considerable detail some of the insights about political systems associated with certain broad, explicitly political taxonomies that emphasize the relationships among key structures in the political system.

DEMOCRACIES AND DICTATORSHIPS

One of the most common methods by which political systems are classified is to distinguish democracies from dictatorships. Most of us have an intuitive sense of which states are democracies and which are dictatorships. However, these terms become slippery when we try to apply them. North Korea calls itself the *Democratic* People's Republic. Is it? Argentina, France, and Yugoslavia also label themselves democracies. Are they? These examples reflect the fact that *democracy* is such a highly valued label that most states, except systems with hereditary monarchs, claim that they are democratic. Is virtually every contemporary political system to be termed a democracy?

Classify the first six political systems in Table 6.1 on a democracy/dictatorship dimension. If you have been raised in the United States, you probably view the United States and the Philippines as democracies, and Libya, Yugoslavia, Cuba, and South Africa as dictatorships. The qualification in the previous sentence regarding the site of your upbringing is a crucial one—it alerts us to a fundamental problem with any such discussion. Chapter 3 attempted to persuade you that the understanding and use of such political labels is deeply dependent upon one's own political socialization and political environment. Thus you should not

TABLE 6.1. Selected Taxonomies for Some Nation-States

	Region	Rural or Urban	Religions	Dominant Economic Activity
United States	North America	Urban	Christian	Postindustrial
Libya	North Africa	Mixed	Muslim	Agricultural
Yugoslavia	Eastern Europe	Urban	Secular	Industrial
Cuba	Caribbean	Mixed	Secular	Agricultural
Philippines	Southern Asia	Urban	Christian	Agricultural
South Africa	Africa	Mixed	Christian	Industrial
China	Asia	Rural	Mixed	Agricultural
Iraq	Middle East	Urban	Muslim	Agricultural
Kenya	Africa	Rural	Christian/Traditional	Agricultural
Poland	Eastern Europe	Urban	Secular/Christian	Industrial
Italy	Western Europe	Urban	Christian	Industrial
Thailand	Southern Asia	Rural	Buddhist	Agricultural
Venezuela	South America	Urban	Christian	Industrial
Soviet Union	Eastern Europe/Asia	Urban	Mixed	Industrial
Egypt	North Africa	Mixed	Muslim	Agricultural
El Salvador	Central America	Mixed	Christian	Agricultural
Nigeria	Africa	Rural	Mixed	Agricultural
Saudi Arabia	Middle East	Urban	Muslim	Industrial
Laos	Southern Asia	Rural	Secular/Buddhist	Agricultural
United Kingdom	Western Europe	Urban	Christian	Postindustrial

assume that individuals from other cultures will necessarily agree with your labels.

It might be argued that this problem regarding interpersonal differences underscores the virtue of the scientific method, at least in theory. The scientific method requires the analyst to specify what a particular concept means, with great precision and in an empirically measurable manner. This might be the only way in which individuals with fundamentally different ideological bases could agree on which of the six states are democracies and which are dictatorships. Our discussion will proceed in the spirit of the scientific method, although the author acknowledges his own lifetime socialization, which is grounded in the political conceptions of the American/Western world.

How might individuals with dramatically different political worldviews attempt to establish whether the classifications suggested above are correct? For example, consider these issues:

> Assume that we are able to establish empirically that the majority of the Libyan population supports the government of Muammar al-Qaddafi (this is arguably the case, although we do not know it empirically, because there are no genuine elections or reliable public opinion surveys). Under such an assumption, is Libya a dictatorship? The same issue might be raised regarding Cuba under Fidel Castro.
>
> By what criteria is Yugoslavia a dictatorship when the government provides far more extensive social benefits to all its citizens and a far greater proportion of the people vote in Yugoslav elections than in either the U.S. or Philippine democracies?
>
> Isn't there vigorous electoral and governmental competition between different parties in South Africa?
>
> By what criteria is the Philippines a democracy under a president, Corazon Aquino, who seized power with the assistance of the military after she was apparently outvoted in an election?

In responding to these questions, you begin to establish the explicit or implicit standards that you apply when you distinguish between democracy and dictatorship. And these kinds of questions underscore the importance of defining with precision the concepts that we use in political analysis.

Defining Democracy

What are the necessary and sufficient conditions for democracy? In its classic sense, true *participatory democracy* is government of and by the people—there is active, direct participation by all citizens in the authoritative allocation of values. Realistically, there is no such political system; indeed, Jean-Jacques Rousseau (1712–1778) claimed that only a society of gods could be a true democracy. If our definition is less stringent, democracy might entail relatively equal capacity of all citizens to influence the allocation of values. It would be difficult to make a persuasive case that this condition holds in any political system, including the Philippines and the United States. Some are more equal than others in every political system.

You might use a notion of *representative democracy*, wherein the citizens elect people to represent them in the political process and to allocate values on their behalf for the society. South Africa meets this criterion, although few would classify it as a democracy, since only a small proportion of the population is identified by the political system as citizens. The definition could be refined by specifying that the elections for representatives be held under conditions of universal suffrage. Cuba meets these conditions, but few would consider it a democracy, because, among other reasons, there are very limited choices among candidates for governmental office. Is the definition adequate if it includes the characteristics above and also stipulates that the elections provide alternative choices among representatives? Yugoslavia satisfies these conditions, although the alternative candidates are generally controlled by the single party that governs the state. Thus it seems that the definition of democracy must somehow include the notion that the citizenry has genuine choices among alternative candidates—yet even the notion of genuine choice can be rather ambiguous.

More broadly, should a complete definition of democracy have more than electoral components? Such a democracy must allow not only voting rights, but also must allow the citizens and the media some freedom of speech, of assembly, and of political opposition. These rights to additional forms of participation and opposition in the political process seem an essential element of a *liberal democracy*. This system still is less than the literal notion of democracy as "rule by the people." The state does not allow absolute freedom of political participation and opposition. And there is only "contestation" among competing elites, with most citizens exercising no direct control on policy decisions by the ruling leadership group (see Dahl 1971, 1984; Schumpeter 1950; Schattschneider 1960).

Perhaps we have now established one possibility for the sufficient, as well as necessary, conditions for a democracy: *governance by political leaders whose authority is based on a limited mandate from a universal electorate that has some rights to participation and opposition.* In this definition, "limited mandate" means that the authority to govern is granted only for a fixed period of time, and that the electorate/citizenry then has the opportunity to select leaders again from among genuine alternatives.

This is a modest notion of democracy, since it guarantees the people little more than an occasional opportunity to select among the competing elites who govern them. Yet among the first six political systems in the table, only the United States (and the Philippines, once Aquino or someone else is actually elected in a "proper" election) would be classified as a democracy using even this limited definition. All six systems encourage some forms of political participation and allow some political opposition. But the authority of the political leadership in Libya, Yugoslavia, Cuba, and South Africa is not based on its electoral selection, by universal suffrage, among genuine alternatives, and for a fixed period of time.

A more expansive conception of democracy would emphasize not only the processes of selecting political authorities, but also the nature of outputs (value allocations) produced by those authorities. For example, Austin Ranney

(1982:278–284) defines democracy as a form of government in which power to make decisions or select decision makers is granted all adult citizens, based on majority rule, and in which decision makers reflect the will of the majority in their public policy decisions. Notice that the first half of Ranney's definition refers to the processes of selecting political authorities and making value allocations while the second half deals explicitly with the nature of the value allocations. A problem with this definition is deciding how to establish whether public policies do "reflect the will of the majority." Is the will of the majority determined by yesterday's public opinion polls? By the insights of the decision makers? By the votes in the previous election? None of these measures seems promising.

Minimally, a process-and-output conception of democracy must incorporate a vision of the effects of the political system as well as the procedures by which value allocations are made. Thus it insures the population of both participatory rights to select and influence political decision makers empowered for a limited term of office, and also broader political and social rights, such as freedom of speech, press, assembly, and religion. An extremely broad conception of the "output" aspects of democracy might also include provision of such value allocations as the right to employment, health care, housing, and other social welfare.

This discussion might help you to identify the criteria that you think are necessary for an adequate definition of democracy. (It is certainly possible that your definition will differ from any of those suggested above. You should, however, be able to justify your criteria.) Can you now articulate a conceptual definition of democracy and classify the political systems in Table 6.1? Do you think your friends will accept your definition and classification? Would a Cuban student accept it? You might be surprised how difficult it is to develop a generally accepted definition of this most widely used political concept.

Defining Dictatorship

How about *dictatorship?* Is dictatorship more easily defined than democracy? Is a dictator a ruler with absolute power and authority (independently of any consideration of the process through which power was acquired)? Can we define and measure "absolute" power? Is a system not dictatorial if the ruler is unable to or chooses not to exercise absolute power?

Or is dictatorship better defined as the set of conditions opposite to those in a democracy? In this case, a dictatorship might be defined by the *absence* of a critical factor that was included in our definition of democracy: The absence of a limited mandate. That is, if the citizens have no regular and realistic opportunity to replace the political leadership, then the political system is a dictatorship. At least, it was the lack of a limited mandate that seemed to justify the classification of Cuba, Libya, South Africa, and Yugoslavia as nondemocracies.

One form of dictatorial system is when political leaders exercise power without popular support. But even a political leadership that has popular support from the majority but does not provide the citizenry with genuine opportunities to renew the leadership's mandate in competition against alternative leaders could be defined as dictatorial. This might characterize the situation in Libya under Qaddafi and Cuba under Castro.

President Muammar Qaddafi of Libya

Consideration of South Africa suggests that not all states are either democratic or dictatorial. The exclusion of a very large proportion of citizens from the mandate process reveals its lack of democracy. South Africa's government might be viewed as a dictatorship of whites over many blacks, but does it meet the analytic criteria for a dictatorship? A citizenry votes and there is definite leadership turnover. The fact is that many political systems are difficult to classify as democracies or dictatorships, in terms of the limited mandate criterion. Three examples indicate some of the difficulties.

In Kenya, all citizens over 21 are allowed to vote in periodic elections for the national legislature. And there are alternative candidates—in the 1983 election, nearly 1,000 candidates ran for the 158 seats; but only one party is legal, and other opposition groups were generally unsuccessful in electing legislators. The president runs without opposition.

In Egypt, everyone over 18 votes for the legislature. Although there was only one party between 1952 and 1984, other parties were allowed to present candidates in the 1984 and 1987 elections. By 1987, opposition parties received about 30 percent of the votes. But most decision-making power is controlled by the president, not the legislature. And there has been only one candidate for president in these, as in earlier elections.

In Mexico, there are regular elections, universal suffrage, and a limited mandate for the president and the legislature. The legislature has representatives from several parties. Despite alternative candidates, the people of Mexico have elected the presidential candidate nominated by the Institutional Revolutionary Party (PRI) in every election since 1929. In 1988, about one-half the electorate voted for a presidential candidate other than that of PRI. But PRI's opponents claim (with some justification) that the party "stole" the 1988 election by massive vote fraud.

According to these descriptions, Kenya seems more dictatorial than Egypt. And Mexico seems more democratic than Egypt. These three cases suggest that countries might range on a continuum from "more dictatorial" to "more democratic" systems. In fact, the extent to which there is a limited mandate is either unclear or is changing over time in the majority of national political systems.

Of our earlier cases, Yugoslavia is somewhat similar to Kenya, since there are multiple candidates but virtually all are members of the one national party. And the Philippines was not dissimilar to Mexico. Ferdinand Marcos won a mandate in the "official" vote count during the 1986 presidential election, although there were widespread allegations of electoral fraud. The differences between the Philippines in 1986 and Mexico in 1988 seem to be less the criteria regarding the level of democracy than political realities. An extensive, organized opposition to Marcos joined with the international media to attack Marcos's legitimacy, and he was forced to leave the country when both his own military and the United States withdrew support for his regime. In contrast, both the Mexican military and the United States supported the PRI candidate, Salinas de Gortari.

Complex situations, changing conditions, lack of reliable data—these kinds of problems make the development of interesting taxonomies in the study of politics both difficult and subject to disagreement. Do you now have a clearer notion of how to define and operationalize democracy? Do you think that democracy and dictatorship are two ends on a single continuum? (Or do you believe that political "reality" is better reflected by two separate taxonomies since the criteria that classify a country as more or less democratic are not the same as those that determine the extent to which a political system is dictatorial?) Try again to classify some of the states in Table 6.1 in terms of your conceptualization of democracy.

CONSTITUTIONAL AND NONCONSTITUTIONAL REGIMES

A related classification of political systems also emphasizes aspects of the relationship between the rulers and the ruled. In this system, the key question is whether the political system abides by the provisions in the state's constitution or fundamental laws. A *constitutional regime* operates in terms of the rule of law, as defined within the constitution, and insures effective restraints on the power holders. In contrast, a *nonconstitutional regime* is characterized by unchecked power, and the structural arrangements of the constitution are not upheld. In theory, at least, a state might scrupulously follow a deeply repressive and undemocratic constitution imposed by the political leadership, and thus qualify as a constitutional regime. But those who employ this distinction typically assume that the guarantees within the constitution provide for a generally democratic and humane political order.

Constitutions

At the heart of most political systems is a constitution, a set of statements describing the fundamental rules of the political system. Most constitutions are composed of a single, written document, in the manner of the U.S. Constitution. However, some political systems do not have such a document, and the fundamental rules are embedded in major statutes, precedents, and legal decisions, as in Great Britain's "unwritten constitution" or in Israel's "basic laws."

Although the idea of a constitution has a certain timeless quality associated with it, the constitutions of political systems are actually quite changeable. The constitutions of more than two-thirds of the contemporary states have been enacted since 1945. In large part, this is due to the great proliferation of new, postcolonial states. However, constitutions are always subject to change. For example, in 1970, Belgium revised a 170-year-old constitution in an attempt to resolve conflicts between its Flemish and Walloon nations. In 1971, Sweden rewrote the oldest European constitution to alter the structure of the legislature, to reduce the power of the king, and to alter the voting age. Spain struggled for nearly a decade before the 1978 ratification of its eighth constitution since 1812. Canada gained control over its own constitution only in 1982, when Britain "repatriated" it. The Philippines ratified a new, post-Marcos constitution in 1987. The Soviet Union made historic constitutional changes in 1989. And Israel is attempting to ratify its first constitution.

While earlier constitutions tended to be relatively short and general, many recent constitutions are quite detailed. The Nigerian Constitution has 245 articles and the Indian Constitution has fully 395 articles. There is also increasing similarity in the language of constitutions, due to quite liberal borrowing of ideas and even specific language from the constitutions of other nation-states. For example, more than three dozen countries have borrowed Abraham Lincoln's felicitous phrasing regarding government "of the people, by the people, and for the people."

Constitutional Regimes

The defining feature of a constitutional regime is that the state does attempt to fulfill the provisions of its constitution. The constitution declares the existence of the state and it expresses the most important fundamental rules of the political system. Three sets of rules are crucial. First, the constitution allocates governmental activities, defining what actions are within the domain of *res publica* and what political structures will perform these various actions. Second, it establishes the formal power relationships between the political structures, indicating the conditions under which each is independent or dependent upon the actions of other structures. Third, the constitution limits the power of the rulers and guarantees the rights of the ruled, by defining the maximum extent of the state's authority over its citizens and by enumerating citizens' freedoms and benefits from the state.

The third set of rules is most important. A regime becomes more fully a constitutional one to the extent the political system fulfills the constitutional limits on the rulers' power and the guarantee of rights to the ruled. Even among constitutional regimes, the limits on the state and the rights of the citizens are not absolute and are not absolutely implemented. Some states justify suspension of major constitutional provisions as a "temporary" response to circumstances that threaten the stability of the society. Such a suspension can last for months or years. A regime becomes less constitutional as there is a greater disparity between the provisions in the constitution and the actual politics of the society. In fact,

BOX 6.1

Constitution by Fiat: Japan

One of the most extraordinary episodes of drafting a constitution occurred in Japan. The Japanese operated under the Imperial Meiji Constitution from 1889 until their defeat by the Allies at the end of World War II. After the war, Japan was under the control of the American occupation forces, led by General Douglas MacArthur. MacArthur decided to blunt Communist influence in Japan and to commemorate George Washington's upcoming birthday by drafting a constitution for the Japanese. For this task, he gathered 25 American military officers stationed in Tokyo, including four lawyers but no constitutional specialists and no political scientists.

Using their knowledge of the American political system and their imperfect understanding of the British cabinet system, MacArthur and his American officers devised a governmental system and a constitution within a few weeks (in time for Washington's birthday). After the English version was completed, it was translated into two forms in Japanese, one in formal bureaucratic language and one in common Japanese. Some of the Americans' perspectives were so alien to Japanese culture and political traditions that there were concepts in the new constitution, such as "civil rights," that were not even words in the Japanese language and required new ideographs. The constitution copied much of the preamble to the U.S. Constitution, and referred to George Washington, President Roosevelt, and even Douglas MacArthur!

This constitution, written by inexpert foreigners, has been in force in Japan since 1946. It has never been amended and seems to have worked, in the sense that the Japanese have maintained a stable and working political system in the subsequent decades. Can you explain this constitutional "success"? Perhaps the military officers developed a sound constitutional framework for the governance of contemporary Japan. Perhaps the constitution is primarily a symbolic document and its details are unimportant for the actual functioning of the political order. Or perhaps this was an early example of Japan's postwar skill: taking an American product, reflecting on how to improve upon it, and modifying it into a superior product.

the disjunction between promise and reality is frequent and extensive in many political systems.

Ultimately, the force of the constitution depends upon the will of those with political power to enforce its provisions. The actual drafting of every constitution is either directly or indirectly controlled by those with political power in the society. Many groups in a society might offer interpretations of what the constitution means and how it ought to be applied to particular circumstances—governmental officials, courts, political parties, interest groups. But in the short run, at least, political power in the society establishes whose interpretation of the constitution will prevail and how the constitution's provisions will be implemented. In constitutional regimes, the interpretations are generally reasonable and judicious, and the implementation is fair.

Few constitutions provide a precise description of how the political system actually works. Yet constitutions are not without significance. In the turbulent debate over the creation of the new constitution for Spain, the distinguished historian Julian Marais insisted, "If the constitition does not inspire respect, admiration and enthusiasm, democracy is not assured." Even if there are major diversions from the provisions of the constitution, it remains a moral yardstick against which to measure actual performance and it is a persistent reminder of the high ideals and goals that have been set for the political system. As Andre Malraux observed, "Face to face with the unknown, some of our dreams are no less significant than our memories."

Nonconstitutional Regimes

Among nonconstitutional regimes, a distinction is often made between authoritarian systems and totalitarian systems. Indeed, many classificatory schemes, such as that of Macridis (1986), cited earlier in this chapter, treat these as two of the three major categories of political systems (along with democracies).

Authoritarian Regimes. Authoritarian regimes place severe restrictions on the activities of individuals and groups desiring to influence the allocation of values by the political system. Meaningful power over political institutions and public policy is limited to a small group and the great majority of the population are excluded from politics. The people are not allowed to participate in any political activities except those expressly encouraged by the regime. In most instances, this means that occasional public expressions of support for the system, such as mass rallies, are the only forms of political behavior that are acceptable.

No citizens are allowed to question the institutions, procedures, or value allocations of authoritarian regimes. But other aspects of life are not under the direct control of the political system. In some systems, these other areas of life are guided by traditional societal values or by overriding religious values. Recent examples of traditional authoritarian political systems are Saudi Arabia under the Saud family, and Jordan under King Hussein. Other authoritarian systems are dominated by a powerful military and/or bureaucracy, which constrain the citizens' behavior in nonpolitical domains by the implementation of laws and coer-

cion rather than by reliance on traditional values. Examples of authoritarian regimes are Chile under Pinochet, Mexico under the PRI, and the Philippines under
Marcos.

Totalitarian Regimes. In totalitarian regimes, the definition of *res publica* becomes total. The political system's allocation of values penetrates into virtually
every aspect of its people's lives. Every political system intervenes occasionally
in such domains as culture, economics, religion, and morality; but the totalitarian
regime is constantly and deeply involved in prescribing and proscribing behavior
and even ideas in these domains.

   All organizations are subordinated under the totalitarian state, and there is a
fusion of the state and the social order. Every activity of the individual citizen is
subject to scrutiny by the state, in the name of the public interest. As examples
of the penetration of the totalitarian state into all aspects of social life, the North
Korean state defines the acceptability of films and plays, determines what and
how much of each type of crop will be produced on every farm, discourages or
prohibits the activities of organized churches, and decides which families will live
in each housing unit. George Orwell's *1984* (1949) is a literary vision of the totalitarian state, and recent examples include Kampuchea under Pol Pot and North
Korea.

AREAL DISTRIBUTION OF POWER

With the exception of small political systems serving only a few thousand citizens,
most political systems have found it desirable or necessary to create governmental structures at several levels. The *areal distribution of power* describes the allocation of power and functions across these levels of government. National political systems, in particular, can be classified into three major forms of allocating
power and functions: (1) unitary states, (2) federations, and (3) confederations.

Unitary State

In a *unitary state* there is a central government that holds all legitimate power.
While the central government has indivisible sovereignty, it can delegate power
or functional responsibilities to territorial units, which are given such names as
states, departments, regions, or *provinces.* These peripheral governments serve
only at the convenience of the central government, which can revoke their power
or functions at any time. More than 70 percent of the current nation-states are
unitary states. Examples include Japan, France, the United Kingdom, China, and
most Latin American and Asian political systems.

   Why are most states unitary? The major advantage of a unitary state is the
presence of clear, hierarchical authority. While there might be conflict between
the central and the peripheral governments, the center's superior constitutional
power is clear, and center-periphery stalemates are uncommon. In addition, be-

cause the loyalty of all citizens is focussed on the governmental authority embodied in the national government, citizens tend to identify with the nation-state as a whole, rather than regional authorities.

Federations

A *federation* has a constitutional division of power and functions between a central government and the set of peripheral governments. In contrast to a unitary state, there is an explicit sharing of power between levels of government, and no level has legal power to dominate the other level(s) in all policy domains. The essence of federation is coordination, not hierarchy. There are five major rationales for federation:

1. *Large size*. Many states become federations to distribute governmental power when there is a huge area to be governed. Fewer than 25 nation-states are federations, but this group includes over one-half of the land area of the world. Most of the largest states are federations, including the Soviet Union, the United States, Mexico, India, Canada, Brazil, and Nigeria. During the constitutional debate in the United States, Thomas Jefferson observed, "our country is too large to have all its affairs directed by a single government." The assumption here seem to be that responsiveness is higher when government does not become too massive in scale.

2. *The prior existence of strong states*. A federation can be an acceptable compromise when strong peripheral governments create a central government. In the formation of the United States, for example, the already strong state governments were unwilling to give up the bulk of their power to a central government, as in a unitary state. Rather, they agreed to delegate certain functions to the new central government, while retaining all other "residual" powers for themselves.

3. *The attempt to encourage or create unity*. Chapter 5 described the serious problems of conflict between state and nations, especially in the newer states. Federations appear to bond diverse nations into a unified state, while still recognizing the different nations' diversity and desire for power. The peripheral governments represent major ethnic, linguistic, religious, or other nation-based characteristics of regions. India created a federation with 17 states, most of which were related to linguistic-ethnic dominance in the area and a few of which were related to religious dominance. The Indian Constitution defines a complex pattern of power distribution, with the center responsible for 97 governmental functions, 66 functions reserved for the states, and 47 functions shared between the two levels.

4. *The desire to concentrate power and resources*. In some instances, a federation is created to combine several states into a stronger political system. In the effort to create Arab unity and to expand the political and

economic power of the state, Egypt has attempted to forge federations with its neighbors several times. Thus at various times Egypt has been part of federations with Syria, Yemen, Iraq, and Jordan. For similar reasons, Kenya, Tanzania, and Uganda formed the East African Federation. As in both of these examples, federations are often short-lived because the prior states are unwilling to sacrifice sufficient local power and resources to a potent central government.

5. *The desire to disperse political power.* Unlike the previous rationale, a federation can be established to prevent the overconcentration of power in the center government. After the trauma of Hitler, West Germans formed a federation to impede the emergence of another overly powerful central government. The bulk of legislative power was granted to the central government, but most power to administer and adjudicate the laws is held by the *Länder* (peripheral) governments.

Confederation

A *confederation* is an association in which states delegate some power to a supranational central government, but retain primary power. It is a loose grouping of states in which each state's membership, participation, and compliance to the central government are conditional, depending on the state's perception of its own national interest. Confederations are usually created when states decide that the performance of certain functions is enhanced by structured cooperation with other states. To facilitate such cooperation, permanent supranational machinery is set up. The United Nations is a major contemporary example of a confederation. There can be confederations that emphasize economic cooperation, such as the European Economic Community (the Common Market), or military cooperation, such as NATO or the Warsaw Pact.

Although confederations can serve many useful functions for member states, their activities and even their very survival are always contingent upon the continuing support of the members. A member state will often refuse to comply with policies that conflict directly with the state's definition of its own national interest. Disagreements among the members can require negotiation and compromise, as in the periodic adjustments within the European Economic Community regarding farm subsidies to member states. A confederation can wither if the supragovernment is ineffective, as in the case of the Articles of Confederation in colonial America, or if members refuse to support its directives, as in the League of Nations after World War I.

Table 6.2 illustrates some of the major advantages and shortcomings of each approach to the areal distribution of power. While each seems to have relative advantages under certain conditions, none is without considerable drawbacks, and none can assure the effective functioning or even the survival of a political system. The general trend toward the centralization of political power within nation-states has meant that the distinctions between unitary states and federations are less clear than in the past and that confederations have become particularly fragile.

TABLE 6.2. Relative Strengths and Weaknesses of Areal Distributions of Power

Form of Areal Distribution	Strengths	Weaknesses
Unitary state	Clear authority Decisive control No stalemates between center and periphery	Hyperconcentration of power Weak representation of diversity, minorities
Federation	Represents diversity Checks on center's power Creates unity	Duplication and overlap of power Conflicts over ultimate power Sluggish, compromising
Confederation	Facilitates cooperation Subunits retain power	Conditional compliance Weak, unstable

FORMS OF EXECUTIVE-LEGISLATIVE RELATIONS

Another conventional method of classifying and especially of describing political systems is by defining the pattern of power and interaction between the legislative and executive structures. The taxonomy in this section emphasizes the two most common patterns through which the executive and the legislative structures interact to perform the functions of rule making and rule application. These are the cabinet form and the presidential form of government. Three other types of executive-legislative arrangements are also examined briefly.

Presidential Government

The crucial feature of the *presidential* form is the separation of executive and legislative structures. Figure 6.1 portrays the electoral chain of command that is presumed to order the relationships between citizens and major political structures. In separate electoral decisions, the citizens select the chief executive (usually called the president) and the members of the national legislature. This electoral process provides both the president and the legislature with independent mandates to represent the citizens in the governing process. The lengths of the terms of each are predetermined, and thus the tenure in office of each is not dependent on the other (except in the rare case of impeachment of the chief executive).

The separation of executive and legislative powers is explicit and intentional, in order to insure a system of checks and balances in the rule-making and rule-application processes. Primary responsibility for rule making (policy enactment) resides in the legislature. Although the chief executive can veto legislation, the legislature can override that veto. Primary responsibility for the rule-application function (the implementation of the laws) is with the president, who has control of the government's administrative departments. The president also appoints a cabinet whose members are responsible for policy oversight in the government's administrative departments and who are controlled directly by the president.

Although the actions of the executive and legislature are interdependent, neither depends on the other for its power or its tenure in office. In practice, it is common to find a considerable blurring of functions, and especially for the president to have substantial involvement in the lawmaking function. The United States is the model example of presidential government, and this form of government is also found in many Latin American and some African and Asian states, including Colombia, the Ivory Coast, Kenya, Mexico, Venezuela, and the Philippines.

Cabinet Government

In contrast to the presidential system, the crucial element of *cabinet government* is the fusion of executive and legislative functions and structures. As indicated in Figure 6.1, the people elect the legislature, whose majority empowers a cabinet, which then empowers one of its members to be the chief executive, typically called a prime minister or premier. The length of the legislature's mandate is often five years; but its term can be shorter, under the circumstances described below. The complex relationships between cabinet, legislature, and prime minister merit further detail.

Cabinet and Legislature.   The cabinet is a collective leadership group of 6 to 30 individuals who are, in most systems, also members of the legislature. The cabinet is responsible to the legislature. This means that the cabinet serves only as long as it can maintain the "confidence" of the majority of the members in the legislature. As long as the cabinet does have the support of the legislative majority, it has primary responsibility for both the rule-making and the rule-application functions. Although policies must be voted into laws by the legislative majority, it is the cabinet that devises, drafts, and implements most policies.

In an intriguing manner, the cabinet and the legislature are at each other's mercy. At any time, the legislative majority can pressure the cabinet to resign, either by a negative vote on a major piece of legislation proposed by the cabinet or by a general motion of "no confidence" in the cabinet. And at any time, the

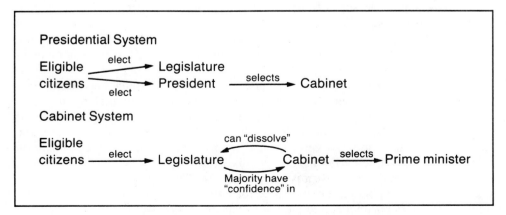

Figure 6.1. Presidential and Cabinet Systems

cabinet can "dissolve" the legislature, requiring immediate new elections. In the subsequent election, voters select a new legislature, whose majority then identifies a cabinet it will support, and the process begins anew. Thus the cabinet and the legislature, rather like two gunfighters standing gun-to-gun in a spaghetti Western, each have the power to eliminate the other, but might also be destroyed in the exchange. Since new elections put everyone's position in jeopardy, it is more common for the cabinet to resign or reconstitute itself than for the cabinet to dissolve the legislature.

Legislature and Prime Minister.   In the cabinet system, the prime minister (or premier or chancellor or whatever the chief executive is called) is not directly elected by the citizens to be the top leader. The prime minister is the member of the legislature who is supported as chief executive by the majority of the legislature. The prime minister can be removed at any time by a no confidence vote of the legislature and might also be obliged to resign if the legislature defeats a major legislative initiative of the prime minister. The prime minister directs the overall thrust of decision and action in the legislative process.

Cabinet and Prime Minister.   The balance of power between the cabinet and the prime minister can be subtle, although both depend upon the majority support of the legislature. Traditionally, the cabinet which had legislative support could select one of its members to serve as prime minister. The prime minister was "*primus inter pares*" in the cabinet—the first among equals. The prime minister exercised broad policy leadership within a collective decision-making body. If a cabinet majority no longer supported a prime minister, either he resigned or he attempted to reconstitute a cabinet which supported him and was supported by the legislative majority.

But in many contemporary cabinet systems, there has been a substantial shift of power from the cabinet to the prime minister. In these systems, the electorate selects legislative candidates from a party committed to support a particular prime minister. If a legislative majority can be created, their leader becomes prime minister. He then appoints the members of the cabinet and clearly dominates the cabinet in the governmental process. In Figure 6.1, the two-headed arrow between cabinet and prime minister indicates these alternate patterns of power.

Thus the cabinet system is characterized by the *fusion of executive and legislative functions* because the cabinet and prime minister formulate policies, guide their passage through the legislature, and administer policy through the administrative departments. However, the actual policy process in a cabinet system depends on whether there is a coherent majority group in the legislature.

In "stable" cabinet systems, there is a clear majority in the legislature (such a majority can be composed of either one party or a coalition). The cabinet and prime minister usually have sufficient power to pass virtually their entire legislative package and the opposition groups are rarely able to block them. In these cases, the prime minister is usually very dominant and remains in office until the time when new elections must be called. A major benefit attributed to a stable cabinet system is that the group with a legislative majority can enact and implement the policies that brought them to power, without the problems of stalemate and confusion of accountability that can result from the separation of powers in the presidential system. Great Britain, Denmark, Canada, Japan, and Australia are examples of cabinet government systems that are usually stable.

An "unstable" cabinet system often emerges when there is not a coherent legislative majority. These unstable systems usually occur in multiparty systems where the legislative majority supporting the cabinet is a coalition of groups who tend to disagree on some important policy issues. In such situations, it is difficult for the cabinet to propose major legislation without losing the voting support of some groups(s) within its majority. When the legislature votes no confidence in the cabinet or defeats it on a major bill, the cabinet usually resigns. Then one hears that a cabinet government has "fallen" or that there are efforts to form a "new government" (a new cabinet, actually). The new cabinet might have almost all the same people as members, or it might be a quite different set of individuals, drawing its majority support from different groups within the legislature. In general, prime ministers are less strong than in stable cabinet systems.

Unstable cabinet systems have been prevalent where stronger ideological differences and multiple political parties have emerged in contemporary legislatures. Italy has had more than one cabinet per year since 1945. During the French Fourth Republic, the cabinet system was so volatile that the average cabinet served for only seven months, and the shortest for less than six hours.

Hybrid Systems

An increasing number of political systems attempts to blend desirable aspects of both the presidential and the cabinet systems. These "hybrid" systems (which have also been termed "semipresidential" systems by Duverger [1980]) tend to fuse executive and legislative power, like a cabinet system. They have a prime minister and an elected legislature that can both enact and implement policies. But they also have a president (selected for a fixed term and having some independent executive powers) who, being a single individual, can act with decisiveness.

Some hybrids are more like cabinet systems. The president has limited power and most control is exercised by the prime minister and cabinet. In India, for example, the president is elected by the legislature for a five-year term and has notable responsibilities, including the appointment of state governors and the right to take over governance of the states during emergencies. However, the prime minister is the dominant political power in the system and the presidents have performed mainly ceremonial roles. West Germany, Austria, and Ireland are other examples of this style of the hybrid.

In some hybrids, there is a more balanced sharing of power between the president and the cabinet. In Finland, for example, the presidential executive controls the administration and has oversight powers. While the president does attend meetings on major legislation and both the president and the prime minister must sign a law before it is enacted, the cabinet and legislature undertake most of the legislation. In these more balanced hybrids, the relative power of the president and the prime minister/cabinet varies, depending on the constitutional rules, the personality of the office holders, and the political situation in the society (see the discussion of France in Box 6.2).

Box 6.2

A Hybrid System in Action: France

An example of a complicated and evolving hybrid system is the French Fifth Republic, based on the "de Gaulle Constitution" of 1962. This hybrid was created to overcome the highly unstable cabinet government system of the Fourth Republic. The premier (prime minister) and cabinet are responsible for the day-to-day functioning of the government, as in a cabinet system. But the president, an office de Gaulle fashioned for himself as a condition for his return to government, has extraordinary power when he decides to exercise it. The president is elected popularly for a fixed seven-year term, and then selects a premier who selects a cabinet. While the cabinet controls the budget and legislative agenda as in a normal cabinet system, it is the president who can dissolve the legislature while retaining the cabinet, and the president can act whenever he deems the cabinet to be "ineffective."

De Gaulle was the first president of the Fifth Republic, serving from 1959 to 1969. De Gaulle was an extraordinarily powerful individual, and he demanded extraordinary power. He created a precedent that the president can act far more extensively than the constitution allows. He dominated all premiers who served during his presidency. The presidents after de Gaulle (Pompidou, Giscard d'Estaing, and Mitterrand) continued to follow the de Gaulle precedent, exercising considerable power. This was made easier because the majority in the legislature, and thus the cabinet and premier, shared the ideological orientation of the president.

But many people felt that the "dyarchy" (dual rule) would ultimately create a constitutional crisis, when a premier and cabinet challenged the president's extensive power. A strong test of the constitution finally occurred in 1986, when Socialist President Mitterrand was faced with a new legislative majority dominated by conservatives. But Mitterrand accepted the situation, appointing the conservatives' leader, Jacques Chirac, as premier. Despite strong ideological differences between the president and the premier-cabinet-legislative majority, there was a reasonable sharing of power and authority, which the French term "cohabitation." After presidential and legislative elections in 1988, Mitterrand was reelected and a sympathetic legislature (although a minority one) was empowered. However, if a president and cabinet ever lock horns over a matter of deep disagreement, the French hybrid could still experience a constitutional crisis.

Council Systems

In a *council system,* a small group shares collective leadership and is responsible for both executive and legislative functions. While one member of the group might be deemed the leader for symbolic reasons, all members of the council are equal in constitutional terms, and decisions and actions are based on the will of the council majority or, ideally, on council consensus. Switzerland has a collegial executive, composed of seven members who are elected from separate regions. The members share legislative power and each is responsible for a particular functional area of administration. In American local government, the weak mayor-council system and the boards of commissioners/supervisors (prevalent in counties and special districts) are council systems.

Where there is no public selection of the top leaders, the informal politics often result in a system of collective leaders, based on factional alliances. Many tribal societies in Africa, for example, were traditionally ruled by a council of elders, who collectively made decisions binding on the members of the tribe. And most of the "juntas" which come to power in Latin America typically begin as council systems, since there is a small leadership group who share power and authority. Finally, some Communist states, such as China, Mozambique, and Yugoslavia, are probably best classified as council systems, since there is collective executive and legislative leadership concentrated in a small group; but as a single, visible political leader increasingly dominates the others, as in Gorbachev's Soviet Union, Castro's Cuba, or Mao Zedong's China, the government less resembles a council system.

Assembly Systems

In *assembly systems,* collective leadership is exercised by a large group, usually constituted as a legislature. There might be an executive officer, but the legislature is clearly dominant. Confederations, such as the United Nations and the European Parliament (the political wing of the European Communities), are assembly systems, since the constituent states participate in a legislative body but are unwilling to delegate much power to a central executive. The New England town meeting in American local government is an extreme version of the assembly system, since all citizens directly participate in key decisions and oversee the administration of policy. There are few, if any, states that operate as true assembly systems, since power for rule making and rule application tends to concentrate in the hands of a single individual or a small group.

In theory, most Communist states are assembly systems, since constitutional power for policy making resides in the legislative body. But in reality the legislatures in such states have traditionally been rubber stamps that authorize the policies and administration of a single leader or a small collective leadership group. Ironically, in states where there have been major reforms, such as the Soviet Union and Poland, the autonomy of legislatures might increase in the early 1990s.

Which Form Is Optimal?

Which form of executive-legislative relations is best? If there was agreement on this question, we might reasonably expect most nation-states to have adopted the same form of government. In fact, each form has its strengths and weaknesses. The cabinet form offers the advantages of a clear and decisive authority structure for the allocation of public values, from the initial formulation of policy through its administration. But it can be argued that there are too few checks on a coherent legislative majority, which can "bulldoze" its policies through the system. Conversely, there might be too little capacity for decisive action in a cabinet system when there is no stable majority. The presidential system offers checks and balances, but does not insure consistency between legislation and execution. And a presidential system can so balance power between legislature and executive that there are damaging stalemates and confusion of accountability.

Because hybrid systems attempt to fuse the strengths of the cabinet and presidential forms of government, more states are adopting some version of the hybrid. However, a significant risk with these hybrids is the increased potential for major power struggles, especially between the cabinet and prime minister, on the one hand, and the president, on the other hand. A council system has the virtue of distributing power among a manageable number of people, but there is a strong tendency for collective leadership to result in persistent internal power struggles, as one or a few members attempt to assert their dominance. And finally, assembly systems are the best approximation of a genuine representative democracy, but they lack the clear and decisive executive leadership that seems to be desired by the populations in most contemporary states.

CLASSIFICATION AND CLARITY

Most theorizing about political systems begins with some classificatory scheme. Classifying political systems in some taxonomies is quite straightforward, especially when the categories are based on clear institutional characteristics (e.g., federations, confederations, and unitary states). But many of the interesting classifications (e.g., democracies and dictatorships) are challenging because most political systems are complex mixtures of characteristics and do not fit tidily into any category. In addition, any classification is time-specific, because evolutionary and revolutionary processes can change the nature of a political system.

Several reasons for classifying political systems have been suggested. First, such classification can provide us with useful descriptive information about political systems. Most people have a vague sense that other political systems are different from their own, and by describing how various political systems are organized between central and peripheral units or between executives and legislatures, we expand our grasp of alternative forms of governmental structures.

Second, such classification helps us to undertake political analysis—to identify patterns of similarities and differences among the political systems of the world. Rather than positing that every political system is unique, the development of a taxonomy assumes that some generalizations can emerge from an analysis of these systems. Sets of political systems that share important characteristics can be compared to each other, or compared to sets that do not share those characteristics. Such taxonomies provide us with a basis for thinking more clearly about the kinds of generalizations that we can articulate. And then comparative analysis can increase our confidence regarding what we know about the political world.

Third, the taxonomies in Chapter 6 might also encourage us to specify with greater precision what we mean by value-laden terms like *democracy* and *dictatorship*. In this manner, the analytic study of political institutions improves our understanding of how these terms are most appropriately used as thoughtful descriptors rather than as rhetorical labels.

Ultimately, the development of greater precision in the use of key political concepts and the increase in our knowledge about the political world can do more than increase the clarity of our thinking. They can also enhance our ability to evaluate the nature and desirability of the political structures in our own nation and in other nation-states and to decide whether there is a "best" form of government.

Would you argue that one form of areal division of power and one form of executive–legislative relations and the same constitution are best for all states? Or do you think that the best institutional arrangements might be contingent upon the major goals and the key characteristics of the particular political society? As a closing puzzle, if your country were to convene a constitutional convention now, would you argue in favor of retaining exactly the same governmental forms that currently exist in your political system?

CHAPTER 7

Political Institutions II:
Structures

The Elysée in Paris, France

When we think about the political world, the names of certain governmental institutions come to mind. These institutions have such names as the *Senate*, the *Chamber of Deputies*, the *prime minister*, the *Ministry of Defense*, the *KGB*, the *Treasury*, and the *Supreme Court*. Each of these labels represents a particular component of one of the four major structures of governance, which are generally termed the *legislature*, the *executive*, the *administration*, and the *judiciary*. This chapter provides some broad descriptive generalizations about the nature and roles of these four common governmental structures that operate within most nation-states.

In Chapter 5, an analytic distinction was made between certain *functions* of governance, such as rule making and rule adjudication, and the institutional *structures* that might be involved in the performance of those functions. This distinction between functions and structures can be confusing, because there is a tendency to identify a certain function with a certain structure. For example, one might assume that the national legislature is the structure that dominates the rule-making function. But the distinction between function and structure is useful because, minimally, there might be other structures besides the legislature that are significantly involved in the rule-making function. In the United States, for example, there are major rule-making activities not only in the Congress, but also from the chief executive (the president), the upper levels of the administration (the cabinet departments), and the judiciary (particularly the Supreme Court). And in China, the national legislature has almost no real power over the rule-making function, which is carried out by the Communist party and the political executive.

This chapter emphasizes the general nature of each major institutional structure, the basic building blocks of most contemporary political systems. It also indicates the primary functions that are typically performed by each institutional structure. As you read this chapter, remember that each of the four major structures can perform a variety of functions in a particular political system and can be composed of many different substructures. For these reasons, the discussions emphasize broad patterns and generalizations, although there are always exceptions and variations across the many nation-states.

THE LEGISLATURE

Most states (about 80 percent) have a legislature as a part of their basic structures of governance. Among the names of legislatures (which can have one or two "houses") are the Senate and the House of Representatives (United States), the Senate and the Chamber of Deputies (Chile, Mexico, and Venezuela, among others), the Legislative Assembly (Costa Rica), the National People's Congress (China), the People's Chamber (East Germany), the National Assembly (Egypt and Tanzania, among others), the Lok Sabha and the Rajya Sabha (India), the Knesset (Israel), the House of Representatives and the House of Councillors (Japan), and the House of Commons and House of Lords (United Kingdom).

Roles of the Legislature

Legislatures have always been structures where policy issues are discussed and assessed. Indeed, the roots of the name of the first modern legislature, the British Parliament, suggests this crucial function—the French word *parler,* "to talk". Most early legislatures were initially created to provide advice to the political executive, typically a monarch, and to represent politically relevant groups. Many legislatures have also been responsible for a second major function—enacting public policies. The roots of the word *legislature* itself are the Latin words *legis,* meaning "law," and *latio,* "bringing or proposing." Some of the earliest legislatures, such as the Roman Senate (from about 500 B.C. to 100 A.D.), had great power to discuss and enact laws.

Although a particular legislature might not exercise these powers, most legislatures are supposed to have three broad roles: (1) enacting legislation, (2) representing the citizenry, and (3) overseeing the executive. In the discussion of these roles that follows, be aware that it is difficult to generalize about the actual functions of the legislatures in all contemporary political systems. First, these actual functions are often quite different from those specified in the state's normative rules, such as those in constitutions. Second, the actual functions of legislatures vary considerably from state to state. Third, they vary through time within a state. Fourth, even in one time period, the role of the legislature within a state can vary because of the particular issue or set of personalities who are active.

Enactment of Legislation.   It might seem obvious that legislatures draft, modify, and then ratify public policy in the form of legislation. But in fact, most contemporary legislatures do not have the dominant role in the rule-making function. As I suggest below, dominance in rule making has passed to the executive in most political systems.

Nonetheless, many legislatures continue to have an active and significant role in the rule-making function. The essence of the legislature's power in rule making is, in most political systems, a constitutional provision that a majority vote of the members of the legislature is required to authorize the passage of any law ("legislative enactment"). The power to enact laws that raise revenue and to authorize its expenditure on public policies ("the power of the purse") has been a central responsibility of the legislative majority. In some systems, legislatures have a system of special committees that thoroughly assess and can amend all proposed legislation that is under the committees' jurisdiction. And in some political systems, many laws are also initiated and drafted by members of the legislature.

Representation of the Citizenry.   A second major role of the legislature is to represent, within the governing process, the opinions and interests of the citizenry. Most legislators are elected by some set of the eligible voters, and it is assumed that a key responsibility of a legislator is to reflect and to serve the best interests of those voters.

However, the concept of representation is not straightforward, because there are at least four different conceptions of the "interests" that a legislator might attempt to represent: (1) the group that is most dominant in the legislator's constituency, possibly a social class or an occupational class or an ethnic group; (2) the political party to which the legislator owes loyalty; (3) the nation-state as a whole, whose broad interests might transcend those of any group or party; or (4) the legislator's own conscience, which provides a moral/intellectual judgment about appropriate political behavior (a position made famous in a brilliant justification in 1774 by British parliamentarian Edmund Burke in his "Address to the Electors of Bristol" [1855/1967:219–222]).

Is it possible for a legislator to represent all four voices simultaneously? In reality, the legislators in most contemporary legislatures do not experience deep conflict in dealing with the problem of representation.

> For some legislators there is no choice, because they hold office in undemocratic systems where their actions are dictated by the political leadership, and thus they act as little more than "rubber stamps." This would characterize the behavior of a legislator in Cuba or Iran, for example.
>
> Some legislators, in both nondemocratic and relatively democratic political systems, are deeply committed to adhere to their political party's line or must obey the party to survive politically. This is usually the situation for most members of the British House of Commons, for example.
>
> Some legislators feel such deep loyalty to particular group or societal norms that they seldom experience seriously conflicting pressures.

There are only a few political systems where most national legislators are *not* significantly constrained by these forces. The U.S. Congress is an example. Legislators can experience underlying tensions, as they attempt to balance legitimate but competing interests that would lead them to support different decisions or actions. Even in such systems, there is predictability in most legislators' choices (on the basis of some dimension such as conservative-radical ideology or party-political loyalty). But there can be considerable variation, as the legislator attempts to balance competing interests, and also as she attempts to do some vote trading, compromising on some issues to insure greater support for the issues about which she cares most deeply.

Oversight of the Executive.   The third major role of legislators concerns their interactions with the executive. In general, the legislature is responsible to oversee the actions of the political executive, and legislators in some systems have substantial capacity to influence what the executive does. The legislature might have the constitutional right to select the executive, to authorize major policy decisions by the executive, and to approve the chief executive's selection of key appointments. In some systems, such as India and West Germany, the president is actually chosen by the legislature (although it is the prime minister, not the president, who is the most powerful executive officer in these systems).

Many legislatures have the right to approve the executive's selection of major appointments. The Israeli legislature must approve the cabinet as a whole. And the U.S. Senate has the right to "advise and consent" on such presidential appointments as cabinet members or Supreme Court justices. The Senate's 1987 rejection of Judge Robert Bork, President Reagan's nominee for the Supreme Court, is an example of a legislature asserting its power over appointments. Also, in cabinet systems, the cabinet and prime minister hold office only if they have the confidence of the majority of the members of the legislature. Also, the cabinet's policies are only enacted if they are approved by the legislative majority.

A second area of legislative oversight involves the right of the legislature to scrutinize executive performance. In many political systems, there are regular procedures by which the legislature can question and even investigate whether the executive has acted properly in the implementation of public policies. At minimum, the legislature serves as a discussion and debating chamber. In subjecting the plans and actions of the political executive to public debate, a modest check on executive power is established. Many legislatures have a more direct right, during legislative sessions, to question the specific plans and actions of particular members of the executive. In Britain, Italy, and West Germany, for example, each minister in the executive cabinet must appear before the legislature and justify any actions taken by her department that are questioned by a legislator.

Most legislatures also have formal investigatory powers on a continuing or a case-by-case basis. Investigations by the U.S. Congress of the Watergate burglary (1972) and of the Iran/Nicaragua arms-for-hostages-for-*contra*-aid deal (1987) are dramatic American examples of such oversight. In addition, some legislatures have followed the innovative idea of Sweden, setting up an *ombudsman*—an independent agency that investigates complaints regarding the actions of the executive branch and its bureaucracies. If legislative questioning, committees, or the ombudsman discover inappropriate behavior by the executive, there is significant political pressure on the executive to correct it. Of course, if the executive resists such pressure, the ultimate resolution of the dispute entails either legal adjudication or, in most cases, a power struggle between the executive and the legislature.

The most fundamental power of oversight held by some legislatures is their capacity to overturn the government. In a cabinet system, the legislature can oblige or pressure the executive to resign from office by a vote of censure or of no confidence or by defeating a major bill put forth by the executive. Even in presidential systems, the legislature has the power to overturn the executive, by means of the extraordinary process of impeachment. Impeachment is quite rare in presidential systems. In the United States, no president has left office due to impeachment, although Andrew Johnson was acquitted on the House's impeachment charge by only one vote in the Senate (in 1868), and Richard Nixon avoided an impeachment trial only by resignation (in 1974).

Structural Arrangements

Number of Houses.   There is one very visible difference in the structural arrangements of different legislatures—the number of houses (often called *chambers*). About three-fifths of the nation-states with legislatures have *unicameral* or one-chamber legislatures. The presumed advantages of a unicameral system are that political responsibility is clearly located in one body and that risks of duplication or stalemate between parallel legislative bodies are eliminated. These arguments sound similar to those put forth in favor of a unitary state. And, in fact, most unitary states have unicameral legislatures. Among the many states with unicameral legislatures are Algeria, Bulgaria, China, Costa Rica, Denmark, Finland, Greece, Hungary, Israel, New Zealand, Kenya, Poland, South Korea, Sweden, and Tanzania.

In contrast, many of the states that have two legislative chambers—*bicameral* legislatures—are federations. These federal states include Australia, Canada, India, Mexico, the Soviet Union, the United States, Venezuela, and West Germany. There are bicameral systems in some unitary states such as Britain, France, Italy, and Japan. Given the apparent advantages of a unicameral system, what is the justification for a second chamber?

One argument is that two legislative houses insure more careful and thorough deliberation on issues and laws. Secondly, the two houses can be based on two different and desirable principles of representation. Thus in the United States, the Soviet Union, and West Germany, one house represents the regional governments in the federal system and the other house more directly represents the numerical and geographic distribution of citizens. Some upper houses also represent functional groups in the society, as in the Republic of Ireland, where most members are appointed as representatives of such groups as agriculture, labor, industry, culture, and public services. Thirdly, in a few bicameral systems some members are selected on more individualistic criteria, as in the Canadian Senate (where all members are appointed for life) and the British House of Lords (where many lords are members because of their families' aristocratic status and the rest are "life" peers appointed for merit).

Over time, some bicameral systems have evolved toward unicameral systems. This has occurred where the need for extensive checks and balances within the legislative branch has not seemed compelling, representation in the "people's" chamber has seemed adequate, and the problems of overlap and stalemate between the two chambers have increased. Some political systems, such as Sweden and Costa Rica, have constitutionally abolished one chamber. And in other systems, such as Norway and Britain, the powers of one chamber have been so reduced that it can delay, but cannot veto, the decisions of the more powerful chamber. In fact, the United States is now one of the few bicameral political systems in which the upper chamber (the Senate) is both directly elected and politically powerful (more powerful than the House of Representatives).

Box 7.1

A Peripheral Puzzle: Nebraska

Nebraska is the only American state government with a unicameral legislature. Can you suggest reasons why Nebraska's decision was a good one or a bad one?

Size of Legislatures.   There is enormous variation in the numbers of members within a legislature. In his comparative study of 108 national legislatures in the early 1970s, Jean Blondel (1973:148–153) reported considerable variation. Lower chambers ranged from 24 to 888 members and second ("upper") chambers ranged from 6 to more than 800 members. The range is even larger now, with the expansion of some legislatures. Currently, the British House of Lords has 1,174 members, the Congress of People's Deputies implemented in the Soviet Union in 1989 has 2,250 members, and the National People's Congress in China has 2,978 members. The U.S. Senate, by contrast, has only 100 members. In the U.S. House, 435 members are elected, proportionate to population. Japan, with half the U.S. population, has 511 members, and the United Kingdom, with less than one-third the U.S. population, has 650 members elected proportionately in their lower chambers. Can you think of an appropriate decision rule for deciding how many members there should be? Are there persuasive reasons for the U.S. Senate having two rather than three—or four or *N*—representatives for each state?

The Decline of Legislatures

Many observers claim that in the twentieth century there has been a general decline in the power of legislatures, relative to executives and bureaucracies. Has the power of the legislature declined, and if so, why? Actually, it is very difficult to provide a definitive answer to these questions about relative power, using the techniques of cross-national empirical analysis. In large part, this is because the precise measurement of power continues to be a puzzle for which political science has no clear solution (see Box 7.2).

Given the difficulty of assessing political power with precision, can *any* answer be provided to the question of measuring the decline of legislative power? An empirical test of the relative decline of legislative power is especially difficult. It requires measurement and comparison of the power not only of the legislature, but also of the executive and the bureaucracy, at several points in time and across several (many?) different countries. Since no studies have provided a rigorous analysis of this issue, we might begin with a more modest question: Is there evidence that contemporary legislatures display significant political weaknesses? Despite the absence of precise measures, there are a few types of circumstantial evidence that suggest legislative weakness.

To begin with, the weakness of the legislature seems undeniable in about one in five contemporary political systems, which have no working legislatures whose power we might assess.

Moreover, in nearly all those states that are classified as totalitarian and many that are authoritarian, the legislature is essentially a "rubber stamp" for the actions of the political executive. This lack of significant power applies to 20–40 percent of the remaining states. Thus in as many as 60 percent of the contemporary political systems, the legislature need not even be considered a major power structure.

Among the 40–50 percent of political systems where there do seem to be

Box 7.2

The Problem of Defining Power

Few discussions about politics can occur without direct or indirect reference to power. There is general agreement that power is exercised when A (one actor) induces B (another actor) to behave in a manner that B would not otherwise behave. This emphasizes a causal relation between what A wants and what B does. But the precise measurement of power has always been one of the fundamental problems that political scientists have never adequately resolved. (For different views, see Nagel 1975; Dahl 1984; Lukes 1974; Bachrach and Baratz 1962.) There are many ambiguities, such as these:

1. Is influence, based on argument or persuasion, an exercise of power?
2. Is power exercised only if B does more or less what A wants, rather than if B merely does what B does not want?
3. How do we know what B would have done in the absence of A's efforts?
4. How substantial has the change in B's actions been?
5. Must sanctions always be negative, such as severe punishment or deprivation, or can the promise of reward (inducements or bargaining) also be a basis of power?
6. Is power exercised if B responds to an important attribute of A other than force, such as social status, knowledge/expertise, or wealth?
7. How do we distinguish B's compliance due to A's exercise of power from B's compliance due to recognition of A's authority, defined in Chapter 5 as B's implicit acceptance that A has some right to be obeyed?
8. Can we be certain that it is the efforts of A rather than of C that have caused B's actions?

Thus, in assessing the significance of the concept of power, the *Dictionary of Political Analysis* (Plano, Riggs, and Robin 1982:112–113) concludes: "Power and the related concept, influence, are central to the study of political science. . . . Because of its wide usage as a general descriptive concept, power is unlikely to disappear from the conceptual treasury of the discipline. Its usefulness as an analytical tool is limited, however, by its ambiguity and the difficulty of finding generally acceptable measures of power. Even descriptively, it does not adequately define the boundaries of the field, since political relationships involve more than the sheer exercise of power or influence, and power relationships appear in all areas of human activity."

It is these kinds of conceptual and empirical problems that have led most political scientists to admit, often with embarrassment, that measurement of one of the central concepts in political science remains elusive. Because most people share a broad common understanding of the idea of power, it is reasonable to continue to refer to it; but it remains difficult if not impossible to undertake a precise empirical test of a question such as, Has the power of legislatures declined in relation to the power of executives?

"real" legislatures, there are indirect indicators of the relative weakness of most national legislatures. First, most legislatures do not provide a coherent structure within which power can be concentrated and exercised effectively. Many legislatures have relatively slow and cumbersome procedures for the lawmaking function, especially where there are institutionalized legislative committees that amend legislation. This complexity in the legislative process is even more evident in bicameral systems, since there is often disagreement between the two chambers.

Second, legislatures almost never have the level of support services available to the executive. Their budgets, facilities, staff sizes, and even the legislators' own salaries are significantly lower than those of top members of the executive and administrative structures. Similarly, the technical expertise and knowledge resources within legislatures are far less than those of the executive and administrative structures, a major liability when legislators attempt to deal with the complex subjects facing governments in modern societies.

Third, such factors put most legislatures at a decided disadvantage, relative to the executive, as a source of major policy. In most national political systems, the executives clearly dominate the legislatures as the source of crucial legislation. Most legislatures react to policy initiatives from the executive more than they create policy. This is particularly true in cabinet systems, where the constitutional power center for lawmaking as well as law application is the executive (the prime minister and the cabinet) rather than the legislature. And in most presidential systems, policy initiatives by the executive are far more extensive than one might expect from examining the constitutional division of power and authority (Blondel 1973; Loewenberg 1971).

Some analysts have argued for a fourth, more social-psychological weakness of legislatures, although there is little empirical data on this point. The claim is that most citizens desire clear, dynamic, and singular political leadership; but legislatures are typically composed of many people who, for most citizens, are either indistinguishable or offer too many different identities. In the United States, for example, it is usually possible to answer the question, What does the president think about issue *Y*? But how does one answer the corresponding question, What does the legislature think? In this case, there are not only two chambers and two parties, but there is also a great diversity of different opinions among the individuals and factions within the legislature. In a sense, even though legislatures usually have spokespersons and leaders, no one can truly speak for the legislature. One might even conclude that the legislature in a domestic society tends to fulfill one of its roles too well—its members too accurately represent the diversity among the society's population, and thus speak with many voices.

Studies of major political institutions often mention the relative decline of many legislatures in the twentieth century. While the empirical evidence on this point is sketchy rather than systematic, the reasons cited in the discussion above suggest why the power of legislatures might not have kept pace with that of other institutions, especially the executive and the administration.

Clearly, not all legislatures are impotent or dying institutions. Certain national legislatures remain extremely powerful political structures, such as those in the United States, Japan, Sweden, and Italy. In most other relatively democratic political systems, legislatures have significant impacts on the authoritative alloca-tion of values through their roles in enacting legislation, in representation, and in oversight. And in virtually all societies that have a legislature, its members can exercise political power in many subtle ways. At least, its members have dramati-cally more political power than most other citizens.

EXECUTIVES

The historical evidence indicates that as long as there have been political systems, there have been individuals or small groups who assume top leadership roles. Such a leader or leaders, who are responsible for formulating and especially for implementing public policy, can be broadly called the *executive structure*. The word *executive* comes from the Latin *ex sequi,* meaning "to follow out" or "to carry out." Thus the particular role of the executive is to carry out the political system's policies, laws, or directives.

One might be tempted to generalize that a few individuals emerge as the lead-ership cadre in *every* political order. But there are some historical counterexam-ples, especially from Africa and Asia, of societies that are *acephalous,* which means that they are "without a head." In such systems, many people in the com-munity share power relatively equally, as a collective leadership. Nonetheless, in most sociopolitical systems a few people do assume the positions of executive power.

At the apex of the executive structure, there is usually a chief executive. This might be a single individual with a title like president, prime minister, chief, premier, supreme leader, or queen. Or there might be a small number of people exercising collective executive leadership, as in a ruling council or a junta.

A broader definition of the executive includes not only this top leadership, but also the entire administrative system. Such a definition derives from the no-tion that the rule-application function (the "execution" of policy) is shared by the top executive group and the administration. The top executive group cannot sur-vive without the continuing support of an extensive system of people who inter-pret, administer, and enforce the policy directives of the executive. But in order to differentiate analytically between the major political structures, we shall exam-ine the top executive and the administration in separate sections of this chapter.

Chapter 6 has already provided some analytic information about the execu-tive structure. The executive was central to the description of different patterns linking the rule-making and the rule-application functions. Typically, the execu-tive structure is partially or primarily responsible for rule making, as well as for rule application. While the executive is clearly differentiated from the legislature in the presidential system, the two structures are more integrated in cabinet, council, and assembly systems.

Also, the discussions of democratic and nondemocratic political systems in Chapter 6 emphasized the mechanisms by which top executive leaders attain power and the conditions under which executives are replaced. Democratic executives are empowered by a limited mandate from the citizens and can be removed by regularized procedures that do not require the use of power. In contrast, nondemocratic executives maintain their position in the absence of a limited mandate. The basis of their position might be heredity or the threat/use of power. Despite the considerable variations across states, this section will attempt to describe the components of the executive structure and certain common roles that most political executives undertake.

Structural Arrangments

The Chief Executive versus the Executive.   The term *chief executive* refers to the one individual or small group (such as a president, prime minister, or ruling junta) at the apex of the executive structure of the political system. The *executive* is a much broader term, including all the people and organizational machinery that are below the chief executive in the executive structure. Thus it encompasses upper- and middle-level decision makers in all the departments, agencies, or other administrative units that are in the chief executive's chain of command. As noted above, a definition of the executive far broader than the one is this book might also include the entire administrative system.

In theory, and usually in practice, this is a hierarchical system of political control, in the sense that the actors in the executive structure are supposed to follow the directives of the chief executive. But the chief executive's power over the rest of the executive is rarely absolute. Among the reasons why the chief executive's directives might not be carried out are these:

1. Units within the executive might be too disorganized to act effectively.
2. The executive might lack the resources to carry out policies in the manner desired by the chief executive.
3. Units might be more involved in competing against other units than in coordinating their actions to meet the chief executive's policies.
4. Units might misunderstand or resist or defy the chief executive.

Can you think of other reasons?

Fused versus Dual Executives.   Many political systems have a *dual executive,* in which one actor performs the more ceremonial aspects of top leadership and another is responsible for the more political aspects of the executive role. The essential virtue of the dual executive is that a citizen can be angry or hostile toward the political executive while still remaining loyal to the nation and to the political system through one's affection and support for the ceremonial part of the top executive.

Constitutional monarchies are obvious examples of political systems with a dual executive. In these systems, there is a ruling king or queen (such as Queen Elizabeth in Britain, Queen Margrethe II in Denmark, or Emperor Akihito in Japan) and there is also a prime minister or other political executive. The monarch has little or no power to make authoritative value allocations; rather she serves mainly symbolic or ceremonial functions, as an embodiment of the nation and the people. Chapter 6 noted some "hybrid" forms of government that have attempted to create a dual executive in the absence of a monarch. They have created a second executive office (such as the presidency in India) that is typically insulated from the daily struggles of politics and thus can be a symbol of national unity.

A different form of dual executive exists in some political systems where the monarch is the strong element of the executive, but there is also a governmental executive that exercises modest political power. For example, in the Kingdom of Morocco, King Hassan II dominates the political process. In 1965, he suspended the constitution and dissolved Parliament, ruling by decree until 1977, when he allowed a new legislature to be elected, with a prime minister as chief executive. Kuwait and the kingdoms of Bhutan and of Swaziland are other examples where the monarch has greater power than the prime minister.

Most political systems have a *fused executive,* in which the ceremonial and political functions of the top executive both reside in a single actor. In such cases, it can be difficult or impossible to distinguish loyalty to a partisan political leader from loyalty to the nation. This is often used to advantage by political executives, who criticize or even punish their opponents by claiming that such opponents are traitors to the political order (although they are usually only critics of the current top leadership).

Roles of Executives

Leadership Roles.   In modern political systems, the crucial role of the chief executive is to lead. The leadership role entails taking the initiative in formulating, articulating, and implementing goals for the political system. In the contemporary political world, political leadership is virtually always identified with chief executives. The effective chief executive becomes the spokesperson for the aspirations of the people, can galvanize the people's support for these goals, and develops strategies that facilitate their accomplishment. The crucial skill of the "great" chief executive is this capacity to lead—to mobilize people and objects in the accomplishment of desirable goals.

To a large extent, initiative in policy formation is centered in the chief executive. Executive policy leadership is especially crucial during times of crisis, because the executive structure has the potential for coherence and unanimity of action that are often lacking in the legislature. Moreover, in most political systems, the chief executive has the capacity to veto, either directly or indirectly, the legislation that is initiated by the legislature. Increasingly, even the drafting of legislation is a function dominated by the executive, since many major bills require the expertise and policy direction of the chief executive and its staff.

Symbolic and Ceremonial Roles.   Whether a modern nation-state has a dual executive or a fused executive, the actors in the executive role usually function as the unifying symbol for the entire society, becoming the ultimate mother/father figures for the people. This is especially true if the chief executive has a strong image, as with such leaders as Britain's Prime Minister Margaret Thatcher, Libya's Muammar Qaddafi, or former U.S. president Ronald Reagan. The executive's presence becomes central to many rituals and ceremonies in the society, whether it is the appearance of the Soviet president on the reviewing stand at the May Day parade in Moscow's Red Square, the Kenyan president's official send-off of the national team to the Olympic games, or the British queen's Christmas Day message on television.

Supervision of the Administration.   In virtually all contemporary political systems, the executive has primary responsibility for the rule-application function—the implementation of the policies and laws of the political order. At the apex of this administrative hierarchy, which might include millions of public employees in the state's departments, bureaus, and agencies, is the top group of the executive structure. Most systems have an executive cabinet, each of whose members is directly and personally responsible for some major area of administration. Given the scale and complexity of the activities that are being supervised, these top executive actors can neither know nor control all of the actions that occur in their domain. But they are supposed to set the broad guidelines of rule application and in many political systems they are accountable for any major failures that occur. In cabinet systems, for example, the minister of a department will usually resign if there is a serious shortcoming or blunder in the area under her responsibility.

Supervision of the Military and Foreign Affairs.   Given the state's monopoly of the legitimate use of force, the military, including internal security forces, is an area over which the top political executive usually has direct control. In such cases, the top executive is the commander in chief of the entire military system of the state, including personnel and other resources (aircraft, nuclear weapons, military intelligence, etc.). The chief executive must set policy and supervise the organization and utilization of the state's military capabilities, a task that can carry the most serious consequences for the security and well-being of the society.

Associated with control of the military is the executive's responsibility for foreign affairs—the state's relations with other nation-states. As Chapter 13 will describe more fully, the relations between states involve complex patterns of cooperation and conflict, as each state attempts to accomplish its own goals in the international environment. The chief executive, or her delegates, represents the state in its dealings with other countries. Particular significance is often attached to situations where the chief executives of different states meet directly, as in a state visit or a "summit conference." In fact, such meetings among heads of state typically are symbolic gestures of cooperation or ratify agreements that have been reached by the chief executives' representatives. But the concentration of the state's political power in the chief executives is so great that such meetings can provide opportunities for major breakthroughs in the relations between the states.

The Age of the Executive?

Although chief executives have nearly always been evident, and usually ascendent, in political systems, some analysts call the twentieth century the "age of the executive." This label reflects the apparent concentration of power in executives and the relative decline of legislatures' powers. Why do analysts claim that this has occurred? To some extent, this is a chicken-and-egg issue: The reduced capacity of the legislature for coherent and decisive state action is linked to the emergence of coherent and decisive executives.

In comparison to legislatures, the executive structure tends to be more streamlined and less prone to stalemate and inaction. And the executive, centered in a single individual or small group, can offer a unified focus for a mass public that desires simplicity and clarity in an age of great complexity. If a contemporary mass public wants some form of heroic leadership, it is most likely to be sought from the chief executive. The chief executive typically speaks with one voice and, when effective, can assure the people that political power will be exercised with certainty and efficiency to respond to the pressures and demands in the society and in the international environment.

Even if a chief executive cannot deliver, she can at least promise decisive leadership in a manner that no other political structure can. Since most political systems have always had a significant or even a dominant executive structure, the twentieth century might merely be more executive-dominated than many other historical periods. Can you specify conditions under which a state would be likely to be dominated by a structure *other* than the political executive?

THE ADMINISTRATION

While the chief executive can be understood as the managers of the rule-application function, the broader executive of a political system—the *administration*—consists of the thousands or even millions of public employees who do the ongoing business of interpreting and implementing the policies enacted by the state. These employees are divided into organizational units called by such names as *departments, ministries, agencies,* or *bureaus.* The state's military and police forces are often a particularly crucial component of the administration.

The administration is the machinery of government without which the political system could barely function. The units perform such important activities as the maintenance of order, the collection of revenues, the keeping of records, the provision of public goods and services (e.g., roads, education, solid waste disposal, health care, monetary aid for the needy), and the regulation or actual control of the factors of production (e.g., production of steel, provision of transportation, growth and distribution of food).

Bureaucracy as One Form of Administration

In most discussions, administration and bureaucracy are synonymous concepts. In the attempt to clarify our language of political analysis, it might be helpful to distinguish them. In this view, *administration* is the general term for the machin-

"Government Bureau" by George Tooker (Metropolitan Museum of Art)

ery and also the processes through which rules and policies are applied and implemented. *Bureaucracy* is a particular structure and style through which the administration can operate. Bureaucratic structure and style have received their definitive description from the great German sociologist, Max Weber, whom we first encountered in Chapter 1. Structurally, bureaucracy is characterized by hierarchical organization and specialization by means of an elaborate division of labor. Weber also defined the "ideal-type" bureaucracy by several key characteristics of its style of operation: (1) Its members apply specific rules of action to each case, (2) so that the resulting treatment of each case is rational (3) and nondiscretionary, (4) and predictable, (5) and impersonal (Weber 1958a:196–244).

Some readers might always have experienced treatment by public administrators that is consistent with these distinguishing features. This is quite possible, since some nation-states have deeply incorporated this bureaucratic style. But there are also many contemporary political systems, and even more examples historically, where there are frequent instances of unpredictable and personal treatment. In these systems, the treatment that you receive can depend on the attitudes of the administrator with whom you interact, as well as who you are, and whom you know. Or it can depend on what favors or benefits you offer to the administrative actor who deals with your case (see Box 7.3).

Among contemporary political systems, situations like that in the imaginary system of Delta are widespread. Personal contacts and bribes (in various societies, these are referred to as *grease, chai, baksheesh,* or *dash*) are often an essen-

BOX 7.3

"Dealing" with the Administration
in Gamma and Delta

An imaginary example might help illustrate the contrast between a classic bureaucracy and one that does not fulfill Weber's criteria. Two citizens, A and B, each intend to undertake an identical activity: to open and operate a small shop selling tea and pastries in the market district.

In the country of Gamma, both A and B apply to the Ministry of Business, where an employee requires each to complete a standard form and to pay a fixed application fee. An inspector from the Ministry of Health examines the premises to insure that all health and sanitation regulations are met. When rat droppings are found in both premises, both A and B are obliged to hire an extermination service. Each receives the health certificate only after pest eradication and a second inspection. Both A and B open their shops.

In the country of Delta, A and B make the same application. However, A is a member of the dominant ethnic group and B is not. When A applies to the Ministry of Business, she is given a form to complete by the clerk, also a member of her ethnic group, and the form is approved. When B applies, she is told that the maximum number of permits for the market district has already been issued. After lengthy discussion, B telephones her cousin, who is an important politician in the local government. The cousin contacts the undersecretary in the Ministry, on behalf of B's request, and the application form is now provided and permission is granted. When the inspector from the Ministry of Health examines A's shop, she finds rat droppings. She threatens to refuse the certificate, and so A offers her a substantial amount of money. The inspector completes a report in which the shop passes the inspection. When the same inspector goes to B's shop, she claims to find evidence of rats. When she can show B no evidence, B demands her certificate. The inspector shrugs, provides the name of the only extermination service she "guarantees," refuses the certificate to open the shop, and leaves.

The contrast between the two imaginary cases is clear. The administrators in Gamma behave in accordance with the bureaucratic ideal. Both A and B receive fair and identical treatment and all rules of procedure are scrupulously followed. In Delta, however, the treatment of A and B is very different. A manages to succeed because she is a member of the favored ethnic group and because she is willing to bribe an inspector. B overcomes the hurdle of her unfavored ethnicity because she has an influential contact; but she fails to open her shop because she is not willing to accede to the extortion attempt by the inspector.

tial element of success in dealing with the administration. Indeed, in some societies, a style like that in Delta is viewed as normal and even appropriate, because it is assumed that individual treatment and personal favors are preferable to rigid application of the rules.

Is there a reasonable argument against a Weberian-style bureaucracy? In complex societies, terming an organization "bureaucratic" is not usually intended to be a compliment. Some criticisms of bureaucracy are really directed at all large administrative structures that exercise increasing control over people's lives and that expand their organizational domain (i.e., their turf) to a level where they are seen as too large and powerful. But at its heart, the negative use of the bureaucracy label has come to connote a system that is too inflexible and impersonal. The application of rules is so rigid that extenuating circumstances tend to be overlooked, and every individual is merely treated as a number. Bureaucrats themselves are seen to be relatively free of political accountability, because they are protected by professional norms and hiring/firing rules, which give them quasi-permanent tenure and insulate them from political pressure.

Despite criticisms of its occasional excesses in practice, the Weberian bureaucracy is celebrated as an ideal form in most contemporary political systems. In the abstract, most people would prefer an administrative system that is overly rigid and impersonal to one that is based on corruption and personal favoritism. Rather like the ideal of democracy, many countries claim to be operating in terms of the ideals of Weberian bureaucracy. But there are enormous differences in the extent to which such ideals are consistently applied, especially in environments where the ideals are inconsistent with traditional practice.

Administrative Functions and Power

The scale of activity of the state's administrative structure depends upon that political system's definition of *res publica*. As the political system penetrates a larger sphere of the society and economy, there is a corresponding need for a more extensive administrative structure, since the administration serves as the basic apparatus through which the state interprets, implements, and monitors its value allocation decisions. Thus the administrative system tends to be larger, in relation to the society, as the political system becomes more totalitarian.

Given the very substantial variations in the definition of *res publica,* there are at least five broad functions that are performed, more or less extensively, by the administrative structures in contemporary political systems.

1. *Information management.* Administrators are responsible for the collection, storage, and analysis of huge amounts of data and information about the individuals and processes in the society. This information provides a crucial data base—recording activities and conditions in the society, measuring the nature and impact of public policies, and informing many ongoing decisions and actions related to the allocation of public values.
2. *Provision of knowledge.* Many administrators develop great expertise within their specialized areas. This knowledge can be of enormous utility for virtually every decision and action undertaken by the political system.
3. *Provision of public goods and services.* The essential work of the administrative structure is the rule-application function. Administrators must constantly interpret and apply public policies that provide public goods and services to individuals and groups.
4. *Regulation and enforcement of public policies.* The administrators are also responsible to interpret and apply many public policies that set

guidelines for the behavior of individuals or groups. These can vary greatly, from monitoring collusion among corporations to enforcing traffic laws to protecting the civil rights of ethnic minorities.

5. *Extraction of resources.* In roles such as collector of revenues from citizens and businesses or operator of state-owned companies producing goods and services, the administrative structure is in charge of many tasks that generate resources for the political system.

This brief and general list of functions suggests the enormous breadth and depth of the administrative structure and its activities. Some observers argue that in the complex, extensive, and knowledge-based political systems of the late twentieth century, the power of the bureaucracy is supreme. Although the administrators are, in theory, "servants" of their political masters and clients, it might be that in reality these roles are reversed. Bureaucrats have such unmatched knowledge and experience in their specialized domains that generalist politicians rarely have sufficient expertise to question the bureaucrats' information, recommendations, or actions. And their power to grant or withhold benefits provides them with considerable leverage over clients. Career administrators have quasi-permanent tenure while politicians and clients come and go. The modern bureaucracy has such wide-ranging power and competence that it is typically credited with maintaining political systems when executives and legislatures are ineffective, as in the Third and Fourth Republics in France and in many modernizing states in Africa and Asia. Max Weber himself might have had the last word when he observed that, "in the modern state, the actual ruler is necessarily and unavoidably the bureaucracy . . ." (1958a:211).

THE JUDICIARY

In a Hobbesian state of nature, disputes among individuals would normally be resolved by force or the threat of force. In such a setting, "might makes right." Thus a primary reason for the social contract is to authorize the state to intervene in the potential and actual disputes among individuals and groups, by creating and enforcing rules regarding proper forms of interaction.

Every society holds that those who violate its rules and laws must be sanctioned. But the rules in each society are deeply influenced by its unique culture, history, and politics, and there are usually ambiguities regarding the rules:

What does the rule mean?
Has a rule been violated?
Who are the "guilty" actors?
How serious is the offense?
What sanctions are appropriate?

These kinds of ambiguities are resolved through the rule-adjudication function in every political system. Many political systems have constituted judicial structures whose primary role is, or at least appears to be, rule adjudication.

Aspects of Rule Adjudication

The rule-adjudication function attempts to interpret and apply the relevant rules or laws to a given situation. When the issue involves civil law—the rules regarding the relations between private actors (individuals or groups)—the main objective of rule adjudication is to *settle the dispute*. Examples of such rules include divorce, contracts, or personal liability litigation.

When an individual or group behaves in a manner interpreted as an offense against the social order, rule adjudication can be an important mechanism of *social control*. Much of this is the area of criminal law, and the offenses are ones like murder, substance abuse, theft, bribery, extortion, or environmental pollution. The state represents the public interest and protects the social contract, insuring that the relations among actors are within the boundaries of "acceptable social behavior." In the same manner that the definition and scope of *res publica* differs greatly across political systems, the definition of acceptable social behavior varies dramatically. In some political systems, such social control entails little more than regulation of the conditions under which people can do physical and economic violence to one another. In contrast, there are other political systems where mere public criticism of the political order or its leaders is viewed as a violation of acceptable social behavior, punishable by imprisonment or death.

In some instances, rule adjudication can center in *arbitration regarding the behavior of the political system* itself. This is especially evident in cases involving constitutional, administrative, or statutory law—the rules concerning the rights and actions of the political system. The main issues for adjudication involve questions about the legitimate domain of action by a governmental actor, in its relations with other governmental units or private actors. Such a dispute might concern a quite technical disagreement over the implementation of a specific policy (e.g., is a person with vision correctable to 20/400 qualified to receive state-subsidized services for the "visually impaired"?) or it might raise fundamental constitutional questions about the distribution of political power (e.g., does the central government have the right, in a federal system, to force the state government to force a locally elected school board to implement full racial integration against the board's wishes?).

Judicial Structures

Most, but not all, political systems have specialized judicial structures—the system of courts and personnel that determine whether the rules of the society have been transgressed and, if so, whether sanctions ought to be imposed on the transgressor. (Some broad definitions of judicial structures even include agencies of law enforcement, such as police and security forces, and agencies that apply sanctions against rule breakers, such as jails and prisons, although I have included these among the administrative structures.)

In the United States we tend to link the rule-adjudication function closely with explicit judicial structures. The United States has one of the world's most complex systems of judicial structures, with a Supreme Court and an extensive system of federal, state, and local courts, including judges, prosecuting attorneys, defense attorneys for the indigent, court clerks, and so on.

While there are significant cross-national variations, most political systems do have a hierarchical system of judicial structures, with appeal processes possible from lower- to higher-level courts. Most judicial systems also have subsystems that are responsible for different aspects of adjudication. For example, the French judicial structure separates the criminal and civil law system from a second system that handles administrative law. In the Soviet Union, one system handles criminal and civil law, but the second major system is composed of special prosecutors who monitor actions in all types of cases and who can challenge, retry, or even withdraw cases from the regular courts. In Great Britain, one major judicial system is responsible for criminal law and a second handles civil law.

The conception of an "independent" judiciary is a particularly interesting one. The legal system and the set of judicial structures in *every* political system are political. By its very nature, rule adjudication entails crucial decisions about the allocation of values and meanings for a society. Thus the only sense in which it is reasonable to speak of an independent judiciary is to assess the extent to which the judicial structures make decisions and take actions that are at variance with other powerful political structures in the society, particularly the executive, legislative, and administrative structures. While there is no systematic research to clarify this question, the judicial structures in most states consistently support and rarely challenge the power and authority of the top leadership groups in their society. In general, the judicial structures are *dependent* on political power for their own power and survival.

However, there are some political systems where the judiciary is relatively independent. By exercising the power of *judicial review,* such judicial structures can reinterpret or even revoke the policy decisions of the other political structures. About one in ten nation-states has a significant level of judicial review. Such states include Canada, Colombia, India, Israel, Italy, Mexico, Norway, Switzerland, the United States, and West Germany. Even in states where the judiciary is relatively independent, it is ultimately dependent upon other political structures, especially the executive and the administration, to enforce its decisions.

The conflict between Franklin Roosevelt and the Supreme Court (see Box 7.4) is a rather visible example of a process that occurs continually in a more subtle manner—the impacts of external political power on judicial processes and decisions. More recent examples in the United States are the refusal of California voters to reconfirm Rose Bird as chief justice of the State Supreme Court in November 1986 and the refusal of the Senate to confirm Robert Bork, President Reagan's nominee for the U.S. Supreme Court in October 1987. In each case, these jurists were rejected on political grounds (Bird too liberal, Bork too conservative).

And even when the judicial structure does strive to maintain some political

BOX 7.4

Packing the Supreme Court:
F.D.R. versus the Judicial Branch

There is a constant interplay of power between the judiciary and other structures. A classic example of this interplay occurred in the United States during President Franklin Roosevelt's New Deal (1933–1940). Roosevelt drafted and pushed through Congress a series of sweeping laws meant to use national government policies to pull the country out of the Depression. However, the U.S. Supreme Court consistently ruled these laws unconstitutional, since the New Deal legislation gave the central government a role far exceeding its constitutional powers, as the Court interpreted them. After considerable grumbling and frustration, Roosevelt devised a different strategy for influencing the court. Since there was nothing in the Constitution that limited the Court to nine justices, Roosevelt implied that he would increase the size of the Court.

Congress blocked President Roosevelt's initiative to expand the Court. But his appointment of two new justices and his threat to "pack" the Court was followed shortly by a change of heart on the Court regarding the constitutionality of New Deal legislation. By 1937, the Court majority no longer objected to the central government's expanded activities. While it cannot be proven empirically that Roosevelt's threat changed the judicial reasoning of the justices, it was punned at the time that "a switch in time saved nine."

independence, it still might respond to political pressure. In most systems, the individuals in top judicial positions are likely to share the values of the ruling groups, since they are appointed by chief executive leaders. And when judicial officials displease the dominant power group, they can be ignored, replaced, or even eliminated. In Argentina during the 1970s, more than 150 high-level judges disappeared and are presumed dead, and it is speculated that the Argentinian government ordered the executions.

Actually, the most common pattern among contemporary states is for the judiciary to be little more than a loyal administrative arm of executive power. While the rituals of the judicial structures offer the appearance of protecting "justice," the reality is that the judicial structures serve the political elite. In short, while most judiciaries exercise some discretion in rule adjudication, the existence of a truly independent judiciary is a rarity.

CONCLUDING OBSERVATIONS

Traditional political science emphasized a description of political structures as the best means to explain how politics worked. But further empirical research has revealed considerable diversity in the roles of particular political structures. There is no straightforward and necessary correspondence between a political structure and the political functions that seem logically associated with the structure. Thus precise behaviorally oriented and process-based analyses of politics now treat political structures more richly.

For a while, political structures seemed so fluid that they were treated as secondary elements, merely forming a context with which various political, economic, and social groups must deal as the groups' actions result in the allocation of values for the society. But in the past decade, many scholars have reemphasized the importance of institutional arrangements. For the "new institutionalists," the particular configuration of political structures can powerfully shape political actions and outcomes (March and Olson 1984). For the "neostatists," the structures of the state—its institutional arrangements, the actors who have major roles in its institutions, and its policy activities—are autonomous and have fundamental impacts on political, economic, and social life (Evans, Rueschemeyer, and Skocpol 1985; Nordlinger 1987).

A full understanding of the political world requires a clear grasp of the essential features of executive, legislative, administrative, and judicial structures. Institutional structures are the skeleton and organs of the body politic. As one could explain certain biological functions and processes of the body without explicit reference to skeleton and organs, so one could explain certain functions and processes of the political system without reference to structures. But such an abstract description of a biological organism would be incomplete without indicating the way in which the structures constrain and shape the functions. Similarly, attempts to describe or explain politics, especially in actual settings, are much richer and more complete if they include a characterization of how political institutions constrain and shape the political process.

CHAPTER 8

Political Economy

In all the political systems of the world, much of politics is economics and most of economics is also politics. . . . For many good reasons, politics and economics have to be held together in the analysis of basic social mechanisms and systems.

—*Charles Lindblom,* Politics and Markets *1977:8*

This book is about the *political* world. But if Lindblom is correct, understanding contemporary politics requires an understanding of its linkages with economics. This combination of politics and economics is called *political economy*. The main aim of this chapter is to provide you with a grasp of political economy. The connections between the economic system and the political system will be described. Then three different types of political economies, labelled (1) the *market economy*, (2) the *command economy,* and (3) the *mixed economy* are characterized. Finally, we can examine how these political economies are related to major "isms" in the political world, especially capitalism, socialism, and communism.

POLITICS AND ECONOMICS

Many of the decisions by the political system can have significant impacts on the economy. Can you think of implications for the economy from such policies of the state as

No state involvement in the construction or repair of highways and roads?
State ownership of all factories producing cars?
High state taxes on the profits of businesses?
State financing of all education for all citizens, from preschool through post-doctoral training?
Absolutely no state restrictions on the right of foreigners to enter and work in the country?
State regulation of the prices of all basic foods?

Similarly, activities within the economic system can have a major impact on the political system. The political order depends upon the economic system to generate goods and services for the survival and prosperity of its citizens. Thus the decisions and actions of the political system can be powerfully influenced by the actions of major economic actors and the performance of the economic system. For example, what policy responses might you predict from the U.S. government to such economic factors as:

A lengthy nationwide strike by automobile workers?
The sale of the nation's major computer company to a Japanese company?
The discovery that there are less than ten years of oil reserves underground within the nation's boundaries?
A disastrous harvest that reduced the nation's grain output by 50 percent?

The more one reflects on modern political systems, the more clear it becomes that the political system and the economic system are inextricably entwined.

Understanding political economy requires the use of some basic economic concepts. Economic systems and the concepts used in economics can seem as complicated as political systems and the concepts used in political science. Thus this chapter describes a framework for the economic system that is similar in spirit to Easton's framework for a political system (in Chapter 5). The framework deals only with some core ideas, without much detail and with considerable simplification. (If you want the full treatment, read an introductory economics book like Heyne 1973 or Baumol and Blinder 1988 or take an Econ 1 course.) Even the discussion here involves some complicated abstractions, so hang in there!

A POLITICAL-ECONOMIC FRAMEWORK

The abstract models presented in Figure 8.1 are our starting point for understanding the idea of a political economy. Figure 8.1 offers an extremely simple characterization of the way in which extraordinarily complex systems of production and exchange operate (see Baumol and Blinder 1988, Chap. 8; Ruffin and Gregory 1986, Chap. 6).

Factors, Firms, and Households/Consumers

In the beginning (according to this model), there are three kinds of important productive resources—the three major *factors of production* (A). Land is the ground and any raw materials (such as coal ore and bananas) on or in the ground. Labor is the productive input of a human (our common understanding of "work"). And capital is the nonhuman productive input from other resources (especially financial resources, machinery, and technology). Each factor of production is controlled by an owner who, in the language of economics, is referred to as a *household* (B).

Some actor called a *firm* (C) (in this book, the terms *firm* and *producer* are used interchangeably) attempts to acquire a combination of these productive resources (factors of production) in order to produce a *good* (D1). A good can be a product (e.g., a pencil, a nuclear missile, etc.) or a service (e.g., a massage, transportation on an airplane, etc.).

A firm might be a single individual who produces a good from his own resources. For example, a masseur (massage giver) provides a massage through his own labor skills. Or a firm might be a large organization that uses many productive resources (of land and commodities, workers and capital). For example, a firm that produces something as simple as a pencil needs such productive resources as wood, lead, tin, rubber, machines, and workers. The firm transforms these factors of production into the final good—here, a pencil. Often, goods are acquired in order to make more complicated goods; these goods used in the firm's production process are called *intermediate goods* (D2). The pencil firm, for example, has probably acquired such intermediate goods as tin (which it acquires from another firm that has mined and refined the metal) and wood (which has come from a firm that owns, cuts, and mills trees).

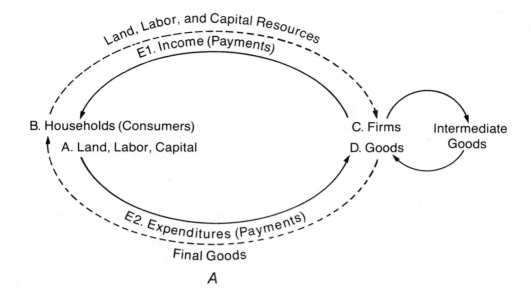

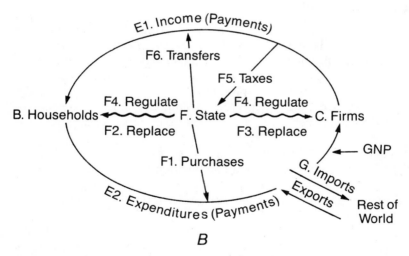

Figure 8.1. A Political Economy Framework. NOTE: The gross national product (GNP) is the sum of household expenditures (including investment via the financial system), government purchases, and exports minus imports.

A household has a second role, as a *consumer,* when it wants to acquire a final good. A consumer offers something of value to the firm in exchange for the good that the consumer wants. What emerges between the household/consumer and the firm is a system of *payments* (E1 and E2). A firm must pay something to those households that control the relevant productive resource(s) necessary for the firm to produce goods. And a household, in its role as a consumer, must pay something to the firm, in order to get the final goods that it wants. (There are a very few "pure public goods," like air, that are owned by no one and thus available without payment to everyone.) Notice that any individual (or group) can act as either a consumer or a firm, depending upon whether he is transforming productive resources into goods or is acquiring a final good.

The size of a payment (the price) is established by how much someone is willing to exchange for something held by another actor. In simple economies, a payment might involve a straight exchange. The actor who has grown a dozen tomatoes exchanges them with someone who will give him a massage (or whatever else he values enough to give up the tomatoes). In every system there are some of these good-for-good exchanges.

But most systems develop an intermediate mechanism (typically, money) that provides a standardized measure of the prices of many goods. The consumer gives the producer some amount of money in exchange for the final good. For example, a tomato might cost 1 dollar (or an equivalent amount of money in francs or yen) and a massage might be offered for 12 dollars.

If no consumer is willing to offer more than 10 dollars for a massage and the masseur wants to get other resources in exchange for his good, the price of a massage is likely to come down. This is how *supply and demand* operate: If demand is low relative to supply, price comes down; and if demand is high relative to supply, the price goes up. In theory, with enough producers and consumers making exchanges, the price of a good reaches a perfect balance point, known as the *efficiency price*.

The payment by a consumer to a firm (E2) might be different than the payments by the firm for the productive resources necessary to produce that good (E1). A firm is successful if it is able to sell the good for more than it paid to produce the good. This return to the firm in excess of its payments is called *profit* or *surplus value*. If the firm must sell the good for less than the cost of producing it, the firm suffers a *loss*. Obviously, firms normally try to increase their surplus value and to avoid loss.

Getting and Spending

So, the system of exchange goes round and round. The households expend their resources on goods and the firms provide the households with income as they pay for productive resources. Ideally, everyone is exchanging things of value for other things that they value even more. As the system becomes more complex, many actors are involved in the production and distribution of goods. In addition to offering goods for money and exchanging money for desired goods, some actors can operate as middlemen, organizing complicated or large-scale exchanges.

As the cycle continues, more and more goods are produced and bought and sold and consumed by all the actors in the economic system. The complexity of the actual exchanges in most economic systems is beyond comprehension. As an example, see how long a list you can develop (in one minute) of the number of different people who contributed some fraction of the value (the one dollar) that you pay for a tomato at the supermarket. (Think about the actors involved in the production and distribution to you of that tomato.) With sufficient time, you could probably identify hundreds of people who share in the resource that you have sacrificed (i.e., the payment you have provided in exchange for the tomato).

To the extent that others are willing to offer substantial payments in exchange for the factors of production or the goods that you control, you have more resource power. You have many choices regarding the use of your own resources. If you have 12 tomatoes, you could (1) eat them all; (2) eat 6 and sell/trade 6 (for as much money or goods as you can get); (3) eat 2, and sell/trade the rest for a loaf of bread and a book of verse; (4) eat 2, sell/trade 2 for a loaf of bread, and use the remaining 8 to make 16 tomato sandwiches that you sell/trade (for as much as you can get); (5) give all the tomatoes to hungry people; or. . . . The possibilities are extensive. And if you chose an approach other than 1 or 5, you now have further choices to make with your new bundle of resources.

Presumably, you attempt to pursue a strategy that maximizes your values (i.e., that results in your most-preferred mixture of goods and resources), and hence enhances your life. Individuals (and groups) can have very different sets of preferences. One person might want to hoard money or beans or precious metals. Another person might want to spend everything on consumption for personal pleasure. One person might actively seek the resources to own a mansion and a Mercedes-Benz while another person might be happiest with no possessions other than the bare necessities he carries in a backpack. One person might work obsessively to increase his total package of resources while another might join a meditation society and give up all work in favor of the contemplative life.

Of course, it's a tough world, and so everyone is not equally capable of maximizing his value preferences. An individual's success in getting his preferred mix of goods and resources can be affected by such things as the kinds and amounts of resources he already controls, his skills in producing desired goods, the constraints in his environment, the actions of others, and even luck. Over time, there are likely to be huge differences in the mix of goods and resources controlled by different individuals and groups.

The State (and the World) Join In

We now have our first approximation of an abstract model of the economic system. The cyclical exchange of payments for factors of production and payments for final goods becomes a perpetual motion machine. This model is extremely simplistic. One crucial omission in our description to this point is the absence of the political system. The state (F) is added in part *B* of Figure 8.1. As we talk about the state in this discussion, it is useful to reiterate that the state, like the other aggregate actors, is really a complex organizational structure composed of many individuals, whose combined decisions and actions constitute the behavior attributed to "the" state. The state can powerfully affect the political economy in six general ways:

F1. It can be a consumer, purchasing any good from a producer.
F2. It can be a household, in the sense that it controls some/all factors of production.

F3.   It can be a firm, producing any good.

F4.   It can regulate the manner in which either consumers or producers operate, by enacting policies that encourage or prevent certain behaviors by those other economic actors.

F5.   It can tax (extract resources from) the payments to any actor.

F6.   It can transfer payments to any actor.

It will be evident in the next section that actions of the state regarding these six dimensions distinguish different types of political economies.

Part *B* of Figure 8.1 also recognizes that there are boundaries that affect the behavior of economic actors. Producers can sell goods outside of the state's boundaries to some consumer in the rest of the world (these are *exports*). Or consumers can purchase goods from producers outside the state's boundaries (these are *imports*). Thus there is a net flow of income into or out of the economic system, based on the levels of imports and exports (G). In addition, a state (the actor's own state or another state) can implement policies that either restrict freedom (e.g., tariff barriers) or facilitate freedom (e.g., conquest of one state by another). In this chapter, the role of political economies in the rest of the world will generally be ignored; but the significant role of such external actors will be emphasized in Chapters 12–17.

Since you probably feel that things are complicated enough already, we'll stop here. There are, of course, many elements of a fully specified model of an economic system still missing. You can readily find them in an introductory economics text. But two more facts about the model should be pointed out: First, part *B* of figure 8.1 does not explicitly identify the role of certain financial actors that would be shown in a fuller model. A household can save some of its income rather than spend it all. These savings are put into the *financial system*. Its investors pay households to use these resources as capital, which the investors offer to firms in exchange for payment and/or a share of the firm's surplus value.

Second, remember also that although all actors are presented as independent individuals in these figures, an economic actor, like a political actor, might be an individual or a collectivity. In an actual economy, some actors will combine their resources with those of other actors in order to enhance their relative advantages in the processes of production and exchange. They might develop cooperative arrangements with other actors, forming groups and institutions that attempt to

Box 8.1

A Gross Product

The total level of production in an economy is measured by a monetary figure known as the *gross national product* (GNP). GNP is the total value of all the final goods produced by a state's economic actors during a certain time period. A related term that is sometimes used is *gross domestic product* (GDP). It is the total value of all final goods produced by everyone within a state's boundaries, whether they are citizens or not. GNP is the production of everyone who is a citizen of the state, whether they are inside the state's boundaries or not.

control the utilization of a resource. Such cooperation might emerge among individual owners of labor, such as a farming collective or a labor union; among those owning a commodity, such as a cartel; or among those controlling capital, such as a syndicate or a diversified corporation.

TWO IDEAL-TYPE POLITICAL ECONOMIES

It is now possible to distinguish the two ideal-type political economies. Recall that an ideal type is a description of what a certain phenomenon might be like in its pure form. An ideal type is illustrative, but it does not necessarily correspond exactly to any real-world example. The two ideal-type political economies are the *market economy* and the *command economy*.

To distinguish the market economy from the command economy, five fundamental questions will be posed:

1. Who controls the factors of production?
2. Who determines what goods are produced?
3. Who establishes the value attached to different resources and goods?
4. Who decides how resources and goods will be distributed?
5. What is the role of the state?

The answers to these questions (summarized in Table 8.1) establish the nature of the political economy in a society. Let us now examine how these five questions are answered for each of the two ideal-type political economies, the market economy and the command economy. Each ideal type is an abstraction meant to reveal a pure form of a political economy. Because these are ideal types, it is likely that no actual political system will correspond precisely to either type. (For other approaches that explain political economy, see, e.g., Alt and Chrystal 1983; Heyne 1973; and Lindblom 1977.)

The Market Economy: Total Private Control

Who Controls the Factors of Production?   In the ideal-type market economy there is total private control. Every actor has direct, personal control over all his own factors of production. The worker decides who, if anyone, he will offer his work to and the type and amount of resources he will accept in exchange for that work. The owner of land or capital similarly decides the conditions under which his productive resource will be employed in the productive system. And the firm determines what productive resources it will acquire.

In general, every household and every firm is motivated to maximize the value associated with the resources and goods it controls. As an actor operates in this economic order, he continually attempts to expand the total package of resources that he controls. Thus he aims to take actions such that every exchange will increase his accumulated value. To the extent that he can exchange some resource(s) and receive an even greater amount of resources in return, he has in-

TABLE 8.1. Two Ideal-Type Political Economies

Key Points	Market Economy	Command Economy
1. Control of factors of production	Every economic actor controls own factors	State owns and controls all factors
2. Production decisions	Sum of all private actors' decisions ("invisible hand" of market)	State decisions defined in detailed plan
3. Value established	Exchange value in the market	State sets values attached to all goods
4. Distribution decisions	Choices by private actors	State determines who will receive what products at what levels
5. Role of the state	Generally passive; enforces rules, provides minimal protection to actors	Dominates process; plans, controls and regulates all economic activity

creased his total resource base. Of course, it is also possible that he can make bad decisions about what to control, and thus reduce his total resource base.

Who Determines What Goods Are Produced?   As all the actors make their own separate decisions in an attempt to maximize their own resources, a pattern emerges regarding what goods are produced. In particular, every firm acts to maximize its surplus value through the process in which it pays to acquire productive resources and then produces goods that are sold to consumers. The firm's decisions about what goods to produce are based on its assessment of how it can achieve maximum profit. In the phrase of the famous Scottish economist Adam Smith (1723–1790), production is guided by the "invisible hand" of the market. This invisible hand is the summation of the actions of every household and every firm regarding the uses of the factors of production.

If one thinks of an economy in terms of the supply and demand for goods, this system is demand-oriented. The most important consideration for a firm that is deciding what to produce is, What good can I offer that others will demand and for which others will offer the highest payments, in comparison to my costs of production? Thus the firm attempts to assess the demand for various goods in the market and then to transform the factors of production it controls in order to provide whatever good it thinks will maximize its own profit.

Who Establishes the Value Attached to Different Resources and Goods?   Similarly, the invisible hand of the market establishes value. Each factor of production and the goods that are produced through transformation of these factors are valued at their opportunity costs—the payment that someone in the market is willing to offer in exchange for them. Hence nothing has value except to the extent that some other actor will exchange resources for it.

In most circumstances, many actors offer similar resources and goods. This results in vigorous competition among private actors, as everyone tries to gain the maximum payment from others in exchange for their own resources and goods. Ultimately, the value of every resource and good is subject to this competition, based on both its supply and the existing demand for it.

Competition is particularly intense where supply and demand are quite unequal. For example, if there are 10 workers who will drill holes in metal (supply) and there is one firm that needs 2 workers with this resource (demand), the firm can bid down the resources it has to pay for the work (this is usually a wage rate, but can also include other resources, such as work conditions, benefits like housing or health care, shares of the firm's profits, etc.) by inducing the 10 workers to undercut each other's wage claim. Conversely, if there are only 2 workers available with this skill and the firm needs 5, the workers can bid up the resources that they will be offered.

A basic economic assumption in a market economy is the continual adjustment of supply and demand toward an equilibrium point. For example, some workers might move to a different place or offer a different labor skill if the wages for drilling holes get too low or there are too few jobs; and a firm might find a substitute for the labor it needs if hole-drilling labor is too expensive or too scarce to enable the firm to make a profit in the market. (Can you think of other supply-demand adjustments that the workers or the firm might make?)

Who Decides How Resources and Goods Will Be Distributed?   Again, it is the invisible hand of the market, rather than anyone in particular, that determines the distribution of resources and goods in the market economy. As everyone pursues his own private interests, actors accumulate dramatically different bundles of resources and goods, depending upon their preferences, the resources they control, and their skill and luck in exchanging and transforming resources in the market.

What Is the Role of the State?   In a market economy, state intervention is minimal. The state is passive in the productive system, allowing private actors to operate in a relatively unconstrained manner. The state is obliged, under the social contract, to prevent private actors from doing violence to each other. And the state protects its citizens from the external environment, preventing or resisting the violation of its sovereignty or its citizens' rights by other states. In meeting these responsibilities, the state might purchase some resources, might levy minimal taxes, and might affect firms' import and export activities. But the general principle in the ideal market economy is that the state does not have a significant role in the economy.

The Command Economy: Total State Control

Who Controls the Factors of Production?   In the ideal-type command economy, the state assumes total control of virtually all the significant factors of production. The state replaces or eliminates the role of private owners of labor, land, and capital whose activities are so crucial in the market economy. The state owns the land, the natural resources, the factories, the machines, and so on. The state even owns labor, in the sense that the state decides the conditions and purposes for which each individual will offer his labor. Thus it is the state that determines how every factor of production will be utilized.

Who Determines What Goods Are Produced? In terms of part *B* of Figure 8.1, the state is the firm that produces virtually all major goods in the system. The state devises a detailed *economic plan* that specifies what levels of each good will be produced from what combination of resources. A political ideal guides this plan for production: the commitment to provide every citizen in the society with the goods that enable each citizen to enjoy a life of material well-being. Thus the state's plan sets production decisions that are supply-oriented (in contrast to the demand orientation of the market economy). The state/firm attempts to use productive resources optimally to maximize the supply of appropriate goods available for consumers. Centralized planning guided by a broad vision of social needs, rather than independent decisions by many profit-seeking actors, guides the complex actions resulting in the production of a particular mix of goods.

Who Establishes the Value Attached to Different Resources and Goods? Since the state controls all the factors of production and is the firm producing all goods, it is also able to set the values (i.e., establish the payments) for all exchanges within its boundaries. Competition is eliminated, since the state, rather than the market, establishes the payments for every factor of production and every good in the society. Thus the state tells a group of farmers to produce a million tomatoes, and then sets the exchange value of those tomatoes. Similarly, the state decides which individuals will have jobs drilling holes and it establishes the wages and benefits they receive for their work. The state is not completely free to set payments—for example, the scarcity of a productive resource can influence its cost—but given availability, value is set primarily by the state's decisions.

Who Decides How Resources and Goods Will Be Distributed? The state is equally active in the decisions on the distribution of goods to the population. The state's plan indicates who will receive which goods in what amounts. The plan will specify, for example, that automobile-producing factory X will receive 46 tons of steel each month, and that a town will receive three tomatoes per family per week. The plan can also indicate precisely where these goods will come from (i.e., steel from factory Y and tomatoes from farm Z).

In the real world, most near-total command economies base their plan on the objective of distributing necessary goods (especially food, shelter, education, health care) to every person on a relatively equal basis. But as an ideal type, a command economy need not be committed to such egalitarianism. The state could decide that one particular group will receive a very large share of the goods and that other, less favored groups will receive very little. The crucial decisions about distribution of goods are made by those with power in the political system.

What is the Role of the State? Clearly, the state has a dominant, even an overwhelming role, in this political economy. The state controls virtually all of the important factors of production, it plans the manner in which they will be utilized in the production of goods, it establishes the official value of all resources and goods, and it decides how the resources of the society will be distributed among individuals. In this political economy, surplus value is accumulated by the state, not by individuals. The state then determines how this surplus value will be used to serve its objectives and to provide goods to certain actors.

KEY PROBLEMS FOR EACH IDEAL-TYPE POLITICAL ECONOMY

There are potential shortcomings in the actual operation of either the market economy or the command economy. It is important to consider a few of the major problems inherent in each. These, along with the benefits, are summarized in Table 8.2.

Market Economy

Resource Inequality.   One problem with a market economy is that substantial resource inequality tends to emerge. In a market economy, competition is everywhere and it tends to become ruthless. As every actor strives to maximize resources and control over the factors of production, some actors are extremely successful and others are total failures. Most importantly, the market system is indifferent to the problems of those who do not succeed. And over time the rich

TABLE 8.2. Benefits and Problems of Market and Command Economies

	Benefits	Problems
Market Economy		
No central plan	Local decisions and "invisible hand" stimulate innovation, facilitate freedom	Economic cycles of boom and bust, inflation and recession
Demand orientation	Goods' cost and quality responsive to consumers' desires	Creation of demand for and proliferation of goods that have limited social value
Competition	Energetic and efficient production	Ruthless interactions; huge inequalities in wealth and resources
Command Economy		
Central plan	Rational use of societal resources	Overcentralized control; limited innovation and lack of responsiveness to changing circumstances
Supply orientation	Production and distribution for social and individual needs	Oversupply and shortages; lack of coordination
No competition	Work for common good; relative equality of wealth and income	Little initiative; shoddy products; low productivity

tend to get richer (especially if they cooperate a bit) while those with few re-sources tend increasingly to lose economic power in the market.

Neither the successful actors nor the state intervene to protect those who fail to capture many resources. Thus some people, and perhaps even large numbers of people, lack the resources to enable them to consume the goods they need for a secure and comfortable life. As inequalities of wealth, power, and status increase, there is greater likelihood of alienation among the less successful and of conflict between the rich and the poor.

Production for Profit, Not Need.   A second problem is that a demand-oriented system of production does not necessarily produce goods that meet human needs. Rather, production decisions are dominated by actors who produce those goods that they believe will maximize their own resources. Thus there can be a proliferation of extravagant or marginal goods that are profitable, while more essential goods are produced in insufficient amounts because they are less profitable. For example, there might be an abundant supply of quality health care for the rich, while large numbers of poor people lack adequate care because private producers see too little profit in inexpensive care and the state is passive in the production and regulation of health care.

There also might be wasteful competition, as many variations of a good are offered. Considerable resources can be spent manipulating demand for these goods, by such techniques as advertising. For example, there might be literally hundreds of different breakfast cereals, most of which are minimally nutritious. A cereal's cost might be based as much on the expense of advertising and packaging (to create demand for the particular brand) and on profit (to the producer) as on the factor payments to produce the cereal.

Severe Economic Cycles.   Third, a market economy can experience major economic cycles. There is no guarantee that the very large number of private decisions about production and consumption (the "invisible hand") will mesh in a manner that insures steady growth and prosperity for the economic system as a whole. The economy is prone to large swings in the direction of either hyperactivity (causing inflation and scarcity) or serious economic decline (causing recession or depression), and the state does not intervene to counteract these swings. Major fluctuations between boom and bust, even if infrequent, can be deeply disruptive and damaging, to the productive system as a whole and especially to those actors whose limited resources make them vulnerable to bad times.

Command Economy

Limited Incentives for Efficiency.   The absence of competition in the command political economy can result in problems as serious as those from excessive competition. First, if there is no competitive market of alternative goods, there is minimal initiative to produce goods of high quality. People are obliged to accept goods that are unexciting or of poor quality. Second, if payments are standardized by the state and there are no major economic incentives for individual initiative and hard work, managers and workers tend to become conservative and even lazy.

Unresponsive Production.   The state's emphasis on a supply orientation means that production decisions are not directly responsive to consumer demand. The supply-oriented political economy is guided by the central planners' ideas of what people should want, not what consumers actually do want and will purchase. Thus it is typical that the plan results in substantial oversupply of some goods and severe shortages of other goods. There is little to force the planners to be responsive to the consumers' desires.

Overcentralization and Inflexibility.   Command economies are usually so centralized that they lose touch with the differences and complexities of individual firms and consumers. The central planners usually do not receive and react effectively to information regarding miscalculations and mistakes in either the development or the implementation of the state's overall plan. Such rigidity and unresponsiveness make the efficient use of productive resources unlikely. In short, the political economy that combines minimal competition, a weak demand mechanism, and inflexibility is prone to low productivity, inferior goods, and inefficient utilization of resources.

THE MIXED ECONOMY

Given the potential shortcomings with the ideal-type market and command political economies, is there an alternative? The *mixed economy* can be understood as an attempt to combine the strengths of the market and command economies, while minimizing the shortcomings of each. As a hybrid, the mixed economy is not a "pure" ideal type. The mixed economy compromises on each of the five key issues considered above.

   Control of the means of production is shared between the state and private actors. That is, the state owns or directly controls some of the major factors of production, such as those relating to key commodities (e.g., coal, oil, steel), and to key infrastructure systems (e.g., transportation, telecommunications), and to key financial resources (e.g., the banks). But there is also a very substantial share of the factors of production that are controlled by private actors (households).

   Production decisions in the mixed economy are primarily demand-oriented, driven by the market mechanism. Most public (state) sector firms are under direct state control, as in a command economy; but they usually must interact and even compete with many private firms when acquiring productive resources and when selling goods to consumers. However, firms and households can be constrained by the state in the mixed economy. The state can regulate the behavior of private actors and it can also implement an economic plan that specifies broad guidelines for all actors in the system.

   In the mixed economy, the *value* of all goods is established in a manner more akin to the market system. Value is generally determined through the market processes of supply and demand, which interact to determine the opportunity costs of most goods. But the state intervenes to insure that national priorities are protected. For example, the state might establish the value of certain factors of production, including wages; it might set guidelines on market prices for goods; it might regulate the manner in which households and firms collaborate and compete; and it might employ taxing and expenditure (purchases in part *B* of Figure 8.1) to influence the productive system. Overall, the state's rules, actions, and direct involvement in the productive system moderate and limit the market of private households and firms.

Decisions on the *distribution* of values is the most complicated element of the mixed economy. Private actors are allowed to take decisions and actions that maximize their profits and their share of the resources. But the state then intervenes by a variety of taxation mechanisms, recapturing some of the payments received by every private actor. In turn, the state uses these taxes to purchase goods or as transfer payments, both of which the state redistributes to certain actors in the social order. The state undertakes only a partial redistribution of resources (unlike the command economy), leaving private actors with considerable resources and freedom to make their own decisions about production and consumption.

In sum, the mixed economy is a middle way between the market and the command political economies. The mixed economy attempts to blend a demand orientation and a supply orientation, to facilitate some competition but to mitigate the effects of ruthless competition, to allow private actors to benefit from their skillful use of resources but to insure a certain level of necessary goods for the less successful actors. The great challenges for the mixed economy concern the difficulties of striking a proper balance between competition and control, between a free market and a planned economy, between private profit and a sharing of society's resources. Real-world economies are so immensely complex and dynamic that the search for such a balance is continual and in some cases impossible.

ACTUAL POLITICAL ECONOMIES: THE "ISMS"

No state in the contemporary world corresponds exactly to any ideal-type political economy. In a sense, all political economies are mixed. But states can be located (in an approximate fashion) along a continuum from a "pure" market economy to a "pure" command economy. Actual political economies are oriented toward one or the other end of this continuum. The vertical dimension in Table 8.3 classifies selected states as fitting into three categories along such a continuum. States can use political power to alter either of the dimensions in Table 8.3. In the early 1990s, for example, the East European states were attempting to shift toward the middle cell, by introducing more market mechanisms and greater elements of democratic politics.

In the more emotionally charged language of politics, a different set of labels is often attached to political economies. Much of the discussion describes political

TABLE 8.3. Political Economy and Democratic Politics

Level of Democratic Politics	Type of Political Economy (late 1980s)		
	Market	Mixed	Command
High	Australia Costa Rica Japan Philippines United States Venezuela	France Italy Sweden United Kingdom	
Medium	Argentina El Salvador Kenya Nigeria Thailand	Egypt Iraq Turkey Yugoslavia	
Low	Chad	Guinea Kuwait Saudi Arabia	Algeria Afghanistan China Cuba Czechoslovakia East Germany Laos Libya North Korea Soviet Union

economies in terms of three "isms": capitalism, socialism, and communism. These terms have strong affective and evaluative content for most people, given their political socialization. Here are some representative emotional renderings:

> Three steps to doom: liberalism, socialism, communism!
> The basis of all human misery is capitalism, and especially its final stage, imperialism!
> The greatest danger to world peace is communist totalitarianism!
> The ideal polity is the middle way: socialism with a human face!

Capitalism, Socialism, and Communism

Can we distinguish analytically between the three "isms," capitalism, socialism, and communism? The three "isms" are related to, but not identical with, the three ideal types of political economies. Unlike the political economies, the three "isms" also include ideological and purely political elements. Although they are more difficult to define with precision, the "isms" can be characterized along the political economy continuum. Most simply, a system near the command end of the continuum is associated with communism. Conversely, with increasing dominance of the private market, a system becomes more capitalist.

While this simple distinction is useful, precise understanding of "isms" is more complicated. How do we determine when an actual state changes from one "ism" to another? There are no precise operational measures that serve that purpose. What is the domain of socialism? Socialism is sometimes equated with communism, and some states use the terms *communism* and *socialism* almost interchangeably (e.g., the Soviet Union is actually called the Union of Soviet *Socialist* Republics). Yet certain Western European states (such as Sweden) are also labelled as democratic socialist states. There are very substantial differences between the political economies of the Soviet Union and Sweden. What is the distinction between communism and socialism?

Communism versus Socialism.   Communism is distinguishable from socialism in an analytic sense, because the state (on behalf of "the people") attempts to control virtually all important factors of production in the society. And communism is distinguishable in an ideological sense, because it has a fundamental commitment to total economic and social equality among all citizens. (Notice that such egalitarianism is not a necessary condition of the ideal-type command economy.) In contrast, socialism (as it is used in this book) is a system where considerable private ownership and control of significant factors of production is retained. And, while policies in a socialist state attempt to reduce inequalities significantly, they do not aim for total economic equality. (See Box 8.2.)

Socialism versus Capitalism.   Socialist countries are far more committed than capitalist countries to active state intervention in the political economy. A significant share of major productive resources are either owned by the state or are managed by state-controlled organizations. There is more state-directed planning of the economic decisions regarding production, distribution, prices, and wages. And the socialist system tends to use public policy to redistribute societal resources towards those citizens who are less advantaged economically.

As a system becomes more capitalist, a larger share of these activities and decisions are made by private actors operating in a market-oriented economy. Under capitalism, private actors are allowed the opportunity to pursue individual economic goals, with minimal state intervention. Private actors own most of the productive resources, have greater freedom to determine what to produce at what price, and retain higher levels of economic surplus, if they are successful in the market. The policy actions of the capitalist state shape the general form of production and distribution. And there are policies to protect individuals and groups from severe economic deprivation.

An Example of Communism: The Soviet Union.   The Soviet Union is still appropriately classified as a communist system (as a command economy) because the political system owns and controls the major means of production in the society and there is a detailed central economic plan. More than 95 percent of the GNP is in the public sector. The Soviet Union has moved away from a more absolute

BOX 8.2

Communism versus Socialism in Marxist Theory

It is worth noting that Marx and Marxist theorists use the terms *socialism* and *communism* in a different manner than do either the political economy approach of this book or contemporary Western media and politicians. In Marxist theory, communism is a higher stage of political economy that follows socialism. In a socialist system, the state strives to achieve social control of resources (of the means of production) by eliminating private property. As private property is eliminated, there will be a reduction in the presence of the different strata (classes) of citizens that are separated by substantial differences in the amount of private property that each controls.

In Marxist theory, communism will emerge only when all classes (and the inevitable conflict between those classes) cease to exist. Thus most Marxists acknowledge that no "socialist" state (e.g., the Soviet Union, China, Cuba) has yet completely eliminated classes and the class struggle; in this sense, communism remains a goal. In the classless society, everyone will work for the good of all, not to gain private value. Thus, under socialism, each provides resources (work) according to his ability and receives resources according to that work, while under communism, each provides according to his ability and receives according to his need.

This book employs the common Western usage: communism exists if a state has near-total control over the major factors of production. Thus the Soviet Union, China, and Cuba are, by this criterion, "communist" states. A detailed description of the class approach to explaining politics is in Chapter 10.

form of communism under Gorbachev, especially due to the considerable reduction in centralized state control over the economy. Like many communist systems, the Soviet Union now allows a limited free market in the provision of consumer goods, such as food and product repairs. But the political system retains a fundamental commitment to egalitarianism through the state's control and allocation of societal resources. Individuals and private collectivities (e.g., families, nonstate organizations) are allowed ownership of modest amounts of resources for personal use (e.g., clothing, household goods, and other personal effects) and for productive use (e.g., tools, intermediate goods).

An Example of Socialism: Sweden.   Sweden is classified as a socialist system (mixed political economy) because, while the state directly controls some of the major means of production, many others are under private control and are constrained by the state only indirectly, through its policies of regulation, planning, and taxation. In Sweden, private citizens and groups have the right to own very substantial amounts of resources, although about 67 percent of the gross domestic product (GDP) is in the public sector. The state then taxes the value of privately held resources at a high rate. (Until altered in the mid-1970s, Sweden's marginal income tax rate—the tax on the next unit of money earned—was more than 100 percent for those in the highest income brackets; i.e., for the extra money earned after a certain level, an individual lost more in taxes than he made!) In turn, the state allocates these revenues to provide many free or highly subsidized goods to society at large (e.g., public transportation, education, health care) and especially to those with relatively less (e.g., income supplements, housing, jobs). In another example, Yugoslavia has a central plan, state ownership of major productive means and strong programs of resource distribution. But it is more socialist than communist in the sense that there are considerable private ownership, many worker-owned enterprises, a large private-sector market, and substantial wage and wealth differentials.

An Example of Capitalism: The United States.   The United States is a familiar and reasonable example of a capitalist system (a market economy). About 65 percent of the GDP in the United States is in the private sector. Since this means that one-third of production is in the public sector, it could be argued that the United States is a mixed political economy. It is classified as a market economy because of the substantial power and discretion exercised by private actors, compared to many other political economies. The state allows very extensive private ownership and control of the factors of production, and most decisions and actions regarding the use of those resources are in private hands. As noted above, private firms are responsible for two-thirds of the goods produced. Apart from defense/military expenditures and education, there is only a modest level of resources allocated to provide public goods, with limited welfare provision for the relatively poor. Thus the U.S. state's role is limited (although certainly evident) in all the domains of action defined for government in part *B* of Figure 8.1.

Corporatism

Recently, many scholars have referred to the political economy of some states by another "ism," *corporatism*. Corporatism is characterized by a blend of public and private control under an activist state. Corporatism is "a system where government grants official recognition to a limited number of interest associations that are given a virtual monopoly in representing a certain sector of the economy before the public authorities. The price paid for such a privileged position is the general expectation that the leaders of the peak associations or other organizations involved will comply with the policy initiatives of government officials" (Hagopian 1984:282–283).

In other words, the corporatist state identifies a few groups that control major productive resources. The key groups usually include the owners of large industries, organized labor, farmers, and the controllers of financial capital. The organizational leaders of these groups are given great influence in working with the state to determine answers to key political economy questions regarding resource value, production decisions, and distribution of resources.

The idea is that there will be consultation, cooperation, and coordination among the state, big capital, big owners, and big labor, rather than conflict and competition. The "peak associations" (organizations that represent those big groups) have some autonomy from the state, but they are supposed to work together for common national interests. In short, corporatism blends features of capitalism (e.g., private ownership, private profit) and socialism (e.g., extensive state economic planning, coordination of major factors of production with the state's conception of the national interest).

Italy under Benito Mussolini created the first modern corporate state—one with a strong fascist bent, as we shall see below—between 1922 and 1943. Twenty-two corporations were established, including ones for chemical trades, textiles, lumber and wood, credit and insurance, and inland communications. Each corporation had owner, employee, and managerial representatives who met with state officials to develop economic policy (Macridis 1987:220–226). There is considerable debate among researchers regarding the extent to which modern states like France or Japan, which do have strong linkages between public economic power and private economic power, are best understood as corporatist systems (see, e.g., Schmitter and Lembruch 1979; Pike and Stritch 1974).

Fascism

Our political economy framework provides criteria for distinguishing between the three big "isms" among contemporary states. There is at least one other political "ism" that has had a major impact in the twentieth century—*fascism*. Fascism is not really a political economy. Rather, fascism is best described as an ideology and a type of mass political movement. As an ideology, fascism is essentially defined by its opposition to forces that might weaken the unity and harmony of all elements of the state. Most importantly, fascism is

1. Anticommunist: It is a reaction against the egalitarian ethic, against the occurrence of a class struggle, and against the seizure of private property.
2. Antidemocratic: It views democratic, multiparty politics as particularistic and unstable.

While the positive elements of fascism are more difficult to specify, fascism has emphasized several central themes. First, the state and society should be unified into a single, organic whole, and all groups must enthusiastically coordinate their activities to achieve the good of the entire nation. Second, the state and especially the top leader are the embodiment of the national will, and all individuals and groups are subordinate to the state and the leader. Third, private ownership of property is protected, although owners of productive resources are expected to pursue profits in a manner consistent with the empowerment of the state, and the owners of labor are directly controlled by the state (Macridis 1986:171–184; Wolf 1969).

The support for fascism comes from a large and active mass movement, based on a coalition of groups threatened by leftist politics. The key groups have typically been the rural propertied class and rural smallholders, the urban lower-middle class, and often the owners of major industry and capital. Each of these groups is threatened by the socialists' and communists' call for collectivization and nationalization. The key conditions for the rise of a fascist movement are strong political activism from leftist political organizations and serious economic downturn.

Although there have been fascist movements in many countries, there have been only two major fascist regimes in the twentieth century—Nazi Germany under Adolf Hitler (1933–1945) and Italy under Benito Mussolini (1922–1943). Apart from these two political systems, few other nonconstitutional regimes of the right are classified as fascist, due to the absence of a mass-based reactionary movement against the left (see Larsen, Hagtvet, and Mykelbust 1976). Most others, such as Spain under Francisco Franco (1934–1975), Chile under Augusto Pinochet (1973–1990), and Zaire under Mobuto Sese Seko (since 1965) are usually described as authoritarian regimes (recall the discussion of authoritarian regimes in Chapter 6), although Germani (1978) labels them "military fascist."

As fascist regimes, Germany and Italy were more noted for their political ideology than for their political economies. Both were characterized by an almost fanatical cult of the leader, through which a single leader is offered total, unquestioning obedience. Both fostered adamant nationalism and, in the case of Germany, this was linked with a notion of racial superiority. "Inferior" racial groups were reviled, persecuted, and even exterminated. The political economy of fascism is usually comparable to what has been described above as corporatism. (Note that Fascist Italy was also mentioned as an example of a modern corporatist system.

Nazi Germany is a clear example of a fascist system. It was a mass-based, antileftist movement, drawing especially strong support from the middle class, the lower-middle class, and the farmers. It developed a corporatist political economy, a cult of the leader (the *Führerprinzip* or "leader principle"), and an intense political ideology (of Aryan supremacy, German nationalism, and persecution of "inferior" groups such as Jews and homosexuals).

POLITICAL ECONOMY AND POLITICS

Another interesting analytical question is whether different types of political economy are inevitably linked with particular styles of politics. It might seem, for example, that it is impossible to have democratic politics and a command economy (see Lindblom 1977:161–169). But can you make an analytic or empirical argument that proves the impossibility of democratic communism? Many advocates of communism either claim that this combination already exists (recall the use of *democratic* in the names of such nation-states as the Democratic People's Republic of Korea) or they insist that it is the ideal blend of politics and economics that will ultimately emerge (after a transition period under a "dictatorship of the proletariat").

If democracy means relatively unconstrained citizen participation in politics, it is certainly possible to imagine a mixed economy that is democratic. How far toward a total command economy might a system move while maintaining democratic politics? Is there a logical or structural inconsistency between state control of the economy and popular control of the state? Conversely, could a capitalist system be highly undemocratic?

The relationship between type of politics and type of political economy has intrigued many political analysts. If these are treated as different concepts, it is possible to undertake an empirical examination of their linkages. A simple method to examine this question is to hypothesize that there is no correlation between type of politics and type of political economy. Table 8.3 classifies 36 states into three types of political economies (market, mixed, command) and three levels of democratic political process (high, medium, low). What does this simple relational analysis seem to indicate? Would you infer causality between the two variables? Are there plausible rival hypotheses that might call this apparent relationship into question? What is your tentative conclusion about the relationship between type of political economy and level of democratic politics?

CONCLUDING OBSERVATIONS

This chapter has introduced you to an approach that classifies and characterizes political systems in terms of their political economies. This might have been difficult, because the concepts are abstract and require the fusion of the language of political science and the language of economics. But these are important concepts, because the linkages between the political system and the economic system are fundamental and pervasive in the contemporary political world. Indeed, the two systems have become so interrelated in most states that it is difficult to separate the two, except in an analytic sense. There can be very substantial variation in the extent to which the political system intervenes in the system of production and distribution of resources. At one extreme, the state can leave virtually all such activities to private actors, while at the other extreme, every activity is planned and controlled by the state.

In considering systems like fascism or communism or capitalism, you might find it particularly difficult to avoid strong normative judgments. This is probably due both to your political socialization and also the tendency to identify an "ism" with particular states. For example, you might associate fascism with Hitler's Germany. That political system engaged in some of the most barbarous practices of any political system in modern history, including the persecution and extermination of more than 6 million Jews and others in its concentration camps.

Yet in assessing fascism, it is important to recognize that other states that have practiced this particular form of political economy, such as Italy under Mussolini and Chile under Pinochet, are not characterized by such morally reprehensible practices. (These two examples are certainly ones in which much violence has been done against citizens, but this does not distinguish them from many other contemporary political systems across all types of political economy.)

Similarly, your evaluative orientations toward communism might be especially negative because you associate it with the governments of such states as the Soviet Union, Cuba, or Vietnam, states that Americans have been socialized to distrust deeply, or even to despise.

In fact, it is certainly reasonable that you will make both analytical and normative judgments about the virtues and shortcomings of every different form of political economy and every "ism." Indeed, there is perhaps no question more crucial in understanding a nation-state in the contemporary political world than an assessment of the appropriateness of its political economy. Despite your own political socialization, you might reflect on a fundamental question: Is *every* state, regardless of its current political and economic development, best served by exactly the same political economy? This will be an important underlying question as we examine political economies in the Three Worlds in Part Five.

PART FOUR

Political Processes

CHAPTER 9

Groups in the Political World

Help us get drunk drivers off the road so you and I can drive without fear. Please don't leave it up to the "other guy." We need you. . . . My husband was nearly killed because of a drunk driver. The driver of a pickup truck crossed the center line and struck us head-on. My husband suffered a broken arm and severe head injuries. As a result of a concussion he contracted spinal meningitis and almost died. I had broken bones myself.

After the crash, I was angry and hurt. But rather than sitting back and feeling sorry for myself, I turned my energies toward working against this problem of drinking and driving. I joined the Mothers Against Drunk Driving crusade because MADD fights to make our roads safe . . . for you, me and our loved ones.

Since our founding in 1980, we've made a great deal of progress–Congress passed the national Minimum Drinking Age Act . . . judges nationwide now impose stiffer drunk driving sentences . . . and government is taking drunk driving more seriously. Yes, we've made progress. But there's so much more to be done. . . . Please help us continue our fight.

—Micky Sadoff, solicitation letter, January 1989

Rather than suffer privately, Mrs. Sadoff decided to take political action. She became a leader, and ultimately the president, of MADD. This group has developed into an effective, nationwide organization in the United States. MADD recruits members and solicits contributions, and then uses its resources to lobby politicians to pass more aggressive policies to punish drunk drivers.

Mrs. Sadoff's story is quite dramatic, but it illustrates the main answer to the question, Why do people join political groups? A person might want to influence the actions of her government, but might believe that her individual actions will not make any difference. People tend to feel that they are relatively powerless in politics when acting alone. But there might be strength in numbers. If a person joins with many others in a political group, it is possible that the group *can* exercise influence in the political world, due to the group's numbers, organization, and capabilities.

This chapter explores the diversity of political groups. Groups are extremely important in politics, because they are often the major mechanism through which individuals are linked to the political system; hence their label as *linkage institutions*. Although there are a few political gladiators who can have a major impact on politics, most individuals, most of the time, have a minimal effect on political decisions and actions.

Even in democracies, casting a vote is the primary individual political act. But if huge numbers of votes are cast (there are more than 90 million votes cast in the U.S. presidential contest), one individual's vote is politically insignificant. To have a greater impact, an individual's best strategy is to combine her political actions with those of others through a political group. Some political groups are wide-ranging in their goals and have a huge membership, like a major political party. Other groups are very focussed in their objectives and have limited membership, like MADD. This chapter describes the nature and activities of various kinds of political groups, political parties, and party systems.

THE CONCEPT OF POLITICAL GROUP

As an analytic concept, a *group* can be defined as an aggregation of individuals who interact in order to pursue a common interest. It is the pursuit of a common interest that is most crucial to this definition, since the individuals do not necessarily interact directly with each other. And the factor that distinguishes a *political* group from other groups is that the common interest is a political objective—an interest in a particular allocation of public values.

A distinction is usually made between political interest groups and political parties, although both types fit under the general definition of political group above. A political group enters the special category of political party when the group seeks not merely to influence political decisions, but also to place its members in the actual roles of government, such as executives and legislators. Although this distinction tends to become rather fuzzy among the most politically active groups, we shall treat political parties as a category of groups that is different from other types of political interest groups.

POLITICAL INTEREST GROUPS

Activities of Political Interest Groups

All political interest groups share the common objective of attempting to influence the allocation of public values; but there is a variety of strategies that groups can employ to achieve this purpose.

Political Action.   The most direct methods to achieve political objectives involve some form of political action. Such action might be taken by all group members or by some members who formally or informally represent the entire group. Depending on the political system, this might entail voting and campaign activities to influence the selection and action of political authorities. Or the group might attempt to articulate its interests to political actors by such communication techniques as letter writing, personal contact, petitions, rallies, or political violence.

Provision of Material Resources.   Political interest groups can also provide goods or services to political actors. Such a strategy assumes that provision of goods and services will influence decision makers to be more favorably disposed towards the interests of group. Each political system develops its own rules about the methods and amounts of money or goods that can legitimately be given to political actors. The line between legal and illegal provision of money and goods varies dramatically across political cultures. In some political systems, all it takes to shock people is the revelation that an interest group has given a political actor a small gift, whereas in other systems, it might take news of a corporation's multimillion-dollar kickback to a politician who helped the company secure a major government contract. Our discussion of administrative systems noted that in many societies it is quite common to provide bribes or favors in exchange for an action by a political actor.

In the United States, extraordinary amounts of money are now contributed to political actors by interest groups. In the 1984 congressional elections, for example, more than $100 million in contributions to candidates was reported. This included $35 million from corporations, $26 million from trade and professional groups, and $24 million from labor unions (Federal Election Commission data in Parenti 1988). Such contributions are legal campaign contributions, but it is obvious that this money is given in the hope of determining who will make what public policies to benefit whom. Although cause-and-effect relationships are hard to establish, the milk producers lobby gave 44 key members of Congress $1 million and the Nixon campaign $500,000 in the 1972 elections, and shortly after the election the federal government enacted new milk price supports resulting in $500 million in new revenues for the milk producers. No one knows the amount of illegal resources that are distributed, although there are occasional scandals regarding bribes and kickbacks, such as the revelation that four oil companies paid $8 million in illegal payments to 45 members of Congress during 1966–1976 (Parenti 1988:202). In a wry comment on American politics, humorist Will Rogers once observed that ''our Congress is the best that money can buy.''

Provision of Information.   Another activity of some interest groups is the provision of data and information to those within the political system. There are certain areas where the interest group has specialized information that the political system would find difficult or impossible to attain from other sources. These private groups have a vested interest in the public policies that emerge, and so most actively provide data that support their own interests.

For example, when the U.S. Congress considered a law requiring mandatory air bags (as a safety restraint) in automobiles, the legislators relied on information from interested groups, primarily the automobile manufacturers and the insurance companies, regarding the increased costs of auto production and the impacts on injuries and compensation if air bags were required (they weren't; Reppy 1984).

Cooperation.   Some political interest groups can also exert influence by their compliance or noncompliance with policy implementation. Government actors realize that successful policy implementation is enhanced when they develop policy acceptable to the affected interest groups. Thus there are clear incentives for the interest group and the political actors to work cooperatively. For example, when the British government was developing its plans to implement a National Health Service (NHS) after World War II, it insured that the interest group representing doctors, the British Medical Association, was actively involved in every stage of planning and policy making. The government recognized that the success of the policy was fundamentally dependent upon the willingness of doctors to accept the framework of the NHS and support its implementation. In return for their cooperation, the doctors won major concessions regarding compensation and peer (doctors') control of professional licensing and performance (Eckstein 1960).

Constraints on a Groups's Behavior

Each interest group must decide what mix of activities is most likely to serve the group's political agenda. This mix is dependent upon many things. Among the most important constraints on the interest group's behavior are the nature of the group's political resources, the objectives it is pursuing, and the political environment in which the group is operating.

Resources.   A group's political *resources* are those elements, controlled by the group, that can influence the decisions and actions of political actors. The particular political resources that are most effective can be different, depending on the situation and the political system. In the previous section, the impact of financial resources and information were emphasized. But certain other political resources can also be influential: control of factors of production, social status, special knowledge or skills, ability to mobilize large numbers of people (who are the source of demands or supports), capacity for social disruption, and access to decision makers. Various groups in a society will usually have dramatically different levels of these political resources. An interest group's behavior will depend on the kinds of resources that it has available and its calculation of the costs and benefits associated with using a particular mix of resources.

Objectives.   The *objectives* that interest groups pursue in the political world are as diverse as the value allocations that the political system might make. One group might want one very specific thing, such as a subsidy for growing wheat, while another group might have very broad objectives, such as a set of policies to eliminate poverty in the society.

Both the group's strategies and the probability that it will be successful are related to the nature of the group's political objective. In general, an interest group is advantaged to the extent its objective (1) is quite similar to existing policy, and (2) is a value allocation that the political system has the capacity to make. For example, the Greenpeace group in France and West Germany is more likely to influence government policies on safer storage of nuclear wastes than to stop the development of new nuclear power stations, and these groups have little capacity to push the superpowers to nuclear disarmament (Dalton 1987).

Political Environment.   At the most basic level, the demands that groups can make and the actions in which they can engage depend on the boundaries of acceptable political action within the particular *political environment*. Every example of interest group action in this chapter has focussed upon a group operating in a democratic political system. An essential feature of democratic systems is that interest groups have quite extensive rights to make political demands and engage in political actions.

Conversely, authoritarian and totalitarian systems tolerate a very narrow range of such activities by interest groups. Even in these systems, groups periodically emerge to articulate demands for various political, social, and economic changes. These groups range from small revolutionary cells like the Sendero Luminoso in Peru to mass movements like the democracy demonstrations in China in 1989. Such groups, and especially their leaders, usually face such extensive harassment and penalties from the authorities that they cease political activity.

Occasionally, the groups do achieve success. Some finally achieve the revolutionary overthrow of the existing regime, as did the Sandinistas in Nicaragua in 1979. And sometimes the authorities eventually grant an interest group a major role in the political process, as happened to the Solidarity movement in Poland, which was transformed into a quasi-political party in 1989.

Types of Interest Groups

To this point, we have not distinguished among political interest groups. A relatively simple and widely accepted taxonomy of political groups is proposed by Gabriel Almond (Almond and Powell 1966). He suggests four types of political interest groups, which he terms (1) associational, (2) institutional, (3) nonassociational, and (4) anomic. Each of these types is described below.

Associational Interest Groups.   The first type, *associational interest groups,* are specifically organized to further political objectives of the groups' members (see Box 9.1). An example is Common Cause, an American interest group whose citizen-members pay a membership fee to support the lobbying activities of a central staff. The leadership of Common Cause identifies political issues that they judge to be of significance to their members. They then attempt to mobilize political action (such as letter-writing campaigns and press releases) in support of a particular position on the issue. The group also provides decision makers with information and data and contributes funds to some political candidates.

Institutional Interest Groups.   Almond's second type, *institutional interest groups,* are organizations that have formed to achieve goals other than affecting the political system but that also act to seek political objectives. Most occupational and organizational groups recognize that there are instances when the decisions of the political system have major impacts on their own interests. Thus many such groups have a formal or informal subunit whose primary purpose is to represent the group's interests to the political system. For example, the University of California is a large institution of higher education. But the university's interests are strongly affected by local, state, and national policies on educational funding, on research funding, on regulation of research, on discrimination in admissions and hiring, on tax law, on patent law, on collective bargaining, and many other policies. Consequently, the university has full-time professional and student lobbyists on each campus, in Sacramento, and in Washington, D.C.

Nonassociational Interest Groups.   In Almond's classification, *nonassociational interest groups* are fluid aggregates of individuals who are not explicitly associ-

BOX 9.1

The British Medical Association:
An Effective Associational Interest Group

The British Medical Association (BMA) is a professional organization for doctors in Great Britain. The group exists primarily to provide technical and professional information to member doctors and to protect the standards and practices of the medical profession regarding important questions of education, training, qualifications to practice, and discipline in instances of malpractice. But the BMA, in protecting the professional and financial interest of its members, identifies many public policies that are relevant to those interests, especially because most health care is controlled by the government through the British National Health Service.

The British Medical Association is a good example of an effective associational interest group. The BMA's professional staff and its members take many actions that attempt to influence the policies of the British political system regarding the health care system. There are many policies of obvious interest to the member doctors, such as those concerning training of doctors, pay issues, client choice of doctors and hospitals, and the quality and quantity of medical facilities. The BMA is also concerned, on behalf of its members, about many other public policies regarding such things as advertising by professionals, judicial rulings on liability, personal and business taxation policies, certification of health care paraprofessionals (e.g., chiropractors), support for medical research, and so on.

Given the wealth of its members, the BMA can contribute substantial amounts of money to influence policy makers directly or to finance public information campaigns. Its members command respect from political actors due to the doctors' high status and social standing, and because they tend to have a common social class and educational background with many political actors. The BMA is also a source of vast information and expertise about health care issues for those public officials who must formulate and implement health care policy. But the BMA's greatest leverage on political actors is its capacity to cooperate or withhold cooperation, since it can powerfully influence the extent to which most doctors support the nationalized health care system in Britain. Thus the British Ministry of Health works extremely closely with the BMA, as the interest group representing most doctors, in all public policy decisions relevant to health care.

ated with permanent organizational entities. Individuals are members of such a group only in the sense that they share some common interest over certain value allocation issues and that some of them become politically active on the issue. It is also possible that a loosely structured organization will temporarily emerge to plan and coordinate their political activities. But the group will be temporary and relatively informal and, once the issue has lost its immediate salience, the group will disappear. If the group does become more formalized and permanent, it is transformed (analytically) from a nonassociational interest group into an associational group.

A nonassociational interest group formed when congressional discussions regarding the Tax Reform Act of 1986 included a proposal to eliminate the tax-free status of fellowships for student teaching assistants. While many graduate students shared a common interest regarding this policy proposal, they did not share

BOX 9.2

Identifying Campus Interest Groups

Can you quickly list a dozen groups on your campus who might temporarily constitute a nonassociational interest group on a specific policy issue?

membership in any organization. However, some groups and spokespersons emerged, and they initiated letter-writing campaigns and articulated their concerns to political actors and the media. Despite their objections and those of university officials, the act did make such fellowships taxable. If an interest group emerges in your community to stop a building development, or recall a public official, or to promote a particular law, it can be categorized as a nonassociational interest group.

Anomic Interest Groups.   Short-lived, spontaneous aggregations who share a political concern are identified by Almond as *anomic interest groups.* For Almond, a riot is the clearest example of this type of interest group—the participants tend to share a common set of political interests or grievances that they express through a generally disorganized outpouring of emotion, energy, and violence. A political demonstration is a somewhat more organized version of anomic interest group activity. It is group political action that emerges with little or no planning and quickly stops that defines an anomic political interest group.

POLITICAL PARTIES

An interest group is transformed into a political party when the group attempts to capture political power directly, by placing its members in governmental office. The political party is the broadest linkage institution in most political systems, because most parties are overarching organizations that incorporate many different interests and groups. While political systems can have thousands of political interest groups, most have only a handful of political parties.

Activities of Political Parties

There are six broad activities, or functions, fulfilled by political parties in most political systems. (1) They serve as brokers of ideas; (2) they serve as agents of political socialization; (3) they link individuals to the system; (4) they mobilize and recruit activists; (5) they coordinate government activities; and (6) they serve as an organized source of opposition to the governing group. Let's look more closely at each of these functions.

Serving as Brokers of Ideas.   The first, most central activity of political parties is to serve as major brokers of political ideas. Many individuals and political groups have interests and demands regarding the allocation of values. A crucial function of political parties is to aggregate and simplify these many demands into a few packages of clear alternatives. To the extent that political parties are effective in this activity, they dramatically reduce the complexity and scale of the political process for the decision maker, who must perceive and respond to individual and group demands, and for the voter, who must select political leaders whose overall policy preferences are closest to her own.

While all political parties are brokers of ideas, parties can be differentiated into two broad categories on the basis of the party's intensity of commitment towards those ideas. *Ideological* parties hold major programmatic goals (e.g., egalitarianism, or Islamic fundamentalism) and are deeply committed to the implementation of these goals to achieve comprehensive changes in the sociopolitical order. Ideological parties are usually ''extreme,'' within the context of their particular political culture. The West German Green party, the Chinese Communist party, the Sínn Fein in Northern Ireland, and the American Libertarian party are examples of ideological parties.

In contrast, *pragmatic* parties hold more flexible goals, and are oriented to moderate or incremental policy change. To achieve electoral success, pragmatic parties might shift their position or expand the range of viewpoints encompassed within their party. Parties of the center are characteristically pragmatic parties. Examples include the Christian Democrats in West Germany, the Democratic and Republican parties in the United States, and the Congress-I party in India.

Facilitating Political Socialization.   A related activity of political parties is their socialization of individuals into the political culture. In many political systems, individuals develop a clear ''party identification.'' This means that a person trusts one political party to represent her political interests. The person's political beliefs and actions are influenced by information that a political party provides or by her perceptions of what the party supports. Even if an individual does not have strong party identification, political parties can be an important source of political knowledge.

Linking Individual and System.   In its role as a linkage institution, a political party connects individuals and the political system. Most individuals rely on political groups to represent their interests within the political system. More than other groups, political parties function in a general manner to formulate, aggregate, and communicate a coherent package of demands and supports. And, if the party gains political power, it can attempt to implement those demands on behalf of the individuals whose interests it serves. Thus political parties greatly facilitate the individual's sense of integration into the political process.

Mobilizing and Recruiting Political Activists.   The political party offers a well-organized and obvious structure within which an individual can direct her political interests. It is a source of political information, of contact with other politically relevant individuals and groups, and of effective access to the political system. In many political systems, involvement with a political party is the primary mechanism through which individuals are drawn into roles as political foot soldiers and, ultimately, as political gladiators. Often it is political parties that select the candidates for political positions or have the power to place individuals directly in positions within the political system. Whether one is considering a highly democratic polity like Great Britain or an extremely nondemocratic one like China, most or all individuals in key positions in the executive and legislative structures have achieved these positions through recruitment and selection by a political party.

Coordinating Governmental Operations. The fifth major activity of political parties is to coordinate the actions of the government. The political party can encourage or require its members to work together to achieve shared policy goals. It can establish an internal hierarchy, with party leaders (e.g., in the U.S. Senate, majority and minority leaders, whips, committee chairs) controlling the actions of the party members in the conduct of government. The parties can also provide mechanisms for facilitating cooperation and regulating conflict among different parties in the political system. Party leaders of several parties might form a coalition in order to secure majority support for certain policies. This is especially important in legislatures where no single party commands a majority. Political parties can also establish forms of power sharing in the conduct of government business. For example, the parties can agree to formulate executive or legislative committees in a manner that reflects the political strength of the various parties.

BOX 9.3

Let's Party!: The Rise
of the Green Party in West Germany

Few political interest groups are transformed into successful political parties. Hence the rapid emergence of the Green party in West Germany is intriguing. The national party was formed only in 1980, but in the 1983 election it won 27 seats in the national legislature and in the 1986 election it increased to 42 seats (8 percent of the total seats).

Where did the Green party come from? Like all political groups, it began with people who wanted to influence politics. There were people in West Germany who were displeased by their government's policies in the late 1960s. The issue that especially mobilized these people was opposition to the West German government's support of U.S. actions in Vietnam and Southeast Asia. (This discussion is based on Mewes 1987.)

But some West Germans were also concerned about other political issues. For these people, their government, and the entire "establishment" in their society had been corrupted in its quest for ever-expanding power and wealth. Some were angered by the social injustice that allowed huge inequalities in wealth and welfare within their society. Some perceived that these inequalities were global, and particularly afflicted the Third World. Some disliked the discrimination against certain groups, like women and ethnic minorities. Some were fearful that the huge buildup of nuclear weapons by the superpowers would result in war in Europe. And some felt that the quest for material well-being and the thoughtless use of new technologies were taking a huge toll on the quality of the environment.

BOX 9.3 *continued*

In the late 1960s, these antiestablishment sentiments appeared in most First World nations. Often, as in West Germany, "leftists" and students were most visible and active in expressing these political views. They demonstrated, they marched, they formed protest groups, they tried all forms of political action that might reduce the political failures they saw.

But in contrast to most other countries, the politically disaffected West Germans did not disappear from politics with the end of the Vietnam War period. Energized mainly by young, countercultural Germans, thousands of small citizen groups (called *Bürgerinitiative*) emerged in many German towns. These citizen groups continued to press policy makers at all levels to respond to the major political issues raised in the late 1960s: concerns about quality of life, elimination of nuclear weapons, environmental protection, local democracy, socialism, and individual freedom.

These local interest groups traced many of the problems in German society to the capitalist political economy, and they criticized the existing political parties for their failure to deal effectively with the problems. By the late 1970s, these groups moved from protest politics to electoral politics, and began to elect some of their members to local office, especially in larger cities. Some of the most dynamic individuals in these local groups developed a national network. They decided that the objectives that the local groups shared could be best promoted by the formation of a single, national political organization. After several conventions, representatives of more than 1,000 of the local groups agreed in 1980 to form a national political party, *Die Grünen* (the Green).

The common concern that holds the many individuals in the Green party together is a commitment to preserving the environment. Thus most Germans initially viewed the new party as an environmental party, and it drew support from the right, center, and left of the traditional German political spectrum. Its electoral support in the national elections of 1982 and 1986 has come particularly from younger voters and from the more educated, higher classes. In Europe, the Greens are viewed as the first important party representing the "postmaterialist values" discussed above in Chapter 2.

The Green party is an ideological party. But it is composed of individuals with quite diverse ideological concerns, and the core activists in both the local groups and the national party tend to be radical in their politics. Thus the platform of the Green party includes strong antiestablishment elements. The ideology of the party increasingly emphasizes the transformation of Germany from capitalism to a political economy in which workers own and control industry; from a militaristic, NATO-based country to one that becomes neutral, eliminates nuclear weapons, and stops preparing for war; and from a leading postindustrial society to one that uses only those technologies that do not damage the environment.

Although the Green party had substantial impact on West German politics in the 1980s, its survival is uncertain. Will the diverse individuals and the broad coalition of local groups from which it emerged support the increasingly radical policies of the Greens? Can it avoid destruction from within caused by the strong ideological differences among its major factions? Will major parties, especially the Social Democratic party, capture the Green's electoral base by effectively promoting moderate policies of environmental protection? Many people believe that this party is too wild to last much longer.

Serving as Opposition.   Finally, where the political system has more than one party, the parties not participating in the governing group can serve as an explicit and organized source of opposition. This is most fully institutionalized in Great Britain, where the major out-of-power party in Parliament is explicitly designated as "Her Majesty's Loyal Opposition." The party should oppose, but never obstruct the actions of the governing party, since the opposition party remains loyal to crown and country. In Britain, the opposition party is guaranteed control of a specified amount of time during legislative sessions. The opposition leaders receive salaries to serve as a "shadow government," with a member of the opposition serving as the alternative, and potential future replacement, for each top official in the government. Hence there is a "shadow prime minister," a "shadow minister of defence," and so on, who articulate what they would do if they held ministerial positions as the governing party.

PARTY SYSTEMS

Party systems are generally classified according to the number of political parties and the interactions among the parties in the governing process. In the comparative study of political parties, four types of party systems are usually distinguished: (1) two-party systems, (2) multiparty systems, (3) dominant-party systems, and (4) single-party systems. Distinguishing features of each type are described below.

Two-Party Systems

A two-party system is characterized by the alternation in governmental power of two major political parties. Each party has a realistic possibility of forming a governing majority and they generally alternate in power, although the electoral fate of each party varies over time. There can be significant third parties in two-party systems, but the third party has limited power unless a major party needs its support to gain a majority.

In two-party systems, there is often a substantial ideological overlap between the parties. In both Costa Rica and Honduras, for example, the two major parties present very similar political orientations and objectives. In the United States, the distinctions between the two major parties are blurred because the liberal element of the more conservative (Republican) party tends to substantially overlap with the conservative element of the more liberal party (e.g., southern Democrats). Great Britain is an example of a party system where the two major parties (Labour and Conservative) have quite distinct ideologies.

Multiparty Systems

As you might expect, a multiparty system has more than two parties whose participation can be essential in the formation and activities of government. In cabinet systems, this means that the creation of a legislative majority (a government) might require a coalition of two or more parties.

Women voting in India

Working Multiparty Systems.   In a "working" multiparty system, there is a relatively clear split between sets of parties capable of forming a governing majority. For example, there might be one or several cooperating center- and right-oriented parties forming one group, and a social democratic or socialist left party, as in the cases of France, Norway, and Sweden. It is also possible to have a working multiparty system where there is a fundamental willingness of various parties to cooperate in a governing coalition. For example, four major parties typically share governing power in Switzerland, and it is viewed as undesirable for any one of the parties to govern independently.

Unstable Multiparty Systems.   Multiparty systems are often unstable. In these cases, the parties that form the government (the majority coalition) have underlying ideological disagreements. At some point, the government's policy on some issue induces a coalition partner to withdraw its support, resulting in a crisis for the government. In cabinet systems, such a crisis often leads to the resignation of the government or the dissolution of the legislature. In presidential or assembly systems, this situation tends to produce paralysis in the legislature. Clearly, the difficulty of forming a governing majority among multiple parties increases as different parties are more firmly committed to their unique ideological orientations.

   Instability is a particular problem in multiparty systems where extreme parties (of the left and/or right) refuse to participate in any coalition. For example, Table 9.1 reveals this problem in the Italian party system in 1987. The very large bloc of Communists refused to enter into a coalition with the other left party, the

188

TABLE 9.1. Examples of Party Systems

Countries	Number of Seats in Legislative Body
Italy, Chamber of Deputies (1987)	
Proletarian Democracy	7
Communist party	198
Socialist party	73
Social Democratic party	23
Republican party	29
Christian Democratic party	225
Liberal party	16
Italian Social Movement	42
Others	17
Total	630
Norway, Storting (1985)	
Left Socialists	6
Labor party	71
Progress party	2
Christian Democratic party	16
Center	12
Conservative party	50
Total	157
Costa Rica, Legislative Assembly (1990)	
National Liberation party	25
Social Christian Unity party	29
Other	3
Total	57
Singapore, Parliament (1986)	
People's Action party	77
Other parties	2
Total	79
Kenya, National Assembly (1985)	
Kenya African National Union party	171
Total	171
Turkey, National Assembly (1983)	
Motherland party	212
Populist party	117
Nationalist Democracy party	71
Total	400
Japan, House of Representatives (1990)	
Communist party	16
Socialist party	141
Social Democratic party	14
Komei (Clean) party	46
Liberal Democratic party	290
Other parties	5
Total	512

NOTE: For each country, parties are listed in order of ideological orientation from left to right.

Socialists, and the array of small right-wing parties also refused to support the center parties in a consistent fashion. Thus the large Christian Democratic party attempted to govern alone or in a minority coalition. The instability of the cabinet system is clear, because the Christian Democrats were assured of only 225 votes in the 630-seat legislature. Under these conditions, several governments fell in rapid succession.

Dominant-Party Systems

In a dominant-party system, the same party repeatedly captures enough votes and seats to form the government, although one or more other parties are free to compete. Japan provides a useful example of a dominant-party system. As reflected in Table 9.1, there are five major parties in the Japanese national party system. Although the center-right Liberal Democratic party (LDP) does not usually obtain a majority of the votes (the LDP typically gets about 45 percent of the votes), the manner in which citizen votes are converted into seats in the legislature (the Diet) has meant that the LDP has enjoyed a majority of legislative seats in the lower House of Representatives after every election since the MacArthur Constitution of 1946 (see Chapter 6). In 1989, the LDP lost its majority in the upper house, the first time it has not been dominant in both houses of the legislature. But the LDP retained its control of the more powerful lower house in the 1990 election.

Mexico, another example of a dominant-party system, has several competing parties; but PRI has controlled the presidency and the national legislature in every election since the 1917 revolution. The opposition parties are convinced that PRI stole the presidential election in 1988, when its candidate, Carlos Gortari de Salinas, barely achieved a majority amid many suspicious circumstances. A few countries are on the margin between a dominant-party system and a one-party system (the next category below). For example, elections in Singapore are dominated by the People's Action party, but candidates who are not members of the party are allowed to run, and a few do win seats in the legislature.

One-Party Systems

In a one-party system, the single party of the governing group is the only legal political party. The clearest examples of one-party systems are in states dominated by the Communist party, such as China, Cuba, and Mozambique. In its effort to control all aspects of public life, the state accepts no institutional opposition to its rule, and a second political party would be the most direct and objectionable form of such opposition. Similarly, many authoritarian regimes do not tolerate the existence of any political parties other than the one that represents the state and its vision of political order.

In some states, multiparty systems are ultimately reduced to one-party systems. For example, many of the nation-states that achieved independence after 1945 initially provided for competition among multiple parties. But these systems have had great difficulty sustaining multiple parties. First, the state has no experience with the transfer of an electoral mandate from one party to another. As one party and its leaders become entrenched in power, they are reluctant to relinquish that power to another group through the electoral process.

And second, there is minimal experience with a system of institutionalized opposition. Thus the governing group views any party that expresses opposition to its rule as disloyal or even as seditious (which means that the party is stirring up resistance or rebellion against the government) rather than as a "loyal opposition." As a consequence, in many newly independent states a brief honeymoon of democratic electoral multipartism is soon followed by increasing repression of opposition parties. In many states, this eventually results in the abolition of any party other than the single "party of the state/government/society." Among the examples of this evolution to one-party states are the West African states of Ghana and Cameroon after 1966.

There are one-party systems that do inject some competition or selection. For example, Tanzania has had a single-party system since its independence in 1963. However, the party offers two alternative candidates for each of the 200 seats in the National Assembly. Thus voters in each constituency have at least some choice, since the candidates have different styles and tend to offer slightly different priorities, despite their loyalty to the single party. In 1980, more than half of the members of the Tanzanian legislature who sought reelection were voted out of office.

It is also possible for one-party systems to evolve into multiparty systems. Fascinating examples of this transformation have emerged in the early 1990s as the Soviet Union and other East European states attempt to establish multiparty systems after decades of rigid one-party rule. In these states, the Communist party is attempting to adjust to a competitive party system and opposition groups are attempting to form effective parties. This change will entail a series of adjustments by leaders and factions as they try to define clear identities and gain a solid base of voters for particular parties. In Poland, for example, the evolution began in 1985, when only 245 seats in the 460 seat Sejm (legislature) were won by Communist party members, although few seats were held by explicitly non-Communist groups. Then, in the 1989 election, Solidarity presented itself as an opposition party. Solidarity candidates won virtually all of the one-third of the seats that it was allowed to contest in the Sejm and it won all 100 seats in the new Senate.

GROUPS AND PARTIES
IN THE POLITICAL PROCESS

Interest groups exist in all contemporary political systems, and most systems also have one or more political parties. Most individuals have interests and values that can be served or harmed by the decisions and actions of the political system. Thus political groups form to shape, express, and promote these interests within the political system. The interest groups that emerge can vary from spontaneous, momentary bursts of political activity to complex and specialized organizations that undertake extensive activities to promote their members' political objectives.

Political parties are a unique form of political interest group, because they are organizations that attempt to place their leaders in official positions within the political system, rather than merely attempting to influence those who make authoritative value allocations.

How do political groups behave and how are their interests converted (or not converted) into value allocations?—these are basic questions in understanding the political world. Answers to these questions depend upon the state's political structures and processes, as well as its political culture, political history, and distribution of power. Chapter 10 characterizes three broad approaches that describe how these political processes operate. While political groups are the basic analytic component in all three approaches, you will discover that the three approaches disagree fundamentally in their explanations of how politics emerges from the interactions among groups.

CHAPTER 10

Politics as a Value Allocation Process

The town meeting: direct democracy in action

One of the most obvious yet most fascinating questions in political science is, How does politics work? Here is one description of how a political system can handle the incredibly difficult and complicated value allocations that are the stuff of politics:

> You may very appropriately want to ask me how we are going to resolve the ever-accelerating dangerous impasse of world-opposed politicians and ideological dogmas. I answer, *it will be resolved by the computer.* Man has ever-increasing confidence in the computer; witness his unconcerned landings as air transport passengers coming in for a landing in the combined invisibility of fog and night. While no politician or political system can ever afford to yield understandably and enthusiastically to their adversaries and opposers, *all politicians can and will yield enthusiastically to the computer's safe flight-controlling capabilities in bringing all of humanity in for a safe landing.* (Fuller 1970:120; emphasis added)

This description from R. Buckminster Fuller probably does not match your idea of how most political decisions are currently made. You probably think that self-interest, ideology, and even irrationality are embedded in many of the actual value allocations by a political system. (It is worth noting that Fuller was a futurist who offered a normative vision of how politics *ought* to work; he was not an analytic political scientist attempting to describe and explain things as they are.)

Earlier chapters have introduced you to many of the major actors and significant structures in the political world and have indicated how these actors and structures operate. This chapter details three extremely "political" analytic explanations of the value allocation process. These three broad approaches are termed (1) the elite approach, (2) the class approach, and (3) the group approach.

Although each approach provides a different explanation of how politics works, they share two important features:

1. All three are constitutive approaches (see the appendix), in the sense that each attempts to define *the* fundamental unit of analysis that explains politics.
2. All three explain politics in terms of the interactions among aggregations of individuals who use the political system to pursue their own particular interests.

Our discussion begins with the elite approach.

THE ELITE APPROACH

Key Concepts

Two key concepts are central to the explanation of the value allocation process using the elite approach. First, *politics* is defined in a straightforward manner as *the struggle for power.* Second, *the political world* is characterized by *political stratification.*

Political stratification means that the population is segmented into separate groups that are in layers (*strata*) with higher or lower power. In the elite approach, there are only two major strata. The stratum of the population that does more of

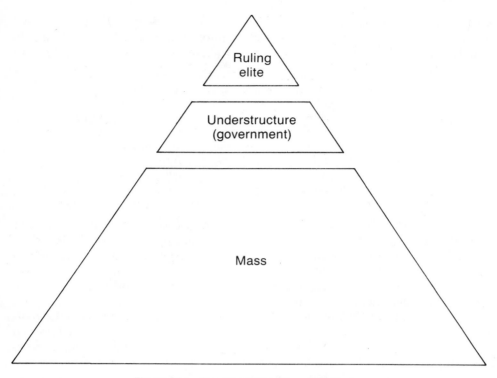

Figure 10.1. Characterization of an Elite System

what there is to do (in the policy process) and that gets more of what there is to get (in the allocation of values) is called the *political elite*. The stratum that does less and gets less is called the *mass*.

Elite theory can be visually represented by a power pyramid, as shown in Figure 10.1. Such a depiction emphasizes that the elite is composed of a relatively small number of individuals who are in a dominant position on top of the large mass. Notice that there is a third stratum between the elite and the mass. This is the *understructure,* composed of political officials and state administrators who carry out the policy directives of the elite.

Major Theorists

The elite approach has been particularly grounded in the writings of European political theorists of the late nineteenth century. Among the scholars most strongly associated with the elite approach are the Italians Roberto Michels, Wilfredo Pareto, and Gaetano Mosca. In *The Ruling Class* ([1896] 1939), Mosca provided one of the fullest explications of the elite approach. He analyzed the political histories of a variety of political systems and concluded that all these political systems had been characterized by two strata, the political class (the elite) and the nonpolitical class (the mass). The political class controlled all political functions, held virtually all political power, and dominated the allocation of values. The basis of elite power has varied across time and location; but Mosca identified broad historical stages during which the primary basis of elite domination has been military power, then religious control, then economic power, and most recently, technical knowledge. According to Mosca, the major role of the political system is as an instrument of the political class, serving the elite's interests in the allocation of values.

A well-known American application of the elite approach is *The Power Elite* (1956) by C. Wright Mills. Mills concluded that political power in American society resides in the controlling positions in the hierarchies of the society's most powerful institutions. In particular, Mills identified three key groups who compose the American power elite: (1) the "warlords" in the military establishment, (2) the "corporation chieftans" in the economic sector, and (3) the "political directorate" composed of those in the top positions in the political system. Mills observed that the members of the elite share crucial values about how society in general, and the political system in particular, ought to operate. The members of the elite tend to come from similar social and educational backgrounds, to circulate between major positions in each of the three key institutional structures, and to have long-standing personal relationships with each other. In common with other elite theorists, Mills did not claim that the elite is a conspiracy that continually plots to retain control. But some of its active members do meet periodically to discuss common interests, and most of its members will act in concert during times of crisis.

Most elite theorists focus upon the elite itself—the identity and socialization of elite members, and how the elite maintains its domination through a variety of techniques such as the manipulation of symbols, the strategic distribution of resources, control of the state, and the use of force. There is a normative element in the discussions of many elite theorists, indicating their disapproval of a system in which there is a high concentration of political power to serve only a small minority within society. But others respond that elite theory merely reveals the inevitable tendency for a few people to take control and to dominate the political order, while those in the mass willingly subordinate themselves to those who are capable of giving coherence to political society.

The Value Allocation Process

The value allocation process is explained primarily in terms of the actions of the elite. Some members of the elite decide that a particular public policy decision is in the elite's interest. A discussion then occurs within the elite, to determine whether this policy should be enacted and how it should be implemented. If there is general consensus among those members of the elite who are concerned about the decision, representatives of the elite instruct the relevant members of the understructure to perform the rule-making and rule-application activities that serve the elite's interests.

In the elite explanation of the policy process, the active elites are subject to little direct influence from the mass or even from the understructure of governmental officials. The mass is politically apathetic and impotent, and policy is imposed upon this large proportion of the population. The understructure follows the directives of the elite because its members depend upon the elite's power and resources as the basis of their own political positions and authority.

The Prevalence of Elite-Based Political Systems

Most contemporary political systems are either authoritarian or totalitarian. Harmon Zeigler (1990: 157, 191, 217–219) classifies 71 percent of the political systems in 1989 as either authoritarian or totalitarian, and only 29 percent as democratic. It is plausible to argue that all authoritarian and totalitarian systems are dominated by an elite in the manner described by the elite approach.

However, whether all the key conditions of elitism are met in a given system (e.g., El Salvador, Saudi Arabia, Singapore, or Zaire) is an interesting empirical question. Here are a few of the analytic questions that might be addressed: (1) Does the political leadership act with unanimity on all major issues? (2) Is there active and effective political participation by various nonelite groups? (3) Are some major political decisions responsive to nonelite demands, even when the decisions are contrary to the elite's interests? (4) Is there dramatic inequality in the distribution of resources between the elite and the mass? While definitive answers to these issues are very difficult, our knowledge of many political systems suggests that they are generally characterized by elite rule. (Consider the brief description of Swaziland in Box 10.1.) In many contemporary states, the power to make crucial political decisions and the benefits from those decisions do seem predominantly concentrated in the hands of a small elite.

The recent "outbreak of democracy," especially in Latin America and Eastern Europe, seems to suggest that more nonelite systems might emerge. But this depends on two crucial considerations. First, will these systems evolve into genuinely democratic regimes? And second, even if a political system meets such basic criteria of democracy as a limited mandate and freedom of expression (recall Chapter 6), does this necessarily mean that the system is not elitist?

This second question underlies a fierce debate among analysts on whether

BOX 10.1

Elite Politics in Swaziland

One of the many contemporary examples of elite politics is found in Swaziland, a small African country between Mozambique and South Africa. Since independence in 1968, the adults in the population of 700,000 have been allowed to vote for some electoral body. Initially, they elected the members of a British-style parliament with competing parties, and more recently they elect part of the members in a nonpartisan parliament. But real political power in Swaziland is concentrated in the king and his small group of advisors. Consistent with the elite approach, virtually all major political decisions are made by this group, with little or no consultation with others in the society.

When one king died in 1982, there was a power struggle among members of the royal family and the king's advisory council. By 1986, one of the princes was installed as the new king. He then dissolved the advisory council, removed many of his rivals from positions of authority, and elevated his own set of trusted advisors to positions of decision-making power. In short, the mass of people in Swaziland have little direct impact on the policies or politics of the state. Moreover, there is substantial resource inequality between the few rich and the many poor, who have one of the lowest life expectancy rates (47 years) in the world (Kranzdorf 1987, Table 7.1).

the elite approach best describes the politics in the most "democratic" political systems. Some, like C. Wright Mills (1956), provide arguments and evidence that there is elite rule, even in most democracies. In this view, a small proportion of the population dominates most significant political decisions and enjoys a hugely disproportionate share of the benefits from the value allocations made by the government. The discussion of the local political system in Oakland, California (see Box 10.2) summarizes an empirical study that concludes that a powerful few dominated the city's development decisions.

Such empirical assessments of the elite approach, whether of a single city or

BOX 10.2

Elite Domination of Development in Oakland

When the Planning Commission in the City of Oakland reported that large areas of the downtown and adjacent districts were blighted and required redevelopment, the residents and property owners in the area were threatened and outraged (this discussion relies on Hayes 1972). The city council even passed a resolution declaring that there was no blight in Oakland. But Oakland's economic elite could see that its members would realize great benefits from redevelopment. Thus its members initiated a strategy to insure that their redevelopment plan would be implemented.

First, the city's real estate board hired costly outside consultants to advise the city's business leaders on how to accomplish their objectives. Then the elite persuaded the newly elected mayor to appoint a committee to lay the groundwork for redevelopment. This committee (called OCCUR, the Oakland Citizens' Committee for Urban Renewal) was led by a top manager from a major local industry, the executive vice president of the home builders association, the past and present presidents of the real estate board, a corporate attorney, and the manager of a large department store.

OCCUR has raised, refined, and promoted redevelopment proposals and coordinated the public and private activities necessary for their enactment and implementation. The committee soon offered a comprehensive plan for redevelopment and conservation in all areas of the city. The city council rejected the plan. Over the next four years, OCCUR mounted an extensive campaign to assure support for the plan from the council and from other local groups. The national association of large real estate developers sent its president to assist the process. The local chamber of commerce prepared a promotional film on redevelopment that was shown to scores of local groups. Oakland's major newspaper ran countless articles and editorials in support of redevelopment. The council was even provided with a chartered airplane trip to successful urban renewal projects in cities around the United States. By this point, the council had initiated the first of several large redevelopment projects proposed by the business elite.

Overall, these projects displaced the poor, increased the tax burden on the middle class, provided subsidized new facilities for major local and national business corporations, and generated huge profits for the local building, real estate, and banking elites. In short, although there was an apparently democratic process of policy making, the economic elite dominated the formulation of policies, guided their passage, and reaped a very large share of the benefits from those decisions. The political understructure implemented the policies formulated by the elite, and the mass of citizens were politically ineffective and relatively passive bystanders.

a country, are highly controversial and ideologically charged, since they are a direct attack on the existence of democracy. A definitive "proof" of the elite approach in most political systems would be a massive undertaking, since it would be necessary to document systematic elite dominance on a large number of key decisions across a variety of issue areas.

THE CLASS APPROACH

The class approach shares certain fundamental concepts with the elite approach, but it offers a very different explanation of the continuing dynamic processes of politics. The most important shared concept is the notion of *stratification*, the basic fact of *structured inequality* in the distribution of values in society.

The strata identified in the class approach are called *classes*. *Class* is an analytic concept that denotes a large group of individuals who are similar in their possession of or control over some fundamental value. The most fundamental value that distinguishes classes differs for different class theorists. Karl Marx (1818–1883), the best-known class theorist, differentiated classes primarily on the basis of a group's relationship to the major factors of production in the economic system (Marx [1867] 1981, Chap. 52). At the simplest level, Marx divided society into two classes: (1) the *capitalist* class, which includes those who own significant amounts of the major factors of production in the society (especially, financial resources, raw materials, and the physical facilities to manufacture goods); and (2) the *proletariat* class, which includes those who own little more than their own labor.

Analysts have suggested a number of modifications to refine Marx's distinctions between classes. Some have argued that in most modern societies, it is control (rather than ownership) of the means of production that tends to be important in determining the power of individuals and groups. Others have observed that in many non-European social systems there are other values, such as status or kinship or tradition-based authority, that might distinguish different strata within the class system. Still others suggest that possession of significant data resources and knowledge have become the crucial resources distinguishing classes in information-based societies. Class theorists identify more than two major class strata in most contemporary societies, with each class characterized by its particular levels of social, political, and economic power (see, e.g., Dahrendorf 1959; Bottomore 1966; Habermas 1975; Foucault 1979).

Figure 10.2 portrays several attempts to represent visually the relationships among classes. These representations reveal different conceptions of the size of classes, the number of classes, the extent of precise differentiation between classes, and the extent of hierarchy among the classes. While diagram *A* is similar to the elite approach in its hierarchical and pyramidal form, the clear separation between classes is also emphasized. Diagram *B* highlights the overlapping nature of the classes—the boundaries between classes are permeable rather than distinct, and some members of "lower" classes have as much or even more political power than those in the class above them (see Lenski 1966:284). And diagram *C* attempts to emphasize the interactive and even reciprocal nature of power in

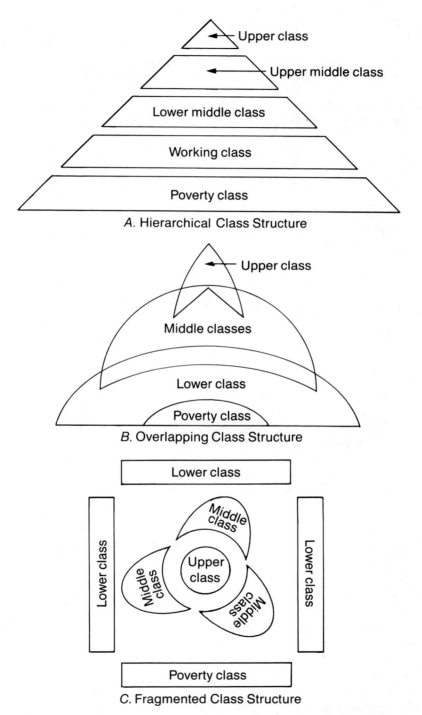

Figure 10.2. Different Characterizations of Class Structures. SOURCE: Based on Bill and Hardgrave 1973:181.

interclass relations. Although there is still substantial inequality in system *C,* and the higher classes clearly dominate the lower classes, there is more interdependence between classes, and the lower classes do affect the actions and domination of the higher classes by means of a variety of constraints and obligations.

The third crucial concept of the class approach is *class conflict.* It is assumed that classes lower in the class system can increase their share of key values only at the expense of the classes above them. Given the fundamental inequalities in the distribution of values, struggle between classes is inevitable. The higher classes employ various strategies, and ultimately coercion, in order to prevent a significant loss of values (and relative advantage) to the classes below them. Lower classes find that only violence enables their class to increase its relative share of values. Thus class conflict is systematic and ubiquitous, although its most visible and violent manifestations (such as strikes, riots, and rebellion) might be suppressed for periods of time, if the higher classes are effective in their distribution of benefits and coercion.

Most class analysts do not explain in detail how policy decisions are actually made. Like elite theorists, class analysts assume that the common interests shared by members of a class will result in general consensus on what public policy decisions should be enacted. And, similar to the elite approach, the political system is viewed as a set of structures that are subordinate to the dominant class. Thus the policies and actions of the state serve the preferences of that class and preserve the existing distribution of values.

The class approach centers on the examination of the tactics of class domination and the dynamics of the class struggle. Not every value allocation by the state is coercive or of direct benefit only to the dominant class. The state might implement policies to shorten the length of the working day or to increase health care benefits to the middle classes. Such policies either ameliorate the worst conditions that might provoke violence or they provide certain classes with advantages over classes below them. In such uses of public policy, benefits are provided to some classes in an effort to buy their support, or their acquiescence, or at least to dampen their propensity for conflict.

Despite such strategies, the systematic inequalities in fundamental values generate continuing conflict between classes in the society. Periodically, this conflict explodes into class violence. And ultimately, in an episode of the class war, a lower class succeeds in overthrowing the highest class. At this point, a new class gains dominance in the system, including control over the political system and superiority in the distribution of values. In the view of Marx and many other class theorists, major class conflict can end only when the elimination of dominant classes reduces the system to a single class, and hence a "classless" society. In the absence of class inequalities, the state serves all groups and there is no cause for further conflict among groups.

THE GROUP APPROACH

The group approach offers a very different account of the political process, although it also describes politics in terms of the interactions among aggregations of individuals. This approach is grounded in the concept of the *group,* which is any aggregate of individuals who interact to pursue a common interest. A political group, as an analytic concept, exists whenever individuals have a shared interest regarding some allocation of values by the political system.

The explanation of politics as a complex web of group interactions has many historical roots, but this approach is particularly identified with American social scientists. For many, the crucial work was *The Process of Government* ([1908] 1967), by American political scientist Arthur Bentley. Other scholars who have provided major elaborations of this approach include David Truman (1951), Earl Latham (1952), and Robert Dahl (1961, 1967, 1971), who is the contemporary political scientist most strongly associated with the development and defense of the group approach.

According to the group approach, any particular individual can belong to many different groups. Individuals are not stratified into large, permanent groups, as described by the elite and class approaches, because the aggregation of people who share common identity on one political interest is not the same as the people who are part of groups regarding other political interests. Table 10.1 shows six hypothetical people whose group memberships overlap in different ways, depending upon the particular issue. The group approach begins with this assumption that an individual's group memberships are multiple and nonreinforcing.

The second important notion of the group approach is that there are *many different political resources* that might influence those who make value allocations for the political system. The discussion in Chapter 9 suggested the kinds of resources that might be used to influence political decisions: money, numbers of supporters/voters, monopoly of expertise, political skill, access to information, and status. A key assumption of the group approach is that every individual (and hence every political group) has some political resources with which he can attempt to influence policy decisions.

In the group approach, politics can be understood as the interaction among groups that are pursuing their political interests. The political process is a giant system of interacting groups and the role of the state is to manage the interactions within this system of groups. The particular functions of the government are (1) to establish rules of the game for the group struggle, (2) to determine the interests of competing groups and the levels of political resources mobilized by those groups, (3) to find a public policy that approximately balances the interests-and-resources positions of all active groups, (4) to enact these balance points as public policy decisions, and (5) to enforce the resulting value allocations.

The state is not merely a cash register or a weighing machine that totals the value of each group's influence resources. First, the state can place greater emphasis on some broad objectives rather than others. For example, it might emphasize assistance to the most disadvantaged groups, by enacting some policies and rules that help those groups gain skills (e.g., extra educational or occupational opportunities). Or it might emphasize procedures and decisions that support the most advantaged groups, since those groups are perceived to be crucial to the stability and prosperity of the political economy. In addition, certain state actors have their own personal and institutional interests (e.g., for political support, for growth of their unit's power, for personal wealth). When such interests are relevant, state actors can become active as groups that participate in the decision

TABLE 10.1. Group Memberships of Six Hypothetical Individuals in the United States

Groups	Person # 1	Person # 2	Person # 3	Person # 4	Person # 5	Person # 6
				Individuals		
Democratic party	✓				✓	
Republican party		✓				
AFL-CIO unions	✓					
Alliance for Survival		✓				✓
Mothers Against Drunk Driving					✓	✓
Moral Majority	✓		✓			
National Rifle Association	✓		✓			
Parent-Teacher Association	✓	✓				

NOTE: Each checkmark (✓) indicates a group with which the individual is affiliated. This distribution supports the concept of *nonoverlapping* group memberships. An individual shares group membership with different people across various groups.

process (with obvious advantages because they are inside "the system"). But government, as an analytical construct in the group approach, is best understood as a neutral arbiter in the competition among groups. And hence public policy is defined as the balance of the group struggle at a given moment in time (see Box 10.3).

BOX 10.3

Two Analyses Applying the Group Politics Approach

Health Care Policy as a Hypothetical Example

The provision of health care in a society is one policy domain that concerns various groups. At one policy extreme, all health care (doctors, hospital services, drugs, etc.) might be provided by the private market system and each individual receives the health care he desires and can pay for. At the other extreme, state agencies might provide all health care services to every citizen, free of any direct charge. Between these extremes, the state might engage in many activities, such as providing care for certain health problems, providing care only to certain groups, subsidizing care, or regulating the private provision of care.

To illustrate how the group approach explains the political process, let's develop a greatly oversimplified example for a society like the United States.

1. Identify the four or five groups that you think would have the largest stake in decisions in this policy area.

2. On a continuum of possible policy outcomes, locate the preferred policy decision of each group.

3. Estimate the level of political resources each group is likely to focus on this policy (represented as a "weight" on the continuum).

4. Find the equilibrium point that balances the "weights" of the political resources mobilized by each group.

5. Describe this equilibrium point as public policy decision(s) that correspond to this position on the policy continuum. According to the group approach, these decision(s) will be the state's value allocations.

Figure 10.3 offers one estimation of the outcome in this example. The key groups who mobilize resources include

1. *The professional association of doctors.* Objective: a totally private health care system where prices and practices are determined by a free market. Political resources: substantial, including money, strong interest, organizational coherence, professional lobbyists, and ability to withhold necessary services.

2. *The insurance companies.* Objective: a mainly private health care system, with some regulation of prices, in which they can profitably sell health care insurance to individuals and groups. Political resources: considerable, including money, organization, lobbyists, high interest.

3. *The relatively poor citizens.* Objective: quality health care, provided directly by the state or at least subsidized by the taxation system and with regulated prices. Resources: interest in the issue, numbers who might mobilize their votes during elections.

BOX 10.3 *continued*

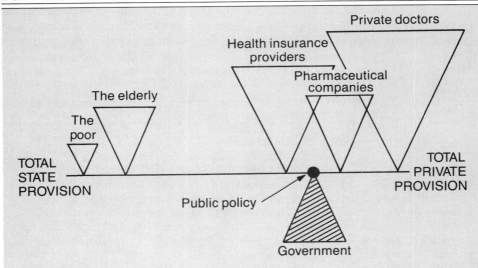

Symbols:

  — = Continuum of possible public policies regarding health care policy

  ▽ = Interest group mobilized on this issue, with volume of triangle
      representing the group's political resources applied to the issue

  ◿ = Government, which determines the equilibrium point and ratifies
      that point as public policy

  ● = Public policy position, which is the equilibrium point in the com-
      petition among groups, given each group's political resources

Figure 10.3. Group Approach Characterization of a Policy Decision on Health Care Provision.

   4. *The pharmaceutical industry.* Objective: higher profits from minimal
state regulation of the production and sale of drugs, except for regulation of
quality. Political resources: substantial financial power, strong interest, a few
highly organized producers, professional lobbyists.
   5. *The elderly.* Objective: subsidized or free health care for their group.
Political resources: high interest, a large voting bloc that can be mobilized,
a general societal sense of responsibility and empathy for the needs of the
elderly.

   Actually, there are likely to be many other groups with substantial stakes in this
decision, such as nurses groups, public and private hospitals, taxpayers in higher tax
brackets, and so on. In this case, the weights for key groups in Figure 10.3 suggest
that most group influence is clustered on the end opposing much state intervention.
Thus, according to the group approach, the government is likely to establish an equilibrium point in the group struggle that entails mostly private control of the health
care system, with some regulation of costs and subsidies for some services and/or
some individuals.

BOX 10.3 *continued*

An Actual Development Decision in New Haven, Connecticut
The two Lebov brothers were wealthy local businessmen in New Haven, Connecticut, who acquired 65 prefabricated metal houses from military surplus. (This section is based on Robert Dahl's seminal advocacy of the group politics approach, *Who Governs?* [1961:192–199]). They received permission from the city's building department to erect these houses on a site that was zoned for industry in a neighborhood called "The Hill." Their proposal also had the support of the mayor and the city's lawyer.

But the (mainly) Italian-American residents of the working-class neighborhood were outraged. They viewed the metal houses as an "instant slum" that would threaten the property values of their modest but well-kept houses and would bring black residents to "The Hill." Miss Mary Grava emerged as the improbable leader of the residents' opposition to the project. An elderly spinster, she had never been very involved in politics. She was tireless in contacting people who might influence the city's decision. She mobilized the residents to telephone members of the city council and others in city government, and she played Republican politicians against Democratic politicians in order to gain support from both groups for the neighborhood's opposition to the metal houses.

Under severe pressure from the neighborhood, the city council drafted legislation to stop construction of the metal houses. But the Lebov brothers began building anyway, with added support from the local newspaper, which saw the houses as low-cost housing for needy blacks. The city's lawyer ruled that the council had no legal power to stop construction. The council nonetheless voted to stop the project. The mayor vetoed the council's legislation. In response, the Hill residents organized a neighborhood association led by Mary Grava's brother, who happened also to be the mayor's godfather. This local association widened its base, gaining support from the middle-class League of Women Voters (who wanted to expand their membership among ethnic working-class groups), from the current mayor's chief Republican rival on the council, and from the Democratic candidate for mayor. The council overrode the mayor's veto. After an arson fire destroyed one of the metal houses, the fire inspector withdrew his support for the project. Ultimately, the metal houses were never placed in the neighborhood.

For Robert Dahl, this is a compelling example of how a group can emerge when it cares deeply about an issue and can concert its limited political resources to influence policy on the issue. In this case, "just plain folks" had fought city hall and had beaten the rich developers, the mayor, and the city's lawyer.

The group approach explicitly rejects the notion that a small elite dominates the resource allocation process. Rather, many different groups become active in the political process on a narrow range of issues relevant to their interests. Mobilized groups use their political resources to affect the decision. While a group might not always win, its participation can affect the policy decisions made in the area.

Critics of the group approach argue that some groups *are* likely to win almost every time that they play the game of politics, because they have a huge advantage in their political resources, such as wealth, access to decision makers, political skill, and so on. Even though "the little people" might occasionally win one particular episode, the powerful groups in the system are persistent winners and big winners—the system perpetuates very substantial inequalities in the distribution of benefits (Bachrach and Baratz 1962; Parenti 1988). Indeed, even in the metal houses case the biggest losers are probably the poor families in New Haven for whom this housing would have been a substantial improvement over their existing conditions.

THE THREE APPROACHES COMPARED

Which Approach Is Correct?

The three approaches offer powerful answers to the basic political questions of who gets what, why, when, and how. Which of these three approaches is correct? Is one the most accurate explanation of politics for all political systems? For most political systems at a given historical moment? Do different approaches best account for the politics of particular systems? For particular kinds of issues?

Advocates of each position offer both theoretical and empirical evidence to show that the politics of actual systems correspond to the description provided in their approach. And, as an indirect method of providing support for their approach, advocates have provided considerable evidence indicating the inaccuracies and contradictions of the other approaches. As you might suspect, the debate has been most acrimonious between, on the one hand, supporters of the group approach and, on the other, supporters of the elite and class approaches, which both assume persistent stratification and deep inequality. In the United States, this debate has been most intensive among those who study power at the local level, prompted by the dispute three decades ago between such "elitists" as sociologist Floyd Hunter (1953) and such "pluralists" (supporters of the group approach) as political scientist Robert Dahl (1961).

Political scientists and other social scientists have not yet established a critical test that reveals which of the approaches best describes or explains politics. After hundreds of studies in various political systems at the local, regional, and nation-state level, the disagreements between the advocates of the three approaches remain as deep as ever. How might you decide which approach provides the greatest insight into the politics of a particular political system? Some key conceptual and empirical questions that you might consider in assessing the validity of each approach are listed below.

The Elite Approach

Are there criteria by which a small elite can be clearly identified, in an analytic sense and also in an empirical study?

Is there evidence of actual collaboration among the elite in the formulation of preferred public policy?

How often (if at all) does the elite lose on policy decisions of significance to its members?

Does the overall pattern of policy decisions clearly benefit the elite? At the expense of the mass?

Are there no instances where the elite truly loses on a policy decision of concern to its members?

Is the mass of citizens uninformed, inactive, and impotent regarding its society's politics?

Is the competition among elites so limited that it does not undermine their overall cooperation?

Is the understructure of government actors always responsive to the will and values of the elite?

The Class Approach

Does the same fundamental value separate virtually all people in a society into a few distinct strata?

Are the group identities of most people reinforcing rather than crosscutting?

Is the concept of class still valid if most people do not identify themselves with the classes specified by the analyst?

Does the state always operate to serve the interests of a dominant class group?

Are the relationships among most groups characterized primarily by conflict?

In their political activities, are most groups limited by force or other mechanisms of coercion?

Are most significant social changes directly attributable to violence?

The Group Approach

Is there clear evidence that large groups of people do not share major political interests with a single broad group?

Does every group "win some and lose some" on policy decisions that matter to the group, or are there persistent winners and persistent losers?

Does the state apply rules and policies fairly and equally to all groups?

Is the competition among groups fair if there are huge inequalities in the levels of political resources available to different individuals and groups?

Doesn't one political resource—money—dominate (or convert into) all other major resources in the competition to influence policy making?

Essential Similarities and Differences

In attempting to explain the value allocation process, the elite, class, and group approaches all focus on the interactions among aggregates of individuals. The elite and class approaches share certain crucial premises. For both approaches, the fundamental feature of society is stratification—the unequal distribution of values across distinct groups. In both approaches, the government is one of the key mechanisms controlled by the dominant group and the government's policy deci-

sions are intended to maintain that group's domination. Thus in both approaches the political system and the value allocation process operate of, by, and for the dominant group.

But the elite and class approach differ in their conceptions of the nature of the groups and their interactions. For the elite approach, there are two broad groups, the elite and the mass. For the class approach, there can be more than two distinct class groups. Most discussion by elite theorists focuses on the elite— its membership, the basis of elite domination, and the strategies employed by the elite to maintain its control. The mass is assumed to be inactive politically, and is rarely subjected to detailed analysis.

In contrast, most class theorists emphasize the dynamic interactions among the classes. There is substantial political energy inherent in the lower classes, and they are the active agents of major political change. The class approach attempts to explain why class conflict is inevitable, how it manifests itself, and how it produces transformations in the sociopolitical system. In short, the elite approach tends to provide a top-down perspective in a two-group system, while the class approach often takes a bottom-up perspective, emphasizing the dynamic processes of conflict and change among multiple groups.

The group approach differs fundamentally from both the elite and class approaches, beginning in its rejection of the notion of social stratification. Rather, the group approach conceptualizes a sociopolitical world composed of many groups, with overlapping (and hence nonreinforcing) group memberships among individuals. Different groups emerge on each particular political issue, and each group has an array of resources that can be organized in order to influence decisions on that issue.

For the group approach, the government is a relatively neutral referee in the process by which various groups compete to influence public policy decisions, rather than the instrument of only one particular group or class. The state insures that the policy competition among groups is fair, and all participants accept the outcome of any given competition. According to the group approach, there is a dispersion of power, of resources, and of benefits from policy decisions, rather than a pattern of "structured inequality." Overall, different people, as members of many different groups, prevail on particular issues. Everyone wins some and loses some; but the losers can always win on the next issue.

There has been a vigorous and often hostile debate between the advocates of these three different conceptions of how politics works. This debate is deep and serious, for it reflects fundamental disagreements about the very nature of society and politics. The elite and class approaches are based on a *coercive* view of society. Conflict and change are ubiquitous features of the relations among groups. Social coherence is maintained by means of power and constraint, of domination by the most powerful class and its agent, the state. In contrast, the group approach reflects an *integrative* view of society. Society is essentially stable and harmonious, in the sense that there is a moving equilibrium maintained by a "fair" competitive game, refereed by the state and played by many groups who accept the rules and the outcomes. Social coherence is grounded in cooperation and consensus (see Dahrendorf 1959).

CHAPTER 11

Change and Political Development

Oman is a medium-sized country west of Saudi Arabia, at a strategic point on the Persian Gulf.* Although Oman has a long history of trading with other countries, its rulers have attempted to maintain an extremely traditional society, even in the twentieth century. But the sultan who ruled between 1932 and 1970, Said ibn Taimur, faced a strong challenge after 1964, when vast oil deposits were discovered in Oman. Fearful that this huge wealth would corrupt his people, the sultan took extraordinary steps to prevent modernization. He declared a moratorium on the building of roads, schools, houses, even hospitals. All ten Omani doctors were forced to practice abroad because the sultan distrusted modern medicine. Many objects of modernity were prohibited, including sunglasses, flashlights, and European shoes. One could be imprisoned for travelling after dark with any light other than a kerosene lantern. The gates of the capital were locked after sunset, and no one was allowed to enter or leave. The sultan even confined his son, Prince Qabus, to a house far from the capital, because he feared the ideas that his son brought back from his education in England.

But there was a group of Omani citizens who had some experience or knowledge of Western culture, through education, travel, or working with foreigners. These people increasingly chafed under the sultan's "backward" rule. Finally, they took action in 1970, overthrowing the sultan and replacing him with Prince Qabus. The (now) Sultan Qabus and his advisers moved swiftly to bring improvements in the areas that his father had blocked. There has been a massive school building program (from 16 to 490) and Sultan Qabus University opened in 1986. Hospitals and many health clinics are operating and an extensive road system has been built. Females are now being educated and many Western consumer goods are purchased. Many Omanis now have a life-style that attempts to balance the behaviors of traditional Islamic culture and the material possessions of a wealthy, highly modernized society.

CHANGE

The recent history of Oman indicates the virtual impossibility of preventing change in any society in the late twentieth century. This chapter examines the question of change within the political world. In particular, there is discussion of the nature and processes of development in a society and within its political system.

There are a few examples of cultures that have generally avoided the processes of change and modernization. The Tasaday of the Philippines and the Masai of the Serengeti Plain in East Africa live in a manner that has changed little from the ways of their ancestors of 50 generations ago. The Masai, for example, continue to raise their cattle, ignoring the Kenya-Tanzania border and resisting the attempts of the Kenyan government to alter their long-standing cultural patterns of family and tribal life. But even the Masai have been affected by the modernization surrounding them. It has brought health care and disease, money from

*This discussion is based on Spencer 1988:105–106.

tourists and reduced land for grazing herds, education and cultural confusion. In the modern world, there seems nowhere to hide from the forces of change.

The Greek philosopher Heraclitus articulated this view in the fifth century B.C. His famous dictum, "You can never step in the same river twice," is an extreme version of the viewpoint that everything is in constant flux. From this perspective, change is inevitable. It is presumed that just as individuals undergo a developmental sequence of birth, growth, maturity, decay, and death, social organisms (groups, organizations, societies) also have some form of evolutionary development.

On the opposite side of the debate about the inevitability of change is the wry French observation, *plus ça change, plus c'est la même chose*. This translates loosely as "the more things change, the more they remain the same." Do you believe this? Is this a wise commentary about the human condition? An erroneous cliché?

There is debate about the desirability of change, as well as its inevitability. One normative position, most aligned with modern rationalism, is that change is generally a positive force in human society. Change is the mechanism of growth, development, and progress, all of which are assumed to increase knowledge, extend control over the environment, and thus improve the human condition. This view is reflected in the ideas of Sir Isaac Newton (1642–1727), Immanuel Kant (1724–1804), and Charles Darwin (1809–1882). In the contemporary world, it is especially prevalent among those who believe in the benefits of science and technology.

In contrast, some take the normative position that change and development have significant negative effects, perhaps so many that change is undesirable. Plato (c. 428–347 B.C.), Jean-Jacques Rousseau (1712–1778), and Sigmund Freud (1856–1939) are among those who argue that knowledge, civilization, and excessive control over the environment result in a loss of innocence, goodness, and happiness, and create the capacity for great harm and destruction. Material progress has been achieved at the cost of moral and spiritual decline. In this view, the human capacity to increase our supply of food and material goods cannot be separated from our development of repressive and destructive forms of human interaction and of technologies (e.g., weapons, chemicals) that degrade the environment and eliminate certain species of life including, possibly, human beings. Most people now recognize the paradox that change and development simultaneously increase and reduce the quality of life. And most accept the serious problems and dangers associated with progress in order to enjoy the material benefits.

DEVELOPMENT

Characteristics of "More Developed" Social Systems

Contemporary changes of social, economic, and political systems are usually discussed in terms of *development* or *modernization*. While both of these concepts can be slippery, social scientific research usually employs the concept of develop-

BOX 11.1

What Makes Millie Thoroughly Modern?

Suppose you were asked whether you like "modern music." What does that mean? What kind of music does it bring to mind? Atonal? Rock and roll? Electronic? Postpunk? The determination of what is "modern" is extremely difficult. It depends very much upon the particular historical moment and it also depends upon the values and culture of the analyst. What seemed modern in the United States 20 years ago does not seem so modern now, given a world of rapid social and technological change. For example, the United States in 1970 was a world virtually without personal computers, videocassette recorders (VCRs), cable television, AIDS, or economic competition from Japan.

ment, because modernization is particularly fuzzy (see Box 11.1). The designation of a social system as more developed (or more modern) indicates that certain key characteristics are evident at relatively high levels. The concept of development can also be used to refer to the processes through which these characteristics become more pronounced.

Several packages of characteristics are general indicators of more developed social systems. These characteristics tap social, cultural, economic, political, and personal dimensions and can be classified in various ways. For simplicity, we can specify three packages of dimensions that are particularly associated with more developed social systems (Bill and Hardgrave 1973:63):

1. The *organizational* dimension emphasizes specialization, interdependency, and differentiation of roles and functions in groups, organizations, and societies.
2. The *technological* dimension indicates the use of increasingly complex and sophisticated artifacts to control the environment and to produce goods and services.
3. The *attitudinal* dimension reflects cognitive, affective, and evaluative orientations that are dominated by increased knowledge, rationality, secular values, and individualism.

Normally, as a society becomes more developed, it is evident in changes in specific social indicators. These include greater urbanization, more social mobility, higher literacy, increased education levels, decreased death rates, growth in productive capacity, expanded communications, and more extensive social networks.

The Process of Development

Stage Typologies. Many scholars have attempted to define the process(es) through which development and modernization occur. One approach is to define a series of stages or phases that each society passes through. Best known are the simple typologies, many of which have only two or three stages. For example, these stages are given such labels as *traditional* and *modern, mechanical* and *organic, folk* and *urban, less developed* and *more developed*. These labels are so broad that they provide minimal conceptual clarity.

Karl Marx proposed a more complex typology, in which most societies pass through six stages of development. A society's particular stage of development depends on the existing distribution of control over the major productive resources in the society. Marx posited an initial stage of primitive communism, where all individuals share control jointly over any available productive resources. The development process then continues through a series of stages in which there are increasingly subtle forms of domination by some classes over others: slavery, then feudalism, and then capitalism. Eventually, capitalist systems are transformed into socialist and finally to communist systems, an ultimate stage where differentiated social classes and inequality in control of resources are eliminated (recall Chapter 10).

Response to Key Challenges.   Most explanations of the process of development do not share Marx's conviction that history and/or logic reveal a single, inevitable sequence of stages. Rather, analysts identify a series of key challenges in the developmental process. Different processes are possible, depending upon the sequence in which the challenges occur, upon the particular response that is made, and upon crucial features of the society and its environment. Some of the key challenges can be the tension between traditional ideas and values and modern ones; the transition from a rural, agrarian society to an urban, industrial society; the transfer of social and political power from traditional elites to modernizing ones; the fit between geographical territory, national identities, and state boundaries. Barrington Moore (1966), whose approach is discussed in Box 11.2, is one theorist who explains modernization in terms of the pattern of responses to key challenges facing the society; others include Black (1966), Rustow (1967), and Wilber (1979).

Dependency within the International Political Economy.   As the focus of research shifted to the countries that have been attempting to develop and modernize since 1945, there has been growing recognition that a state's development can be powerfully affected by other states in the international environment. This is most explicit in a set of explanations of development known generally as the *dependency approach.*

The dependency approach often has both ideological and descriptive elements. This approach argues that Third World states cannot follow the same development processes that occurred in the more developed countries. The ideological element asserts that this is because the developed political economies of the "capitalist"/"imperialist" states of the First World exploit and control these less developed countries, in order to maintain their economic domination of the global economy. They manipulate such factors as capital, markets and prices, and technology so that the economies of the developing states remain dependent upon the developed states.

BOX 11.2

Barrington Moore's Explanation of Development

Barrington Moore's study, *The Social Origins of Dictatorship and Democracy* (1966), illustrates one approach to the study of societal development. A social historian, Moore analyzes the changing patterns of relations among key groups in a society. While many analysts focus primary attention on the interactions in the urban areas between the bourgeoisie (those who operate factories, shops, commercial establishments) and the working class, Moore places particular attention on the landed aristocracy and peasants in the rural areas. He does also examine the role of the bourgeoisie and of governmental bureaucracies. He details eight historical case studies—China, England, France, Germany, India, Japan, Russia, and the United States—and concludes with analytic generalizations.

Moore's key questions about development concern the shift from agrarian society to modern industrial society. Does the landed aristocracy take the lead in the commercialization of agriculture? Are the peasants cohesive and do they support or resist state authority? Is the urban bourgeoisie strong and effective in economic development? Whose interests do the governmental bureaucracies represent?

Moore distinguishes three different modes of modernization, depending upon the dominant actions and evolving relationships among the key groups. There are *bourgeois revolutions,* which are driven by the modernizing efforts of the urban bourgeoisie, who dominate the urban workers and gain control of the rural sector, as in England and France; there are *revolutions from above,* in which development is effected by a coalition of the landed aristocracy and strong governmental bureaucracies, as in Germany and Japan; there are *peasant revolutions,* in which the peasants are more cohesive than the upper classes or the bourgeoisie, resist the powerful state apparatus, and eventually overthrow the old regime, as in Russia and China; and finally there are some societies where no groups have been able to lead a modernizing revolution, as in India.

Moore's most powerful assertion is his conclusion that all forms of development and modernization are essentially revolutions from above—the great majority of the population does not want these changes and the changes are implemented by a ruthless minority at great cost to the large majority. But Moore also argues that, despite the widespread suffering generated during the developmental process, the costs (in terms of cumulative hardship to the population) of going without a modernizing revolution are even more severe for a state in the contemporary world.

The descriptive element provides a similar analysis, but without heaping such blame on the capitalist states. Rather, all the developed states, whether capitalist or communist, are the "core" of the global economy. Their domination of capital, markets, and technology enables them to maintain enormous competitive advantages over the other states on the "periphery" of the global economy. The periphery states remain suppliers of raw materials and providers of cheap labor for core states. The economic choices and options available to the developing states are thus severely constrained by other actors in the international environment. In short, the developing states in the economic periphery experience continuing dependency (Cardoso and Faletto 1979; Wallerstein 1974, 1980).

The dependency approach attempts to describe and analyze how the major capitalist states employ the factors above, as well as their military and political power, to insure their continued dominance of the international political economy. Within the developing states, certain modern sectors and some prosperous actors do emerge, because these sectors and actors operate for the mutual advantage of their members and the international capitalists. But development in such a state is extremely uneven. The organizational and technological dimensions of a modern society are primarily evident only within the state (typically a repressive military and bureaucracy) and within a few limited sectors of the economy. A large proportion of the population remains trapped in conditions of underdevelopment and poverty (Cardoso and Faletto 1979; O'Donnell 1973). For example, in Evans's (1979) analysis of development in Brazil, there is an alliance of three key actors: (1) the multinational corporations, (2) the Brazilian capitalist class, and (3) the Brazilian state apparatus. Only the groups in the alliance, and especially the multinationals, share in the benefits from Brazil's rich resources, while the great majority of the population remains poor and backward.

It is certainly clear that the process of development in virtually all countries is now substantially affected by the international political economy. The ideological aspects of the dependency approach, given its emphasis on the pernicious impacts of First World capitalists, draw the most vigorous criticism (Almond 1987). But there is also empirical disagreement about the key contentions of the dependency approach. For example, is economic inequality greater or are rates of growth slower in underdeveloped countries that are more dependent upon international capital? Although the evidence is mixed, it seems that the penetration of foreign capital initially stimulates growth, but that this pattern is not necessarily sustained and does not produce economic diversification (Russett 1983; Sylvan et al. 1983).

On a related issue, recent evidence seems to indicate that there is no clear relationship between higher rates of growth and the level of income inequality in most developing countries (Morawetz 1977). The reemergence of democratic politics in many Latin American countries in the 1980s is presented as evidence that repressive state power is not a necessary condition for states in a situation of economic dependency. And the contrast between the developmental success of some Asian states such as South Korea and Taiwan in comparison to the failure of most African states suggests that cultural factors might be more crucial to development than dependency on foreign capital (Huntington 1987).

Individual-Level Change.   Most analyses of development, whether emphasizing stages, sequences, or international political economy, focus on the macro-level structural dynamics—that is, on the nature of the organizational and technological dimensions of social systems. But attention to the attitudinal dimension shifts the analysis to micro-level dynamics. This perspective emphasizes the social psychological factors that might account for variations in rates and patterns of development. Such analyses are similar to the political behavior studies described above in Chapters 2–4 (e.g. the political culture analyses and Pye's study of the Burmese leaders), although the focus here is upon a broader array of beliefs (not just political beliefs) and upon the implications of such beliefs for modernization and development. While the approaches have often characterized the attitudes of groups and nations, most of the research actually focusses upon the distinctive patterns of political beliefs of *individuals* within a given nation (Pye 1962; Lerner 1958; McClelland 1961; Inkeles and Smith 1974; Inkeles and Smith 1983).

In the attempt to establish the attitudinal traits associated with modernity, the work of Alex Inkeles and his colleagues (Inkeles and Smith 1974; Inkeles and Smith 1983) is noteworthy. This group gathered extensive survey data from more than 5,500 men in six developing countries (Argentina, Bangladesh, Chile, India, the "Oriental" Jews of Israel, and Nigeria). Statistical analyses produced a set of seven qualities that constituted a "syndrome of modernity"—that is, the general traits of a modern man in a developing society:

1. Openness to new experiences, regarding both people and behaviors
2. A shift in allegiance to individuals representing modern institutions (e.g., government leaders) from those in traditional authority structures (e.g., parents, religious leaders)
3. Belief in modern technologies (e.g., science, medicine) and a less fatalistic attitude about life
4. Desire for social mobility for oneself and one's children
5. Belief in the value of planning and punctuality
6. Interest in local politics and community affairs
7. Interest in news, especially national and international affairs

Inkeles and his colleagues conclude that there is remarkable similarity in these clusters of beliefs among the modern men in all six societies. On this basis, they claim that there is a "unity of mankind in terms of psychic structure" (Inkeles and Smith 1983:102). This means that the same traits are present in the modern individuals in virtually all cultures.

In the large literature on traditional and modern personality, many issues are unresolved (Banuazizi 1987). For example, most studies have not established the existence of a single syndrome of modernity that exists across all cultures. Even more importantly, it is not obvious that individuals with modern orientations will necessarily be more likely than others to engage in modern actions. And, in a related point, it is unclear whether the existence of modern attitudes among a certain proportion of the citizens causes any measurable increase in economic or political development. Indeed, in cases of Islamic resurgence like Iran, it seems that many leaders in the return to traditional societal forms display some of the activist and outward-oriented psychological traits associated with the "syndrome of modernity" (Banuazizi 1987).

An associated issue is the factors that seem to facilitate psychological modernization. Karl Deutsch (1961:496) describes these individual-level changes as *social mobilization*—defined as "the process in which major clusters of old social, economic and psychological commitments are eroded or broken and people be-

BOX 11.3

How Ideas Undermine Culture:
Things Fall Apart in Nigeria

You might be able to understand individual-level change intuitively if you think about what happens to a society when it is infused with such major threats to existing values as education, new religions, television, and travel. As a popular post–World War I song asked about the returning soldiers, "How are you going to keep 'em down on the farm, after they've seen Paree?" The erosion of traditional values and behaviors can be rapid or slow, but, as the Oman case suggested, it is difficult to prevent change in the face of major unsettling forces. The Islamic religion explicitly recognizes the importance of personal values in shaping culture. As one Koranic verse observes, "Lo! Allah changeth not the condition of a people until they first change what is in their hearts."

A rich illustration of these change processes, in a fictionalized version of the actual history, is Chinua Achebe's 1959 novel *Things Fall Apart*. Achebe's novel describes the dramatic and traumatic changes experienced by the Ibo people of Nigeria at the turn of the twentieth century. The key theme is the conflict between the binding power of the Ibo's traditional views of life and religion and the disruptive ideas introduced into the culture by the Christian missionaries and the British colonial administrators. The story centers on the members of one Ibo village, who are increasingly divided between those who continue to be guided by traditional patterns of behavior and religion and those who no longer accept those traditions.

The major character, Okonkwo, is a great farmer and a strong leader. He follows the traditional patterns very rigidly, even participating in the murder, decreed by tribal law, of a boy whom he has treated like a son for years. This murder so alienates his own son that the boy becomes one of the first in the village to be persuaded by the missionaries to convert to Christianity. Because Okonkwo continues to follow the traditions of his tribe, he experiences a series of major setbacks, even being banished for seven years and losing his land and his possessions. Eventually, Okonkwo's anger and frustration at the collapse of Ibo village life leads him to murder a messenger of the colonial administrator. Rather than be executed by the white men, he finally violates a basic Ibo law, by commiting suicide.

Before Okonkwo dies, his friend Obierika articulates how these external ideas have caused the collapse of the village (and of Ibo) society. In a key passage, he says,

Our own men and our sons have joined the ranks of the stranger. They have joined his religion and they help to uphold his government. If we should try to drive out the white men in Umuofia we should find it easy. There are only two of them. But what of our own people who are following their way and have been given power? They would go to Umuru and bring the soldiers. . . . [The white man] says that our customs are bad; and our own brothers who have taken up his religion also say that our customs are bad. How do you think we can fight when our own brothers have turned against us? The white man is very clever. He came quietly and peaceably with his religion. We were amused at his foolishness and allowed him to stay. Now he has won our brothers and our clan can no longer act like one. He has put a knife on the things that held us together and we have fallen apart (Achebe 1959:161–162).

come available for new patterns of socialization and behavior." In general, such social mobilization seems to be associated with elements of socioeconomic development, including increased education, exposure to modern media, and work within modern industrial or bureaucratic organizations (Inkeles and Smith 1983).

In most developing societies, some people and groups enthusiastically embrace the new beliefs and new behaviors while others cling tenaciously to the old ones. You probably think it is obvious that development and modernization involve an interplay between the emergence of modern individual-level behavior (both beliefs and actions), group behavior, and societal development. Virtually all the researchers agree with you. But there are still many interesting and generally unanswered questions: Why do old patterns erode? Which kinds of people are most inclined to accept new patterns? Are there certain proportions and sectors of the population whose social mobilization is crucial to macro-level change? What macro-level conditions seem particularly conducive to individual-level change? And, most broadly, what are the precise causal linkages between psychological modernity and development?

Culture and Change.   Recently, some studies of development have particularly emphasized the importance of culture as a determinant of the processes of change. Since Max Weber's (1958a) classic study of the linkage between the culture of the Protestant religion and the rise of capitalist political economies, there have been continuing efforts to clarify the relationship between broad cultural systems and economic development. Some, like Weber, argue that Protestantism has motivated people to make substantial, even irrational, sacrifices of the pleasures of life and material consumption in order to work extraordinarily hard and accumulate wealth rather than spending it. (Weber [1951, 1958b] also tried to apply his cultural explanation of development to India and China.) Other scholars argue that the religions of developing European societies have promoted passivity to the hardships associated with the transformation to a modern society and economy (Davis 1987:223–234).

In contrast to the limited development in much of the Third World, there has been a recent dramatic surge of economic development, following the earlier pattern in Japan, in certain Asian countries, including Hong Kong, Singapore, South Korea, and Taiwan. There is great interest in trying to explain the success of the latter group, termed the *newly industrialized countries* or NICs. Many explanations focus on the particular approach to economic development in the NICs (see Box 11.4). But the relative failure of the strategy outside of Asia has provoked an attempt to find a cultural element in the explanation (Davis 1987; Morishima 1982; Huntington 1987:21–28). For example, Davis (1987) argues that the Japanese work ethic is primarily motivated by normative expressions of the cultural and national uniqueness of Japan. These cultural norms encourage the Japanese people to work hard and be loyal and sincere in order to protect and build their nation.

BOX 11.4

The NIC Way

The successful "newly industrialized countries" have a broadly shared formula that is grounded in three strategies:

1. An open-door policy regarding foreign capital and corporations
2. Agrarian reform supporting private small-farm entrepreneurs
3. A gradual expansion of urban industrialization, moving from production of labor intensive goods (e.g., textiles, shoes, toys) to manufacture more advanced goods (e.g., shipbuilding, automobiles, electronics)

The political regime in the NICs has generally been effective in maintaining stability and in providing an infrastructure for development. The state is repressive, restricting political freedoms and participation and discouraging group politics. The state has been efficient in implementing policies that insure a disciplined and docile labor force. Apart from educational expenditure (to produce effective workers), most NICs have distributed only modest levels of surplus resources to citizens in the form of public goods and services. The economic surplus has primarily been shared between external actors (such as multinational corporations) and the state, which reinvests most of its surplus to support further internal economic development and which regulates such sectors as finance, transportation, and commerce. (Notice that the pattern in the NICs is comparable to that described in the dependency approach.

Assembly line, Seoul, South Korea

BOX 11.4 *continued*

But the NICs have managed to foster economic development despite their initial subjugation in the international political economy. By the early 1990s, the most successful NICs enjoy considerable power in the world economy.)

The major NIC success stories have all been in Asia, beginning with Japan, and more recently in Singapore, South Korea, Taiwan, Hong Kong, and to a lesser extent Malaysia. Other Third World states that have attempted variations of the Asian strategy have had partial success. Brazil, India, and Mexico are sometimes classified as NICs because they have established a modern industrial sector, which utilizes high technologies and produces for export. But these states fall far short of the Asian NICs. Economic development is narrowly based and heavily dependent upon external actors, loans, and markets. Labor is difficult to control. The rural sector produces insufficient food to feed the population and there are violent conflicts over the distribution of land between large landholders and peasants. There is a cosmopolitan elite enjoying a high standard of living. But huge segments of the population continue to live in conditions of deep poverty. And the probability that the benefits of prosperity will be widely shared in the near future is quite low. Until this NIC approach generates significant development in countries outside of Asia, the cultural element of the strategy will continue to seem very important.

POLITICAL DEVELOPMENT

There are no precise measures to distinguish systems that are modern or developed from those that are not. In fact, relative rather than absolute language is most commonly used in describing social, economic, or political systems. Political actors and the media, as well as scholars, usually refer to the *more developed countries,* or MDCs, and the *less developed countries,* or LDCs. MDCs are presumed to be relatively high on such characteristics as urbanization, literacy, productive output, complexity, specialization, and secularization. To this point, the discussion has broadly considered development in any sphere of human activity, including the social, economic, cultural, and intellectual spheres. Let us turn our attention to the specifically *political* aspect of development.

Characteristics of Political Development

The study of modernization and development of the political system also begins with attempts to list the defining characteristics of development. Some scholars (e.g., Cutright 1963) define political development as the establishment of the rule of law, legitimate elections, and representative institutions. What do you think of this definition of a developed political system? Many scholars object that this conception of political development is extremely biased. Why? What concept do such characteristics seem to measure?

Recent attempts to define the key characteristics of more developed political systems emphasize four dimensions:

1. *Concentration of power in the central state.* Traditional sources of political authority weaken and most power and authority are increasingly cen-

tralized in a single state-level governmental system. The citizens recognize the right of the state to allocate public values and their own responsibility to accept those allocations as authoritative. The legal-formal apparatus of government (e.g., constitutions, laws) is established.

2. *"Modern" forms of political organization.* Specialized political structures emerge to fulfill most key political functions. There are complex, organized political institutions such as legislatures, executives, political parties, and political interest groups. The actions of these institutions are generally guided by such bureaucratic principles as rationality and efficiency.

3. *"Modern" forms of political behavior.* Individuals develop a strong identity with the political system and the nation-state as the entities, beyond familial groups, that receive their primary loyalty and support. Active political roles become widespread, as individuals become participants in the processes of politics, as voters, communicators, and so on (recall Table 2.2).

4. *Expanded capabilities of the political system.* The system becomes better able to generate support, and to respond to demands from its population and to control the environment. Overall, its organization is more stable and coherent, its structures are more efficient, and its actions more effectively serve its goals and objectives.

The capabilities of the political system (item 4) are probably the best measure of the level of political development. Almond and Powell (1966) have elaborated the key elements of a "capabilities analysis" for a political system. As a political system improves in any of these capabilities, it achieves a higher level of political development. There are five types of capabilities:

1. *Extractive:* utilizing human and material resources in the environment
2. *Regulative:* controlling individual and group actions
3. *Responsive:* making decisions and policies that react to demands for value allocations
4. *Distributive:* allocating values through institutionalized structures and procedures
5. *Symbolic:* manipulating images and meanings, and distributing nonmaterial rewards and values

The Process of Political Development

The process of political development is a topic of great interest to those attempting to shape their society as well as to those attempting to understand the political world. In one view, political development occurs primarily in response to development of the economic and social systems. Because of increases in the elements of modernization, such as greater economic development, urbanization, and social mobilization, there is a need for a more complex and more efficient political system. A more developed political system is needed to provide the infrastructure for economic activities and urban life, and to serve the expectations and needs of a modern citizenry.

The elements of modernization also provide the material and human resources that make political development possible. Greater economic capability produces resources that the political system can distribute. An urban population with increasingly modern beliefs is more willing to accept the authority of government and to participate meaningfully in politics. In short, the political system develops the more complex and specialized structures in order to respond to changes that are occurring in the society and the economy. As characterized in diagram *A* of Figure 11.1, political development is essentially a *dependent* variable. (The *dependent* variable, as explained in the appendix, is the phenomenon that changes because of the impact of other significant forces, termed *independent* variables.)

This view of political development was generally based on the historical political systems that evolved in the eighteenth and nineteenth centuries. But consideration of societies whose development has occurred primarily during the last 40 years revealed the growing power and impact of the political system as the

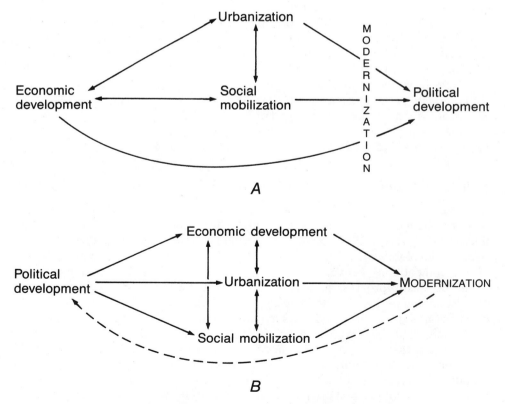

Figure 11.1. Models of Development

independent variable. From this perspective, the political system is the crucial force for modernizing the social and economic systems.

Kwame Nkrumah, the first president of Ghana, observed: "Seek ye first the political kingdom, and all things shall be added unto you." This widely quoted, near-religious invocation assumes that if the political system is developed first, it can then serve as the instrument through which social and economic development are achieved. Value allocation decisions by the political leadership can guide or even determine the directions of changes in individual and group behavior, in the political economy, and in the society. Obviously, development in the political, social, economic, and other domains are interdependent. But diagram *B* of Figure 11.1 emphasizes the central importance of the political system as an agent of change in other societal characteristics.

When a new political elite takes control, it is the political system over which the elite has most direct control. By explicit policy decisions and actions, an assertive leadership group can create modern forms of political organization and encourage modern forms of political behavior. The leaders can, for example, enact policies that establish new governmental structures, diminish the power of traditional authority sources, empower governmental bureaucracies to perform particular functions, create political parties, mobilize certain groups into the political process, or assert state control over human and natural resources.

Given its direct control over the political system, the political leadership can also employ public policy in direct or indirect efforts to modernize other domains of social and economic life, such as the political economy, the educational system, the culture, national identity, the media, or religious practice. Earlier chapters have provided examples of such attempts to use the political system and public policy as the mechanisms for broad changes in many spheres of life. The efforts of Chairman Mao in China and of Pol Pot in Kampuchea are representative examples of using the political system as a powerful instrument of social change. Kemal Atatürk's effort in Turkey (see Box 11.5) is another example.

Political Institutionalization and Political Decay

As the example of Turkey suggests, even when the forms of the political world appear to be modernized, the changes might lack "staying power." Samuel Huntington (1965, 1968, 1987) offers incisive commentary regarding the illusion of political development. Huntington observes that many studies assumed a fundamental compatibility between economic, social, and political development. There would be steady progress in all domains from a traditional society to a modern one. But in the period since the late 1950s, there has been a deterioration of political structures, processes, and roles in many political systems that appeared to be developed. And this reversal of political development has not necessarily been associated with the direction of change in other areas of society.

Huntington (1968) argues that political development must be measured not by outward forms, but by *political institutionalization*. This concept means that political organizations and procedures have acquired *value* in the eyes of the population and *stability* to withstand significant pressure. To a large extent, Huntington's operational measures of political institutionalization correspond to the indi-

BOX 11.5

Political Development
and Modernization in Turkey

The modernization effort in Turkey is an example of "seeking the political kingdom first." Historically, the area of the Turkish nation was part of the large Ottoman Empire ruled by a sultan. After World War I, an army commander named Mustafa Kemal led a fierce military struggle for national independence. Victory resulted in the creation of the sovereign state of Turkey in 1922. Mustafa Kemal, who seized political power in the new republic, was committed to rapid modernization. At the time, Turkey had very traditional political, economic, and social systems, with Islamic law dominating the actions of the 98 percent Muslim population. The new leader decided that the key to modernization was to reduce the hold of Islam on the people.

In a stroke of symbolic politics, he began his modernization drive at the personal level, changing his name to Mustafa Kemal *Atatürk*, which means "father of the Turks." (*Kemal* was also a fortunate name, since it means "perfect one".) Atatürk initially focussed on political development, establishing a new state based on the principles of independence and democracy. A constitution was approved in 1924, executive power was granted to a president, the sultan was exiled, a legislature was elected, and a single political party was established. Atatürk thus created a political system with modern structures of governance and modern forms of political participation. This political system then became the instrument for Atatürk's broader efforts to reform Turkey.

From 1925 until his death in 1938, Atatürk employed his great political power to implement three major sets of public policies that were meant to modernize Turkey and to separate it from the traditional Muslim world. First, he promulgated laws that prohibited the wearing of religious garments in everyday life, abolished religious schools, and closed religious tombs as places of worship. Second, he encouraged the emergence of an educated, cosmopolitan elite, by such steps as replacing the Ottoman script with the Latin alphabet and establishing literacy programs, especially in urban areas. Third, he established a new civil code to govern the legal relations between individuals and collectivities, relegating Shari'a law and the Koran to peripheral status in guiding public life. For example, he reduced the subordinate role of women, encouraging them to work, providing them with rights of divorce and inheritance, allowing them to vote and hold public office, and banning polygamy.

Politically, the attempt to create an effective, multiparty democracy in Turkey remains unfinished. There have been periods of serious social instability and governmental corruption, and three periods of military rule since 1960, although in each case the military returned power to civilians when order was restored. Most recently, a new constitution was adopted by popular vote in 1982 after two years of military rule, and a parliament was elected from among four main political parties.

Many changes prompted by Atatürk (who died in 1938) have occurred in the last generation. While 70 percent of the population lived in villages in 1964, Turkey is now 65 percent urban. The economy was 75 percent rural in 1978 and is now 70 percent industrial and has diversified considerably. Turkey's 52 million people remain 98 percent Muslim, but the country now has the most educated and modern women in the Muslim world. Atatürk's strong policies have not totally transformed Turkey, but they are an illuminating example of the use of political power to achieve considerable modernization and development within a society.

cators of capabilities analysis described earlier in this chapter. Hence political institutionalization is measured by the political system's capacity to:

Regulate its citizens
Respond flexibly to citizen demands
Extract and distribute resources efficiently
Adapt to changing circumstances

Rather than assuming inevitable progress in political development, *political decay* is always a possibility. Features of the modernization process, such as social mobilization, economic growth, urbanization, education, and so on, are inherently destabilizing. Social mobilization can undermine the traditional values and beliefs that sustained social order; economic growth produces new resources over which there is competition; urbanization concentrates heterogeneous groups into large, densely packed masses; and increases in education and communications make these masses aware of the many resources and values that they do not currently enjoy.

These circumstances can generate a huge increase in the volume and nature of demands that are directed at the political system. Groups begin to demand that the state provide them with many values, such as better education, decent health care and housing, good jobs, a free and open political process. Most developing political systems lack the capacity to extract the requisite resources from the political economy and also lack the authority to persuade the citizens to accept value allocations that they judge insufficient. In the face of growing citizen dissatisfaction with the political system, Huntington argues, a common strategy for the political leaders is an attempt to "buy off" the population by increasing their political participation and mobilization rather than providing tangible (scarce and costly) goods and services. Increased political activity might satisfy people in the short run, but it soon generates even higher levels of demands that cannot be met. At this point, rising social, political, and economic frustrations erupt into political demonstrations and protests, and even riots and rebellion.

Given low levels of support and excessive citizen demands, the political system must employ other mechanisms to maintain social order. In some cases, a charismatic leader emerges. She gains the support and obedience of the people, but only by personalizing power and thus weakening the overall processes through which power and political structures are institutionalized. In some cases, the one organization in most societies that *is* institutionalized—the military—forcibly takes over political power, under the justification of restoring order. And in some cases, there are periods where no individuals or institutions have the capacity to reestablish social peace, and there is widespread disorder and violence.

What can be done to achieve political institutionalization? Huntington suggests two general strategies. In the most direct approach, the political system acts to increase the value and stability of political institutions. For example, traditional authority structures (e.g., chiefs, religious leaders, tribal councils) might be adapted to the modern system. Or there might be a long incubation period under colonial rule, while new political structures and processes slowly gain value and stability. Or political parties might be created, as a locus of legitimacy and basis of stable governance. The problem with creating or transforming institutions, according to Huntington, is that this is the very approach that has been attempted and has failed in many developing states.

In the second approach to institutionalization, the political system substantially limits the processes of political participation and social mobilization. This requires policies that minimize visible political issues by limiting the activities of political parties and the media, the open competition among political elites, and citizen participation in politics. More fundamentally, citizens' political beliefs and actions can be manipulated by controlling the educational system and the media.

A third approach to institutionalization, not suggested by Huntington, is to mobilize the population, but to encourage only those forms of participation that support the political order. That is, individuals and groups are mobilized by the political system to "serve the people," not to make demands on the political system. This is the ultimate form of U.S. President John F. Kennedy's famous inaugural exhortation, "Ask not what your country can do for you; ask what you can do for your country."

China under Mao Zedong is an example of the effective use of this technique. People were inspired by Mao's principles of revolutionary change to work very hard in cooperation with many other people to develop China. Large numbers of minimally skilled workers constructed buildings, canals, and roads, increased productivity in food and manufactured goods, and provided educational and health services to the population. But this reliance on mobilization can be a problem. The political system can lose control of the process, as it did during the Cultural Revolution (1962–1968). During that period, Mao encouraged an overmobilized and overzealous segment of the population (led by the Red Guards) to revitalize the revolutionary spirit of the society. But the methods were primarily ones of persecution, violence, and disruption. Skilled people were ridiculed and forced to do menial work, while unskilled party loyalists were given positions requiring organizational and technical knowledge that they did not possess. The result was chaos in all spheres of Chinese society and a severe decline in economic productivity.

In Huntington's analysis, as indicated in Figure 11.2, the political leadership must balance participation and demands, on the one hand, against political institutionalization and system capabilities, on the other hand. As the modernization process generates social mobilization and economic development, there is a tolerable range for the ratio between participation and institutionalization. If the system overemphasizes institutionalization, there is what Huntington terms *political order;* if participation is overemphasized, there is *political decay.*

From this very choice of terms (*order* rather than *repression, decay* rather than *activism*), it should be evident which overemphasis Huntington believes is preferable. Huntington insists that in societies undergoing change and development, "the primary problem is not liberty, but the creation of legitimate public order" (1968:7). There can be order without liberty, he continues, but there can be no liberty without order. What do you think of Huntington's preferences and

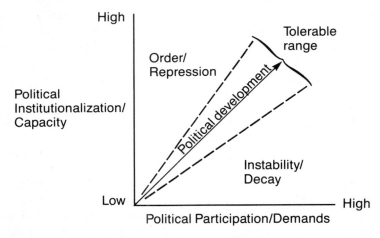

Figure 11.2. Political Institutionalization and Political Decay. SOURCE: Based on Huntington 1968.

assumptions here? If stability is preferred so absolutely, what kinds of objectionable actions by the state might be justified?

ACHIEVING POLITICAL DEVELOPMENT

Ultimately, all political systems aim to increase their capabilities and to increase their level of political development. There is general consensus that a more developed political system should enable the political actors to more fully accomplish their objectives. But there is considerable disagreement about the specific shape that political development should take.

In general, the people in most states assume that political development in other states should result in political systems and political economies that resemble those in their own state. It is debatable, however, whether all states should or even can follow the same developmental path. Some, perhaps most, newly developing states might have basic value systems, cultures, histories, economies, or social systems that are not compatible with the patterns of development or the kinds of political structures and processes that "worked" in states that emerged in earlier eras, whether France or Hungary or Japan or the Soviet Union or the United States.

The leaders in most developing states try to assess whether the prior experiences and the development strategy of some other state provide a model for their own development. This could help the developing state to benefit from the successes and avoid the mistakes of that state. Even if a model is selected that does seem compatible with the developing state's own goals and unique characteristics, achieving political development and political institutionalization are extremely difficult in the contemporary world. In addition to all the problems discussed in this chapter, the remainder of this book will continually illustrate the extent to which the choices and actions of states are influenced and sometimes controlled by other states in the international system. Most current states cannot shape their own destiny and cannot create their own political society free of intervention by other, more powerful political systems. This is a particular problem for states with low capabilities and minimal stability—that is, in states that lack political institutionalization.

Huntington is certainly correct that the challenges to political development are great. There have been periods of major political instability even in some European and Latin American states—and these states had the advantage of a long period in which the structures of a modern state could evolve into more complex and effective forms and in which the citizens could come to accept and value their political system.

In contrast, most nation-states in the contemporary political world began creating their own modern political systems after 1945. While these systems have the appearance of modernity—complex, specialized political structures, widespread political participation, and so on—they lack the stability and value that come with a long evolutionary development. The fundamental dilemma for the political elites in these states is how to allocate public values effectively while maintaining political order, expanding political participation, and strengthening the political economy.

How much political participation and political opposition should be allowed? How large should the domain of *res publica* be? To what extent should the state control the political economy? What levels of what values should be allocated to particular groups? All states continually deal with these issues. But in the absence of strong political institutionalization, determining and implementing appropriate answers to these issues can be nearly impossible. In virtually every state, it is assumed that effective political development is essential to accomplishing its major goals.

CHAPTER 12

Political Violence

Military action, Nicaragua

Yesterday, in the political world . . .

> Political rallies were forcibly broken up by police in such places as Atlanta, Georgia, United States; Managua, Nicaragua; Mexico City, Mexico; Nagomo, Azerbaijan, Soviet Union; and Seoul, South Korea.
>
> Seventy-four South Africans were injured during the aftermath of an anti-apartheid rally in Soweto.
>
> Three Palestinians were killed by Israeli soldiers during demonstrations/riots on the West Bank.
>
> A political group killed seven passengers on a luxury boat sailing in the Greek Islands.
>
> Two British soldiers were killed by a bomb near Belfast, and a splinter group of the Irish Republican Army took credit.
>
> A few Afghani *mujahideen* were killed in a battle with Afghan soldiers near the Afghan-Pakistan border.
>
> A few Sri Lankans were killed in a raid of an electrical power installation near Columbo.

Such incidents of violence are often at the center of our awareness of the political world. On a given day, the media rarely report that the great majority of countries and billions of people experienced no bombings, kidnappings, riots, or revolutionary acts that had an explicit or implicit political motivation. Rather, the media are likely to report on the settings that do experience armed conflict, riots, assassinations, terrorist incidents, and so on. In part, this selective reporting reflects our general fascination with the horror of violence. And in part it indicates our underlying sense that such political violence is extraordinary, or even an aberration, from politics-as-usual.

Violence is excluded from some definitions of politics, such as the group approach, since violence is viewed as a breakdown of politics, understood as consensus building and conflict resolution. For example, one recent textbook defines politics as "bloodless conflict" (Donovan, Morgan, and Potholm 1984). However, other definitions, including the class approach, treat conflict and violence as one possible, and perhaps even inevitable, form of politics. The purpose of this chapter is to discuss the nature and dynamics of political violence.

VIOLENCE

Before the discussion can unfold, we need to consider briefly the concept of violence itself. The most common notion is that violence entails the use of physical force, usually with the purpose of injuring or damaging the object of the violence. The tools of such violence can range from flying fists and feet to clubs and bullets to nerve gas to nuclear missiles.

But notice that some analysts take a much broader view of violence. First, the threat of violence might sometimes be understood as a form of violence, even if the violent act is not actually committed. If someone points a gun in your face and you give him your money, you will probably view this interaction as a violent one, even if the gun is never fired. In parallel, then, if a state points many nuclear missiles at the state across its border, would you classify this as an act of violence? Is it a violent act if an interest group threatens to blow up a public building unless its demands are met? Is it a violent act if a group shouts down a speaker at a public rally? Do you think that such acts of intimidation and show of force have a violent element, even if there is no actual physical injury or damage?

Second, an even broader view of violence includes various forms of subjugation and manipulation that do not involve physical harm. For example, consider a group that is an ''underclass'' within a society. The group is subjected to discrimination in education, in health care, in jobs, in housing. This intentional pattern of systematic deprivation continues over time. The group is not targeted for any specific physical violence, but the economic and cultural system provide the group with minimal opportunities to gain a significant share of the values in the society. Some would classify such oppression as a form of violence by the dominant group(s) against the fundamental rights of this group as it pursues the goals of life, liberty, and happiness. The extensive use of propaganda techniques on a people might be considered an even more subtle form of violence against those people.

The central topic in this chapter is the use of actual physical violence or very serious threats of such violence to achieve political goals. But as you assess the role of violence in politics, you should also consider the other ways in which the world of politics generates actions and impacts that ''do violence'' to many people. Although the resort of physical force is quite evident in politics, the more subtle forms of coercion and manipulation are pervasive.

POLITICAL SOCIETY

For Thomas Hobbes, the formation of political society was an attempt to overcome the frequent reliance on force and violence in human interaction. The state of nature described by Hobbes was pervaded by interpersonal violence. Consequently, individuals submitted to the social contract in an attempt to submit force to reason—to insure that force would be the *ultima ratio* (the final resort), not the *prima ratio* (the first resort) in human interactions. In essence, individuals ceded to the state a monopoly over the legitimate use of violence, sacrificing their own right to do violence in exchange for a similar sacrifice from others.

Some individuals and groups argue that the existing political society has no authority over their actions, and that they are therefore not morally bound to refrain from engaging in ''justifiable'' violence. Indeed, those who commit political violence offer a justification for their actions in virtually all cases. Among the most common rationales for political violence are the preservation of values, the restoration of order, self-defense, and retribution. Broadly, all such justifications are based on a claim either that their group has never accepted the right of a particular government to command their obedience or that the political system has failed to act properly (it has gone too far or it has not gone far enough in its value allocations).

TABLE 12.1. Types of Political Violence

Actor	Target	
	Individual/Group	State
Individual/Group	Crime Terrorism Nation-based conflict Class conflict	Riots Rebellion Secession Revolution
State	Order maintenance Establishment violence	War

TYPES OF POLITICAL VIOLENCE

A simple taxonomy of political violence can be based on specifying the actor who perpetrates the violence and the target of the violence. Either party may be a state or an individual/group. Table 12.1 categorizes the four types of political violence that result. In this chapter, we discuss three types, deferring the discussion of war to the next chapter on the relations between states. While the categories in Table 12.1 help organize and clarify our discussion, this taxonomy is imperfect and the boundaries between categories are imprecise. This is because the states, groups, or even individuals who engage in political violence are often motivated by multiple objectives and employ complex strategies.

State Violence against Individuals or Groups

Because the state has a monopoly of the legitimate use of violence, there are many instances where the application of political violence by the state seems justifiable. The state typically characterizes its own use of violence as an *order maintenance* activity. There are many instances where the state acts as policeman, judge, and executor of punishment when individuals or groups seem to have violated the society's legal system. The state's agents might arrest, try, and punish an actor who breaks a criminal law, such as robbery, or a civil law, such as tax fraud. In such cases, most citizens are likely to support these efforts to create and maintain public order.

But some uses of violence by the state are more problematical. Recall from Chapter 5 Lenin's definition of the state as "a body of armed men, weapons, and prisons." Because the state has the capacity to define the nature and severity of all "crimes," it is possible for the state to be highly repressive and discriminatory in its use of state violence. To those opposed to the regime, excessive reliance on force and oppressive laws are viewed as *establishment violence* rather than as the state's legitimate use of violence to maintain public order.

The boundary between a crime against society and a crime against the existing political order can blur. In many societies, "political crimes" include mere opposition to the actions of the current political leadership. Thus political opponents become "enemies of the people," and are subject to constraints on freedom of action, deprivation of resources, imprisonment, and death. The state can also institute systematic policies of violence against certain groups who are not overt opponents of the regime, but who are blamed for problems faced by the state and thus are made scapegoats.

A key instrument of state power against its enemies is its security forces. This can include official groups such as the regular military (e.g., the Chinese People's Liberation Army) and the secret police (e.g., the Soviet KGB), or force can be applied by unofficial groups such as paramilitary forces (e.g., the "death squads" in El Salvador) or civilian vigilante groups (e.g., the Red Guards during the Cultural Revolution in Mao's China). Another form of state power is judicial systems and prison systems, which punish those whose behaviors displease the state. According to Amnesty International, a group that monitors violations of individual civil rights by agents of the state, there are substantial numbers of political prisoners who experience establishment violence in the majority of contemporary states. And the state can cause great suffering or even death to individuals through its power to withhold access to such rewards as good jobs, shelter, and welfare services.

In the contemporary world, there is extensive attention to certain forms of political violence, especially violence between states (war) and individual/group violence (such as terrorism and civil war). This is understandable, because such violence is dramatic and terrifying. But, according to an extensive analysis of "politically caused deaths" by political scientist R. J. Rummel (1986), the death toll from establishment violence far outweighs the deaths from war in the twentieth century. These data are summarized in Table 12.2.

According to Rummel, the deaths of more than 155 million people in the twentieth century are directly attributable to government violence and war. There are 37 politically caused deaths in each 1,000 deaths in the population. The most staggering aspect of these data is that fully 77 percent of these politically caused deaths are establishment violence—that is, it is (conservatively) estimated that

TABLE 12.2. Politically Caused Deaths in the Twentieth Century

Cause	Total Deaths (millions)	Percent of Total	Deaths per 1,000 Population
All causes	155.1	100.0	37.1
Government	119.4	77.0	34.9
Communist	95.2	61.0	47.7
Totalitarian and extreme authoritarian	20.3	13.0	49.5
Other authoritarian	3.1	2.6	4.8
Democratic	0.8	0.7	2.2
War	35.7	23.0	2.2
International	29.7	19.0	1.7
Civil	6.0	4.0	2.6

SOURCE: Adapted from Rummel 1986. Data reprinted by permission of *The Wall Street Journal*, © Dow Jones Company, Inc. 1986. All right reserved.

governments killed 120 million of the people they are supposed to serve. Examples include the deaths by execution and starvation of several million Cambodians under Pol Pot's regime (Chapter 5); the elimination of more than 15 million Jews and other "dangerous" groups by the German Nazi regime (Chapter 8); the deaths of more than 7 million "enemies of the people" by Stalin's Soviet regime in the Great Purge of the 1930s. If you need evidence regarding the fundamental importance of the state in determining the quality of citizens' life, the 120 million deaths attributable to the citizens' own governments should be compelling.

Individual Violence against an Individual

In most instances when an individual is the actor and another individual is the target, the violence is not explicitly political. Most such violence (e.g., such crimes against people as murder, robbery, rape, assault, and also certain crimes against property, such as burglary and arson) is best characterized as *ordinary crime*. Only the state (and its agents) have a legitimate right to use violence, and thus an individual who does violence independent of the state is normally in violation of the law. Thus such violence has a political component in the sense that the state usually is involved in determining what behavior is criminal, in apprehending actors, in judging them, and in punishing them.

Explicit political motives are evident in some instances where one individual commits violence against another individual. Some assassinations of political actors are of this type. For example, in 1981, San Francisco Board of Supervisors member Dan White resigned and then requested reinstatement. When Mayor

The assassination of President John F. Kennedy on November 22, 1963 in Dallas, Texas. A secret service agent climbs onto the presidential limousine moments after the president was shot.

George Moscone denied his request, White returned to the City Hall with a gun and murdered Moscone and Supervisor Harvey Milk, White's main political opponent. The evidence generally supports the view that several American presidents, including Abraham Lincoln (1865), James A. Garfield (1881), and John Kennedy (1963) were assassinated by individuals acting at least in part on political motives. There seem to be many other cases where one person directs violence at specific individuals against whom he has a personal grudge or vendetta, especially during periods of broader social unrest, such as riots and civil wars.

Analyzing individuals' motivation in violent ordinary crimes is complicated by the fact that in most societies, members of deprived or subordinate groups tend to engage in these crimes far more frequently than members of the more advantaged classes. Can you suggest ways in which this pattern might suggest that the commission of some violent crimes has, at least in part, a subtle political origin? If most violent crimes are committed by subordinate groups, what is the likely response of the political system?

Group Violence against an Individual

A group can target an individual for political violence. Groups often direct their political violence against individuals who are perceived as representatives of the enemy state or enemy group. For example, members of the Irish Republican Army (IRA) might maim or murder such political enemies as members of the Protestant paramilitary forces in Northern Ireland, traitors or informers against the IRA, or individuals who are seen to represent British power and authority (e.g, Lord Mountbatten, a member of the Royal Family, who was assassinated on his pleasure boat in 1979).

When the individual against whom the political violence is directed is an "innocent," the action is often termed *terrorism*. Terrorism entails premeditated violence against individuals, in order to serve an underlying political objective. Bombs can be planted in public places such as pubs or airplanes, civilians can be kidnapped or murdered, harmful chemicals can be planted in food, water, or air. Also, those committing the violent act usually claim credit for their actions.

Why harm innocents? The motives of political terrorists vary, but several rationales guide most such acts. A common motive is to use the terrorist act as a means to gain international publicity for the group's cause. Unlike those committing ordinary crimes, terrorists typically claim credit for their violent actions. Another motive is to secure financial resources to support the group's political activities or to demand the release of imprisoned members. Many of the acts of violence entailing hostages and ransom demands are of this type. While innocents are the direct target of these actions, some existing state is usually the ultimate target, and the objective of the terrorist violence is to promote revolution. Terrorism as a strategy to overthrow a political system by violence will be discussed later in this chapter.

There are ambiguities in the assessment of terrorism. One problem is that in many acts labelled "terrorism," the targets are not truly "innocents," but rather are agents of the enemy state. For example, when a Palestinian group bombed and killed more than 100 U.S. marines in their barracks in Beirut, Lebanon, in 1984, U.S. spokespersons termed the attack "terrorism"; yet marines can hardly be construed as innocents. Another common target of terrorists is police officers or judges who have done violence to individuals associated with the terrorist group. In such cases, the political violence can be terrible, but one must decide whether group violence against agents of the state is appropriately defined as terrorism.

Ironically, some groups labelled as terrorists are actually employees of a political system, which uses them as "death squads" to keep the citizens in line. And some terrorist groups are mercenaries, who are subsidized by one state to perform violent acts against a rival state. In such cases, the actor actually causing the political violence is best understood as a state, not a group. Such actions can be labelled *state-sponsored terrorism*.

With the proliferation of groups employing terrorist tactics, the wry observation has been made that "one person's terrorist is another person's freedom fighter." The root problem with using *terrorism* as an analytic concept is that it has become a powerful and negative label in political rhetoric. In the manipulative language of politics, the label is sometimes used regardless of the innocence of the victim, the identity of the actual sponsor of the violence, or the justifiability of the ends. It communicates a disgust for extreme political violence against innocent individuals; but it can also be used to discredit any group that uses violent means to achieve its political ends or to condemn a group whose political ends, as much as its means, are unacceptable. Ultimately, the issue centers in moral and political values: Are there any circumstances in which group political violence against individuals is justifiable? If so, what kinds of violence are acceptable under what circumstances?

Group Violence against a Group

When one group engages in political violence against another group, it is usually motivated by a deep animosity based on some element of the two groups' identities, such as ethnic or religious differences. This can be termed *nation-based violence*. The discussion in Chapter 5 of the political violence among different nations on the Indian subcontinent is a clear example of such intergroup violence. The conflict between the Hindus and Muslims at the time of independence resulted in more than half a million deaths, as neighbors in the villages and cities engaged in bloody and protracted violence. And the violent civil war between East and West Pakistan, while regionally based, was essentially a struggle between two ethnic groups, the Bengalis and the Punjabis. A religious cleavage is again the basis of the group political violence in the Punjab between Hindus and Sikhs. Recent examples of such nation-based political violence are the struggles in Lebanon and in Northern Ireland among groups distinguished mainly by religion, and in Sri Lanka between groups distinguished by ethnicity.

In many cases, an underlying intergroup *class conflict* is associated with an ethnic or religious cleavage. In Lebanon, Northern Ireland, and Sri Lanka, for example, one of the groups in the conflict has dominant social, economic, and political power over the other group(s). Thus class theorists argue that the "real" conflict in many settings is not actually due to religion or language or ethnicity, but is the inevitable class struggle that emerges from stratification and inequality. Of course, class conflict can occur between any strata, such as the peasant class against the landlord class or the capitalist class against the worker class, independent of any nation-based cleavage that might reinforce the distinction between conflicting classes.

When group political violence entails the murder of many members of one ethnic group by its rival, the term *genocide* is often applied. The political system is often a partner in such situations, since its machinery of violence is employed by the dominant group. Examples of this situation include the killing of Armenians by the Turks (mid-1920s), of the Tutsis by the Hutus in Rwanda (1963–1964), and of the Hutus by the Tutsis in neighboring Burundi (1988), and of the Hmong by the Laotians (1976–1979).

Individual or Group Violence against the State

Individual or group political violence directed against the political system can stem from several bases. At one extreme, such violence might be a spontaneous outburst of frustration with a person's or group's life conditions. At the other extreme, there might be such deep-seated hostility against the existing political system that the individual or group undertakes a lengthy series of violent actions in order to overthrow that political system.

Riot and Rebellion.   When political, social, or economic conditions become intolerable, in comparison to the conditions that people expect, frustration and anger are one possible response. Such frustration can lead to apathy or it can be expressed by political action, beginning with normal demands on decision makers. If demands are still not met at an adequate level, individuals' political actions might become more intense, taking such forms as demonstrations and civil disobedience. The next escalation of political action for those who remain dissatisfied might entail violence.

Riots are a sporadic and relatively disorganized form of such violence. Riots involve group violence against property, against agents of the political system, or against perceived opponents in the society. Riots often arise spontaneously out of a specific incident that is a catalyst for latent frustration. For example, a riot might begin with an action by the police, such as the shooting of an individual, or with an economic problem, such as a sudden large increase in the prices of basic foodstuffs. Once riots begin to occur, such political violence can spread, as others within the society are motivated to use the same means to demonstrate their dissatisfaction with the political system or social conditions. The total pattern of political violence might be termed *rebellion* once riots become more frequent, premeditated, widespread, and involve more people. It is such a deterioration of citizen support and escalation of political action into political violence that is at the heart of Samuel Huntington's description of political decay (see Chapter 11).

Riots and rebellion are expressions of frustration in which there is an implicit or explicit demand for redress of grievances. There is an expectation that the political system will perceive the nature of the grievances and will enact public policy that is responsive to the unmet demands. The basic demands might involve opposition to certain political leaders or public policies. Examples of this include the riots against the Vietnam War in America during the late 1960s and the riots against apartheid in South Africa in the late 1980s. Alternatively, the demands underlying riots might involve support for certain leaders or policies. Riots by blacks in urban America in the 1960s were essentially demands for constructive economic and social policies that would benefit racial minorities and the poor.

Separatist Violence.   Many groups with strong national identity take political action to achieve greater autonomy or independence from the nation-state that governs them. If the desire for independence is very strong and the existing political system is unresponsive, groups might engage in separatist violence to achieve their goal. If the separatist group is small and lacks political resources, the probable forms of political violence are acts of terrorism or attacks against specific individuals or structures within the political system. The actions of the Irish Republican Army in its efforts to separate Northern Ireland from the United Kingdom and unite it with the Republic of Ireland are an example of this form. Targets of the IRA's bombs and murders are usually the British "occupying army" and the leaders of Protestant opponents in Northern Ireland. Similar forms of separatist violence have characterized recent activities by Basque separatists against Spain, by Palestinians against Israel, by Tamils against Sri Lanka, and by Sikhs against India.

In most colonial settings, violent uprisings against the colonial power have usually been one element in the political struggle for independence. In some cases, organization of the separatist violence has been weak or nonexistent. But in most cases, the separatist violence has been coordinated by an organized group, such as the Mau Mau versus the British in Kenya (1950s), the Muslim League versus the British and Hindus in the Indian subcontinent (late 1940s), FRELIMO versus the Portuguese in Mozambique (1962–1975), and the Vietminh/Vietcong versus the French and then the Americans in Vietnam (1940s–1970s).

When a significant proportion of the population in a region actively supports a separatist movement and political violence emerges on a large scale, *civil war* is the likely form of the political violence. In the United States, the political leaders of the slaveholding Southern states decided that they no longer wished to maintain their participation in the federation, and they announced that their states were seceding (withdrawing formal membership) from the federation. The central government rejected their request to secede, forcing 11 Southern states to declare their independence, create a confederation, and initiate a military struggle against the central government. In the bloody Civil War of 1861–1865, the Union forces of the central government ultimately defeated the army of the Confederacy and forced the Southern states to remain in the federation.

A similar civil war occurred in Nigeria (1967–1970). The Ibo tribe, differing from other major tribes in religion, language, and political traditions, attempted to secede from the federation and create a separate state called Biafra. After four years of civil war and nearly 1 million deaths, the central government's army was victorious, and Biafra was stillborn as a nation-state. In contrast, the Bengalis were successful in their separatist civil war against the central government of Pakistan (recall Chapter 5), and thus the new nation-state of Bangladesh was created (in 1971).

Coup.   A coup occurs when the top leader or part of the leadership group is replaced by violence or the explicit threat of violence. There is no intention to overthrow the entire political-economic order, although the opposition to the existing leadership can be based on differences in policy preferences as well as personal rivalry. This is a common form of leadership turnover in political systems that have no institutionalized procedures for leadership succession. Political violence against the top leadership group is typically organized by other members of the political leadership, by a rival political group, or by the military. Coups are especially common in many Latin American and African states. An extreme example is Bolivia, where 190 coups have occurred in a 156-year period. Coups in 1988 included the overthrow of the leaders in Burma, Fiji, and Haiti.

Revolution.   As Lennon (John, that is) observed, "You say you want a revolution, well you know, we all want to change the world." In contrast to the other forms of political violence against the state, the explicit object of revolution is the use of violence to destroy the existing political system. In a revolution, there is a rapid and fundamental transformation of the state organization and the class structure (Skocpol 1979). The ultimate goal is a fundamentally different distribution of value allocations. The extent of transformation that must occur for "revolutionary" changes in the state organization, class structure, or distribution of values is sometimes difficult to specify. Determining when changes are revolutionary has analytic difficulties similar to those, discussed in Chapter 5, for determining the "death" of a political system.

There are many instances where new leadership takes power, claiming that it will serve a new ideology and will allocate power and resources to new/different groups. When Colonel Muammar Qaddafi overthrew the hereditary king and installed a revolutionary council committed to total egalitarianism (in 1969), it was clear that there had been a revolutionary change in the Libyan political system. But there are many instances where it is not clear whether the essential features of the political system have dramatically changed. This can occur either because the attempt to transform the political system is a charade or because it falls far short of its objectives. This issue will be considered further at the end of this section, in discussing the outcomes of revolution. First, let us describe four broad strategies that can be employed to achieve a revolution.

Strategy 1: Terrorism.   The problems of defining the boundaries of terrorism were raised earlier in this chapter. There are many instances where an "innocent" appears to be the target of political violence, but where the state is the actual target and its revolutionary overthrow is the ultimate objective of terrorist acts. As a revolutionary strategy, *terrorism* involves selective acts of violence, usually by small organized cells of political activists. Terrorism is a strategy for a group that lacks sufficient membership and resources to sustain a direct struggle with the existing state.

Terrorists use political violence in an effort to undermine support for the state. Their tactics are to disrupt public life, by such means as bombing in public places, interrupting basic services such as electricity and food distribution, and disabling key political actors within the regime. Terrorists believe that these tactics might further their revolutionary objectives in two ways. First, the acts of terrorism might provoke harsh and repressive order-maintenance actions by the state, such as large-scale detention of citizens, crackdowns on opposition groups and opposition media, and so on. In this situation, terrorists assume, many citizens will become alienated as they see the "true" repressive nature of the political system, and these citizens will become radicalized, shifting their political support away from the existing regime, either towards the terrorists' position, or at least towards an unstable situation where survival of the existing political system is in jeopardy. Second, terrorist acts might prevent the political system from effective allocation of such values as distribution of food, provision of transportation, and, most fundamentally, maintenance of public order. This will undermine citizen support for the system and decrease resistance to (possibly even increase support for) revolutionary change.

The anticolonial resistance in Algeria is a clear example of the successful use of terrorism. A mixture of random public bombings, disruptions of infrastructure services, and violence against the agents of the colonial French led to a dramatic decline in the quality of life and provoked highly repressive responses from the political and military authorities. As conditions deteriorated, France decided to abandon the ungovernable country, whose anticolonial/terrorist leadership, under Ben Bella, formed a new political system. (Pontecorvo's powerful film, *The Battle of Algiers,* documents this period.)

Obviously, terrorism, like other revolutionary strategies, does not always produce the expected results. Often the terrorists are crushed without achieving any of their objectives, as was the case with terrorist groups in the United States in the 1960s, including the Weathermen and the Symbionese Liberation Army. And sometimes, the repression evoked by terrorism merely makes things worse. The leftist terrorists in Iran were successful in destabilizing Shah Reza Pahlavi's regime; but it was the Islamic fundamentalists supporting the Ayatollah Khomeini who succeeded in grasping political power and forming a new fundamentalist political system even more unappealing to the leftists than the shah's. The situation in Uruguay (see Box 12.1) is another example of revolutionary terrorism that backfired.

Strategy 2: Revolution from Above. The essence of the revolution from above is the swift overthrow of the elite. There are three key characteristics in revolution from above (Johnson 1966). First, activity is primarily centered in the urban capital. Second, some members of the existing political elite are usually supportive of the revolution and thus the existing political structures have to some extent been

BOX 12.1

Terrorism Makes It Worse: Uruguay

Between 1903 and the early 1960s, Uruguay became widely respected as the exemplary Latin American democracy (this discussion based on Goodwin 1986: 79–80). A stable two-party system was the basis of a liberal democratic government that facilitated increasing social welfare and economic prosperity. But political decay emerged in the 1960s, grounded in economic decline, high inflation, and governmental incompetence and corruption. These failures spawned the Tupamaros, an urban guerrilla group that engaged in violence and terrorism to overthrow the state and establish a more just political order. The civilian government was overthrown, but by the conservative military in a 1973 coup.

The Uruguayan military dictatorship then launched a massive campaign to suppress not only the Tupamaros, but all civilian opposition. During this period, Uruguay became known as "the torture chamber of Latin America," with widespread human and civil rights abuses. By 1979, more than 1 in 100 of all Uruguayans were political prisoners, estimated to be the highest proportion in the world. And one-sixth of the population (a half million people) were in exile. The economic crisis worsened under the military regime, with inflation of more than 60 percent and unemployment higher than 30 percent. When the military promoted a referendum on a new constitution in 1980, 60 percent of the population rejected it. Eventually (in November 1984) the military allowed elections, returning governmental power to civilian rule in March 1985. But Uruguay has not regained the stability and political institutionalization of the pre-1960 period. Economic problems and foreign debt are substantial. And the military is constantly watching the situation and especially the Tupamaros, who now act as a nonviolent political group. It is a continual possibility that the military will reassert its domination of the political order.

infiltrated by those who intend to create a new political system. And third, toleration or support of the revolution by the armed forces is important.

In this form of revolution, the old regime is eliminated in a few minutes or a few days. The revolutionaries might storm the leader's residence and capture and/or execute key figures of the old regime. Sometimes the revolutionary group takes control while the leader is away from the capital on business or pleasure. In either case, the new leadership uses the media to declare the elimination of the old leadership and the creation of a new political order, and it then proceeds to create new political institutions. There follows a slow penetration of the new political system into the hinterlands outside the capital city.

Historically, many revolutions most closely resemble the revolution from above. The Russian Revolution is a version of this strategy, although the armed forces did not all acquiesce to the change. This lead to Trotsky's observation that if the forces of coercion are split, there will be civil war rather than a decisive revolutionary victory. Other twentieth-century examples of revolution from above include Gamal Abdel Nasser's replacement of King Farouk in Egypt

(1952), Muammar Qaddafi's victory over King Idris in Libya (1969), the creation of the Lon Nol regime in place of Prince Norodom Sihanouk's regime in Cambodia (1970), the overthrow of Salvador Allende's government by General Pinochet in Chile (1973), the execution of President Tolbert by Sergeant Samuel Doe in Liberia (1980), and the execution of Premier Nicholae Ceausescu in Romania (1989).

Strategy 3: Guerrilla War. The strategy of revolutionary guerrilla warfare has been highly refined in the twentieth century, especially during the Chinese Revolution. Guerrilla war contrasts with the revolution-from-above strategy in four crucial ways. First and most importantly, the essence of guerrilla war is a long, protracted campaign from rural bases, although the fighting can be in both rural and urban areas. Second, it is an explicit struggle against the military. The strategy, rather like that of the young boxer Muhammad Ali, is to "float like a butterfly and sting like a bee." The guerrilla's forces persistently harass the regime's army by fighting in a hit-and-run style, suddenly attacking an exposed point and then literally disappearing into the population and the countryside.

Third, guerrilla war entails an extensive and continuing effort to win the support of the peasants. This effort mixes two techniques: (1) propaganda—promises of land reform, exhortations for resistance against domestic traitors and foreign invaders; and (2) terror—disrupting village stability, eliminating local leaders loyal to the government, demanding food and shelter, and dragooning locals into the guerrilla army. China's Mao Zedong, as a revolutionary leader, was the first to emphasize the crucial role of the peasants. He observed that if he had 10 points to give for success in the revolution, he would award 3 points to the urban dwellers and the military and 7 points to the peasants, for "without the poor peasants, there can be no revolution."

Fourth, guerrilla warfare mobilizes the mass into the struggle and creates new political institutions *prior* to the collapse of the old regime. Thus the political violence expands and escalates as the guerrilla forces disrupt, demoralize, and eventually defeat the regime's military. Ultimately, the guerrilla army marches victoriously into the capital city, the previous leadership having fled or been killed, and the political institutions developed in the countryside are empowered in the capital and in the urban areas.

Many of the successful Third World revolutions in the last 40 years have employed the strategy of guerrilla warfare. With the Chinese Revolution as the model (victory in 1949), this strategy has been the method of revolutionary political violence in Cuba under Fidel Castro (1959), in Vietnam under Ho Chi Minh and his successors (1975), in Zimbabwe (formerly Rhodesia) under Robert Mugabe (1980), and in Nicaragua under the Sandinistas (1979). It is evident in current struggles in El Salvador, in Cambodia, and in Afghanistan. Guerrilla war is interesting because it directly contradicts two key principles of the Marxist-Leninist-Trotskyist conception of revolution. First, it undermines the principle that revolution emanates from the urban proletariat. And second, it rejects the view that revolution cannot be made against the elite's armed forces.

Strategy 4: "Democratic" Revolution. It seems there can also be a democratic strategy for revolutionary change. In this case, legal, nonviolent political action is effectively mounted to achieve a fundamental transformation of the political system. In one form, the population uses the democratic electoral process to select a new leadership elite, which then dismantles the existing political system and creates a new one. This form might describe the rise of Hitler and the establishment of the Third Reich in Germany (1933), the election of Salvador Allende's Marxist-Leninist government in Chile (1970), and the election of the anti-Sandinista coalition in Nicaragua (1990).

In a second form of democratic revolution, widespread but generally nonviolent resistance to a regime forces the elite to resign. The new leadership, although not initially elected, implements fundamental transformations in the political system. This occurred in such Soviet bloc states as Czechoslovakia, East Germany, and Poland in the late 1980s. When Soviet leader Gorbachev indicated that the Soviet Union would no longer support unpopular leadership groups, citizens in these states participated in mass demonstrations against the existing Communist governments. With a minimum of violence, the regimes rapidly collapsed and the repressive, one-party Communist states were replaced by more democratic, multiparty systems. (The revolutions in Eastern Europe are discussed further in Chapter 15.)

The Conditions for Revolution. The conditions under which political revolution occurs is an issue that has fascinated many people, especially those who want to analyze revolution and those who want to lead a successful revolution. Many different explanations are offered to account for the occurrence of revolution. The most widely cited studies of major historical revolutions include those by Hannah Arendt (1963), Crane Brinton (1957), Chalmers Johnson (1966), Barrington Moore (1966), and Theda Skocpol (1979). The contemporary revolutions in Third World states are analyzed in works by such scholars as Migdahl (1974), Paige (1975), and Wolf (1969).

One long-standing explanation of revolution is the "theory of rising expectations," associated with Alexis de Tocqueville (1835, 1945), James Davies (1971), and others. In this view, the key cause of revolution is a sudden growth in the disparity between the values that the population expects to enjoy from the government and the actual value distribution they receive. Contemporary research calls this the "J curve" theory because, as indicated in Figure 12.1, the disparity resembles an inverted J. At the point where this gap between expected and actual values becomes substantial, political violence emerges and can escalate into rebellion and then revolution. Although this explanation is intuitively appealing, most scholars find the empirical research testing the J curve to be unconvincing. In particular, it has been difficult to establish the size of the gap that provokes revolutionary violence and the approach does not specify which/how other economic, social, and political conditions affect this pattern.

Another example is the theory of Chalmers Johnson (1966), who claims that there are three necessary conditions for revolution:

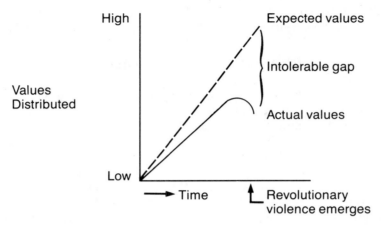

Figure 12.1. "J-Curve" Description of Revolution. SOURCE: Derived from Davies 1971.

1. The sociopolitical system must be very significantly disrupted, through such forces as a rapid change in fundamental social values or an extreme environmental change such as a natural disaster.
2. There must be a serious decline in the authority of existing regime leadership, such that substantial subsets of the population no longer accept the legitimacy of its decisions and actions.
3. Some unexpected event, such as a mutiny, a violent response to public protest, or an action in the international environment, must serve as a catalyst for massive political violence against the regime.

It seems that a fourth important element might be included in this list: some visible image of leadership, embodied in an individual, a group, or an ideology, must emerge as an alternative to the existing regime.

Although the various theories of revolution have evident differences in the specific causes and dynamic process, most theories of contemporary revolutions share certain commonalities (Hagopian 1984, Chap. 6). First, the state has experienced *broad, destabilizing forces* that have affected the culture, the economy, and/or the political system. These might include the decline of traditional social and religious values, the emergence of a modern state, a transformation of the economic system, social mobilization (recall Chapter 11), or the global expansion of capitalism into a world economic system. Second, there are more *direct and immediate forces of disruption,* such as violent conflict with another state, major economic decline, serious financial problems for the state, or incompetence or division within the ruling elite.

The Outcome of Revolution. Since the ultimate objective of revolution is a fundamental transformation in the political system, an assessment of the outcomes of revolutions is at least as important as an analysis of causes and processes. Many scholars still distinguish the three postrevolutionary phases identified by Crane Brinton (1957), based on his extraordinary study of the French Revolution of 1789:

1. *Rule of the moderates.* After the revolution, the leadership group that comes to power attempts to fashion a new political order, but not to use governmental power to transform drastically the social and economic system. Often, the moderates are committed to increasing the democratic nature of the politics in the society.
2. *Rule of the radicals.* The moderates are displaced by more ideological and aggressive political groups. These radical groups want to use political power to implement a far more extensive transformation of society, including greater centralization of political and economic power in the state. The radicals also direct substantial and continuing political violence against any groups who are viewed as obstacles to this transformation.
3. *Reaction and moderation.* At some point, a new set of moderates regains control from the radical groups. There are various reasons why the radicals might lose control: They might destroy each other through internal struggles over power or ideology; the revolutionary violence might become so extreme that there is insufficient popular support to sustain the radicals; or the new entrenched elite might begin to enjoy the privileges associated with power and lose its revolutionary fervor. At this point, the "old regime" is dead, but the resulting political system is far less extreme than that during the rule of the radicals.

The three-phase model of outcomes is based on the French Revolution, and its phases do not fit many revolutions, especially those in the post–World War II world. First, in many recent revolutions, initial rule by moderates is either fleeting or nonexistent. The groups who seize power after many of the revolutionary guerrilla wars in peasant societies come to power committed to move quickly into a phase that resembles the rule by radicals. This is certainly true in such postrevolutionary states as China, Cuba, Iran, Kampuchea, and Vietnam. And second, the third phase is either limited or emerges only very gradually in many states. Rather, the new society forged during the radical phase is institutionalized. Periods of significant revisionism can alternate with periods of renewed radicalism. But the key question is whether a transformation to a more democratic and moderate politics (as described in phase three) occurs. This is the intriguing question regarding the changes in the Soviet Union under Gorbachev, in China since the death of Mao Zedong, and in Iran after Khomeini.

EVALUATING POLITICAL VIOLENCE: MEANS AND ENDS

Political violence must be understood as a failure of institutionalized political action. A strong and persuasive normative perspective is that political violence is unacceptable, deviant behavior. Others glorify political violence as a mechanism for human liberation from tyranny and oppression. Political violence can be either the midwife of progress or it can be the source of nearly universal suffering and chaos. Clearly, there are fundamental issues about means and ends tied up with one's assessment of political violence.

If a crucial objective is the maintenance of public order and political institutionalization, one must consider that the resort to political violence not only causes obvious disorder, but it also deeply undermines longer-term prospects for peaceful, orderly governance. If a crucial objective is political justice, it is important to consider whether the ultimate outcomes of the process of political violence seem to serve justice. Many cynics would share Ignazio Silone's assessment, which you may recall from Chapter 1: "Every revolution begins as a movement of liberation but ends as tyranny." But those who would justify some forms of political violence might sympathize with Eldridge Cleaver's claim that "a slave who dies of natural causes will not balance two dead flies of the scale of eternity."

There are no tidy answers to the question of when political violence is justifiable. Perhaps one way to organize your own assessment of political violence is to reflect on three basic questions:

1. Are the means of political violence unacceptable under *all* circumstances?
2. If you answered no, could an outcome emerge from the use of political violence that is so preferable to the existing situation that establishing the precedent of using political violence is justifiable?
3. If you answered yes, what specific circumstances would be necessary to justify the resort to political violence?

In the current technological era, the mechanisms for violence are more efficient, powerful, and horrifying than at any time in human history. The implications of this are especially evident in the relations between states, which is a topic of the next chapter. But even subnational political groups can now inflict such massive and destructive political violence. Thus, questions about the balance between liberation and destruction have never been more pressing at any time in human history.

PART FIVE

Politics among Nations

CHAPTER 13

Politics between States

Meeting at the White House. From left to right: President George Bush, Foreign Minister Eduard Shevardnadze, and Secretary of State James Baker.

Imagine an island nation-state, Buena, blessed with temperate climate and rich natural resources that provide sufficient food and other necessities for the population. A few hundred miles to the south is a similar island, Malo; but Malo is cold and windy and has few resources. Each island is located about 50 miles off a large landmass composed of several nation-states.

If you knew nothing more about either island, could you make any educated guesses about the political and economic relations of each with the other island and with the large landmass?

In considering the relations between these states, many considerations might emerge, including these: Is either island more needful of trading relations with outsiders? Does either island have strong reasons to protect itself from intervention by outsiders? How could such protection be accomplished? If either island establishes a military, what kind of forces make most sense? What kind of political alliance would each island be most likely to forge (with states on the landmass or with each other)?

One traditional method of thinking analytically about nation-states is based on precisely these kinds of assessments. This method of *geopolitics* assumes that the geography of a state—that is, its physical characteristics (e.g., location, topography) and its natural and human resources (e.g., population size, fossil fuel resources, arable land, water)—might significantly affect the politics of the state.

While only a few argue that "geography is destiny," it does seem reasonable to assume that a state's geography can be the source of both opportunities and constraints on its actions. Consider, for example, the effects on a state of conditions such as insufficient domestic food production, abundant fossil fuel resources, a small population relative to land area, the absence of any natural barriers separating the state from surrounding states, being snowbound eight months per year, enormous variation in yearly rainfall, or strategic location in a major international shipping lane.

It should also be obvious that other important features within its boundaries besides physical setting and resources might powerfully affect the state's behavior toward other political systems. Among the important features are the nation-state's history of relations with other states, its political culture, the style of its major political leaders, the nature of its political structures, and the behavior of other actors outside its boundaries.

Poet John Donne wrote that "No man is an island entire unto himself." In the contemporary political world, it is clear that not even an island is insulated from the world around it. Indeed, our imaginary Buena and Malo (or actual islands like Great Britain or the Falkland Islands or Japan or Cuba or Grenada) will find that their politics are heavily dependent upon what other states are doing. In the model of the political system in Chapter 5, this point is made explicitly in the concept of the extrasocietal environment. The behavior of every political system is affected not only by its own characteristics but also by the actions of political systems outside its boundaries, as well as by other types of external systems, such as economic, cultural, demographic, and social ones.

Most contemporary states expend much, and in some cases most, of their political energy on their relations with other states. When these actions are studied from the analytic perspective of the individual state, such decisions and actions are usually classified as the study of *foreign policy*. When the *inter*actions among two or more states are studied, such decisions and actions are termed *international relations*.

This chapter explicitly considers the political system in its extrasocietal environment, with particular emphasis upon the interactions among states. First, the three major sets of goals pursued by all states are detailed. Second, there is a discussion of the means by which states can attempt to facilitate cooperation and resolve conflict with each other. Third, key forms of interstate competition, such as balance of power and colonial domination, are examined. The final section of the chapter considers the nature and causes of political violence between states.

THE GOALS OF STATES

The political system of each nation-state will attribute different levels of relative importance to the wide variety of goals it might pursue. However, crucial political goals of virtually all political systems can be subsumed under three overarching goals: security, stability, and prosperity. Each of these three goals includes component goals that the political system might act to serve. The significance of each component goal and also the capacity of the political system to achieve each goal depends on many factors. As noted above, these include the state's geopolitical situation, history, culture, leaders, political structures, and interactions with other states. Figure 13.1 illustrates this framework of basic goals. In the lists below, major components of each overarching goal are presented in the general order of their priority for most states.

Security

1. *Survival* is the fundamental element of security. It entails the very existence of the state, such that other states do not conquer it and absorb it.
2. *Autonomy* refers to the capacity of the state to act within its own boundaries without intervention into or control of its affairs by other states.
3. *Influence* involves the state's ability to alter the actions of other states in desired ways, by means of persuasion or the use of inducements.
4. *Prestige* is the desirable situation where other states will admire and respect the state.
5. *Dominance* is the use of power or violence to enable the state to impose direct control over other states.

Stability

1. *Order maintenance* is the capacity of the state to insure social peace for its citizens through the prevention of individual and group violation of social norms, especially those involving violence.

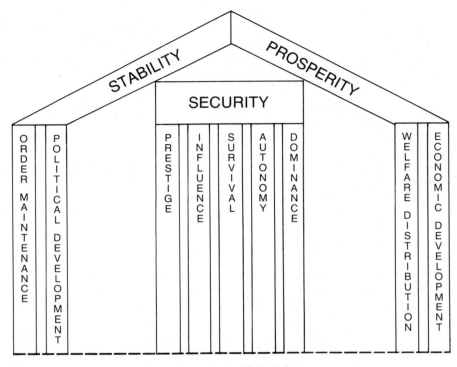

Figure 13.1. Basic Goals of States

2. *Political development* refers, as in Samuel Huntington's conception of institutionalization (recall Chapter 11), to the concentration of political authority in a state that has strong capabilities to make and enforce effective policies and to gain support from its citizens.

Prosperity

1. *Economic development* reflects both (a) the increasing scale, complexity, and specialization of the productive system and of the goods produced; and (b) the capacity of the political economy to obtain, manage, and transform resources into valued goods.
2. *Welfare distribution* refers to the private and/or public allocation of adequate and increasing levels of valued goods to enhance the quality of life of the citizenry.

Few, if any, states can fully achieve their desired level on even one of these nine major goals, and the pursuit of multiple goals entails difficult trade-offs. In an obvious example, expansion of the welfare goods and services allocated to the citizenry is costly and absorbs resources that might otherwise be reinvested in the economic system to facilitate economic development. This is often referred to as the fundamental policy choice of "growth versus welfare." And resources allocated to the military for major security goals are not available for either welfare or for economic development. The policy trade-off between security and welfare is often characterized by the phrase "guns versus butter." Some political systems justify extensive resource allocation to security and stability goals by claiming that greater achievement of these goals will indirectly enhance prosperity goals. Of the nine major goals listed in Figure 13.1, which sets do you think are most complementary? most competitive?

The politics between most states, most of the time, is characterized by cooperation or mild competition. As each state pursues its own goals, other states are relevant only to the extent that they represent opportunities for or constraints on goal achievement. While there are many elements of competition as each state pursues its own national interest, there are few interactions that might escalate into a major confrontation. The political and economic interdependencies among many states in the global era mean that there are substantial incentives for states to emphasize cooperation and coordination in their interactions.

Many forms of competition between states do contain the potential for serious disagreements and conflict. While every state has a monopoly on the legitimate use of force within its territorial boundaries, in order to enforce its laws and to control the behavior of its citizens, there are not such strong mechanisms to control the relations between states.

MECHANISMS OF COOPERATION BETWEEN STATES

Diplomacy, Treaties, and Alliances

Under most circumstances, a state is likely to accomplish more of its goals at lower costs if it can develop mutually advantageous cooperative arrangements with other states. States formalize and coordinate their interactions through many mechanisms, the most widespread being *diplomacy*. Diplomatic practices developed as states attempted to insure that their own skilled and sensitive representatives could engage in regular discussion and negotiation with the representatives of other states. Thus most states maintain an array of actors (e.g., ambassadors, cultural attachés) and institutions (e.g., embassies, trade delegations) whose objectives are to further interests shared with other states and to resolve potential problems by means of "normal diplomatic channels" and informal communications.

More explicit cooperation among states is usually manifest in bilateral (between two states) or multilateral (among three or more states) treaties and alliances. *Alliances* are informal or formal agreements between states that they will cooperate or assist each other in the military, economic, or political sphere. *Treaties* also deal with the same areas, but tend to be more formal and legalistic. These agreements can range from a rather straightforward arrangement for a cultural exchange between two friendly nations to a complex nuclear arms reduction pact between many hostile states. In contemporary international politics, many of the most crucial treaties are trade agreements and mutual security pacts among a large number of nations (e.g., the General Agreement on Tariffs and Trade [GATT], the North Atlantic Treaty Organization [NATO], and the Warsaw Pact). The European Communities (EC) is an example of a multistate, multipurpose confederation for economic, political, cultural, and military cooperation among twelve Western European nations with a combined population of 180 million people. For ultimate survival in a world of extensive nuclear weapons, the arms control treaties among rivals, such as the Strategic Arms Limitation Treaties (SALT) between the United States and the Soviet Union, might be the most crucial form of cooperation.

The direct, day-to-day interactions among most states are substantially governed by such treaties and alliances. Like other forms of international cooperation, treaties and alliances are binding only as long as the participating states are willing to abide by the conditions of the agreement or are willing to submit disputes to some form of resolution. But such agreements can collapse. First, some participants might find their national goals are not well served and the agreement is ignored or violated. Thus, for example, the needs of particular Organization of Petroleum Exporting Countries (OPEC) member-states for additional revenue have resulted in recurrent violations of the agreements on production and pricing. Second, participants can disagree on what actions are acceptable. Thus, the United States and the Soviet Union repeatedly accuse each other of violating its interpretation of the SALT I (1972–1977) and SALT II (1979) treaties limiting offensive nuclear weapons. Third, fulfillment of the key objectives in an agreement might be impossible. For example, the Treaty of Locarno (1925) between Britain and Italy failed in its attempt to insure the border of France and Belgium with Germany, because Britain and Italy were not strong enough to counteract the reemergence and assertion of Germany's military power, and Italy's national interest eventually became more pro-German.

International Law

The broadest attempt to formalize and constrain the interactions among nation-states is international law. In 1625, Hugo Grotius, the ''father'' of international law, published *De jure belli ac Pacis (On the Laws of War and Peace)*. This document emphasized *natural law*—sensible forms of behavior that ought to guide the relations among states and restrain hostile or destructive interactions.

Unfortunately, ''sensible'' action is often defined by a state's political needs and is uncommon when deep disagreements or violence emerge between states. Thus, by the nineteenth century, natural law had been supplanted by *positivist law*—explicit, written agreements between states, in the form of international treaties or conventions. Positivist laws have attempted to adjudicate geographic boundaries (e.g., the three-mile limit on the waters around states), to regulate states' uses of environmental resources (e.g., laws limiting whale hunting in international waters), and to establish states' rights and limits over nonnational resources (e.g., the law of outer space).

The treaties and conventions of positivist law also attempt to distinguish acceptable from unacceptable behavior during conflicts between states. For example, the Helsinki Agreement binds the combatants to use no glass-filled projectiles

The World Court, The Hague, Netherlands

or other forms of violence that produce "unnecessary suffering." And the Geneva Convention on "fair" war making prohibits the use of poison gases and insists that captured soldiers be treated with dignity, although it does not preclude most of the terrible forms of suffering or death that a soldier can experience before she becomes a prisoner.

While positivist law has the great advantage of being formulated in explicit, written agreements, such agreements ultimately depend upon the willingness of states to comply. Some states refuse to sign particular agreements, sometimes signatories openly violate the agreements, and states often deny accusations that they have violated the agreements.

The International Court of Justice (the World Court) at the Hague can rule on alleged violations of positivist law; but the court has jurisdiction and binding decision authority only if both parties to the dispute accept its ruling. The court has occasionally provided a valuable mechanism for conflict resolution. But when the political or economic stakes are high or even when emotional elements of the disagreement are intense, states typically refuse to accept the court's jurisdiction or to be bound by its judgments.

One study found that of the 52 major cases considered by the court between 1946 and 1975, only 3 concerned violent conflicts between states (Holsti 1983:433). And only about one-third of the members of the United Nations have agreed to accept automatically the court's jurisdiction in matters affecting them.

The United States is one of those who reject the court's jurisdiction, as in a 1984 case regarding covert U.S. actions against the Nicaraguan government (such as mining Nicaraguan harbors). In fact, juridical resolution between states is more likely in the domestic court system of one of the disputants rather than in an international court.

An intriguing question: Is it reasonable for a state to refuse the court's jurisdiction? What do you think would happen to international politics if all states automatically accepted the court's jurisdiction?

International Organizations

Another overarching mechanism for conflict avoidance and conflict resolution is *international organizations*. A supranational government is created to provide a forum for communication between states, to implement policies that respond to problems that transcend national boundaries, to enact international laws and treaties, and to intervene in disputes between states. Two major efforts at international organizations have been created in the twentieth century. The League of Nations was formed in 1921 as a mechanism for collective security against aggression. But aggression by Italy in Ethiopia and by Japan in Manchuria in the 1930s revealed that the league lacked the diplomatic, political, or military power to achieve its goal.

After World War II, the United Nations was created (in 1946) as another attempt at international organization. While the United Nations has a mixed record of success and failure in its central objective of keeping the peace, it has improved the international political climate during its nearly 50 years. In a few instances, its multinational military force has performed a "peacekeeping" function by intervening between combatting groups (e.g., in Korea since 1950, in the Congo in 1960, and in Lebanon since 1978). In this sphere, it is especially effective at what former U.N. Secretary-General Dag Hammarskjöld (1953–1961) termed "preventive diplomacy"—the insulation of between-state crises from extensive political and military involvement by the major powers.

The United Nations also provides many nonmilitary services that enhance states' security, stability, and prosperity. In a quiet manner, its committees and agencies, such as the United Nations Educational, Social, and Cultural Organization (UNESCO), improve the quality of life and level of understanding among nations. Through its debates and resolutions, the United Nations can focus international attention on dangerous or irresponsible behavior by states. And, perhaps most importantly, the United Nations serves as a continuous open forum for formal and informal communication among the representatives of virtually every state.

COMPETITION AMONG STATES

Balance of Power

When the competing interests between states are stronger than their mutual interest, the states are unlikely to agree upon a cooperative strategy. In such situations, another way in which direct conflict can be avoided is if a balance of power emerges. This occurs if there is a rough equality in the power resources (political, economic, and especially military) that can be exercised by competing states. It can be understood as a situation where an actor is prevented from taking advantage of others because of the power that other actors have to retaliate.

The term *balance of power* is widely used and has many meanings. But there are a few key elements in the classic notion of balance of power, which is especially associated with political scientist Hans Morgenthau's 1948 book, *Politics among Nations: The Struggle for Power and Peace* (see also Gulick 1955; Kaplan 1957).

1. It is an attempt to maintain a general stability in the relations among states and to preserve the status quo.
2. It assumes that peace can be assured only by a balancing of contending states, because potential aggressors will be deterred only by overwhelming opposing power.
3. There are typically a few (usually four to six) major power states that are decisive in insuring that the balance is sustained.
4. These states, and others, constantly create shifting alliances, based only on self-interest and system equilibrium, never on friendship or ideology.
5. One or more power states must intervene in the relations between states or into the affairs of a single state to prevent actions that seem to threaten the overall balance of the system.
6. There will be periodic political violence and war, because states must use force to preserve themselves and because the system is not always in such balance that all between-state conflict is deterred.

Since the emergence of nation-states in the seventeenth century, there have usually been only a few states that, at any point in time, had both the desire and the power to project their interests over many other states. Some scholars characterize international relations during most of the period from the Peace of Westphalia in 1648 to the beginning of World War I in 1914 as a period of classic balance of power politics. This description applies primarily to relations among the European states, which tended to be the most significant in international politics during these 300 years. There were shifting alliances and the system did resemble that described above. Actually, Great Britain often played a major role as the "balancer." As Winston Churchill (1948) observed, "For 400 years the foreign policy of England has been to oppose the strongest, most aggressive, most dominating power on the continent, in joining the weaker states."

However, by the late nineteenth century, there were changes in the international system that made balance of power politics less possible. The growing importance of ideology and of nationalism were especially significant, because these factors hindered the ease with which alliances between states were made and broken. This was most clear in the deep antipathy that developed between France and Germany, who would inevitably be on opposite sides of any conflict.

The driving force of ideology became even more evident after World War II, with the hostility between the U.S. bloc and the Soviet bloc. The old pattern of flexible, nonideological balancing between a handful of independent states had broken down. In addition, the arena of between-state power struggles expanded from its narrow European base to a worldwide one. And the newer technologies of war reduced the ease with which war could be employed and controlled as a tool of foreign policy.

Thus the classic balance of power system no longer seems possible in the post–World War II era. Many observers still use the balance of power concept to describe contemporary international relations. They posit that a new type of *bipolar* balance emerged with the cold war in the late 1940s. In this view, the United States and its allies are generally balanced against the Soviet Union and its allies. The bipolar system is characterized by only two major power blocs. They are rather rigid in their ideological antipathy to each other and are inflexible in their alliance formation, but they do check each other's desire for hegemony (i.e., for clear domination of the international system).

Since the early 1970s, however, there has been a decline in the coherence of the U.S. and Soviet blocs and the emergence of additional power sources. Some analysts still describe the system as bipolar, since there is no state or coherent bloc of states that approaches the power of either of the two superpowers. But others characterize the current system as *multipolar*. In this view, major power actors now include not only the United States and the Soviet bloc, but also Western Europe, China, and groupings of "nonaligned" nations. While there has not been a return to classical balance of power politics—there is too much ideology and too little flexibility shaping alliance formation—there is a variety of sometimes stable and sometimes shifting alliances that prevent any single power bloc from asserting international hegemony. Occasionally, there is a surprising alliance shift, such as the conflict between China and the Soviet Union and the subsequent cooperation between China and the United States after 1972.

In the current *multipolar* system, open conflict between states does occur, as particular power groups attempt to gain advantage on specific issues and to expand their spheres of influence. Empirical research suggests that in the twentieth century, unlike the nineteenth century, (1) the more extensive the pattern of alliances, the more likely there will be war in the international system; and (2) the states that are in alliances are more likely to be involved in wars (Small and Singer 1982; see also Russett and Starr, 1989:99–123). But the complex distribution of power resources has been sufficiently balanced to discourage any bloc from a direct, general military confrontation with another bloc. Rather, as is discussed later in this chapter, the major powers tend to fight "proxy wars" against each other in third states.

Another intriguing question: What will be the next pattern of power relations in the international system? One scholar's provocative answer is that there will be a bipolar system, with Germany, France, and the Soviet Union on one side, and the United States, Japan, and China on the other (Brucan 1984). What is your prediction?

Balance of Terror

While the idea of a loose equilibrium among states might appear attractive and sensible, it has not prevented considerable conflict and violence in the relations among states. And, perhaps even more important than the changes noted above, the balance of power system has been perverted by the enormous destructive capacity of modern military technologies. War is no longer a subtle and controllable option among states with the capacity to wreak massive devastation on their opponents and to risk equal destruction at home.

Among those states with nuclear weapons, the balance of power goal in the contemporary world is a broad equilibrium: Each bloc must believe that it has sufficient military and nuclear capacity to discourage others from attacking. But the problem with such a strategy of mutual deterrence is that each bloc fears vulnerability: Does a rival have a numerical superiority in weapons or firepower? Does a rival have a technically superior system? Could a rival's first strike destroy one's capacity for second-strike retaliation? (A more detailed discussion at the end of this chapter [see Box 13.2] describes how deterrence is analyzed using a version of game theory called *expected utility theory*.)

To overcome such uncertainties, destructive capacity, numbers of weapons, and technical development are expanded to a point where a state or bloc of states has great confidence that it can inflict catastrophic and unacceptable damage on any other state. Thus, the balance of power has evolved into a balance of terror, a system of "mutually assured destruction" (MAD). Even at this point, the fear of technological breakthroughs by rivals and the inherent desire for superiority induce each bloc to expand military capability to an extraordinary, and excessive, magnitude. This continual expansion of the level of military power a bloc believes it needs to balance potential rivals results in an arms race that produces arsenals capable of massive, even total, annihilation of humankind. In short, balance of power politics has become a dangerous and possibly irrational mechanism for regulating the relations among powerful states in the nuclear age.

Domination and Dependence

While all states enjoy sovereign equality, it is obvious that some states are far more powerful than others. Few relations between states are perfectly symmetrical, in the sense that neither state enjoys greater ability to influence or control the actions of the other. This section discusses the situation where one state has very substantial power over another state. The capacity of one state to alter the actions of another state can be based on different forms of leverage, although there are three primary mechanisms of control:

1. *Economic* leverage is based on the advantageous trade, financial interactions, or economic aid that the state can provide (or withhold from) another state.
2. *Military* leverage can be applied either negatively, via the use or threat of military action against a state, or positively, via military assistance in the form of protection, provision of military resources, or training.
3. *Political* leverage is derived from the ability of a state to affect the actions of another state by the application of its political resources, such as its negotiating skills, its effective political institutions, or its influence in interstate relations.

Colonialism/Imperialism.   In the twentieth century, particular attention has focussed on extremely uneven patterns of dominance and dependence between states, and especially on the master-servant relations usually termed *colonialism* or *imperialism*. Various goals might motivate a state to attain mastery over another state. First, the subordinate state can provide resources, both human and physical, for the master state. Second, the subordinate state can be a controlled market for the products of the master state. Third, the subordinate state can serve important strategic functions, either as a buffer between the master state and its rivals or as a staging area for the master state's political or military objectives. Fourth, a state with a missionary zeal might dominate another state to insure that its values (usually political or religious) guide the subordinate state. Fifth, a state might want to dominate another state to gain international prestige.

While all forms of colonial domination entail a mix of economic, military, and political control, master states have employed different emphases.

1.   In the *segregationist* style of colonialism, the master state is quite explicit in its exploitation of the servant state. There is little or no attempt to improve the economic, political, or social systems in the servant state. This style generally characterized the relations of Belgium, Germany, and Portugal with their African and Asian colonial territories.

2.   In the *assimilationist* style, there is some attempt to transform the servant state into an external extension of the master state. While still exploiting the servant state, the institutions, knowledge, and culture of the master state are introduced to the elite of the servant state and become a basis for political, economic, and cultural development. This style is particularly associated with French colonialism in Africa and Asia and with Soviet colonialism.

3.   In the style of *indirect rule,* the master state uses the traditional leaders and institutions of governance and culture in the servant state as intermediaries in its control, but it also introduces the modern forms of the master state that will eventually supplant traditional forms. The British approach to its vast empire (prior to the independence movement after 1945) is the classic example of indirect rule, and this mode of colonialism also seems to correspond to the style used by the United States in some Latin American and Pacific Rim states.

Neocolonialism.   In the nearly half-century since World War II, most states have, willingly or reluctantly, granted independence to their colonial holdings. But it is not the case that political independence has liberated all those servant states from fundamental domination by a master state. The label *neocolonialism* is given to new forms of domination and dependence that are nearly as powerful as those under colonialism. These new forms were described in Chapter 11, in the discussion of dependency approaches to explaining the lack of development in many of the states gaining political independence in the postcolonial era (i.e., after 1945).

Despite official withdrawal by the master state, especially of its direct political and military presence, domination has been maintained, especially by economic leverage. Through the use of foreign aid, loans, technology transfer, military support, and economic intervention, the master state can continue to control many of the actions of a supposedly independent state. The actions of the master state become relatively invisible, and its interests are also served by a subtle alliance of a small internal elite, transnational corporations, and other transnational actors, such as the International Monetary Fund (Evans 1979; Cardoso and Faletto 1979).

Some analysts such as Immanuel Wallerstein (1980) take this perspective a further step, arguing that individual master states have been replaced by a *world system* of domination and dependence. Some states (especially the United States, the European Communities, the Soviet Union, and Japan) compose the "core" areas, which control the production and sale of most modern goods and services for the international market by means of a diversified economy and skilled labor. Other "periphery" areas (especially the Third World states) produce mainly raw materials and simple goods for export, and are subject to systematic exploitation by and subordination to the core states. As a consequence, the peripheral state's economy is severely distorted. There is minimal economic development and welfare distribution. This results in social disorder and political decay, leading to repressive government and increasing dependence on external actors. In general, the dependency approaches emphasize the capacity of a handful of powerful states to manipulate the international political economy to their enormous advantage. The recent history of Zaire (see Box 13.1) exemplifies the impacts of colonialism and neocolonialism on vulnerable Third World states.

BOX 13.1

The Faces of Colonialism: Zaire

Zaire is in the hub of Africa, a large, resource-rich state (one-fourth the size of the United States) located in the center of the continent. It encompasses more than 30 million people and 250 ethnic groups. King Leopold of Belgium sponsored expeditions down the Congo River and in 1879 he claimed the area as his own private kingdom. Leopold's companies extracted the natural resources ruthlessly and treated the people with brutality. In 1908, the area was placed under Belgian colonial administration. Military forces were used to "pacify" the population and local men were forced into virtual slavery as workers in the mines and on the plantations. The colonial regime provided only minimal education to the population, and encouraged Catholic missionaries to teach the population the great virtue of obedience to authority.

The Belgians continued to exploit the resources of the Congo until the point where internal unrest and the general liberation of African colonies made it clear that the time of Belgian colonial rule in the Congo was over. Within about one year after substantial resistance to Belgian rule emerged, Belgium granted the Congo its independence on June 30, 1960. Belgium withdrew its military and administrative personnel and also most of its financial and technical support from the new state.

BOX 13.1 *continued*

Unprepared for self-rule, and without the Belgians' order-maintaining institutions, the Congo soon found its political system in disarray. The Congolese elite broke into competing factions and the country collapsed into civil war when the wealthy province of Katanga attempted to secede. The remaining Belgians fled, leaving the country in chaos. The United Nations sent in a peacekeeping force, and the Soviet Union also began to provide support for some groups in the Congo. With assistance from Western countries (and the apparent assistance of the U.S. Central Intelligence Agency [CIA]), an army leader, Joseph Mobuto, led the army of the central government to victory over Katanga and also assassinated the prime minister.

In 1965, Mobuto, now army chief of staff, led a coup that overthrew the civilian government, and installed himself under a one-party system that has continued until today. Mobuto "Africanized" his society, changing his own name to Mobuto Sese Seko and the country's name to Zaire. Another insurrection in Shaba (previously Katanga) was defeated in 1977. Despite the authoritarian rule of Mobuto, the clear evidence of widespread corruption, and the persistent failure of the economy, his staunch anti-Communism has won him substantial economic and military support from the United States.

Since "independence," Mobuto's victories over Katanga/Shaba and his long tenure in office have depended upon foreign aid, loans, technology transfer, and military support from Western countries, especially the United States. Zaire has relied heavily on foreign corporations to build and maintain the mines, factories, and infrastructure facilities in Zaire. Due to volatility in the price of copper, Zaire's major export product, the state has amassed huge deficits, and has received huge loans from the International Monetary Fund (IMF), a consortium of First World banking institutions.

The IMF has agreed several times to extend and restructure Zaire's debt of more than $4 billion (the largest in Africa); but the IMF has demanded "conditionality"— the requirement that Zaire accept crucial economic policies demanded by the IMF, including devaluation of the currency, cutting real wages, and drastically reducing social welfare programs. There have even been extended periods when Zaire has been obliged to allow its national banking system to be run by a six-person group of Europeans sent in by the IMF. The level of education is declining, the country can no longer feed itself, the infrastructure system (e.g., roads, water supply, telecommunications, etc.) is in shambles. The real wages of urban workers are now only one-tenth of what they were at independence. Despite the appalling poverty of most Zairians, Mobuto and his cronies are prosperous and he is rumored to be the wealthiest person in black Africa, with holdings of more than $10 billion outside of Zaire.

Zaire's political leaders and economic system are deeply dependent upon Western capital. After 80 years under a brutal and exploitive colonial system, 30 years of "independence" have brought no blossoming of democratic politics, no sharing of the society's abundant resources among its people, no economic development. Rather, contemporary Zaire is a tragic product of colonialism and neocolonialism, a state characterized by poverty, corruption, oppression, economic chaos, and dependence on foreign states and foreign economic actors.

One of the most ideologically charged issues in international politics is the extent to which a few states do reap enormous benefits through their domination of many less developed countries. The dependency approach provides both an explanation for underdevelopment and also a basis for demands that the prosperous states redistribute their resources to those states that have been exploited. And it describes the global elaboration of the patterns of dominance and dependence that were established under colonialism.

Evolution to Transnationalism?   In most versions of the dependency approach, the major beneficiaries have been a few capitalist/imperialist states. But the current international system might be evolving beyond a state-centered approach to one that emphasizes *transnational relations*. From the perspective of transnationalism, the crucial resources of goods, wealth, and information move across national boundaries without significant, direct participation or control by governmental actors (Keohane and Nye 1972; Russett and Starr 1989:492). The most powerful actors are multinational corporations (e.g., General Motors, Matsushita, Exxon, Siemens, Nissan, and IBM) and other nonstate actors (that is, actors whose members and interests are independent of any particular state, such as the International Monetary Fund, NATO, and OPEC).

State boundaries have little significance for transnational actors. This is a system where the economic interests of these actors shape international relations more than the military security concerns of individual states. Actors pursue economic gain in a world economy and their behavior is primarily guided by the pursuit of profit, not loyalty to a particular state. Comparing economic power (GNP or gross sales in 1985), only 60 of the top 100 economic units in the world were countries, and 40 were multinational corporations (Todaro, 1989: 471–473).

In short, it is possible that international relations in the world after the year 2000 will be determined as much by transnational actors as by nation-states. Would the relentless pursuit of profit produce a more peaceful or more just world than the relentless pursuit of state power?

VIOLENCE BETWEEN STATES

War is sustained, organized violence between states. Such violence, especially when employed by military forces, is the ultimate mechanism for resolving conflict between nations. Chapter 12 indicated that political violence, especially war, represents the failure of politics for those who define politics as conflict resolution. But most people probably agree with Karl von Clausewitz's (1833/1967:87) famous dictum, "War is a political instrument, a continuation of political activity by other means." Thus war is the use of violence by one state to achieve its political goals at the expense of another state.

Robert Ardrey, a well-known ethologist (a person who studies animal behavior to better understand human behavior) wryly observes that "human war has been the most successful of all our cultural traditions.'' That is, history is marked by recurrent episodes of organized violence between groups, nations, and states. Indeed, world history is usually presented to us as a subject dominated by wars, which are treated as the exceptional and notable phenomena through time.

The elimination of war is not among the accomplishments of the modern world. One author estimates that for the past 40 years, an average of 12 wars are being conducted throughout the world on any given day (Sampson 1978:60). And a major analysis of wars between 1816 and 1980 found that while the number of wars that break out has been relatively constant over time, the number of wars at any given time, measured as the total number of nation-months of war, fluctuates and has increased substantially since 1900 (Small and Singer 1982). In short, the outbreak of wars is not more frequent than in the past, but there is more ''war in progress'' in the contemporary era.

There also seem fewer *conventional wars* in the late twentieth century—that is, wars that entail the direct confrontation of the military forces of two states within a defined space, usually occurring on the soil of one or both combatants. The Iran-Iraq War (1980–1988) is an example of a conventional war. But many recent wars seem unconventional, in large part because of the new technologies of war. Many are what the Pentagon terms *low-intensity conflicts,* involving more geographically dispersed and sporadic episodes of violence. In addition, the combatants include various civilian and paramilitary groups, as well as military forces. And often these wars are sustained by, and explicitly serve the policy goals of, states other than the combatants.

The ongoing struggle in Lebanon (since 1975) seems a prototype of the contemporary unconventional war. (There is further discussion of the Lebanese conflict in Chapter 16.) At one level, it is an internal, civil war between Lebanese Muslims and Maronite Christians, with intermittent fighting at various locations in Lebanon. There are also other internal struggles, particularly between Sunni, Shi'ite and Druze sects among the Muslims. And there are armed hostilities between large families, which operate in a Mafia-like style.

In addition, there are more internationalized conflicts, especially between Lebanese groups and the Syrian army, which has invaded and occupied parts of Lebanon several times. The location of the Palestinian Liberation Organization (PLO) headquarters in Lebanon has also prompted extensive military intervention by Israel. At times, the Lebanese struggle has also been viewed as a *proxy war* between Israel and Syria being fought in Lebanon. France, the United States, the Soviet Union, and other Arab states have been active, attempting to resolve the Lebanese conflict in a manner that serves their own national interests.

In a proxy war, an internal civil war or a war of liberation is sustained in large part because it is a means by which external powers engage in violent competition within the territory of some third state. The external powers can sustain the conflict through military and economic support, or they might actually deploy their own military forces, as Israel and Syria have done in Lebanon. Chad is another country that has become a proxy war battleground. The fighting there, which began 20 years ago as a civil war, now involves about a dozen factions;

TABLE 13.1. Death in Wars, 1820–1965

Period	Deaths (millions)
1820–1863	2.0
1864–1907	4.5
World War I era	8.5
World War II era	80.0
1945–1965	35.0

SOURCE: Adapted from Russett 1965:12–13.

but the conflict has been internationalized through the intervention of Libya and the Western states, represented by France, the United States, and Zaire.

The changing turf and nature of many contemporary wars are most evident in the enormous increase in the proportion of civilian deaths. Whereas in World War I there was only one war-related civilian death for every eight military deaths, in World War II there were two civilian deaths for every military death. Even more distressing is the huge increase in the total number of deaths in war. Russett (1965:12–13), who gathered the data presented in Table 13.1, observes that death from war has increased by a factor of 10 during each 50-year period from 1820 to 1965 and that, if this rate of increase continues, "wars by around the end of this century would kill the equivalent of the [1965] population of the globe." (You should note that Russett has a more inclusive definition of deaths associated with a war than does Rummel, whose analysis in Table 12.2 is probably a more precise estimate of actual war deaths among combatants.)

The technological sophistication and scale of war are also evident in the enormous costs associated with preparations for war. Together, the United States and the Soviet Union spend more than $100 million *per day* just to increase their nuclear arsenals. And worldwide, more than $800 billion was spent in 1985 on military preparedness (Russett and Starr 1989: Appendix B). This massive allocation of resources to support the security objectives of states could, if redirected to prosperity goals, provide a very substantial enhancement of the quality of life for the citizens in those states. The problem, of course, is that the policy makers believe that security goals have highest priority and that security is the *sine qua non* for fulfilling prosperity goals. And, in an era of high-tech warfare, virtually no one feels truly secure, leading every state to push itself and its rivals into an accelerating, unending, and potentially devastating system with the capacity for massive political violence.

What Causes War?

Are there fundamental causes of war? Studies have attempted to determine whether there are some attributes of a state and/or its population that result in a greater propensity of the state to engage in war. Such attributes include the state's size, its economic system, its political system, its cultural features, its geographic position, its wealth, its religion, its rate of modernization. Among the characteristics that do seem correlated with a state's propensity to war are strong nationalism, shorter period of statehood, and lower (but not the lowest) levels of economic development. Some argue that states are most prone to be involved in a war when they are undergoing a substantial power transition in the international pecking order: either (1) when they have substantial new capacity and resources and want to assert their new international power position; or (2) when they are in major decline that is not yet reflected in their existing power position (Organski and Kugler 1980).

At the "ultimate" level, however, three broad alternative explanations of war are usually offered.

1. War can be attributed to scarcity in *nature*. Because the consumption goals of states are greater than the natural resources available, states undertake war to protect or capture resources from other states. Thus states struggle with each other for the control of such resources as people, food, minerals, and strategic locations.
2. War can be attributed to the inadequacy of *institutions*. In this systemic view, neither the existing sociopolitical structures nor the rules governing the conduct among states are adequate to prevent states from using force to achieve their objectives. Thus nation-states are guided by self-interest, and there are no conflict resolution mechanisms that prevent the occasional explosion of large-scale interstate violence.
3. War can be explained by *human nature*. From this perspective, humans are innately aggressive, as a biological species. Humans are virtually the only species that engages in widespread killing of its own kind. And humans, it is claimed, are acquisitive, competitive, and selfish by nature, rather than by nurture. Thus war becomes a predictable group-level manifestation of these inherent qualities.

Each of these three explanations of war also suggests possible "solutions" that might eliminate war.

1. If the problem is scarcity of natural resources, one might look to *technological solutions,* as states develop new techniques for more efficient exploitation of natural resources and for the development of substitutes for scarce resources.
2. If the problem is inadequate institutions, the need is for *social engineering*—for the creation of new organizational arrangements that more effectively structure the relations among individuals and states. In the political domain, this might ultimately entail the creation of viable world government.
3. If the problem is human nature, the solution is found in *human engineering,* by means of comprehensive political socialization or perhaps even

by genetic manipulation to create a population with the "proper" qualities.

The first and second versions of the causes of war are generally associated with a broad interpretation of international relations called the *idealist perspective*. The idealist perspective assumes that human nature is basically good. People's natural tendencies toward altruism, cooperation, and mutual aid are subverted by flawed social institutions. Aggressive behavior by nation-states is not inevitable and can be eliminated with the use of appropriate institutions, including diplomacy, treaties, international law, and organizations.

The third version of the causes of war is generally associated with the *realist perspective,* a less optimistic view of international relations. Both interpersonal life and between-group relations are fundamentally based on a struggle to dominate others. People are neither good nor controllable. The states they form will pursue self-interest and self-preservation. A state makes alliances or breaks them, makes war or insures peace solely on the basis of its leaders' calculations of what will further the state's interests. Political violence is an inevitable element of the relations between states. Clearly, the realist perspective is consistent with the supreme importance attached to national self-interest in the balance of power approach described above.

There is some evidence in support of each of these three general explanations of the causes of war. But there is also sufficient counterevidence so that none of the three positions is compelling as a complete explanation of war. Neither abundance of natural resources nor advanced technology have insured the absence of intergroup violence. And while there are societies whose members have not been driven by human nature into warlike behavior against their neighbors, no set of human institutions has been shown inevitably to generate war or perpetuate peace between states.

Most social scientists assume that war is probabilistic rather than deterministic. That is, war is best explained by a complex set of resource and institutional variables, embedded within a unique context of historical circumstances and chance events, and guided by individual personalities and group dynamics. While the complete elimination of war might be impossible, it does seem that a combination of material abundance, effective institutions, and thorough socialization could reduce the incidence of war. The question is whether this combination can be identified and implemented by political actors.

Is War Justifiable?

Chapter 12 probed your views about the conditions under which political violence might be legitimate. The same issues are germane on an even larger scale regarding the justification of war. Despite the massive human and financial costs of war, few would support the proposition that there are absolutely no conditions under which war is justified. But what are the circumstances which justify war?

A classic justification for war is the doctrine of *self-defense,* a position associated with St. Augustine (354–430 A.D.). A victim of an unprovoked attack has the right to use violence as a means of protection. Apart from total pacifists, there are few who would reject the principle of self-defense as a legitimate rationale for violence. But the application of this principle might be subject to considerable disagreement, especially in the relations among states. Here are some examples: Might state A engage in nonviolent actions that are so provocative that state B is justified in responding with violence? What if the initial violence against state B is by an actor from state A who does not have the sanction or the explicit support of state A? What if the violence by state A was unintentional? What if the initial violence is within the territory of state A but is perceived as directly harmful to citizens or interests of state B? What if state B uses violence to prevent state A from the (expected) use of far more substantial violence? What if the violent response of state B is of far greater magnitude than the violence by state A? Wars sometimes develop because there are such patterns of misperception, accident, preemption, and incremental escalation (Schelling 1960).

Frequently, however, war is justified on the more ambiguous rationale, associated with St. Ambrose (339–397 A.D.), of the *defense of universal principles*. In this view, "man has a moral duty to employ force to resist active wickedness, for to refrain from hindering evil when possible is tantamount to promoting it." But in the contemporary world, it is difficult to identify truly universal principles in whose defense war is always justifiable. Even the interpretations of "active wickedness" and "evil" are not shared across all cultures. Obviously, not all citizens in every state will be persuaded either by the Ayatollah Khomeini's justification for *jihad* (holy war) against the infidels (those who do not believe in Mohammed) or by President Reagan's mid-1980s justification for military action against the minions of the Soviet Union's "evil empire."

In most cases of international political violence, a justification based on universal principles is invoked. State power is used against other states in the name of many principles, such as capitalism, communism, freedom, social justice, human rights, self-determination, territorial integrity, egalitarianism, religious freedom, religious orthodoxy, and so on. But all states do not accept a single vision of natural law that provides universal principles to govern international relations. Moreover, the international system itself has not implemented powerful and effective institutional mechanisms for conflict avoidance. Thus occasional outbreaks of interstate conflict and war are inevitable.

The crucial point is that the context of international politics is essentially *amoral*. Recognition of this fact is the key to understanding most behavior in international relations, whether diplomatic activities, alliances, or war. At some points, a state's actions in the international environment are constrained by *its* view of morality and of universal principles. But at other points, a state's decision makers might decide that virtually any action is acceptable, if the action seems to further the state's achievement of its security, stability, and prosperity goals. If either view is correct, what are the chances that contemporary states will ever meet the requirement of the United Nations Charter that states "settle their international disputes by peaceful means in such a manner that international peace and security, and justice, are not endangered"?

BOX 13.2

Deterring Rivals through Military Power

How does a state decide that it has sufficient military power to deter its military rival from employing violence against it? While there can never be absolute certainty, short of conquering or destroying the rival, there are calculations that are made to provide some measure of the extent to which the rival is deterred. Many of these calculations are based on *rational choice theory* (see the appendix). This section details how a version of the rational choice theory called *expected utility theory* has been used to analyze international relations by those who make foreign policy, as well as by social scientists.

There are several key concepts in expected utility theory. First, each outcome (possible result) has a certain *utility,* which is a numeric value that measures a political actor's perception or judgment of how desirable or undesirable each possible outcome of interstate relations would be. Second, each outcome is attributed a *probability,* which is the presumed likelihood of that outcome rather than some other outcome. The *expected utility* of a particular situation is determined by multiplying each utility by its associated probability, and then comparing different situations that might emerge. These comparisons provide the actor with information about which behaviors that actor should undertake and which behaviors are most likely from others. These are only estimations, and are based on one's best judgments about probabilities. It can be especially difficult to estimate the values of one's rivals. But this approach has been used very effectively by political scientists to predict when nations will go to war, to predict what foreign policy choice a nation is likely to make, and to estimate whether a rival is deterred from using nuclear weapons (see Bueno de Mesquita 1981, 1984, 1985).

Table 13.2 provides a highly simplified application of expected utility theory to determine whether a political rival is deterred from using nuclear weapons. Peace-loving state A has determined the utilities that bellicose state B attaches to four possible situations. In this example, the best of all possible outcomes is given a utility of +100 (it could be any number, all the way to positive infinity), and the worst outcome imaginable has a utility of −100.

In cell a, neither B nor A use nuclear weapons. (This could mean there are no hostilities between A and B or that A and B refrain from using nuclear weapons, despite hostilities.) State A believes that B would find that situation reasonably desirable, since B could carry on its other activities without the threat of nuclear holocaust, and so the estimated utility is 85. Similarly, A estimates that B would be absolutely delighted if it attacked A with nuclear weapons and A did not respond (cell b, utility = +99). If A attacked and B did not respond, it would be quite terrible, but at least the damage might be minimized, relative to a total war, and thus some parts of B might survive (cell c, utility = −95, better A'ed than dead). If there was nuclear attack and retaliation, it is presumed that B would find the outcome a bit more positive than negative (cell d, utility = +10). Similarly, A decides that the probability of B not using nuclear weapons if A does not is .8, and that the probability B might strike first is .2. If A does use nuclear weapons, it is assumed that the probability is .95 that B will also use nuclear weapons, and only .05 that B will refrain from using such weapons.

By multiplying each utility by the associated probability, one gets four expected utility scores. Then the two expected utilities if B does not use nuclear weapons are summed, and compared to the two expected utilities if B does use nuclear weapons.

BOX **13.2** *continued*

Since the total expected utility for not using nuclear weapons (63.25) is higher than the total from using nuclear weapons (29.3), B has been deterred from using nuclear weapons. State B does a similar calculation for A and decides that A also has a higher expected utility from not using nuclear weapons. The world is saved!

From a strategic perspective, notice that the objective is to shift the expected utilities so that B's "not nuke" options have an increasingly higher value relative to the "nuke" options. Most areas that a state can manipulate relate to its own nuclear capabilities. The *utility* B attaches to various outcomes can be altered to the extent that A has the capacity for such a massive nuclear response that the impact on B will be devastating. Thus A is induced to increase the magnitude of its potential response (increase megatonnage and number of weapons) and to increase the effectiveness of its response in reaching the targets (improve the technology of weapons' delivery systems). The *probability* of different behaviors by B can be altered by insuring that A can respond under any circumstances. This means that A must develop a certain second-strike capacity so that B will not believe that it can use a massive first strike to eliminate A's ability to respond. It is also important for A's political leaders to make clear their firm resolve to respond if attacked.

Ultimate Weapons?

The Strategic Defense Initiative (SDI, or "Star Wars") is an effort to develop a system that primarily alters the *rival's* capability to use nuclear weapons (and thus the rival's expected utility), rather than to enhance one's own capability. Opponents of Star Wars have identified two crucial problems with this "defensive" system.

TABLE 13.2. Expected Utility Theory Applied to Nuclear Deterrence

STATE A	STATE B Not use nuclear weapons $U \times P = EU$	Use nuclear weapons $U \times P = EU$
Not use nuclear weapons	a $85 \times .8 = 68.0$	b $99 \times .2 = 19.8$
Use nuclear weapons	c $-95 \times .05 = -4.75$	d $10 \times .95 = 9.5$
Sum of *EU*s:	63.25	29.3

Conclusion: State B is deterred from using nuclear weapons because B's expected utility for not using nuclear weapons (63.25) is higher than its expected utility for using them (29.3).

NOTE: U = the utility (value) attached to an outcome (here, A's perception of B's utility).
  P = the probability of a certain action (here, A's judgment of the probability that B will act in a certain way).
  EU = the expected utility (the utility times the probability for a certain action outcome combination).

BOX 13.2 *continued*

First, most scientists claim that it is not technically possible to create a workable system that would effectively destroy enough incoming nuclear weapons. Second, even if such a system could be built, it would alter the entire framework for current deterrence calculations. Thus the rival, who has no reason to trust its opponent, would be obliged to develop new technologies that cannot be deterred by the Star Wars system. Or the rival might decide that it is forced to attack before the new technologies are deployed. Thus, such a system would be inherently destabilizing, since it would substantially change the entire basis for deterrence.

One "ultimate" deterrent might be "The Doomsday Machine" in the film *Dr. Strangelove*. Recall that the Doomsday Machine is a system of nuclear weapons that will be detonated if *any* nuclear weapon explodes, anywhere in the world. The Doomsday explosion will produce a nuclear shroud that will cover the entire planet and destroy all life. In terms of expected utility theory, it is the perfect deterrent: It has a utility of -100 (everything and everyone is destroyed) and it has a probability of 1.00 (it would be activated automatically, with no human decision involved). Of course, the irony of this ultimate deterrent, in the bleak vision of the film, is that the Doomsday Machine has been activated but its existence has not yet been announced, since the Soviet Union's leader is planning a dramatic media event to reveal its existence. In the meantime, a technical mistake leads to an accidental nuclear strike against the Soviet Union by a gung-ho U.S. bomber.

The calculation in Table 13.2 is obviously quite simplified. Pentagon planners use supercomputers to develop extraordinarily complex scenarios about possible interactions among rivals, but most are based on the kinds of assumptions in this game-theoretic framework. It is crucial to gain the best possible information about the capabilities of the rival; hence the need for continual surveillance (spying) on the rival is essential to these calculations.

Notice how the "logic" of deterrence leads toward mutually assured destruction. Each side is compelled to expand its nuclear capabilities to a level where there is no doubt about its capacity to inflict massive damage in a nuclear confrontation. Of course, one of the problems with such extensive and devastating capabilities is that any small mistake can have the most horrendous consequences, and it is more difficult to limit violence if a nuclear exchange does somehow begin. Hence there is a real madness to MAD.

CHAPTER 14

The First World

The House of Parliament, London, United Kingdom

THE FIRST, SECOND, THIRD, AND FOURTH WORLDS

Chapters 14–16 aim at the impossible: to characterize the key features of politics, both within states and between states, for the more than 160 nation-states in the contemporary political world. As you discovered in Part 1, a central goal of political analysis is to develop more general descriptions and explanations of political phenomena. In order to allow for some generalizations in discussing all these states, it is obviously necessary to use some taxonomic system. Given the vast complexity and variations among states, no taxonomy is really satisfactory. These chapters will use one of the classifications that is commonly employed, based on the concept of different "worlds."

Both social scientists and the media frequently refer to a category of nation-states termed the *Third World* and there are occasional references to a *Fourth World*. It is less common to see the terms *First World* and *Second World,* because these groups of states are usually labelled the *Western democracies* and the *Soviet bloc*. Chapters 14–16 examine these four worlds, describing their characteristic approaches to achieving the key goals of prosperity, stability, and security.

In order to provide you with a broad understanding, we shall emphasize general patterns within each world, highlighting similarities within worlds and differences between them. But you should recognize that

There are substantial differences between states within each world, especially in the vast set of states lumped together as the Third World.

Each state has unique features that will be lost in such generalized discussion.

There are some instances where a trait is more similar among some states across worlds, rather than among all the states within one world.

This method of grouping the states for analysis and generalizations is not perfect. As you read these chapters, you should assess the extent to which this classificatory scheme is accurate and provides a useful means of organizing a discussion of more than 160 nation-states.

How are the four worlds distinguished? The First and Second worlds share some crucial characteristics. Both are composed of nation-states that are relatively modern and industrialized. These states are urbanized, secularized, and have highly specialized and institutionalized political and economic systems. But First World and Second World states are particularly different on the dimensions introduced in Table 8.3: level of democratic politics and type of political economy.

The *First World* states have (1) relatively democratic politics, in which people enjoy broad political and personal freedom and citizens have a genuine choice among political leaders; and (2) political economies with rather high levels of private control, ranging from mixed economies toward market economies. The two dozen First World states are listed in Table 14.1. This group includes such countries as Australia, Canada, Japan, Sweden, the United States, and West Germany, and has a total population of about 675 million.

TABLE 14.1. Classification of States into Four Worlds

First World

Australia	Iceland	Norway
Austria	Ireland	Portugal
Belgium	Israel	Spain
Canada	Italy	Sweden
Denmark	Japan	Switzerland
Finland	Luxembourg	United Kingdom
France	Netherlands	United States
Greece	New Zealand	West Germany

Second World

Albania	East Germany	Romania
Bulgaria	Hungary	Soviet Union
Czechoslovakia	Poland	Yugoslavia

Third World

Algeria	Guatemala	Oman
Argentina	Guinea-Bissau	Panama
Bahrain	Guyana	Papua New Guinea
Barbados	Honduras	Paraguay
Bolivia	Indonesia	Peru
Botswana	Iran	Philippines
Brazil	Iraq	Qatar
Cameroon	Ivory Coast	Saudi Arabia
Chile	Jamaica	Senegal
China	Jordan	South Africa
Colombia	Kuwait	Swaziland
Congo	Lebanon	Syria
Costa Rica	Liberia	Thailand
Cuba	Libya	Trinidad and Tobago
Cyprus	Malaysia	Tunisia
Dominican Republic	Malta	Turkey
Ecuador	Mauritius	United Arab Emirates
Egypt	Mexico	Uruguay
El Salvador	Morocco	Venezuela
Equatorial Guinea	Mozambique	Vietnam
Fiji	Nicaragua	Zambia
Gabon	Nigeria	Zimbabwe
Ghana	North Korea	

Fourth World

Afghanistan	Cambodia	India
Angola	Central African Republic	Kenya
Bangladesh	Chad	Laos
Benin	Ethiopia	Lesotho
Bhutan	Gambia	Malagasy Republic
Burkina Faso	Guinea	Malawi
Burundi	Haiti	Mali

TABLE 14.1. *continued*

Fourth World		
Mauritania	Rwanda	Togo
Mongolia	Sierra Leone	Uganda
Myanmar (Burma)	Somalia	Western Samoa
Nepal	Sri Lanka	Yemen
Niger	Sudan	Zaire
Pakistan	Tanzania	

Newly Industrialized Countries (NICs)		
Hong Kong[a]	South Korea	Taiwan
Singapore		

[a]While it is classified as a NIC, Hong Kong is not an independent state but rather a crown colony of the United Kingdom, which has leased the territory from China since 1898; the 99-year lease is due to expire in 1997.

The *Second World* includes the Soviet Union, its seven East European bloc allies, and Yugoslavia (Table 14.1). The total population of these states is about 450 million. This group has shared key characteristics since World War II: (1) they are generally modernized, industrialized and urbanized; (2) they have had relatively totalitarian politics, with limited political and personal freedom and minimal control over the selection or actions of political leaders; and (3) their political economies have been close to the command economy end of the continuum. This category might soon become obsolete. Most of them might become similar to First World states, *if* the recent sweeping changes in these states' politics and political economies (see Chapter 15) are institutionalized in the 1990s. But their political systems have been very distinct from those in the First World for more than forty years, and thus your understanding of the political world will be enhanced by examining these states as a separate group.

Between the late 1950s and the early 1970s, the *Third World* was a term applied to those states that, by their own definition, were "nonaligned" states—that is, their political spokesmen claimed they were not under the strong control of either the United States and its allies or the Soviet Union and its allies. Others used the term Third World quite broadly, to refer to all nation-states that achieved independence after 1945. The latter approach is closest to the one used in this book, and thus the term includes virtually all states not classified in the First and Second worlds. This category is huge, with more than 140 nation-states and a population of 3.4 billion people.

Most of these states have forms of politics and political economies that are similar to those in the first two worlds. Thus some Third World states have command economies and others have market economies. Some have very democratic politics and others are quite totalitarian. The crucial analytic difference that seems to distinguish Third and Fourth World states from states in the First and Second Worlds is that the levels of economic development and modernization in Third

BOX 14.1

A Note about Bias in Political Analysis

In its pure form, the method of science might be value-free. But in the analysis of politics, it is impossible for the analyst to describe and explain without being influenced by his own values. This fact is especially important as you consider the chapters in Part 5. It is likely that most readers of this book (like the book's author) have lived primarily in First World states. In most of these states, the patterns of political socialization are strongly biased in favor of First World politics and economics and against any other forms, especially those of the Second World. Notice that even the language of the classificatory scheme itself subtly seems to award "first" place to the industrialized Western democracies, "second" place to the industrialized socialist systems, and "third" place to the developing countries.

As I wrote these chapters, I attempted to be sensitive to my own political biases (I recognize some of them, but others are subconscious) and I attempted to be fair in describing, analyzing, and generalizing about the different political systems. But in Part 5, and throughout the book, there are value judgments embedded in every choice about what content is included and how it is presented. In these chapters, every paragraph includes generalizations to which there are exceptions, and observations that might be at variance with your own views.

It is very appropriate for you to assess whether the basis of the claims in these chapters is sound and to consider what biases affect the discussion. The chapters are based on my study of social science research (which is mainly from First World researchers and mainly in English) and on my personal experiences, which have been in all three worlds. I have asked many students which of Chapters 14–16 they judge to be most negatively biased, and they have selected the chapters in about equal proportion—that is probably a positive indicator that the treatment is not systematically biased against one area.

I am aware that my own assessment regarding the achievement of the goals of prosperity, stability, and security varies among the three worlds. There is particular emphasis on the gap between aspirations and reality in the Second World and on the very serious problems facing many Third World states. The First World states do generally receive a more favorable overall evaluation regarding their achievement of these goals. These emphases might reflect my bias (as an American First Worlder), or they might reflect political reality. It will take far more than this book to help you make your own judgments regarding these political realities. As you read, try to become more conscious of *your* biases, which will undoubtedly influence your ultimate assessments of these political systems, and even your openness to the claims made about the political world.

and Fourth World states are considerably lower. Some analysts refer to all these states as the Third World. When a distinction is made between a Third World and a Fourth World, the *Fourth World* refers to those states that are so poor and so underdeveloped economically that modernization seems impossible.

Some of these distinctions within the Third World will be elaborated in Chapter 16. But you should be aware, in all these discussions, that by the late 1980s, the Third/Fourth World category is so large and diverse that it is a confusing array of states. The level of economic development in some of these states is no longer easy to classify. This category now includes some extremely wealthy yet socially traditional oil states (e.g., Bahrain), some increasingly modernized and developed economies (e.g., Singapore), some states with prosperous modern sectors amid vast poverty (e.g., Brazil), and some extremely poor states (e.g, Bangladesh).

It is reasonable to ask whether the categories of First, Second, and Third/ Fourth Worlds are sufficiently useful to be employed in this book. As groups within a taxonomy, they have clear shortcomings. Nonetheless, they are used in this book because the classifications are still widely used and understood and because they seem more defensible than the alternatives for dividing states into a very few broad categories that facilitate generalizations.

FIRST WORLD IMAGES

When you think of First World countries, what images come to mind?

Anyone reading this book has probably lived in at least one of the two dozen states in the First World, as listed in Table 14.1. This can make the images you select for First World states somewhat more accurate than those you might offer for countries in the other three worlds.

Among other things, you might envision large and tall cities, extensive use of high technologies like computers and VCRs, representative government and electoral politics, individualism, a generally high standard of living, freedom of speech, quality medical care, rock and roll, colonialism, and so forth.

What traits do you think best characterize life in the First World? As you try to provide your own list, you might become aware of how difficult it is to capture complex reality with straightforward descriptors. The "First World life" of a poor farmer in rural Mississippi is rather different from that of a wealthy banker in Zurich, a secretary in Yokohama, an unemployed factory worker in Milan, or a teenager in the New Zealand countryside.

The list of different First World lives could be extended. This is a further reminder that the generalizations offered in these chapters regarding the three worlds will, at best, capture broad tendencies that seriously oversimplify the diversity of political situations. Given that shortcoming, we can begin with a discussion of the political culture of the First World.

POLITICAL CULTURE

Because the First World states, like most nation-states, are composed of a variety of political cultures and subcultures, it is not possible to describe the First World in terms of a uniform political culture. Nevertheless, the political cultures of most First World states can be characterized broadly in terms of the balance between two sets of fundamental ideological tenets: classical liberalism and social welfarism. As these tenets are described in the following paragraphs, you will notice the tension between them.

Classical Liberalism

The concept of *liberalism* has a long history, but it has always emphasized individual freedom. "Classical" liberalism, which is outlined here, has a quite different orientation from that associated with the contemporary American use of the term *liberal*. In fact, as you will notice below, those labelled "liberals" in the late-twentieth-century United States are likely to support elements that are more closely associated with social welfarism than with classical liberalism. Among the most important thinkers contributing to the classical liberal perspective are John Locke (1632–1704), Jean-Jacques Rousseau (1712–1778), Adam Smith (1723–1790), and John Stuart Mill (1806–1873). Three central themes are emphasized in classical liberalism (Macridis 1986, Chap. 2):

1. The *moral* emphasis affirms the natural rights of the individual to life, liberty, and the pursuit of personal happiness. Justice is based on fair and equal treatment of all individuals, whose personal rights are protected from government intervention.
2. The *economic* emphasis celebrates economic freedom, especially the freedom of the individual from constraint or intervention in the economy by the state. Competition, the free market, and enlightened self-interest are the mechanisms that should regulate economic activity.
3. The *political* emphasis favors limited government, based on the contractual consent of individuals and on democratic participation within a framework of representative government.

Social Welfarism

The values of social welfarism emerged in the late nineteenth and early twentieth century. Among the contributors to this perspective are utopian socialists such as Charles Fourier (1772–1837) and Claude-Henri Saint-Simon (1760–1825), Fabian socialists such as George Bernard Shaw (1856–1950), Sidney Webb (1859–1947), and Beatrice Webb (1858–1943), and more recently by "liberal" economists such as Richard Musgrave (see Musgrave 1959). The key premise of social welfarism is the belief that the state must intervene actively and positively in order to mitigate the negative effects of the free market celebrated by classical liberalism. According to the social welfare perspective

1. In the *economic* sphere, the free market fails to provide sufficient levels of important goods and services, which cannot be sold profitably by private providers. Moreover, the competitive market is unlikely to provide decent jobs for all desiring work, and it does not adequately control the impacts on society of strategic economic sectors, such as energy and transportation.
2. In the *moral* sphere, the distribution of values emerging from a free market, characterized by very substantial inequalities, is unacceptable. Many people have so few resources that they cannot adequately provide

themselves with even the basic essentials of food, shelter, and health care. Social justice requires that every individual should enjoy a decent life. And individual freedom and self-interest must be balanced against the protection of the public interest.

3. In the *political* sphere, there is need for an active and positive state, empowered by the processes of participatory democracy, to intervene in the political economy to reduce the negative effects of the free market. The state must allocate resources positively in order to promote social justice.

The concept of the *welfare state* was explicitly articulated by Englishman Sir William Beveridge in 1941 (it is now also termed the *social welfare state*). In a major policy statement to the British government, Beveridge argued that the state had clear responsibility to employ public policy actively in order to overcome five tragic effects on some individuals in a society based on classical liberalism:

1. *Disease* must be combatted by public provision of subsidized or free health care services, including doctors, treatment, hospitals, and medicines.
2. *Want* must be eliminated by public provision of sufficient money and other services to raise people above poverty.
3. *Squalor* must be reduced by publicly owned and subsidized housing affordable to all.
4. *Ignorance* must be eliminated by universal, free public education.
5. *Idleness* must be overcome by government policies that insure meaningful work for all individuals.

Each First World state has developed its own compromise between classical liberalism and social welfarism, as it pursues the major political goals of prosperity, security, and stability. The extent to which classical liberalism or social welfarism is favored in the state's political culture, and is implemented in the state's policies, changes over time, depending upon the state's political and economic situation. Many of the political debates in First World states, particularly those regarding domestic policy, are grounded in disagreements about the proper balance between classical liberalism and social welfarism.

GOAL: PROSPERITY

In First World states, the goal of prosperity (and its components of welfare distribution) is pursued with great energy. The emphasis is on economic development, under the assumption that this will increase resource control and generate an expanding economic base with which to finance greater welfare for the population.

Mixed Economy

To achieve prosperity, First World states have relied on the dynamics of a mixed political economy. There is considerable private ownership and control of productive resources (land, labor, and capital) and substantial freedom in their use. Private actors are encouraged to use their productive resources aggressively in order to acquire the goods and resources they desire and to maximize their profit. The state has two key roles in the mixed economy of First World states. First, the government intervenes to regulate the worst aspects of the free market, employing policy to reduce ruthless competition among private actors and to limit the nature and extent of economic swings. Second, the state extracts some surplus (as taxes) in order to redistribute money and other welfare-oriented goods and services towards the less advantaged individuals in the society.

The extent to which particular First World states have a more market-oriented or a more mixed political economy varies considerably. In some states, the public sector actually owns or exerts very strong direction over many major productive resources and has direct responsibility for producing many intermediate and final goods, such as education, utilities, communications systems, transportation systems, and financial services. In other states, most productive resources are privately owned and the state primarily sets rules that regulate the behavior of private economic actors.

One broad comparative measure of the public-private mix is the percentage of the gross domestic product (GDP, which was defined in Box 8.1) that is in the public sector. This percentage provides a general measure of the proportion of final goods for which the state is the firm. Table 14.2 indicates that the proportion of productive capacity (measured as GDP) that is directly under state control varies enormously, from 67 percent in Sweden to less than 30 percent in Japan.

The mixed political economy designation seems to be appropriate for coun-

TABLE 14.2. Total Public Expenditure as a Percent of Gross Domestic Product in Selected First World States

State	Percent of GDP (1985)
Sweden	67.3
Denmark	60.1
Netherlands	59.4
Italy	50.3
France	48.7
West Germany	48.5[a]
Canada	47.5
Norway	44.5
United Kingdom	44.4
Greece	39.9
United States	34.9
Japan	28.6

[a] Data for 1983.
SOURCE: Mouritzen and Nielsen 1988:49.

tries in which public expenditure is about half or more of total GDP. This is the case for 7 of the 12 First World states in the table, and this group includes such countries as the Scandinavian states, the Benelux states (Belgium, the Netherlands, and Luxembourg), Italy, France, West Germany, and Canada. Countries that are closer to the market end of the political economy continuum include Japan, the United States, Switzerland, Spain, and Greece.

There are also cross-national differences in the mix of final goods that the public sector produces. Some sectors, such as education, public safety, utilities, and national defense, are usually in the public sector. In the mixed political economies, the state also tends to be very active in the provision of such goods as health care, housing, transportation, and income support.

Performance

First World states tend to assess their prosperity primarily in terms of economic activity, which is usually measured as GNP per capita and especially as the rate of change in GNP per capita over time (GNP was also defined in Box 8.1). Former U.S. Secretary of State George Schultz probably reflected the views of others at the 1983 Williamsburg, Virginia, conference of First World leaders when he stated: "The immediate international imperative is to restore adequate growth. Without that, no one's objectives are achievable". But some accuse First World states of "growthmania," claiming that societal health and citizen satisfaction are better measures of performance than an increasing GNP.

Table 14.3 provides comparative data on First World states for two prosperity measures. The first is a conventional measure, GNP per capita. If one accepts the idea that the total value of a society's total production of goods (relative to population size) is a reasonable indicator of its prosperity, the First World states

TABLE 14.3. Prosperity Measures for Selected First World States

State	GNP per Capita 1987	"Index of Social Progress" 1983
Switzerland	$21,330	82
United States	18,530	76
Norway	17,190	86
Japan	15,760	85
Sweden	15,550	90
Canada	15,160	80
Denmark	14,930	92
West Germany	14,400	93
France	12,790	88
Netherlands	11,860	85
Australia	11,100	81
United Kingdom	10,420	83
Italy	10,350	93
Israel	6,800	62
Spain	6,010	76

SOURCE: World Bank 1989: Table 1 for GNP data and Estes 1988: Table A.1 for Index of Social Progress data.

enjoy considerable prosperity. In a rank ordering of GNP per capita among 125 states (120 reported by The World Bank 1989 plus five Second World states), 12 of the top 15 states are in the First World. As a point of comparison, the top 15 includes only two oil-rich ministates (United Arab Emirates and Kuwait) and one Second World state (East Germany) in this group. On GNP per capita, the top three states are Switzerland, the United States, and Norway.

An "index of social progress" is the second measure in the table. This is one scholar's attempt to develop a sophisticated and complex index which measures the state's ability to provide for the basic material and social needs of its population (Estes 1988:4). What would you include in such an index? How would you weight the components? Box 14.2 describes how the index of social progress was constructed.

BOX 14.2

Measuring the Quality of Life

Richard Estes wanted to understand the social, economic, and political factors that seem to sustain social inequality among the countries of the world. Thus he attempted to develop a measure that revealed changes in the "level of human welfare" and to track the factors that account for changes in this level over time (Estes 1988: xvi). He selected an array of social indicators to create what he termed an "index of social progress" for 124 contemporary nation-states. Estes cautions that the index is not a measure of personal happiness at the individual level; rather, it indicates the level of the society's "social safety net."

The index is composed of ten main subindexes, and each subindex is measured by 1 to 5 specific indicators for a total of 36 indicators. One form of the index simply aggregates the 36 specific indicators, but most emphasis is on a second form which attaches weights to each indicator to reflect its relative importance.

The crucial question is what subindexes and indicators to include and how to score each measure. Estes (1988:4) chose these ten subindexes (with representative examples of specific indicators):

   1. Education (pupil–teacher ratio, percentage of GNP spent on education).
   2. Health Status (life expectancy, daily calorie supply).
   3. Women's Status (percentage of girls attending school).
   4. Defense Effort (percentage of GNP spent on the military, with higher percent as a negative factor).
   5. Economy (GNP per capita, food production).
   6. Demography (death rate, population under 15).
   7. Geography (proportion of deaths from natural disasters).
   8. Political Participation (violations of political rights and civil liberties).
   9. Cultural Diversity (percentage of people sharing the same language and religion).
   10. Welfare (old age, sickness, unemployment provision).

Would you have deleted any of the ten that were used? Would you add any others? There are some that Estes did not include because he judged that reliable comparative data were not available (e.g., access to safe water, crime levels, inequality of wealth).

The states in Table 14.3 score very high on the index of social progress. Of the 15 states in the table, only Spain, the United States (!), and Israel score below 80. Moreover, among the 124 states studied, the 15 states with the highest ranking on the index are all First World states. These states generally have very high rankings on education provision, economic performance, and political rights and most also rank high on health measures. Thus by these two measures, at least, First World states seem relatively successful in achieving their overall prosperity goals.

Problems

Erratic Economic Growth.   Despite the clear accomplishments of First World states, there are problems evident in the quest for prosperity. Most of these states have periods of solid economic growth (about 4 percent or more per year); but there are also extended periods, such as the early 1980s, when states have not sustained the high levels of economic growth that are essential to their vision of prosperity. Either there is low growth, or more seriously, there are periods of recession. Some underlying problems seem to contribute to the problem of economic growth.

First, increases in *productivity* have been lower than is desirable if goods are to be competitive in the market. Several causes of low productivity gains in First World states have been proposed. Some emphasize the failure of First World firms to develop and fully exploit new technologies. Some claim that labor (workers and unions) have too much power to push up wages without a corresponding increase in production. Still others claim that the state-controlled areas of the economy are the problem, because they lack the efficiency and profit incentives that vitalize the private market sectors of the economies.

Second, these states have experienced periods of significant *inflation,* which occurs when there is high demand for productive resources and/or goods. While high demand might seem good for the economy, high inflation undermines economic stability, planning, and development. It can also result in more expensive goods that are less competitive in the world market. And if continued demand is based on extensive borrowing, it can also undermine the value of the currency.

Third, most First World economies are suffering from the increasingly *competitive international economic system*. In the postcolonial world, producers in First World states control fewer resources and markets. There is more competition among firms in First World states who try to sell goods in each other's markets. And firms in all First World states face increasing competition from Second and Third World states, which have lower production costs. Under such conditions, imports (goods produced abroad and purchased by the state's consumers) can exceed exports (goods produced in the state and purchased by consumers abroad).

This can result in a reduction of income in the national economy, lower levels of production, higher levels of unemployment, trade deficits, balance of payments problems with other states, and other factors slowing the national economic machine. A few First World states, especially Japan and West Germany, have prospered in the competitive international economic marketplace. But many First

World states have experienced serious problems from stagnant economic growth and inflation. At times, there has even been an unexpected combination of these, termed *stagflation*.

And some states have temporarily avoided the most serious elements of economic downturn by financing current shortfalls through increases in the national debt. A dramatic case in point is the United States, which has shifted in the past 15 years from the world's largest creditor nation to the world's largest debtor nation. The U.S. national debt has increased in recent years as much as $150 billion per year. Such deficit financing is not the basis of a sound growth economy.

Inequality of Prosperity.   A more serious indictment of the nature of prosperity in some First World states is the unequal distribution of that prosperity. Classical liberalism is explicitly opposed to extensive state intervention to reduce the inequalities that tend to emerge among individuals in a market-oriented economy. Even with the emergence of greater social welfarism and state control of the political economy, substantial economic inequalities remain in many First World states.

Economic inequalities can be measured in various ways. The measure of household income in Table 14.4 indicates the magnitude of the economic inequalities. Virtually every First World state now has a proportion of the citizenry who are severely disadvantaged and do not enjoy the benefits of prosperity that are experienced by many in the society. In comparison to the wealthiest households, the poorest 20 percent of households (which also tend to have more members) have only about 11 percent as much disposable income in Australia and 13 percent as much in the United States, France, and Canada.

The states emphasizing social welfare have implemented programs to mitigate these effects. One strategy is to use the system of taxation and transfers to supplement the low (or nonexistent) payments that the poor receive for the (labor)

TABLE 14.4. Income Inequality in Selected First World States

State	Ratio of Household Income, Highest to Lowest 20 percent of Households
Australia	8.7:1
France	7.7:1
United States	7.6:1
Canada	7.5:1
Italy	7.1:1
Denmark	7.1:1
Switzerland	5.8:1
United Kingdom	5.7:1
Sweden	5.6:1
West Germany	5.0:1
Netherlands	4.4:1
Japan	4.3:1

SOURCE: The World Bank 1989: Table 30

resources they sell to firms. Moreover, because the free market sector does not provide goods to consumers who lack sufficient resources to afford market prices, essential goods, such as health care and housing, are heavily subsidized for the poor.

But the harsh effects of economic inequality are particularly severe in states where the values of classical liberalism are most powerful among the political decision makers. In the United States, for example, about one in eight citizens is ''in poverty'' according to the government's own statistics, and one in five children is born poor. Moreover, the gap between the rich and poor is growing wider, with the top 20 percent controlling an increasing share of wealth and family income, and the lowest 20 percent having a decreasing share. Such substantial and persistent inequality can produce a permanent *underclass* of citizens who are also disadvantaged in such areas as education, job skills, housing, health care, and, most broadly, quality of life (Saikowski 1988; Wilson 1987).

Policy Responses

The combination of limited economic growth and economic inequality puts some First World states under enormous cross pressures. At this point, a central political issue becomes *growth versus welfare*. Should the state reduce the taxes and state regulation imposed on private actors, under the assumption that the market economy is most likely to stimulate greater production and higher economic growth? Or should more of the surplus be captured by the state, which then redistributes it as welfare to the groups (the underemployed and unemployed) who are least successful in an economic downturn?

Classical Liberalism.   When those more committed to classical liberalism control a First World political system, public policy regarding the political economy emphasizes individualism and the free market. The state becomes less interventionist, allowing private actors greater freedom in the productive process. This means fewer constraints on competition (e.g., fewer antitrust actions, less protection of unions, more industry deregulation). Private ownership and control of major productive resources is extended, relative to public ownership.

Market incentives are extended in order to encourage efficient production for private profit, and the state extracts little surplus, operating a lean, limited government with low taxes and a balanced budget. Social welfare services are reduced toward a basic ''safety net,'' with which the state protects individuals only from the harshest consequences of the marketplace. To encourage companies to be strong and competitive in the international market, state protections such as tariffs or quotas on imported goods and subsidies for domestic production are reduced. Among First World states, this general philosophy is particularly reflected in the policies of the Reagan administration in the United States (1981–1989) and the Thatcher government in Britain (since 1979). (See Box 14.3.)

Social Welfarism.   When political power belongs to those oriented to social welfarism, public policy regarding the political economy is directed to insure a decent life for all citizens. The state is an active force in the political economy, planning,

guiding, and controlling the productive system in the service of "the public interest." Individuals and aggregates are protected against ruthless competition (e.g.,
monopolistic practices, price-fixing, abuse of workers' collective bargaining
rights, unsafe working conditions). The public sector controls or owns some major productive resources that have strategic importance for the political economy
and the society.

The state provides such goods and services as free health care, subsidized
housing, meaningful work at decent wages, public educational and cultural opportunities, and so on. In the international marketplace, domestic producers are protected from aggressive or "unfair" foreign competition by means of tariffs and
quotas on imports and subsidies for domestic production and consumption.

In most First World states the 1980s was generally an era of retrenchment,

BOX 14.3

The "Womb to Tomb" Welfare State: Britain

Great Britain provides an example of the constant tensions and the compromises
between classical liberalism and social welfarism in a First World state. Since the
Atlee government in 1945–1951, whenever the Labour party has been in power it has
used its majority control in the cabinet system to push the political economy in the
direction of social welfarism. This has resulted in publicly provided (free or highly
subsidized) health care (including doctors, treatment, hospitals, dentists, and medicine), education (preschool to university), public housing (for about one-third of all
families), and public transportation; in payments to people who need financial support, including the elderly, the unemployed, the handicapped, and the poor; and in
state ownership or control of major economic sectors, such as telecommunications,
transportation, power, and banking.

When the Conservative party has controlled the government, it has generally
reduced the role of the state in the political economy. The Conservatives have accepted the basic policies of the welfare state, but they reduce the extent of social
welfarism in nearly every area and they attempt to limit government control or
involvement in economic policy and labor policy, to reduce taxes, and to denational-
ize industries (i.e., the state relinquishes ownership, selling its share to private sector
actors). Similarly, the Labour governments after Atlee have often accommodated
their policies to more liberal orientations regarding free market economic principles
in such areas as labor relations, external trade, and currency support.

Only the most recent period under the extended leadership of Margaret Thatcher
(since 1979) has been characterized by a strong break in the trend to social welfarism.
The Thatcher government has aggressively pursued policies that emphasize classical
liberalism, such as reducing the power of the unions and reducing taxes. Many key
economic sectors, including the gas utility, the electric utility, the major airline, the
major auto manufacturer, and the major airplane manufacturer have been denationalized. Moreover, there have been sharp reductions in many welfare programs, such
as reducing the staff and facilities of the National Health Service and the university
system, cutting payments to the unemployed, selling public housing units, and raising
the fares on public transportation.

marked by some policy shifts from the social welfare orientation to that of classical liberalism. But there is still broad support for social welfarism among the citizens and the political decision makers in many states, including Denmark, Sweden, Norway, the Benelux countries, Canada, and West Germany.

GOAL: STABILITY

First World states have been generally successful in achieving their basic stability goals of political institutionalization and order maintenance. Within a framework of representative democracy, most states maintain a politics characterized by the group approach, with multiple competing elites and groups. There are substantial pressures on some First World governments, because problems exist that are exacerbated by the group politics approach. But overall these states enjoy relatively high levels of social and political stability while allowing widespread participation in the political process.

As suggested by Chapters 6 and 7, there is variation in the political structures of First World states. Most have a cabinet government, based on coalitions emerging from a multiparty system. Some are very stable, with alternating left and right coalitions (e.g., Canada, Denmark, Great Britain, Sweden, and West Germany) or dominant parties (Japan). Others experience substantial instability, due to the fragmented nature of the party system (Israel, Italy, Greece). While there are some hybrids, with an elected president in addition to the cabinet and prime minister (France and West Germany), the United States is an exception as a presidential government with a two-party system, and Switzerland is an exception as a council system. Many First World states have dual executives, often with a constitutional monarch. Some are federations (such as Canada, the United States, and West Germany), while most are unitary states. Even in the unitary states, most human services and welfare services are the responsibility of local governments. In general, these states have large, efficient bureaucracies and relatively independent judiciaries.

Most of the states have national legislatures that are unicameral (or with one clearly dominant chamber) and are actively involved in the policy process. In many First World states there are high levels of political participation by citizens, at least in terms of electoral involvement and interest in politics. As the discussions and data in Chapters 2 and 3 indicated, the forms and levels of participation vary among different states.

Political Institutionalization

The political systems in most First World states have high levels of political institutionalization—that is, substantial value and stability are attached to political structures and processes. Most First World states operate as constitutional democracies. Leaders and policies are constrained by the rule of law and the rights of individuals are guaranteed by law and tradition. Individuals and groups have substantial freedom to criticize and oppose the government and to take a wide variety of nonviolent political actions to change leaders and policies. Leaders operate with a limited mandate, leadership succession is regularized, and the selection of many public officials is based on citizen elections among genuine alternatives.

Some First World governments have evolved over centuries, by means of gradual and generally nonviolent mechanisms of political change. This pattern applies to such states as Belgium, Canada, Denmark, Great Britain, Sweden, Switzerland, and the United States. The distribution and uses of political power have changed as new groups gain admission to and influence in the political system, extending participation steadily until mass representative democracy is created. This politics of inclusion has drawn important groups into the political process and built their support for the political system, by reducing their need to use extraconstitutional mechanisms such as political violence to capture political power. (See Box 14.4. While this emphasis on the relative absence of violence in First World states is accurate, it is useful to recall Barrington Moore's observation, discussed in Box 11.2, that development in virtually all societies has involved a considerable amount of violence against some groups.)

Some First World states have substantially restructured their political systems by means of constitutional procedures. In the last 40 years, most such transformations occurred after involvement in World War II had undermined the legitimacy of the previous political regime, as in Austria, France, Italy, Japan, and West Germany. Despite the shorter period during which these political systems could acquire value and stability, democratic political processes appear to be firmly established. It is revealing, for example, that these states tend to have among the highest levels of voter turnout among the world's democracies. While these countries have relatively strong leftist or Communist parties, those parties are generally committed to working within the democratic parliamentary system, not to overthrowing it. Only in a few First World states, particularly those with a quite short history of democratic, representative politics (e.g., Portugal and Spain), is the level of political institutionalization, and thus political stability, more problematic.

Order Maintenance

First World states have had varying levels of success in meeting the stability goal of order maintenance. This goal can be interpreted as the *absence of disorder* in the political, social, and personal domains. (See Box 14.5.)

Table 14.5 provides representative data on the relative success of various states in maintaining public order. These data suggest that First World states are neither the most orderly nor the most disorderly in the political world. Overall, most citizens in most First World states enjoy orderly and secure lives. The differences among the states can be very substantial, although it is difficult to generalize. Switzerland, for example, has little disorder, at the personal, social, or political level. France and the United States, in contrast, are relatively high on most measures of disorder. The problems of substance abuse and drug-related crime have become so severe in the United States that the state has become increasingly aggressive (if ineffective) in a "war on drugs." The Scandinavian countries have

BOX 14.4

Building Political Institutionalization by Political Inclusion: Britain

Great Britain is an excellent example of the evolutionary approach to building political institutionalization. Britain has the longest-lived modern political system in the world. During the 775-year period since 1215, the powers of the hereditary monarch (the king or queen) were established, then constrained, and finally limited markedly. Now, in the late twentieth century, the monarch formally exercises some political functions, but has virtually no direct political power. The monarch still performs certain political functions, such as dissolving Parliament for new elections, summoning an individual to form a government and become prime minister, and delivering the opening speech in Parliament, which sets the year's legislative agenda. But by convention, these activities are done in a politically neutral manner, with the monarch serving a symbolic role, merely implementing the decisions of the real executive power base, the prime minister and the cabinet.

In parallel, the political power of the legislative bodies, the House of Lords and the House of Commons, was gradually extended after 1215. The elective Commons, which began as a weak second house, slowly gained equality and then clear dominance over the Lords. As the legislative body that directly represents the population, the Commons' emergence as the powerful house that selects the cabinet and authorizes legislation indicates the increasing influence of the citizens over the political process.

Over the same period, the electorate expanded steadily, enfranchising new classes of citizens as wealth, gender, and age barriers to political participation were dropped. The Reform Act of 1832 increased the electorate from 500,000 to 813,000. Another Reform Act in 1867 increased the electorate from 1,358,000 to 2,477,000. Legislation in 1884 reduced property requirements for voting so that virtually every working man could participate in the election of the House of Commons, as well as for the local council. In 1918, all adult men were allowed to vote, as were women over 30 (if married or property owners!). In 1928, voting rights were extended to all adult women, and the voting age for men and women was reduced to 18 in 1969 (Norton 1984).

The political parties also changed, becoming more representative of, and responsive to, the major groups in the society. As new groups entered the electorate, each political party altered its program by including policies to attract the groups' support. Most importantly, the Labour party, which explicitly represents the interests of the working class and the trade unions, emerged after 1906 and soon became one of the two major parties. An extensive set of policy decisions, which implemented the British welfare state and hugely benefitted the working class and lower class, was enacted by the Labour government of 1945–1951.

In general, the great majority of the British population believes that governmental bureaucracy serving it is honest and efficient and the politicians have been relatively responsive to its needs and interests. (Recall the data on the British political culture in Chapter 2.) The period since 1945 has been difficult for Britain, as it has declined from a major world power to a marginal actor in international politics with a struggling economy. Thus there have been periods of substantial political unrest and occasional outbreaks of internal political violence by groups (especially ethnic minorities and workers in declining industries) who are frustrated by the failure of the political system to serve their interests. But the British political system is highly institutionalized, with strong support from its population, stability, and effective performance of its functions.

BOX 14.5

Problems in Measuring Order and Disorder

It is difficult to obtain accurate, comparative data on the level of disorder in most states. Revealing indicators of explicitly political violence, as discussed in Chapter 12, include measures of illegal demonstrations, riots, rebellions, coups, and revolutions. These more political forms of disorder are possibly the ones most accurately measured for most states because they are both the most visible and the most infrequent. But the failure to maintain public order also involves such social disorders as murder, rape, robbery, white-collar crime, and organized crime, and such personal disorders as suicide and substance abuse (alcohol, drugs).

Few societies enthusiastically report the level to which there is a breakdown of public order. (It is particularly difficult to obtain accurate measures of these problems in states outside the First World.) There are also substantial differences in the manner in which disorderly behavior and "crime" are defined, since these are defined through the political process. Even in the First World, many states provide self-serving data or do not know the actual level of the problem. For example, Catholic states typically underreport the level of suicides, and few states have accurate measures of the extent of organized crime or the extensiveness and severity of substance abuse among the population.

TABLE 14.5. Measures of Public Disorder in Selected States

State (World)	Riots[a]	Deaths from Political Violence[b]	Armed Attacks[c]	Homicides[d]	Suicides[e]
Afghanistan (4)	0	9	1	na	na
Argentina (3)	7	620	32	3.1	70
Australia (1)	0	0	2	1.9	106
Czechoslovakia (2)	2	3	0	na	189
East Germany (2)	0	0	0	na	na
Egypt (3)	1	9	2	na	.3
France (1)	8	5	22	9.8	212
Kenya (4)	2	11	2	5.1	na
Philippines (3)	3	542	18	7.1	7
Poland (2)	0	0	0	1.8	136
Sweden (1)	0	1	0	2.4	193
Soviet Union (2)	2	2	1	na	na
United Kingdom (1)	27	133	314	.9	75
United States (1)	14	16	22	9.1	116

[a]Average yearly riots, 1969, 1971, 1973, 1975, 1977. "Riots" are demonstrations or disturbances (against the government, its leaders, or its policies) that become violent.
[b]Average yearly deaths, alternate years, 1969–1977.
[c]Average yearly attacks, alternate years, 1969–1977. "Armed attacks" are acts of violent political conflict carried out by (or on behalf of) an organized group with the objective of weakening or destroying the power exercised by another organized group.
[d]Murder and homicides per 100,000 population, 1973.
[e]Suicides per 100,000 population.
SOURCE: Data derived from Taylor and Hudson 1977 and Archer and Gartner 1984.

very low levels of political violence and crime, but tend to have relatively high levels of substance abuse. Continuing problems with violent nationalist groups (as in Britain, Israel, and Spain) or with extremist political groups (as in Japan) result in particularly high levels of political disorder.

Several alternative explanations can be offered for the seemingly high levels of social and personal disorder in some First World states (especially in comparison to the data for developed states outside the First World). Can you identify several of these explanations? Which seem most plausible to you?

Challenges to Stability

Conflicts and Disputes.   First World states face difficulties in fully achieving their stability goals. Where an open group politics is allowed, even fundamental value disagreements can become active issues. Some enduring conflicts in First World states center on unresolved disputes about the domains where the state can legitimately prescribe or proscribe behaviors that some individuals and groups perceive to be private and others perceive to be within the public interest. The need for order maintenance implies that the state must limit the behavior of the individual in order to preserve social peace and to protect the freedom of others.

In the United States, for example, state constraints on private behavior are particularly controversial political issues in such areas as

Abortion
Development and use of private property
Educational curriculum (religious instruction, sex education)

Ownership and use of firearms
Personal discrimination (based on age, sex, ethnicity)
Sexual conduct
Substance abuse (alcohol, drugs)

Issues concerning the political economy have been another area of conflict between classical liberalism and social welfarism in First World states. In the group politics environment there is constant competition, sometimes very conflictual, between well-organized interest groups and effective political parties that promote each approach. Many of the states have introduced considerable state ownership and control of major productive means and have substantially increased the provision of social welfare since 1945.

Not surprisingly, many groups in First World states, especially the "have-nots" (those who have not shared in the prosperity of their society), attempt to use the political process to increase their proportion of the societies' resources. In states where public policy has not been responsive to the "have-nots," there is a greater incidence of crime and other social disorders within these groups. And many in advantaged groups (the "haves") attempt to use their considerable political power to protect and expand their share of resources. Thus there is constant political pressure from many groups to shift public policy in directions compatible with the groups' views on how the state should reallocate resources and on when and in what form the state should restrict individual freedom of action.

Of course, making these kinds of policy decisions is the primary function of the political system. A key measure of a government's effectiveness is its capacity to resolve such conflicts among competing groups. The political elites and the governments of First World states are generally committed to representative democracy and the group politics approach. Thus the governments attempt to establish compromises on issues that can become highly politicized among groups with strong and irreconcilable preferences.

Hyperpluralism and Political Polarization.   Where value conflicts are intense, efforts to maintain political order are particularly difficult in First World states. Chapter 10 suggested that the processes of group politics are not well suited to situations where there are strong, competing demands. The persistent risk is hyperpluralism, in which dissatisfaction with policies results in increasingly aggressive political demands, frustration, and substantial political instability.

In some First World states, the risks of instability are especially high because of political polarization. In such cases, center parties and centrist policies are only weakly supported, and politics becomes a battleground between large and mobilized groups of the right and of the left. When most citizens support active and ideological parties of either the right (promoting classical liberalism) or the left (promoting social welfarism), the political system is subjected to enormous pressures. Conflict resolution and decision making become extremely difficult, since it is often impossible to satisfy advocates of both orientations. Such polarization and instability have occurred periodically in several First World states, including Britain, France, Italy, and Japan.

Most analysts do not see these factors as a fundamental risk to political order in First World states. But a few scholars, such as Samuel Huntington (Crozier, Huntington, and Watanuki 1975:59–118), argue that this situation has already created a "crisis of democracy." Rather like his analysis of political decay in the Third World (Chapter 11), Huntington claims that the extensive political mobilization of new groups with strong political demands might undermine the authority of First World governments. Fearing that hyperpluralism is causing social and political instability, Huntington argues that political and social freedoms should be limited by constraints on the media, the educational system, and the public political process.

Some First World governments prefer to tolerate hyperpluralism and some level of disorder rather than apply repressive and undemocratic controls in the pursuit of stability goals. Thus states such as Britain, France, Italy, and the United States have experienced quite high (in international comparison) levels of civil disorder during the past 30 years. Other states, such as the Netherlands, Norway, and Switzerland have successfully reduced the incidence of more serious forms of disorder by nurturing a cultural style of social tolerance and/or by developing political institutions that accommodate competing groups (Eckstein 1966; Lijphart 1978).

Domination and Control.   There are some analysts who offer a far more critical assessment of the nature of order maintenance in many First World states. In this view, First World states primarily serve the interests of dominant groups in the society. The state blends some welfare-oriented policies with extensive socialization (by such agents as the schools and the media) to insure that most citizens will acquiesce to the unequal distribution of power and resources in the society. Moreover, many explicit and subtle mechanisms of control are exercised by the state apparatus (e.g., the police, the bureaucracy, the judicial system) to sanction individuals and groups who threaten the social order.

This view of order maintenance is consistent with Dahrendorf's (1959) description of a society based on coercion rather than consensus (see Chapter 10). It is also that of class and elite theorists who argue that First World societies are controlled by hegemonic elites (Mills 1956; Miliband 1969; O'Connor 1972). As Chapter 10 noted, those who explain politics by the class and elite approaches disagree fundamentally, at both the theoretical and empirical levels, with those who use the group approach.

It is clear that the First World state has powerful and effective means to contain the level of instability within a tolerable range. And the group politics explanation offers a problematic account of how democratic politics can work amid the huge inequalities in political resources available to different groups (Dahl 1961; Parenti 1988). Yet most analysts and most citizens in First World states see no compelling evidence that their political systems are controlled by a self-serving, nondemocratic elite. Radical (Marxist) theorists interpret such citizen views as tragic evidence that the state can fool most of the people all of the time. One of the great (and perhaps impossible challenges) for political scientists is to develop an indisputable empirical analysis of how political power is exercised, values are allocated, and order is maintained in First World states.

GOAL: SECURITY

A First World state's beliefs and actions regarding its security depend on many factors, including its geopolitical position, its history, its military strength, its perception of the objectives of other states, and the extent to which it wishes to assert influence and power over other states. Since World War II, the security goals and security-oriented actions of virtually all First World states have been powerfully influenced by the international struggle between the United States and the Soviet Union.

Most First World states, whether enthusiastically or reluctantly, find themselves covered by the security blanket of American military power. The United States spends more than 3 times as much of its GNP per capita on military expenditure as Canada does, 6 times as much as Austria, and 12 times as much as Finland. Although every First World state can and sometimes does act independently, U.S. security policy usually is the most powerful factor affecting those states' security policies.

Differing Perspectives on Foreign Policy

Table 14.6 summarizes three alternative belief systems (first discussed in Chapter 2) that might be held by foreign policy elites in First World states (Rosenau and Holsti, 1986; Holsti and Rosenau, 1984). Rosenau and Holsti (1986) applied the framework to analyze the foreign policy elite in the United States during the 1980s. They concluded that its members have been guided primarily by the cold war internationalist perspective.

This perspective is consistent with the broad thrust of American foreign policy from the outbreak of the "Cold War" in the late 1940s until the end of the 1980s. Key foreign policy actors in the United States perceived a bipolar international system in which there has been a fundamental conflict between the First World and the Second World. In this view, the freedom, influence, and even the survival of First World states have depended upon a strong military posture towards the Soviet Union and its allies.

There were at least three core elements of U.S. foreign policy. First, the United States attempted to use military power to constrain the international actions of the Second World. The United States developed a massive capacity for nuclear war and has extensive military personnel and hardware stationed at strategic locations around the world. Second, to gain support for its approach from other First World states, the United States has used a variety of strategies. These strategies include energetic diplomacy, multilateral military alliances, especially NATO, numerous bilateral agreements in the political, economic, and military spheres, and extensive efforts to influence public opinion in other states.

Third, the United States has also applied its considerable military, economic, and political power to affect the actions of many Third World states, because the support and resources of such states marginally affect the bipolar power system. For example, the United States has provided extensive support to pro-American, anti-communist regimes and varying levels of support to other Third World states

TABLE 14.6. Three Belief Systems among First World Foreign Policy Elites

Issue	Cold War Internationalism	Post–Cold War Internationalism	Semi-Isolationism
Primary threats to First World	Soviet and Soviet-sponsored aggression; Soviet military superiority	Problems between rich nations and poor nations; nuclear war	Domestic problems (inflation, racism unemployment, drug use, crime)
Soviet foreign policy	Aggressive expansionism (highly successful)	Defensive; seeks parity with First World (partially successful)	Limit First World dominance (generally unsuccessful)
Soviet-American conflict	Basic conflicts of interest	Limited level of conflict of interest	Few important conflicts of interest
Primary danger of war	Soviet aggression encouraged by military imbalance	Misperception leading to unwanted war	U.S. and Soviet meddling in volatile regions
Impact of the Third World on First World interests	Primary target of Soviet subversion and aggression	Primary source of unresolved social and economic problems in world	Peripheral and largely irrelevant
Appropriate foreign policies	Rebuild First World military strength; active support to states experiencing Soviet aggression or of strategic importance	Stabilize relations with Soviets; economic and other nonmilitary assistance to Third World states	Stabilize relations with Soviets; reduce all commitments (military and economic) abroad; major effort to control arms race

SOURCE: Adapted from Rosenau and Holsti 1986, Table 2.

that are not aligned to either major power. This support has taken such forms as (1) foreign aid and loans; (2) the provision of goods, services, and technology; (3) favorable trade arrangements; and (4) military assistance, in the form of financial aid, provision of military hardware, training and advisors, and even actual military support. This foreign policy has been used in the attempt to bolster some political regimes, especially those in such client states as El Salvador, South Korea, and Zaire. The policy suffered its most catastrophic setback in the direct military involvement and ultimate defeat in Vietnam. The United States also supported efforts to destabilize certain leftist or pro-Soviet regimes. These included military and political support for ''counterrevolutions'' (e.g., Afghanistan, Nicaragua), attempts to eliminate political leaders (e.g., Allende in Chile, Castro in Cuba), and direct military action (e.g., the Grenada invasion in 1983).

One of the interesting tensions among First World states has resulted from the fact that not all foreign policy elites in the First World have shared the United States' perception of a clear bipolar struggle between the forces of good and of evil. Some First World states (e.g, Switzerland, Austria, Finland) have generally maintained a position of neutrality. Others (e.g., Denmark, France, Greece, Italy,

New Zealand, and Sweden), especially when their governments have been controlled by socialist or social democratic parties, have emphasized a foreign policy perspective that is closest to post–cold war internationalism.

The central tenet of post–cold war internationalism has been that the First World should be conciliatory toward the Second World. The First and Second World states are relatively modern, industrialized, and prosperous. They have strong common interests in maintaining their superior position in the international order. Aggressive power politics by First World states actually reduces their security, by increasing the probability of a violent confrontation between the First and Second Worlds and by provoking political instability in Third World settings. A further, pragmatic consideration in many states in Western Europe has been the fear that their countries would be the battleground in a war between the United States and the Soviet Union.

Particularly when open hostility between the United States and the Soviet Union has been low, many governments and interest groups in the First World have emphasized *"détente"* ("relaxation" of tensions) between the Western bloc and the Soviet bloc. They have promoted the negotiation of agreements that reduce the levels of nuclear weapons, military equipment, and military personnel in Eastern and Western Europe. And they have supported expanded trade with the Second World and numerous other forms of communication and exchange, especially in such areas as tourism, sports, and culture.

Since the late 1980s, Soviet leader Gorbachev's extremely effective peace initiatives and the dramatic shifts in politics and political economies in Eastern Europe (see Chapter 15) have substantially increased the support in First World states for the post–cold war internationalist position. The reunification of Germany represents the most dramatic initiative to transform the nature of First World—Second World relations. Even American foreign policy reflects a stronger responsiveness to tenets of the post–cold war internationalist and the semi-isolationist positions. For example, President Bush used direct military force against an *anti*-communist leader who threatened U.S. interests in the 1989 invasion of Panama and the arrest of General Noriega on drug trafficking charges.

The changes in foreign policy, domestic policy, and political stability in the Soviet Union and Eastern Europe will probably be the crucial factor to which First World foreign policy will respond. These changes might have major effects on the arms race, security alliances such as NATO, and foreign policy towards the Third World. And as economic power shifts from the United States to East Asia and Europe, American domination of First World security policy might also be transformed.

Performance

During the twentieth century, First World states have enjoyed some success in the pursuit of their basic security goals, especially survival and freedom. There have, however, been two massive multistate wars among First World states. While most of the states survived intact (there are notable exceptions, including Austria-Hungary after World War I, and Germany after World War II), many states were devastated in human, material, and political terms by these wars.

Some First World states have also been extremely successful at extending their influence or domination over other states in order to further enhance their own security goals. By means of political, economic, and military power, many of these states managed to assert colonial/imperial control over vast territories that are now Third World states. Belgium, France, Germany, Portugal, Spain, and the United States are among the First World states that have dominated colonial territories in the twentieth century.

And the imperial control by Great Britain of more than one-fourth of the world's population (circa 1945) is the most dramatic example of the capacity of First World states to protect not only their survival and freedom, but also to promote such other security goals as influence, prestige, and domination. By the late 1980s, most such colonies have achieved official independence although, as we

BOX 14.6

A Day in the Life: First World

There are 675 million stories in the First World. This is one of them. . . .

Poul-Erik works as an accountant for a private Danish company that builds and exports furniture. His wife leaves to drive the two children to the state-subsidized nursery school, and then drive on to her job. Because his family can afford only one car, due to the very high taxes on auto purchases, Poul-Erik rides to work on the excellent public bus system. On his job, he works at an unpressured pace on a sophisticated computerized accounting system that links his records with those at branch locations in other cities. He also has a meeting with colleagues, to discuss their union's policy on further computerization of their jobs.

After work, Poul-Erik stops at the market to purchase food for supper. Food and other consumer goods are expensive, and they are subject to high taxes. His family uses its money carefully to buy quality food and the many nice consumer items (e.g., furnishings, electronics equipment, household conveniences) in their comfortable home. They also save enough for summer camping holidays in Western and Eastern Europe. But money is always a concern for Poul-Erik's family, because prices are high, the government takes nearly 50 percent of their wages in income tax, and there are additional high taxes on most purchases.

In general, Poul-Erik is very satisfied with the quality of his life. Although he grumbles about taxes and the family budget is always tight, the state provides his family with many excellent services, including free health care, efficient public transportation, good roads, quality day care and schools, cultural activities, beautiful parks and enjoyable recreation programs, well-stocked libraries, and so on. He rarely sees a truly poor person, since the government's policies tend to provide everyone with a reasonable standard of living. He feels that life is safe and stable for himself and his family.

He and his wife prepare the evening meal and then put the children to bed. He bicycles to the local recreation facility to practice with his soccer team. The men on his team have quite different life-styles, but they always enjoy sharing a few beers after practice. Their animated discussion is not diverted by the bland programming on the state-operated television, although they do watch the news about politics and sports with interest. When Poul-Erik (unsteadily) rides his bicycle home through the dark late-night streets, he feels relatively contented.

saw in Chapter 13, dominance often continues through neocolonialism. From the perspective of most Third World states, the First World has very much "had its own way" in promoting its security interests and projecting its will in the international political arena.

As the discussion of political violence in Chapter 13 should make clear, no First World state is able to insure its own security independent of other states. In the current international environment, far more than in the past, all states recognize the fragility of their security in a world of superpower competition, scarce resources, complex economic interdependencies, and nuclear weapons. Thus, even the most powerful First World states are constantly devising new policies that might enhance the elusive quest for greater security.

CONCLUDING OBSERVATIONS

In terms of pursuit of the broad goals of prosperity, stability, and security, the states of the First World generally have the highest levels of "success" in the world. These states have the most highly developed systems of economic production, especially when measured by the standard indicator of gross national product per capita. The political economies of these states are mixed. In the last four decades, the broad trend has been to expand significantly the extent to which the state is actively involved in control of the economy; but in most First World states the majority of productive resources remain under private control. In comparison to those in the rest of the world, most First World citizens enjoy a relatively high standard of living.

By exercising their considerable economic, military, and political power in the international system, the First World states have also met their security goals. They have a strong record of survival, influence, and even control over other political systems. Among the most assertive First World states, the approach to international balance of power politics was most extreme during the period of colonialism. But the leading First World states continue to apply their power in order to maintain their advantages relative to other states. Leaders and citizens in most First World states believe that they are the guardians of an approach to political freedom and economic prosperity that would be destroyed if greater power and influence were to pass to the Second or Third World. The mix of economic, military, and political power exercised by a particular First World state depends upon such factors as that state's resources, political culture, and perception of national self-interest.

The First World states' success in achieving prosperity and security is not unqualified. Many citizens in these states have been excluded from the general prosperity in their societies. While most First World citizens enjoy a high material standard of living, others live in relative poverty and despair. And many critics, especially in Second and Third World states, argue that the First World has maintained its prosperity by exploitation—historically, of the poor within its own societies and, more recently and more systematically, of the population and resources of other states, by means of neocolonialism and military intervention (see also

Chapter 16). In the competitive international system, the First World states have not reached the top by being passive or generous.

First World states, perhaps because of their prosperity and security, have maintained a relatively open, fair, and stable politics. First World politics is generally characterized by the group approach, since many individuals and groups are able to mobilize their political resources in the attempt to influence the processes of government and decision making. In every First World state, some are more equal than others in terms of political influence and political power. But there is tolerance of a wide range of political actions, and citizens do have the right to select among leadership elites at regular intervals. At the base of much of the political instability that does exist are significant inequalities in the distribution of values, especially economic resources, and disagreements about whether, how extensively, and by what means these inequalities should be reduced.

Thus the politics of First World states is broadly democratic and constitutional. This politics does face challenges from underlying tensions between the commitment to individual freedom and limited government, on the one hand, and state intervention to increase equality of outcomes, on the other hand. To the extent such tensions manifest themselves in highly active and polarized politics, the governing style of pluralism might become paralyzed. But such a breakdown in governance has, to this point, been more a potential problem than a major crisis. In comparison to other nation-states, the states of the First World receive high marks for their maintenance of a constitutional, participatory politics.

CHAPTER 15

The Second World

St. Basil's Cathedral, Red Square, Moscow, USSR

SECOND WORLD IMAGES

The Second World consists of the Soviet Union, the seven satellite states of Eastern Europe that are under its broad influence, and Yugoslavia. These states, listed in Table 14.1, have a total population of about 450 million. Because of the massive changes that are occurring in the Second World states at the beginning of the 1990s, this taxonomic category might eventually disappear. That is, the politics and political economies of the Second World might evolve so that they are no longer analytically distinguishable from those of the First World. But these states do still differ from First World states and share strong commonalities from the past four decades. Thus it remains illuminating to discuss them as a group.

When you think of these Second World countries, what images come into your mind about their society and politics?

Negative imagery. For some people, and especially those socialized in First World countries like the United States, the dominant images of the Second World are unflattering or unfavorable. These are grey, dull, and joyless societies, where people have no incentives, and where goods and services are of poor quality and are often unavailable. In these images, people in the Second World experience little freedom, behavior is constantly monitored in a police-state atmosphere, and a small clique makes all major political decisions. Although they are constantly being propagandized, most of these people long for "the good life" in the First World.

Positive imagery. For other people, these images miss the essential points about the Second World. The positive imagery might emphasize that virtually all citizens in these societies have peace of mind that their lives are secure. Regardless of individuals' conditions at birth or their level of income, they are assured of sound housing, decent food, professional health care, employment, financial support in their old age, and all the education they merit. And the citizens feel safe at the societal level, confident that there is little crime, drug addiction, or violence against people. Internationally, these states have not only survived in the face of hostility from major First World states, but their bloc of states has also achieved superpower status militarily and is able to protect their interests throughout the world.

This chapter considers the nature of politics in the Second World in the context of these alternative images. Much of the discussion will focus on the Soviet Union, which is clearly the dominant state in the Second World. But each Second World state has its own unique history and characteristics. Yugoslavia has always been quite independent of the Soviet Union, belonging to neither the military security pact nor the economic association of Second World states. In the early 1980s, Hungary and East Germany had diverged from the Soviet economic model. Romania had asserted considerable autonomy in foreign policy. And by the early 1990s, most Second World states had asserted substantial independence from the Soviet Union.

BOX 15.1

Who's on First?

The states of the Second World, like those of the First World, have relatively well-developed political, economic, and social systems. They are distinguished from First World states because, as communist systems, they have had command political economies, with very extensive state ownership and control of firms and also of productive resources in the society. (Recall that these Second World states are not in second place, except in the sense that the taxonomy we are using was developed by social scientists in that group of countries that was given the title *First* World—surprise!). Second World states are distinguished from Third World states by their high levels of development. The classification of Second World states in this book differs from that used by many other commentators, who include some (but for unknown reasons, not all) communist states, regardless of level of economic, political, and social development.

The broad conclusion emerging from this chapter is that both the positive and negative images described above seem to be generally accurate. The Second World states have committed substantial resources to achieve their goals of security against external states and of stability of the internal social order. And they have attempted to provide all citizens with the peace of mind associated with a decent material life. There is considerable success in achieving these goals, but there are also significant costs. In general, the productivity of the economic systems has been poor, the standards of the material life have been modest or low, and individual freedom has been sacrificed to social order.

But things are in flux at the beginning of the 1990s. Since the emergence of Soviet leader Mikhail Gorbachev (in 1985), dramatic changes in theory and in practice have been introduced in Second World states. Most states have repudiated central elements of their political culture and there are major attempts to restructure their politics and the political economies. How successful—and how permanent—these new structures will be is impossible to assess at present. Therefore, although this chapter characterizes the major changes, it also emphasizes the patterns that have dominated the political systems of the Second World since World War II.

POLITICAL CULTURE

The peoples of the Second World have a rich and complicated history of different political cultures. Most of the Soviet Union was ruled autocratically by the Russian czars for three centuries before the Russian Revolution of 1917. And the rest of Eastern Europe was controlled for much of the same period by great empires, including the Ottoman Turkish Empire and the Austrian Empire. Only in the late nineteenth century did independent nation-states emerge in Eastern Europe. The political cultures of Second World states are strongly influenced by these historical patterns of oppressive rule and by the many nationalities comprising their populations.

The dominant influence on political culture in the contemporary period has been the political philosophy of Karl Marx (1818–1883), and its evolution after the Russian Revolution through the decisions of such Soviet leaders as V. I. Lenin (in power 1917–1924), Joseph Stalin (1927–1953), Nikita Khrushchev (1953–1964), Leonid Brezhnev (1964–1982), and Mikhail Gorbachev (since 1985). Our under- standings about the actual nature of their elite and mass political belief systems remain somewhat speculative due to the minimal amount of empirical social sci- ence research and the relatively closed nature of these societies. Moreover, the discourse of Second World politics has been so dominated by the language of Marx and Lenin that it is often difficult to penetrate the rhetoric of the leaders and others in the society. Although it is supposed to be a description of reality, this political culture is also normative (i.e., about how things *should* be).

Three central concepts help us understand the broad political orientations of the Second World. First, consistent with the class approach to politics, societies and the international system are subject to historical patterns of stratification and class struggle. Second, the ultimate goal of the political system should be the transformation of society into a classless system, where all citizens share equally in the production of and benefits from the society's resources. And third, politics is dominated by an ideological vanguard, the Communist party, until the condi- tions emerge for a true people's democracy.

Stratification and Class Struggle

The class approach described in Chapter 10 suggests the broad framework within which people in the Second World understand politics. Every society is character- ized by social stratification, with the people divided into a few class strata. There is systematic inequality in the classes' possession of some fundamental resource. In each society, there is a natural evolution of stages, during which particular classes rise to dominance and then are overthrown by the lower classes.

At each stage, the society is characterized by a particular political economy, related to the pattern of class relations at that stage. Each type of political econ- omy is presumed to have crucial internal contradictions that reduce the capacity of the dominant class to resist the next revolution. The major stages, according to Marx, are primitive communism, slavery, feudalism, capitalism, socialism, and finally, communism. Ultimately, all societies are expected to reach the classless utopia of communism, a system where there is no further political violence. The inevitable breakdown of advanced capitalist states has been delayed by their suc- cessful use of imperialism and neocolonialism to exploit less developed states.

Egalitarianism and Economic Justice

The proletariat (working) class is empowered in a revolution. For the first time, this class gains control of the key resources (for Marx, this meant the major pro- ductive resources) in the society and takes control of the political system. After a period of socialist transition, during which remnants of other classes are eliminated or absorbed, the ideal communist society emerges.

No one, including Marx, has provided a clear and detailed description of this society. One of its major features is equality in the control of and benefits from societal resources, regardless of status, role, age, gender, ethnicity, and so on. And the second key feature is economic justice, based mainly on Marx's well-known injunction: "From each according to his ability, to each according to his need". Leaders of Second World states acknowledge that neither egalitarianism nor social justice has been fully achieved, yet. In every state, some groups continue to have relative advantages; but a society based on egalitarianism and economic justice remains the basic goal.

People's Democracy

Before the stages of socialism and communism, the state is essentially a coercive system that protects and maintains the resource control and power of the dominant class. In the Marxist vision, the coercive state is finally eliminated with the institutionalization of socialism. But the nature of the future state is unclear. In the language of Engels (1878/1978), when the coercive state is no longer necessary, the state will "wither away," to be replaced by "the administration of things" and by widespread democratic participation in politics at the local level.

But the reality of an underdeveloped political economy and a hostile world of capitalist states led Lenin to argue that there must be a prior transition period, during which a strong government, led by a party elite, is necessary to create the political and economic conditions for people's democracy. Until recently, the members of the Communist party have been this elite in every Second World state. Party members have provided leadership and made all key political decisions.

The Counterculture

An alternative political culture has always existed in the Second World, although it was generally repressed by the state and the Communist party until the mid-1980s. By 1990, this alternative political culture was ascendent in most Second World states. It is articulated by citizens and groups who have opposed the Communist party as well as by some party moderates. It differs most importantly from the political culture described above in its alternate vision of people's democracy and political economy.

In this conception, genuine democratic participation, including civil rights and personal freedom, is an essential feature of the political system. The monopoly of power by the Communist party is repudiated, in favor of a group politics approach with multiple competing groups. In economic terms, the shortcomings of the command economy are judged to be so substantial that the political economy must allow greater freedom of action to firms and to individuals. However, the commitment to egalitarianism and social justice remains a strong theme, and thus the state must continue to be very active in controlling and redistributing society's resources.

The clash (in the Second World) between the traditional political culture and the counterculture has become one of the most dramatic political phenomena of the twentieth century. The resolution of this clash and its effects on the politics in these states remains uncertain. But the dimensions of the clash can be better understood by examining how and how well Second World states have achieved the basic goals of prosperity, stability, and security during the past 40 years.

GOAL: PROSPERITY

The prosperity goals of Second World states, like those in the First World, are to facilitate economic development and to provide welfare to their populations. There is a difference in emphasis, however, because Second World states stress that the fundamental objective is to distribute material welfare and social well-being to the entire population, not to maximize rates of economic growth or the overall GNP per capita without regard to the inequality of benefits. Pursuit of economic growth should not take precedence over the essential objective: enhancing the quality of everyone's life, with relative equality of resource distribution.

Command Economy

The core strategy for achieving prosperity in Second World states has been the command economy. The state, on behalf of "the people," controls most significant factors of production in the society, including land, labor, and capital. Citizens do own their personal and household goods and can use some of their labor and other resources in the private production of certain goods (including services).

The state decides what goods will be produced by the system, and also how and to whom values and goods will be distributed. The main guide for the production and distribution of goods is the *central plan*. The plan is developed and administered by central, regional, and local bureaucracies that are controlled and monitored by Communist party members. The plan replaces the market, providing detailed targets regarding production, costs, prices, and allocation. The Soviet Union has devised its thirteenth Five-Year Plan for 1991–1995.

Ideally, the plan provides a framework for insuring that society's valued resources are controlled by the state (on behalf of the people), rather than by private households (for their own private profit). And the plan directs the resources into areas of the economy and the society that merit support, in order to stimulate economic development, provide jobs for everyone, and distribute welfare. This welfare includes free or highly subsized goods such as food, roads, schools, hospitals, power, transportation, and so on.

Performance

Table 15.1 presents the same prosperity measures that were used in Table 14.3. The states of the Second World have achieved reasonable levels of economic performance, as measured by GNP per capita. In comparative terms, most are in

TABLE 15.1. Prosperity Measures for Second World States

State	GNP per Capita 1988	"Index of Social Progress" 1983
East Germany	$12,500	73
Czechoslovakia	10,130	71
Soviet Union	8,700	52
Hungary	8,670	74
Bulgaria	7,540	71
Poland	7,280	68
Romania	6,570	67
Yugoslavia	6,540	62
Albania	990	55

SOURCE: *C.I.A. World Factbook 1989* and *U.S.S.R. Facts and Figures Annual 13*, 1989 for GNP data; Estes 1988: Table A.1 for Index of social progress data.

the upper ranks within the set of 125 states, ranging from fifteenth (East Germany) to forty-ninth (Yugoslavia). Only Albania is far outside this range, at eighty-third. Growth rates in GNP have been adequate, although considerably below the targets set by the states' economic plans. In the Soviet Union, the growth rate has averaged about 3 percent per year, despite a target in the 5 percent range.

Given their declared objectives of improving the general quality of life of their citizens, the index of social progress might be a measure more aligned to these states' own definition of prosperity. These countries do reasonably well on the index, with most achieving index scores in the seventies or high sixties. Among the 124 nation-states in Estes's (1988) study, all but two Second World states rank between twenty-first and thirty-first place. These states tend to score quite high on measures of education and health. Their scores are low on political and civil rights and on excessive military expenditure. Most Second World states compare very favorably with First World states on a similar index measuring "physical quality of life"—that is, "important elements that should be included in a humane existence," (including infant mortality, life expectancy, and literacy) (Morris 1979:20–40).

By worldwide standards, the states of the Second World are relatively prosperous on these measures. However, their levels are unimpressive if the yardstick is performance in the states of Western Europe (should it be?). A comparison of Table 14.3 with Table 15.1 reveals that most Second World states score lower than most First World states on both measures of prosperity. An East Germany–West Germany comparison is probably the most appropriate and dramatic one. Since these two parts of a single state were separated at the end of World War II, West Germany has promoted extensive economic development—its GNP per capita is about $2,000 higher than that of East Germany, and it is the top ranking country on the index of social progress, while East Germany is twenty-second on the index. (Like most cross-national comparisons, this one is subject to qualifications. For example, much of the German industrial base before World War II was in the area which became West Germany; West Germany received substantially more post–war economic aid for reconstruction from the United States Marshall Plan than East Germany did from the Soviet Union; East Germany does outrank West Germany on two of the ten subindexes of social progress, most notably on health status.)

It is the more difficult to describe prosperity at the individual level. Generally, most people's material lives are, like the objective measures, adequate but not great. On the negative side, the quality of goods is often poor and there are recurrent shortages, even of basic consumer goods. Consumer products are more abundant in East Germany, Hungary, and Czechoslovakia than in other Second World states, but are still at considerably lower levels than in Western Europe. One study estimates that the average Soviet citizen's level of consumer goods has a market value of only one-half of that of the goods consumed by a comparable citizen in Western Europe (Schroeder 1987:13–30). Basic necessities such as housing and health care are available to all, but few enjoy high standards of provision (see Herlemann 1987). Luxury items (e.g., electronics equipment, dressy clothes, fancy foods, cars) are expensive, yet demand nearly always outstrips supply. (In the Soviet Union and Hungary, for example, people can be on a waiting list to buy a new car for up to ten years.)

On the positive side, each state's allocation of resources provides a decent standard of material life for a large proportion of the citizens. Virtually every citizen has access to inexpensive or free health care, education, food, and shelter. People have jobs and nearly all are secure against the economic problems associated with disability, illness, and old age. The state provides extensive public facilities for transportation, culture, and recreation. Second World leaders emphasize that very few of their citizens need to fear the devastating effects of poverty and relative deprivation experienced by as many as one-fourth of the citizens in some of the most prosperous First World states.

Problems

These states begin with admirable objectives: (1) to produce goods that serve social needs, and (2) to control wages and prices in order to insure affordable goods for all. But Second World states are plagued by substantial underproduction and poor quality of many goods and services due to some of the inherent problems with command political economies (recall Chapter 8).

Inadequate Incentives.   One key problem is that individuals do not receive substantial material incentives for exceptional productivity. Contrary to the Marxist ideal, workers seem less inclined to work hard for the good of the collectivity than for their own private benefit. Because wage incentives are low, many workers have low morale, high absenteeism, and minimal commitment either to productive efficiency or to the production of high-quality goods and services. And managers are cautious and noninnovative, because the penalties for failing to follow the plan are greater than the rewards for successful innovation. Thus productivity problems are evident in all sectors of the economy.

Overcentralization.   A second key problem with Second World economies is the commitment to central planning and control. Large state economic planning bureaucracies simply cannot foresee the precise needs of producers and consumers.

They are not sensitive to local variations, they are not responsive to short-term opportunities or problems, and they stifle local initiative. Excessive centralization is a particular problem in the industrial sector. Given the rigid adherence to the central plan, in the absence of a strong demand mechanism, there are continual inefficiencies of the following sorts:

> Miscalculations in the central plan (e.g., too many heavy coats are produced and not enough light coats, relative to consumers' desires)
> Supply bottlenecks (e.g., production of the coats is delayed for weeks because the button factory did not send enough large buttons)
> Lack of innovative management (e.g., factory manager waits for buttons to come "through channels" rather than improvising to find buttons from another source)

Inadequate Capital Investment.   Due to the emphasis on development of heavy industry and military equipment, there has generally been insufficient capital investment in machinery and modern technologies to stimulate productivity gains in agriculture, light industry, and consumer goods (Goldman 1988). Much of the machinery in these sectors is old and in disrepair. The computer technologies and automated systems employed in the production process are in short supply and are often unsophisticated. The low level of capital expenditure also results in poor distribution systems for many goods (e.g., there are serious deficiencies in the systems for storing and transporting farm products).

Responses and Innovations

Even in the 1970s, a few Second World states had begun to reform their political economies (see the discussion of Hungary in Box 15.2). By the late 1980s, leaders in most Second World states openly acknowledged that their command economies have failed to create the economic vitality necessary to achieve their prosperity goals. Thus most have modified their political economies in the effort to spur productivity (Toma 1988).

Decentralization.   First, the economy has been decentralized, with less government control. Some industrial and agricultural enterprises have considerable independence to (1) determine their own mix of what is produced, (2) organize their technologies of production (i.e., decide what combinations of workers and machines will perform specific tasks), (3) set wages and provide wage incentives, (4) retain some surplus ("profit") and decide how to distribute it between expansion and wage rewards, and (5) negotiate their own arrangements with suppliers and buyers.

Private Market Development.   Second, a private market sector has emerged. Small enterprises are allowed to offer goods and services at a free market price. While the state extracts a substantial tax, successful firms can generate considerable profits, which managers and workers distribute among themselves or reinvest in the firm. Also individuals and groups are now allowed to produce and sell prod-

BOX 15.2

Hungary's Goulash Communism:
Early Economic Innovation

Hungary, one of the smallest East European states, shares borders with the Soviet Union, Czechoslovakia, Austria, Yugoslavia, and Romania. In 1945, Soviet troops liberated Hungary from the Germans, and assisted the Hungarian Communists as they took control of the postwar government. A loyal satellite of the Soviets, Hungary followed the repressive politics and economics of Stalin for the first decade. When reformists in the Hungarian Communist party seized control in 1956, announcing major political and economic reforms, the Soviet Union intervened militarily, brutally suppressing the popular uprising and installing Janos Kadar as a hard-line loyalist to the Soviet view of Second World politics and economics.

In fact, Kadar proved to be a moderate who promoted innovative reforms in the extreme command political economy model implemented in other second World states. Guided by the New Economic Mechanism of 1968, the reforms reduced the role of the central plan, encouraged local initiative, and allowed work groups and individuals to enjoy the benefits of their labor. Individual firms and their managers made production decisions, established workers' wages, and set prices on the basis of market demand and profit, rather than being constrained by the central plan. Farmers were allowed to produce for private or group profit on state-owned lands. Unprofitable state enterprises were closed.

Over the next decade, more and more aspects of the market were introduced, emphasizing greater economic entrepreneurship. By the late 1970s, Hungary's economic system was labelled "goulash communism," because it mixed in everything that worked, regardless of its consistency with the pure model of the command economy. Hungary also developed many linkages with First World economies, borrowing substantial sums from Western banks and forming many cooperative enterprises with "capitalist" corporations. For example, Levi Strauss built and managed factories in Hungary that produced "May Day" levis, and shared in the profits as the pants were sold throughout Eastern Europe.

The reforms stimulated productivity and enabled many of the 10.6 million Hungarians to enjoy one of the highest standards of living in Eastern Europe, with ample consumer goods. These economic innovations became a model for those implemented in other Second World states in the late 1980s.

But the difficulty in finding the appropriate balance between command and market elements is also very evident in Hungary. Hungary's openness to market-oriented reforms exposed its people to substantial inflation, unemployment, and a very high per capita foreign debt. Ironically, modest prosperity also seemed to cause many Hungarians to feel considerable unhappiness, due to unfulfilled expectations for even more consumer goods.

According to a 1987 survey, the standard of living has been declining throughout the 1980s, and 83 percent of Hungarians live under "intolerable economic strain." Hungary has one of the highest suicide rates in the world, as well as rapid increases in divorce, alcoholism, and social alienation (discussion based on Goldman 1988:92–95; 188–190). In short, goulash communism seemed to falter in its attempt to achieve prosperity through a mix of command economy and market economy elements.

ucts in their spare time. For example, agricultural families can cultivate small private plots and sell their products to state distributors or in the market. In Poland, for example, the private sector now produces 35 percent of the marketable (nonfood) goods and 55 percent of the basic services (Goldman 1988:102). Equally important, the state is releasing its tight control on the prices of goods, allowing prices to move substantially closer to a market-based price.

Transactions with First World.   The third innovation is the increased involvement with First World firms and capital. Second World states have purchased considerable First World technology in an attempt to modernize their productive systems, and have developed extensive trading relations with the First World. Yugoslavia, Romania, and Hungary have been especially outward-looking, establishing official joint ventures with First World firms. The managerial capabilities, productive systems, and technology of the capitalists are used in combination with local workers, materials, and markets, and profits are shared. Hungary and Poland have borrowed substantial sums of money from First World financial institutions, and now face major debt obligations.

Perestroika.   For nearly four decades, from the late 1940s to the late 1980s, the Soviet Union attempted to prevent other Second World states from deviating far from the Soviet approach to political economy. The Soviets used economic and even military power to limit innovation. But after Gorbachev came to power in March 1985, he began to promote *perestroika* (''restructuring'') of the Soviet economic system (Goldman 1987; Naylor 1988). Like the innovations described above, *perestroika* shifts the system toward a more mixed political economy. It encourages greater initiative by producers, more incentives to those who are productive, a reduced role of central planners, and more market-based prices. Private economic actors operate legally in certain sectors of the economy, including food production and consumer services. And there is greater worker self-management in enterprises, with profitability now a major determinant of the enterprise's survival.

So far, however, these economic innovations have been associated with a worsening economic situation. There are serious shortages of basic goods, inflation is up, debt is up, productivity has not improved, and there seems greater economic inequality than before the reforms. These problems are especially severe in states that have been least willing to implement economic innovations, like Romania. But even the most innovative states, which enjoyed economic success in the early 1980s (e.g., Hungary), are now experiencing such problems. In the face of inflation and growing debt, these governments have introduced income taxes and other taxes and are trying to determine how much change toward a market economy is desirable.

While these economic reforms are major, their permanence is an open question. If economic conditions deteriorate seriously under the reforms, the new leadership might face a severe counterattack from the supporters of a more traditional command economy. Powerful groups (especially the military and the advantaged *nomenklatura,* which includes the higher levels of the party and state bureaucracies) have been the losers in these reforms, and they constitute a strong base from which a counterrevolution might emerge. And many citizens might become so disillusioned with the further decline in prosperity and the reduction in equality that they would not resist a return to earlier economic approaches.

GOAL: STABILITY

A basic assumption in the Second World is that prosperity + equality → stability. That is, social and political stability will result from the relatively equal distribution of abundant goods and services. The use of the economic system to serve all the people instead of to exploit them and the elimination of pervasive competition and class conflict will replace human alienation with a sense of personal well-being. And effective socialization will create "new" citizens who have a collective and communal consciousness instead of antisocial personal values like acquisitiveness and individualism.

Risk of Instability

Second World states have not achieved stability in this manner. First, they are not classless societies of total equality. Novelist George Orwell's ironic observation in *Animal Farm* (1945/1964:114) that, "all animals are equal, but some animals are more equal than others," applies to citizens in Second World states. In general, there are some advantages in material goods and status for certain groups, such as professionals, urban citizens, men, and favored ethnic groups. The greatest benefits have been enjoyed by Communist party members, especially those near the top of the power hierarchy.

But in comparison to the pre-Communist period, most Second World states have substantially reduced major forms of inequality (Kolosi and Wnuk-Lipinski 1983). The basic components of social welfare, such as housing, health care, jobs, and education are provided to all citizens either free or deeply subsidized. In general, the overall distribution of wealth is more equal than in First World states. For example, the wage differentials between the top and bottom 20 percent of wage earners in the Soviet Union are in a ratio of about 2:1, compared to 5:1 in Sweden and 12:1 in the United States. In a specific example, a doctor and a bus driver in East Germany each earns about $1,000 per month, but the bus driver works five fewer days (*Newsweek,* November 20, 1989:32).

Disparities related to gender, ethnicity, and so on have been reduced, although not eliminated. In the Soviet Union, for example, 90 percent of adult women now have jobs or are students. Women constitute 70 percent of the physicians, nearly one-third of the members of the national legislature, one-third of the ordinary judges, and one-fourth of the (Soviet equivalent of) Ph.D.s. But women still do most of the housework and are concentrated in the lower-paying occupations (Goldman 1988:42–44).

In terms of the stability equation, the greatest problem has been the insufficient level of prosperity, not the level of equality. The failure of the political economy to generate material abundance for all is a major source of citizen dissatisfaction in all these states. Alienation and instability have been evident in countries that have promised far more than has been delivered (e.g., the Soviet Union), and in countries that experienced a substantial increase in material abundance during the early 1980s but have been unable to meet people's growing expectations since then (e.g., Hungary). At the political level, this frustration is manifest in growing criticism and electoral repudiation of the Communist party and the political leadership.

To the extent there is insufficient prosperity, Second World states have relied upon a rather pervasive system of repression to insure political and social peace. In Samuel Huntington's (1968) terminology, these states preferred to err in the direction of order/repression rather than in the direction of freedom/instability. To insure stability in the absence of prosperity, Second World states have imposed control over many aspects of peoples' lives. Prior to the 1990s, the key instruments of control were the use of rewards and sanctions, system-supporting socialization, and the Communist party. This traditional approach to control is discussed first, followed by a description of the recent changes in these control instruments.

Sanctions and Rewards

Those who support the system have been rewarded in a variety of ways. Communist party membership has been a significant reward to loyalists because the party was the route to power and status and also to additional material benefits such as preferential access to desired goods, including housing, social services, entertainment, and even food. Hard workers who fulfill their production quotas also receive job advancement, modest wage differentials, and status rewards such as plaques, medals, and public recognition. Additional material rewards are also provided to those who bring recognition to their country through exceptional talents (e.g., in areas such as science, the arts, and sports).

Although positive rewards are a major part of the system of order maintenance, these states also rely heavily on sanctions to insure stability. Individuals' behavior has been closely monitored by peers, by Communist party members, and by an extensive apparatus of secret police (such as the Soviet KGB and the Romanian Securitate). While few states of the Second World have been as pervasively totalitarian as those described in George Orwell's novel *1984* (1949/1967), individuals have lived with the constant possibility that any person they see might be "spying" on them and that any place they go might have surveillance equipment. Given such possibilities, most people were cautious about publicly violating social norms in action or even in speech.

Antistate behavior is viewed as a severe threat to the stability of both the political system and the society. Crimes against other people, such as murder or rape, are obviously unacceptable. And, given the significance of material resources in Marxist thinking, crimes against property, such as theft or embezzlement, are generally viewed as far more serious offenses in the Second World than in the First World. Both the state bureaucracies and the Communist party seek to identify and punish individuals who violate the state's rules. Informal punishment might be reduced access to desired resources such as job advancement and better housing.

Minor offenses are usually dealt with by the lower, citizen-staffed comrades' courts, but the penalties are slight and rarely involve imprisonment. The small proportion of people who commit more serious offenses have faced the sanctions meted out by the state's security forces and its judicial system. First World images of Second World justice are perhaps overly influenced by the writings of Soviet emigré Alexander Solzenitzyn (e.g., his books *One Day in the Life of Ivan Denisovitch* [1963] and *The Gulag Archipelago* [1973]). While most offenders do not face decades in mental asylums or at hard labor in Siberia, the judicial systems do levy swift, certain, and harsh punishment for serious offenses, and Siberian-style imprisonment does exist.

Socialization

A second main technique of control has been extensive political socialization. The educational system emphasizes that loyalty to the system and obedience to rules are appropriate behaviors that will be rewarded in all aspects of life. The content of education explicitly presents the Soviet (Marxist) view of history, social sciences, the arts, and even the sciences. The school system rewards conformity to the rules of the society as much as it rewards outstanding scholarship.

From an early age, people are required to participate in mass social organizations that reinforce the principles and behavior promoted in the schools. Children must join youth groups such as the Young Pioneers (from age 8–12) and Komsomol (through the teenage years), which mix the social, entertainment, and training activities that First World children might find in diverse organizations like sports teams, Boy or Girl Scouts, teen clubs, and church groups. Adults are also supposed to participate in mass organizations based on special interest groups and unions. A central function of all such organizations is political socialization, through their recurrent emphasis on the benefits and values of life in the Second World.

Until recently, the media and culture have been carefully controlled by each Second World state in order to insure that these agents of socialization continually affirmed the goals and ideology of the society. The state has owned all television, radio, and news media. All media have presented high-quality, selective content that is meant to educate and entertain. Material that might disturb the stability of people's political or social beliefs has been avoided. Similarly, literature, theatre, music, film, visual arts, and other cultural forms have been required to conform broadly to the principles of "socialist realism," which essentially meant they reinforced the basic tenets of Second World political culture.

Communist Party

The members of the Communist party have been the third crucial element in maintaining stability in Second World states. The party is an elite, and the honor of membership is extended only to about 10 percent of the adult population. Those at the apex of the Communist party are the most powerful individuals in the society, for the party, not the state, has been the ultimate source of political power. Top party leaders have made all crucial policy decisions for the political system and thus for the society. And throughout the society, party members are represented at every level in every organization (e.g., in factories, social clubs, collective farms, schools, etc.). In the Marxist jargon of the Second World, this policy process is based on *democratic centralism:* Ideas and information move up the hierarchy and are clarified by top leaders into explicit decisions, which are then communicated downward. The decisions are imposed upon all institutions, groups, and individuals at lower levels, with the expectation of unquestioning obedience.

The Communist party members have had three central roles in insuring stability:

1. Party members *transmit* policy. Operating in the strongly hierarchical fashion of democratic centralism, the top party leaders make the public policy decisions that allocate values. Then party members throughout the society receive these policy directives, adjust them to local conditions, and communicate them to local actors. They also provide those at higher levels in the party with information about local problems and issues that threaten the stability of the system.

2. Party members *mobilize* the population. There are party members in virtually every organization in the society, and they attempt to promote enthusiasm and commitment for the leaders' policies among the people in the organization.

3. Party members *monitor and control* behavior. Because they have penetrated all organizations at all levels, they can observe the extent to which individuals behave in accordance with policy. They warn people who deviate from the norms and, if necessary, can recommend sanctions against those who act improperly.

Party-State Relations

In terms of political structures, most states have an assembly form of government, with policy-making power residing, in theory at least, in a national legislature. The legislature is elected by universal suffrage, although there has traditionally been only one candidate per district, proposed by the Communist party. The large legislatures have acquiesced to the policy directives of an executive body composed of 10–30 top leaders. In the Soviet Union, for example, the legislature consists of an elected 2,250-member Congress that meets only once or twice a year, from which a 450-member full-time two-house legislature, the Supreme Soviet, is appointed. At the apex is the 20-member Presidium serving as an executive body, and the chief of state, the president of the Congress.

There are parallel party structures for each governmental structure. To this point, primary political power in Second World states has been held by individuals who are in the party's top executive body (e.g., the Politburo in the Soviet Union), regardless of their positions in the government. In most states, the leader (general secretary) of the Communist party has also been the head of state. In this parallel party-state framework, the party membership and the entire governmental system have been a pervasive system of institutions and individuals who administer the policies established by the Communist party leadership.

Is the Party Over?

Until recently, the leading role of the Communist party has been absolute in Second World societies. Only minor, subservient political parties were tolerated. Any association such as a church or trade union that gained the loyalty of a subset of the population was treated as a threat to the stability of the political order. There have always been limits on the liberalization that the state's Communist party and, behind it, the Soviet Union's leadership would allow. When a flowering of public participation occurred in Czechoslovakia in 1967–1968, the population became so enthusiastically mobilized that the Soviet Union feared uncontrollable instability might emerge. Thus the Czech experiment in "socialism with a human face"—socialist economics with democratic politics—was quickly squelched by Soviet military intervention (see Box 15.3).

BOX 15.3

A Preview of Socialism with a Human Face: Czechoslovakia 1968

An early attempt to create a more open and democratic society within the context of a command economy occurred briefly in Czechoslovakia in the late 1960s. A multiethnic nation of 15.6 million, Czechoslovakia is at the crossroads of Europe, bordering West Germany and Austria as well as East Germany, Poland, Hungary, and the Soviet Union. The Communist party had considerable support from the population after World War II. During the 1950s and 1960s, Czechoslovakia closely followed the Soviet model of politics and political economy.

However, internal Czech opposition to the leadership's rigid adherence to the Soviet approach emerged in the 1960s. Some Czechs felt that economic development would be best served by a less centralized approach and looked favorably at the flexible approach in Yugoslavia. Others wanted to return to the historical pattern of greater trade and cultural interaction with Western Europe. These forces led to the ouster of the party's very conservative leader, Antonin Novotny, in January 1968, and his replacement by the leader of the party's Slovakian region, Alexander Dubček.

Dubček immediately introduced major reforms that emphasized liberalization. Economic planning and policy-making powers were decentralized from the national party and the central ministries to the regions and to the managers and workers of individual enterprises. Even more important was Dubček's encouragement of greater personal freedoms. Open public discussion of political and social issues was permitted, and censorship of the media and of culture was virtually eliminated.

Many Czechs, especially in the capital city of Prague, were exhilarated by the new freedoms. The streets and cafés were filled with people engaged in animated discussion about politics and society. Unofficial newspapers and flyers circulated widely. Even the official media featured frank examinations of the problems with the Czech political and economic systems and of innovations that might yield improvements. Performances of the works of playwrights, poets, and other artists proliferated. People were genuinely excited about their ability to participate actively in the discussion of public issues and to influence the formulation of policy.

BOX 15.3 *continued*

Dubček himself was highly visible, enthusiastically leading and encouraging the new openness in Czech life. His vision came to be termed "socialism with a human face." He made clear his continued commitment to socialist economics—the state's organization and control of society's productive resources for the material benefit of all citizens. But he also emphasized democratic liberalism—a humanistic system granting each person greater power and discretion over her life, especially regarding personal freedom of expression. Thus the basic features of a command political economy (although with greater private initiatives) were to be combined with the basic features of a democratic politics (although with the continued dominance of the Communist party).

The outpouring of energy and political support for these reforms among Czech citizens alarmed Leonid Brezhnev and other leaders in the Soviet Union. Brezhnev had been moving the Soviet Union and other Second World countries toward greater ideological orthodoxy and he opposed open criticism of the party's economic and political policies. Brezhnev feared that the liberalization in Czechoslovakia might be uncontrollable there and, even worse, that it might spread to other Second World states.

When Dubček would not moderate his policies under pressure from the Soviets, they moved decisively. On August 20, 1968, the Soviets led a joint invasion of Czechoslovakia by Warsaw Pact troops from Bulgaria, East Germany, Poland, and the Soviet Union. Prague was occupied overnight by tanks and soldiers, who took control of the government and the major cities. There were mass demonstrations and some violence against the occupying forces, but the soldiers firmly suppressed all protests. The Czech leaders, including Dubček, and others who resisted the invasion

BOX 15.3 *continued*

were arrested. The Soviets installed a new leader, Gustav Husak, who was told to implement a policy of "normalization." This meant that all of Dubček's liberalization policies were reversed. Instead, there was ruthless suppression of freedom of expression, severe censorship of media and culture, and strong central control of the society and the political economy by the party. Warsaw Pact troops remained in Czechoslovakia until the return to orthodoxy was assured.

Many point to the extraordinary freedom of expression during the "Prague Spring" of 1968 as an example of how Marxist socialism can coexist with democracy. From this perspective, the combination failed not due to a basic contradiction between socialism and democracy, but because of the intervention by the Soviets. Others argue that the two are incompatible, and that the Czech experiment would have led to political decay, with sufficient time.

Epilogue. For the citizens of Czechoslovakia, the period from 1968 to 1989 was decidedly undemocratic. While Czechoslovakia is one of the more prosperous Second World states, social and political life under Husak was very repressive. Some groups (e.g., Charter 77) advocated a return to the liberalization and human rights that existed briefly in 1968, but they had little impact. Fearful of another direct Soviet intervention, the Czechs generally remained an obedient Soviet ally on social, economic, and foreign policy. Hungary and Poland were the leading states in the sweeping reforms toward democratic socialism in the 1980s, not Czechoslovakia.

Husak was replaced in 1987 by a more moderate leader, Milos Jakes, and then Jakes was swept out of power in November 1989, near the end of an astonishing year of change in Eastern Europe (see Box 15.4). At the beginning of the 1990s, Czechoslovakia was also on the path to a multiparty system and a mixed political economy. Its transitional president was a man from the counterculture, a playwright (Vaclav Havel) who had been a leader of Charter 77 and a symbol of defiance against the party. In a dramatic gesture, Alexander Dubček was welcomed as a returning hero and was elected speaker of the new Czechoslovak Parliament in December 1989. It seems socialism with a human face emerged in Czechoslovakia 20 years too early—before changes in the Second World made its survival possible.

Suddenly, in the late 1980s, the Communist parties in Eastern Europe seemed unable to suppress criticism of and opposition to their longstanding domination of society. And 1989 seems like a watershed year in the post–World War II era—the year of the collapse of the Iron Curtain and of the popular overthrow of Communist party hegemony in most Second World states (see Box 15.4). The near-total dominance of the Communist party over the political system, a fundamental Leninist tenet of these political cultures, was rapidly eliminated.

Between October 1989 and January 1990, the leading role of the Communist party was officially abolished from the constitutions of Hungary, Czechoslovakia, East Germany, Poland, Romania, and Bulgaria. The Central Committee of the Soviet Communist party agreed to amend the Soviet Constitution in the same manner. During this same period, the party suffered massive electoral defeats in the first multiparty elections held in forty years for the legislatures of Poland, East Germany, and Hungary. Despite widespread recognition that the Communist party was unpopular with most citizens in the Second World, few analysts within or outside these states anticipated either the explosion of open political opposition to the party or the disintegration of the party's control of the government and society.

In retrospect, the growth of political opposition can be traced in most states. Although Albania, Bulgaria, and Romania did attempt to sustain an utterly totalitarian regime, the party leadership in the other states abandoned this commitment during the 1970s and 1980s at various rates of speed. Maverick Yugoslavia had traditionally allowed its citizens considerable personal freedom, even in political behavior. Several other states (especially East Germany, Hungary, and Poland) allowed moderate expansion in the level of personal and political freedom, especially during the 1980s. East Germany, for example, tolerated organized dissent groups which publicly promoted such issues as nuclear disarmament, the demilitarization of East German life, and strong political and economic linkages with Western Europe. The Evangelical Church became a major force in peoples' moral lives and the East German government allowed the church to speak out on many social and political issues. And while culture was supposed to be "socially useful," there were few explicit restraints on forms of cultural expression in East Germany (Goldman, 1988:89).

As explicitly political associations emerged, the response of the Communist party and the state apparatus was to ignore them officially and to attempt to undermine them covertly by means of the many bureaucratic actions through which the association's operations could be made more difficult. Individual critics of the regimes were also subjected to this pattern of responses, although some suffered the more traditional forms of sanctions.

The tolerance of opposition received an enormous boost with Gorbachev's policy of "glasnost." The word has been translated in the West as "openness," but it is better interpreted as a willingness by top leadership to allow public discussion and criticism. In the Soviet Union, top-level authorities encouraged and participated in explicit public criticism of the political, economic, and social system. This was accompanied by the rapid emergence of critical cultural and media expressions that were previously repressed.

In most Second World states, political opposition groups began to test the limits of the states' tolerance. It became increasingly clear that Gorbachev would not use the military or economic power of the Soviet Union to support a Second World political regime attempting to repress the personal and political expressions of its citizens. While Box 15.4 details many key events in 1989, two seem pivotal in the undermining of Communist party hegemony. First, in March 1989, the Soviet Union followed several other Second World states in allowing its citizens to elect a legislative body in which there was genuine competition among alternative candidates, some not proposed by the party. Governmental roles were taken by individuals who were critical of the party. In a second key event at this time, the Polish government allowed Solidarity, the independent (of the Communist party) trade union movement, to sponsor non-party candidates in elections to the national legislature. Its candidates won a stunning victory, defeating Communist party candidates in virtually all the seats it contested.

With the whole world watching, the streets of East Germany, Czechoslova-

BOX 15.4

That's the Way the Curtain Crumbles:
1989 in Eastern Europe

In 1989, there was a series of tumultous changes in the Second World that are unparalleled since its creation. Events occurred at a dizzying pace, and each incident usually had impacts in other states. Some of the most notable events are described below.

January and February
Hungary takes the lead in the reform movement when its Parliament legalizes freedom of assembly, and the Communist party allows the creation of legal, independent political parties. In Poland, tens of thousands of citizens openly insist on their political and economic rights, staging demonstrations and wildcats strikes.

March, April, and May
The pivotal event, again in Hungary, is the dismantling of parts of the barbed wire fence that had long separated Hungary from Austria. This is the first physical break in the "Iron Curtain," a system of travel restrictions, guards, walls, fences, and other obstacles that had physically prevented East Europeans from free entry into Western Europe. Party leaders recognize that the Soviet Union will not interfere with reforms and the Soviets begin to cut back their troop levels in Eastern Europe. Public protests intensify and broaden, particularly in Poland and Czechoslovakia.

May, June, and July
In Poland, Solidarity deals the Communist party a devastating defeat in legislative elections, creating a formal political opposition in the legislature. Moderates take control of the Hungarian Communist party and attempt to negotiate with opposition groups.

August, September, and October
East Europeans, including more than 30,000 East Germans, pour out of the Second World via the new openings in the borders of Hungary. There are massive demonstrations in East Germany, and the party chief (Erich Honecker) is forced out of power after 18 years. In Poland, a new government is formed in which non-Communists are the majority. Hungary establishes a "free republic" and plans for open multiparty elections in early 1990.

November and December
East Germany removes restrictions on foreign travel in an attempt to discourage the massive, illegal exodus. Then, on November 11, it opens the Berlin Wall, the most dramatic and notorious symbol of the Iron Curtain. A million East and West Germans begin an exuberant reunion in the streets of West Berlin. A new East German government is formed in which the interim president and one-fourth of the cabinet are non-Communists. Free elections are promised for May 1990. After massive demonstrations, several reformations of the Czech government are attempted, leading to the replacement of the Communist party leader, the prime minister, and the president, and the installation of the first non-Communist-dominated government in 41 years. Public demonstrations in Bulgaria force the government to promise free elections by June 1990. Violence explodes in Romania, as the state's security police kill hundreds of demonstrators. After a brief civil war, a reformist group takes political control in Romania, and executes Nicolae Ceausescu, the hardline party leader since 1965.

kia, and other states filled with citizens demanding political and human rights. But, unlike a similar situation in the major cities of China in 1989, the party leadership lacked either the will or the capacity to suppress the citizen demands for democratization. The power of the Communist party in most states seemed to shrivel up. But the party and its members remain entrenched in every institution in these societies. Hence the citizens' euphoria was mixed with uncertainty. Had the party merely made a tactical retreat to regroup? Would the party accept the role of loyal opposition in the governmental system? Was the party really finished?

Democratic Revolution. With the notable exception of Romania, the dramatic changes of 1989 occurred with so little political violence, either establishment violence or revolutionary violence, that the transitions of these political systems seem consistent with the concept of the "democratic revolution" discussed in Chapter 12. (Romania seems to correspond more closely to the model of "revolution from above," with a violent urban struggle between factions of the military and their civilian supporters, and the swift overthrow of the leadership of the "old regime.") Leaders in Czechoslovakia, for example, termed this transformation "the gentle revolution." With minimal violence, the population rejected the authority of the Communist party and the regime, which lacked the will and/or means to reassert its control. In each case, the new leadership has committed itself to sweeping changes in the political system and the political economy.

The End of Stability?

Overall, the Second World states have been successful in maintaining a high level of stability. There have been occasional outbreaks of collective instability, as in the uprisings in Hungary in 1956, Czechoslovakia in 1968, and Poland in 1956, 1968, and the 1980s. But these were firmly suppressed, and the normal pattern of collective life has been stable, with the state and its agents in firm control.

In most Second World states, some periods since the late 1940s are appropriately characterized by imagery of a totalitarian, "police state" atmosphere. But most people's private behaviors have generally been free from repressive state control, as long as individuals did not call public attention to their activities. Like their First World counterparts, most people enjoyed a life of friends, family, eating, working, playing, loving, and so on. In every Second World state, people had developed a broad understanding of the point where their personal freedom of expression and action began to threaten the state's sense of social stability and they usually behaved within those boundaries. When their actions seemed too defiant of the state's or Party's authority, the authorities imposed repressive measures.

In such oppressively stable systems, frustration often manifests itself at the personal level. The levels of substance abuse (e.g., alcoholism, drug use) and family problems (e.g., divorce, child abuse) have been increasing (Goldman 1988:42–43, 95). Per capita alcohol consumption is among the highest in the world, and widespread alcohol abuse has caused major social, health, and economic problems (Treml 1987:151–162). Polish anti-drinking laws include the rationing of alcohol and a ban on alcohol sale after Wednesday of each week, laws that merely produce extremely long lines. Gorbachev's government is sloganeering that *"trezvost norma zhizni"* ("sobriety is the norm of life"), which, in the Soviet Union, it clearly is not.

But violent anti-social behavior still seems to be at much lower rates than in the First World. As suggested by the comparative crime data in Table 15.2, violent crimes against people and property crimes are substantially lower in the Second World. These have been societies where, due to the mixture of political culture and state control, citizens generally feel safe from harm by each other.

With the recent liberalization, both the political culture and state control are uncertain. The boundaries of acceptable private and public behaviors have been blurred. These states can no longer presume the dull conformity that enabled them to be among the most stable political systems in the world. Even the conservative states have not been able to avoid a large rise in instability. The most notable case is Romania, which openly denounced the changes in other Second World states and failed in its attempt to sustain a repressive regime. It is uncertain whether the new personal and political freedom in these states will reduce personal pathologies or increase them. The initial evidence in the political sphere has been an outburst of political disorder. Open political conflict and negative support for the political system have been unleashed in most Second World states.

Another manifestation of the changing context is the large scale mobilization of long-repressed nationality groups. Such resurgent nationalism is a particular problem, because it challenges the very survival of the nation-state. Most Second World states are ethnically diverse. Nationality-based political violence, including demonstrations, protests, and rioting, has surfaced in several Second World states, such as Yugoslavia, where the fragile amalgamation of ethnic groups has begun to fragment. Resurgent nationalism has been a major problem for the Soviet Union, one of the most diverse multinational states in the world, with more than 100 ethnic groups, 22 major nationalities, and more than 50 languages (Silver

TABLE 15.2. Crime Rates in the Soviet Union and the United States, 1987

Type of Crime	Cases per 100,000 Population	
	Soviet Union	United States
Aggravated assault	13	350
Rape[a]	6	37
Property crimes	191	4,906
Violent robbery	4	NA
Murder[a]	6	8
Overall crime rate	657	5,550

[a]Soviet figures include "attempted rape" and "attempted murder" while U.S. figures include only rape and murder.
SOURCE: *Los Angeles Times*, February 15, 1989, based on reports of the Soviet Foreign Ministry and the U.S. Federal Bureau of Investigation.

1985). Groups in the western republics of the Soviet Union, such as Armenians, Azerbaijans, Estonians, and Lithuanians, have been extremely aggressive in demanding cultural and political autonomy. The republics' efforts to establish independent states resulted in major political and military confrontations with the central Soviet government.

A Prediction for the 1990s.   It seems the early 1990s will be characterized by the emergence of a multiplicity of political groups, of free elections, and of the establishment of non-Communist governments in most Second World states. But there are many uncertainties about the evolution of this group politics. Will the Communist party accept electoral defeat and the role of "loyal opposition"? What are the agendas and political effectiveness of the new activists? Will they be able to govern effectively and retain the support of the citizens? Is Gorbachev's continuation in power essential to maintaining the balance of change and stability in the Second World? No one can be confident in the accuracy of her answers to these questions.

The high levels of stability in the period from the early 1950s to the mid-1980s are unlikely to continue in the 1990s. Indeed, the effects of democratizing the political system and transforming the political economy might be so destabilizing that they severely undermine social order. It is clear that in the short run these states will not be able to provide their citizens with the level of material well-being they desire. As state control of the society's resources is reduced in favor of the market, the state cannot sustain the levels of subsidies on goods that Second World citizens have traditionally enjoyed. Citizens' demands and expectations will far exceed the capacity of the political systems. Thus the conditions seem ripe for the kinds of political disorder and political violence indicated by such analyses as Huntington's (1965) conception of political decay (recall Chapter 11) and Davies's (1971) "J-curve" theory (Chapter 12).

GOAL: SECURITY

History and Geopolitics

The fundamental goal of all states is survival. And the Soviet Union places exceptionally high importance on security goals. This priority is understandable in both historical and geopolitical terms. For the last 200 years, Eastern Europe and the Western areas of the Soviet Union have been recurrent battlefields. From the west have come devastating invasions by the French under Napoleon and by the Germans under Hitler. In World War II, for example, 15 million Soviet citizens were killed—1 in every 22 people in the society. In contrast, 1 in every 150 British were killed and only 1 in every 500 Americans. The culture of the Soviet Union emphasizes a tragic history of invasion, destruction, and brave resistance in "Mother Russia" and the desire for peace combined with the necessity to prepare for future war.

Geopolitically, the Second World is a crucial pivot in the political power bases of the Northern Hemisphere. In fact, in Mackinder's famous nineteenth-century geopolitical analysis, Eastern Europe and Russia were the essential "heartland," whose control would ensure dominance of the world. From its contemporary geopolitical perspective, the Soviet Union perceives potential threats everywhere:

> To the *east,* the huge population of China on the Soviet's long eastern border is viewed as a direct threat. And Japan is both a historical military adversary and a current, major capitalist economic power.
>
> To the *south,* the militancy of Islamic fundamentalism presents an explicit and growing danger, given its strong antipathy to communism. And there are also large Arabic/Asian ethnic groups in the Soviet Union, who share identity and nationalistic impulses with the states to the south.
>
> Most importantly, to the *west* are massed the major capitalist powers, with their own deep animosity to the communist systems and with devastating military (including nuclear) capabilities stretched along almost half of the Second World's border.

Military Power

To protect itself against all these real or perceived threats to its survival, the Soviet Union emphasizes unchallengeable military power. Its geopolitical location and its international political interests mean that the Soviet Union needs military strength on land, sea, and air, and in nuclear weaponry.

The broad objective of the Soviet Union has been to maintain military parity with the United States and its NATO allies. The Second World now has arguably the most powerful military in the world for conventional warfare, and it is not far behind the First World in air power and nuclear capabilities. Through the Warsaw Pact, a mutual security treaty including most Second World states, such power increases these states' capacity to protect themselves on their eastern, southern, and western borders (Nelson 1984).

A strong integrated military through the Warsaw Pact has also been the final, powerful force to suppress instability within any Second World state, as in Hungary in 1956 and Czechoslovakia in 1968. Warsaw Pact military power has supported internal leadership changes in the face of major disorder, as in the ascendency of Wojciech Jaruzelski in Poland in the fall of 1981. Most broadly, military power has become a useful mechanism for projecting and protecting Soviet interests internationally, especially in the Third World.

The Soviet Union allocates a substantial proportion of its economic and human resources to support its military power. Soviet leaders from Stalin until Gorbachev have consistently opted for guns over butter. The Soviets reported spending 9 percent of their GNP on defense in 1989, compared to about 6 percent in the United States. (Some Western analysts argue that the Soviets devote as much as 15 percent of GNP to military expenditures. In either case, the United States spends more in absolute terms: about $305 billion in 1988 vs. Soviet expenditures of $119–200 billion). The military has always been a major power bloc in the internal politics of the Soviet elite. Both the loyalty and the capabilities of the military have been essential to the security and stability goals of the Soviet Union. But the cost of allocating such massive resources to military power is a substantial reduction in the societal resources available to achieve economic growth and distribution of welfare.

Buffer States

The Soviet Union also attempts to increase its security by surrounding as much of its territory as possible with buffer states between itself and its competitors. Historically, the Baltic states and Eastern Europe were the route by which the Poles, Swedes, French, Austrians, and Germans invaded Russia. Thus a foreign policy objective of the Soviet Union is to guarantee its clear sphere of influence over these states.

Political Relations.   Early in World War II (1940), the Soviet Union annexed some Baltic areas, including Estonia, Latvia, and Lithuania, directly into the Soviet federation, as Soviet republics. In the late stages of the war, it extended its control over the other nation-states now included in the Second World category. This was accomplished by military conquest and then partial withdrawal once loyal local groups had taken political and military control of the state. Although the annexed areas and the other Second World states share neither a common history nor unique ethnic identity with the Russians, they do buffer the Soviet Union from the hostile capitalist powers of Western Europe.

In foreign policy, the other Second World states generally conform to the position of their 'big brother.'' But nearly all these states assert their independence from the Soviet Union on some issues. For example, Romania has differed quite openly with important aspects of Soviet foreign policy. It insists on the autonomy of national Communist parties from external interference. Thus Romania refused to support Soviet attempts to isolate China from other Communist states (in the 1960s and 1970s), was the first Second World state to restore relations with West Germany (1968), opposed Soviet military intervention in Czechoslovakia (1968), condemned the Soviet intervention in Afghanistan (1979), defied the Soviet boycott of the Los Angeles Summer Olympics (1984), and has been a leader in advocating an end to the deployment of missiles in Europe. The Soviets have tolerated such independence because Romania has generally conformed to Soviet domestic and economic policy and has been a loyal ally, supporting the overall stability and security of the Second World.

Economic Relations.   In addition, there is a cooperative economic market among the Second World states, the Council for Mutual Economic Assistance (CMEA). Through resource sharing and free trading within CMEA, most Second World states are able to strengthen their own economies. Originally, the arrangements were structured primarily to advantage the Soviet economy; but in recent decades there has been more subsidization from the Soviet economy. In general, the Soviet Union sells raw materials at low prices to other Second World states and purchases manufactured products from them at high prices.

Given their own resources and their economic cooperation, Second World states have attempted to limit their dependence on external resources. For reasons of ideology and goodwill, they trade actively with Third World states. But the Second World has become dependent on the First World both for the importation of food, since it usually fails to produce enough for its own population, and also for the purchase or theft of advanced technology.

With the attempts to modernize their economies and introduce more elements of the mixed political economy, most states have become more involved with First World capital. A few states have borrowed substantial sums from First World financial institutions to pay for imports. These states are now saddled with significant debt repayment and balance of payments problems because they have few exports that can be sold profitably for hard currency outside of Eastern Europe. For example, the hard currency debt in 1990 for Hungary is $16.0 billion and for Poland is $39.4 billion (Kaslow 1989). But most states have limited their involvement with foreign capital, conducting most of their major international economic exchanges within the CMEA, and thus have very low foreign debt.

In sum, the Soviet Union has been willing to pay a considerable price for the security it attains through the loyalty and stability of other Second World states. During periods of political unrest in those states, the Soviets have provided additional financial subsidies to support cheap food and other commodities and have also financed much of the military power these states employ to prevent internal instability. The Soviet attempt to install a puppet regime in Afghanistan and the protracted Afghan civil war, fought with Soviet resources and personnel, is a recent example of Soviet willingness to expend very high levels of resources to extend and maintain its buffer, in this case between itself and the Islamic world. The assertion of independence by East European states as well as border republics within the Soviet Union is undermining the Soviet's system of buffer states.

Promoting Revolution

According to the Marxist-Leninist view of international relations, the survival of every communist state depends ultimately upon the creation of a world of "comradely" communist states that are classless and peace loving. Pragmatically, it is assumed that many existing states are hostile to the continued existence of communist states and are committed to overthrowing such states. And it is recognized that the "inevitable" revolutions that establish communist states can always use help. This leads to a two-pronged strategy: (1) vigilance against conquest of or counterrevolution in any current communist state; and (2) constant support of "wars of liberation" in states that are noncommunist. The implementation of this strategy is primarily planned, financed, and carried out by the Soviet Union, with other Second World states generally supporting Soviet foreign policy.

The First World objected to but acquiesced in the Russian Revolution (1917), the Soviet expansion of its sphere of influence and control over the Baltic states and eastern Poland before World War II, and the occupation of the remainder of

Eastern Europe at the conclusion of the war. But the security policies of the First and Second World have been in great conflict since that time, reaching a level referred to as a "cold war" (no direct fighting but extensive and hostile interactions) in the 1950s.

The leaders in the Second World believe, probably correctly, that their own military power has been a necessary defense against a hostile, well-armed First World. In turn, leaders in the First World judge, probably correctly, that the military power of the Second World has been excessive and threatening. Each side in this bipolar balance of power system has tried to insure itself against military vulnerability, by attempting to achieve its own definition of military parity; but the other side interpreted this as an attempt to achieve superiority. This spawned a huge military buildup and arms race, and resulted in the kind of mutually assured destruction (MAD) discussed in Chapter 13. In such a context, no state can ever feel secure.

A second factor complicates the security relations between the First and Second World. The Soviet Union actively promotes "wars of liberation" in the Third World. Communist ideology assumes that political violence is an essential part of the revolutionary class struggle. Thus the Soviet Union views the support of such violence as appropriate. The Soviets provide (either directly or indirectly through such Soviet client states as Cuba, Angola, and Nicaragua until 1990) financial, military, and ideological support for indigenous groups anywhere who are committed to overthrowing their noncommunist political system. This support has facilitated communist revolutions in such states as Angola, China, Cuba, Mozambique, Nicaragua, Vietnam, and South Yemen. In addition, the Soviet Union committed itself (in the "Brezhnev doctrine") to protect all communist-oriented states against counterrevolution. In the 1980s, this resulted in the costly Soviet involvement in Afghanistan.

Second World support of revolutionary activities is deeply objectionable to First World states. They are distressed over the emergence of additional pro-Soviet communist political systems, they claim that revolution by political violence is unacceptable, and they believe that such activities destabilize the international balance of power. On the one side, First World states tend to hold the Soviet Union directly or indirectly responsible for virtually all political unrest aimed at substantial change in the distribution of power in First or Third World states. On the other side, Second World states assume that much of the class oppression and establishment violence in most noncommunist states and the instability in communist states is directly or indirectly supported by the First World. Such contrasting perceptions heighten the tension and increase the conflictual interactions between the First and Second Worlds, and they cause the Second World states to be even more concerned to protect their security (Garthoff 1985).

Thus, whenever there is an international hot spot, one or both superpowers usually interprets it as a threat to security that requires some political-military action. In this complex multipolar system with two superpowers, the international balance of power remains fragile, at best. To this point, however, the First and Second World have managed to avoid a direct, hot war in the nearly half-century since the Second World War.

Foreign Policy Shifts

As in his economic and political policies, Gorbachev's foreign policy represents a significant break with previous approaches in the Second World. His approach has evolved significantly toward the post–cold war internationalist perspective or possibly even the semi-isolationist perspective (Chapter 13). While Nikita Khrushchev boldly predicted that communist political economy would bury the First World through its economic vitality, Gorbachev seems intent on burying the hatchet and copying many features of First World economics.

Gorbachev has made sweeping and dramatic proposals for reductions in Warsaw Pact defense expenditure, nuclear weapons, and conventional forces. He authorized unilateral reductions of military personnel and hardware in Eastern Europe and a lengthy cessation of nuclear weapons tests. And Gorbachev has taken the initiative in reaching signed agreements with the United States regarding bilateral (Soviet–U.S) and multilateral (Warsaw Pact–NATO) military reductions.

The more reformist Second World states had developed strong cultural and economic ties to Western Europe. But substantial reduction of tensions between the First and Second World was possible only when the Soviet Union was incorporated into the process. Gorbachev achieved this with his conciliatory approach to demilitarization in Europe and in his entrepreneurial efforts to increase economic cooperation with the First World. The dismantling of the Iron Curtain has had a dramatic effect on the interactions between and the attitudes of East and West Europeans towards each other. This is most evident in the actions to reunify East and West Germany.

Under Gorbachev, the Soviets have abandoned the Brezhnev doctrine, most concretely with the withdrawal of Soviet troops from Afghanistan. More broadly, the Soviet bloc's direct military support for wars of liberation in the Third World has been limited. Many (but not all) observers believe that the Soviet Union and other Second World states are making a genuine effort to reduce their commitment of resources to security concerns in order to allocate more resources to achieving their prosperity goals. But both the Second World and the First World continue to have massive military power, both conventional and nuclear. In a MAD world, the possibility of a devastating conflict between the Second World and the First World remains.

A RECKONING

In the three-quarters of a century since the Russian Revolution, there has been a very mixed record of success and failure in the communist states of the Second World. These states have clearly achieved their fundamental *security* goal—they have survived in a world that has generally been hostile to their very existence. And in terms of international conquest, the Soviet Union probably has the world's most notable record of successes in the period since 1940. It is largely responsible for creating and controlling the new political systems that emerged in all other Second World states.

Moreover, the Second World has exerted great influence on the behavior of

BOX 15.5

A Day in the Life: Second World

There are 450 million stories in the Second World. This is one of them. . . .

Anna wakes first and quietly prepares breakfast for herself, her husband, and son. Her husband worked late at the battery factory to make some extra money, but he must be up soon for his regular shift. She moves quietly around their crowded, two-room flat in the outskirts of Warsaw, since her son sleeps in the larger room, which also serves as living room, dining room, and kitchen. She wakes her son so that he can get ready for school. He has aptitude in science, and she is very optimistic that his exam results will qualify him for technical training at the university and a better job than she or her husband have.

She rides the bus to her own assembly line job in a factory that manufactures radios. She talks and jokes with the other workers while her production group works steadily to meet their daily quota. At lunch, Anna walks down the road to see if she can buy some groceries. She is pleased that the lines are not long and that milk, bread, and some vegetables are available. She is even able to buy a small piece of meat, mainly because she has done some free repair work on a radio owned by the butcher. (As a second job, Anna privately repairs radios for extra money.) But there is no fruit or sugar today and vodka cannot be purchased on Fridays.

After lunch, her supervisor, who is a Communist party member, reminds her that her production group will be meeting on Monday to discuss changes in work organization. She dislikes her supervisor, and shows no enthusiasm for the meeting. Her group works hard to surpass its quota, since the members will share some extra wages if they maintain their current output rate for the entire month.

When her nine-hour shift ends, Anna walks by the department store that sells the color television that is her family's great desire. She is on a waiting list to buy it, and had hoped to save enough money in the remaining months before she reaches the top of the list; but Anna is worried because prices on basic goods have begun to rise sharply. Nonetheless, she and her husband still manage to save, because their rent is very low (less than 10 percent of her wage alone), costs for food and transportation remain modest, some services like health care are free, and there are few luxury items to buy.

Shortly after Anna arrives home, her husband and son also return. Soon, some friends arrive at the apartment. Everyone has brought something to share, and the table is covered with things to eat or drink. There is talk of politics, with much interest in the new government policies to allow higher wages but also to raise the prices of most basic foods. There is an animated debate, in which Anna argues strongly that Solidarity's economic policies are even worse than those of the party, and that everything will be more expensive than ever. Others insist that eliminating the strong control by the party is bound to improve economic conditions, although no one wants the state to eliminate its subsidies on such important goods as food, housing, health care, and education. Only one person argues that Poles would be better off if the country were capitalist. Anna's husband credits most of the positive changes to Gorbachev, although no one expresses much optimism that the Russians want to improve the life of Polish people. Everyone does agree that Gorbachev is doing a good job of reducing the danger of war in Europe and of softening the aggressive foreign policy of the United States. When Anna's husband does his imitation of George Bush, the serious mood is broken by laughter.

BOX 15.5 *continued*

As more vodka is drunk and more food is eaten, everyone becomes more jovial and there is talk, laughter, and some singing. Most watch a soccer match on television featuring two top European teams; but the rest of the evening's programming is dull, including an old German film and a Polish children's choir, and the television is generally ignored. As soon as the friends leave, Anna snuggles up to her husband and sleeps.

many states. By mixing military support and an attractive ideology of development and egalitarianism, it has deeply influenced the politics in many Third World states and has played a major role in transforming the political systems of about two dozen of these states. In such states, revolutionary leaders have decided that the Second World's approach to politics and political economy offers the most promising solution for achieving basic goals.

But there are also negative effects of these extensive Second World efforts to create and support other communist systems. First, the Second World has expended many resources abroad that might have been used to enhance life within its own states. And second, some other states, especially in the First World, judge the Second World to be the most dangerous threat to their own quest for prosperity, stability, and security. These other states have taken many actions to disrupt or undermine the foreign policy, economic health, and internal politics of Second World states.

Thus the Second World, led by the Soviet Union, has become an international power whose military prowess is unsurpassed. But these states have not made themselves secure in a world of socialist states. They rely on outsiders for technology, capital, even food. They are still surrounded by strong states that would be delighted to see the death of their current political systems. Their opponents have military capacity that is as formidable as their own. If enormous military power provides security, the citizens of the Second World should feel secure. Yet they do not.

Second World states have been more successful in achieving their *stability* goals. Stability and very gradual, controlled change characterized the political, social, and economic orders of these states until the late 1980s. The political systems, although generally nondemocratic and repressive, have had high levels of political institutionalization, measured as capability and stability. The decision-making dominance of a small elite and the strong leadership role of the Communist party have been the central features of Second World political systems. The elite resolved its disagreements behind closed doors, and offered few political choices to the citizens. An extensive and costly state apparatus insured order maintenance, and the state allowed only modest personal freedom within a generally repressive framework.

If stability is assessed by conventional measures of revolutions, coups, and large-scale political violence, Second World states have been among the most stable political systems in the modern world. Crimes against people and against property also are relatively low, in comparison to the rates and the seriousness of such crimes in comparable First World states.

But there are now fundamental changes occurring in these states. The repressive, authoritarian politics is being supplanted by democratic reforms allowing freedom of expression and opposition, multiple parties, and elections with genuine alternatives. Elements of the mixed economy, including market prices, a demand orientation, and private profit are being introduced into the rigid command political economies. These innovations are inherently destabilizing, and it is unclear whether the elites will be able to govern effectively and to insure social and political order in the face of such instability.

It is in the pursuit of their *prosperity* goals that the performance of Second World states is most problematic. On the one hand, the citizens of the Second World enjoy lives characterized by social and economic security and relative equality. Most citizens have basic necessities, and there is a very deep safety net for those in need. Individuals lack the freedom of choice available to economic actors in the First World; but this is in large part due to the attempt to enhance and equalize the lives of all the citizens. Overall, these states have made substantial progress in providing shelter, food, jobs, health care, education, and other social welfare goods to their entire population, regardless of the individuals' wealth or social position.

On the other hand, the political economies of the Second World have failed to satisfy their populations' desires for goods and services. Their command economies have revealed the weaknesses that arise in the absence of a demand-oriented market and strong material incentives. Economic growth has been only modest. In general, the economic systems have been characterized by low productivity, inefficiency, and poor quality in the production of goods. Material abundance has been the major unfilled promise of the Second World states.

The current economic reforms are intended to stimulate productivity and increase the availability of goods by introducing major elements of the market political economy. But the economy will be very disrupted in (at least) the short run and there will be greater inequality in the distribution of benefits. As the example of Hungary indicates, it is not clear that these systems can establish an effective mixed economy. The future of Second World states seems especially problematic if prosperity does not increase at a rate that compensates for the reduction in social and political stability.

As this point in human history, no society can have it all. Each must decide which goals are most desirable, and then attempt to implement strategies to attain them. This entails *evaluative* choices, given the constraints of political culture, resources, and the environment. In the Second World states the maintenance of vast military power, international influence, and extremely high levels of internal stability has absorbed resources that might have provided greater material abundance for the citizenry. While the general welfare of the population has been increased, economic shortcomings have obliged these states to expend even more resources on order maintenance.

To this point, at least, the Second World has followed an approach that has produced considerable stability and security within a framework of egalitarianism—but in the absence of material abundance and individual human freedom. The fascinating question for the 1990s is whether these states will be able to create and sustain socialism with a human face by blending egalitarianism and *freedom from* disease, want, ignorance, squalor, and idleness for all in the society with individualism and *freedom to* behave with minimal constraint in the economic, social, and political spheres.

CHAPTER 16

The Third World

THIRD WORLD IMAGES

What is your image of the Third World? It might be of dusty villages where poor and uneducated people scrape out a subsistence diet from their small farm. It might be of large cities where some live and work in modern, technologically advanced settings but are surrounded by a huge, dense population living in abject poverty and squalor. It might be of traditional religious societies where petrodollars have provided high levels of material goods and a high-tech environment to people who had previously been relatively untouched by modernization. It might be of a huge nation-state attempting to govern 1 billion people or of a small island state with a population of less than 50,000. It might be of a state successfully adopting European political forms of representative democracy, popular participation, and freedom of opposition, or of one reeling under a despotic regime where the small leadership clique ruthlessly eliminates all opposition and leadership change occurs only by political violence.

Developmental Classification

Somewhere among the 140 states and 3.4 billion people in the Third World, all of these images are accurate. As we have noted above, the concept *Third World* is usually employed rather loosely to encompass all states not in the First or Second worlds. Broadly, the common traits shared by the states in the Third World are that, relative to the first two worlds, they are less developed—less modern, less industrialized, with a lower standard of living, high birth rates (often higher than economic growth rates), youthful populations (often more than half the population is less than 25), and a history that includes a significant period of domination by a colonial master.

The Third World states are often defined developmentally as the *less developed countries* (LDCs) in contrast to the *more developed countries* (MDCs) of the First and Second worlds. The terms *South* and *North* are also used to distinguish these two groups, because the great majority of the Third World is geographically south of most states of the First and Second worlds. Although the labels *LDC* and *South* are generally accurate, it is not true that every state in the Third World is poorer than all those in the First and Second worlds. In fact, the two states among those with the world's highest GNP per capita are oil-rich Third World ministates in the Middle East (the United Arab Emirates and Kuwait).

Some discussions by social scientists and in the media refer to a *Fourth World,* which includes the poorest Third World states. The World Bank (1989) makes this differentiation among the LDCs, distinguishing 53 *middle income countries* (MICs) with annual GNP per capita of $520 to $5,810 from 42 *low income countries* (LICs) with annual GNP per capita of $130 to $450. It is the LICs that are generally classified as the Fourth World states. (Other international organizations like the United Nations and the Organization for Economic Cooperation and Development have similar classifications, in which there are about 45 and 30 countries in the lowest group.)

In developmental terms, Fourth World political economies show few signs of progress toward overcoming their development gap in relation to other countries. In a Fourth World state, the political system and the economic system are so disorganized and/or the resources are so meager that the political economy seems unlikely to attain even limited success in achieving the prosperity goals of economic development and resource distribution. In these states, most people live close to subsistence, hard pressed to provide themselves with the basic essentials of food, clothing, and shelter.

Regional Classification

While most approaches classify Third World states on developmental criteria, it is also possible to distinguish four regional groupings, which have somewhat different characteristics.

Latin America.   The Latin American subset (including Central American and South American states) tends to be relatively advanced, with a modern, technological sector. Direct colonial control of these states came early, with most of the states having been granted independence by the mid-nineteenth century. In most there is a strong national identity that corresponds to the geographic boundaries of the state and the state has considerable institutionalization. There are also other well-institutionalized structures in the society, particularly the army and the church, and there is an indigenous upper-class elite. Finally, most of these states are highly urbanized, and it is estimated that more than 80 percent of the population in Latin America will live in cities by the year 2000.

There is a subsubset in Latin America, composed of the Caribbean states. These hundreds of islands are extremely diverse in culture and geography. In comparison to the rest of the Latin American region, these island states tend to have longer colonial legacies, to be less developed and less urban, and to have an ethnic heritage that is more African and Asian (and secondarily English and French) rather than Indian and Hispanic (who predominate in the rest of Latin America).

Asia.   A second regional subset consists of most of the states in Asia. This is a vast regional area, covering one-third of the earth and including about two-thirds of its people. The area is characterized by great ethnic, cultural, and geographic diversity, although it is dominated in human and historical-cultural terms by China (with its 1.1 billion people) and India (with its 800 million). These and other populous Asian states (e.g., Indonesia, Bangladesh, and Pakistan) are Fourth World states on the basis of per capita GNP. They are predominantly rural and agrarian, and there is a large gap between the traditional society and the smaller modernized and technologically advanced sectors in a few major cities. Yet Asia also includes some successful developing MICs, such as Malaysia, and all of the major NICs—the newly industrialized countries (see Box 16.1). India and most of South Asia have experienced considerable direct European colonial influence since the seventeenth century, while much of Southeast Asia has historically been more under the direct or indirect control of China. There are substantial national-

BOX 16.1

Neither First nor Second
nor Third: The NICs

A small set of countries no longer seem to fit the classification as LDCs but have not yet evolved into more developed countries. In general, this group has been termed the *NICs* (the newly industrialized countries). These states have undergone substantial economic development, with a diversified and technologically based productive sector.

Chapter 11 described the development strategy of the "classic" NICs, all of which are in East Asia: Singapore, South Korea, Taiwan, and the British crown colony of Hong Kong. These Asian NICs have developed within a hierarchical and conservative social and political system. The national elite has exerted strong control over the political economy, over other major social institutions, and over the population in order to facilitate the transition to a developed economic system based on manufacturing and knowledge-based industries. Most of these states have depended upon the financial and technological support of a First World patron state, usually the United States or Britain.

To add to the confusing array of labels for Third World states, a few other countries are also sometimes referred to as NICs. Some of these are Third World states that are attempting to copy the strategy of the Asian NICs, usually with only limited success (e.g., various lists include such states as Argentina, Brazil, Malaysia, and Mexico). Some lists of NICs even include the least developed First World states Greece, Portugal, and Spain, which are still evolving into industrialized economies. Indeed, Singapore and Hong Kong have already surpassed the GNP per capita of these and several other First World states and will soon pass others. In this chapter, the occasional references to the NICs will essentially refer to the Asian NICs, since they provide a strategy for development that is widely admired.

ity differences in most contemporary Asian states, which include diverse ethnic, religious, and linguistic traditions. Political forms and the levels of political institutionalization vary substantially from state to state.

North Africa and the Middle East.   A third regional set of states usually includes the 15 states and ministates of Southwest Asia and the five North African states that are on the Mediterranean Sea and are dominated by the Sahara Desert (Algeria, Egypt, Libya, Morocco, and Tunisia). These states (with the exception of Iran and Turkey) are composed of people who are mostly Islamic in religion and culture and mostly Arabic in ethnicity and language (Weatherby 1987:216–217). The area has major geopolitical importance, both for its strategic location, including its waterways, and for its petroleum resources. Much of the region was controlled by the Ottoman Empire between 1453 and 1918. In the nineteenth and twentieth centuries, European colonial power was exercised mainly through indirect economic and military involvement. Despite some brief periods of direct colonial rule, European values and structures did not penetrate most of these states. Although many have modern sectors, the social, economic, and political forms of these states remain generally tribal-feudal and conservative. In a few petroleum-rich states (e.g., Saudi Arabia, Kuwait, and Iraq), this sudden great wealth distinguishes them from other Third World states and has created powerful forces of change and modernization with which these states are struggling to cope.

Sub-Saharan Africa. Despite its substantial natural resources, Sub-Saharan Africa (the African continent excluding the states of North Africa listed above) is the poorest and least economically developed region in the world. About two-thirds of the world's poorest countries (as measured by GNP per capita) are in this region. After the abolition of the slave trade, the direct experiences with colonialism in most of these states were late, occurring between the 1880s and the 1950s, and were extremely intensive and exploitative. These countries are generally dependent in a neocolonial situation, with limited control over their own resources and minimal modern technology. Few have a strong sense of national unity, because colonial powers created states that arbitrarily merged many nationality groups who had no historical commonality. More than two-thirds of the population in these states is rural, although there is an increasing migration to cities. In most countries, the authority of the central, modern state is weak, and state-level political, social, and economic structures lack institutionalization.

Diversity in the Third (and Fourth?) Worlds

These developmental and regional differences underline the fact that the states in the Third World are so diverse that generalizations are perilous and are subject to many qualifications. These states do not share one political culture, but include many different histories, traditions, religions, and political ideologies. As you read this chapter, and especially as you formulate your own understanding about the Third and Fourth worlds, you should be especially sensitive to the enormous variation across these states and, in many cases, within them. The chapter attempts to specify dominant patterns and general trends. At most points, the term *Third World* will be used to refer to all these states; but at some points, the Fourth World will be distinguished when developmental differences are very significant.

You should understand that there is considerable imprecision in *all* of the concepts discussed above. The work by social scientists, journalists, and others constantly uses the Third World concept, as well as the other labels and acronyms such as MDCs and LDCs, the South and the North, and others. These terms can be a useful shorthand for denoting certain types of states or economic conditions. But there is no widespread agreement on which taxonomy is most useful or on exactly which set of states is included in *any* of these categories. Table 16.1 suggests how this book classifies selected states into these categories.

Like all taxonomic categories, these labels are meant to provide some conceptual order for complex reality. The categories are worth using if they facilitate analysis, comparison, and generalization. You might ultimately decide that these widely used labels are so crude that they diminish rather than enhance your understanding of these states.

TABLE 16.1. Developmental and Regional Classification of Selected Third World States

Developmental Classification	Regional Classification			
	Latin America	Asia	North Africa and the Middle East	Sub-Saharan Africa
Oil states			Kuwait Libya Saudi Arabia	
NICs		South Korea Singapore Taiwan		
MICs	Argentina Brazil Costa Rica Cuba El Salvador Mexico Nicaragua Peru Uruguay Venezuela	Malaysia North Korea Philippines Thailand	Algeria Egypt Jordan Syria Turkey	Ivory Coast Swaziland Zimbabwe South Africa
LICs	Haiti	Afghanistan Bangladesh China India Laos Myanmar Pakistan	Sudan Yemen	Chad Ethiopia Ghana Guinea Kenya Tanzania Uganda Zaire

GOAL: PROSPERITY

The states of the Third World strive for the benefits of prosperity associated with economic development and welfare distribution. While the great majority of Third World countries employ the same economic strategies as First and Second World states, most have minimal success in achieving these benefits. Table 16.2 presents our two prosperity measures for a selected set of Third World states.

Although GNP per capita can be difficult to determine in agrarian societies with a limited cash-based economy, it is the common measure of prosperity in these countries. Kuwait is the wealthiest of a half dozen states outside the First or Second World with "high income country" GNPs. The large majority of Third World states have a GNP per capita of less than $1,000. The average GNP per capita for all Third World states is less than $1,300, and the average for all individuals is less than $700. (Do you understand how these two figures are different?) For the quarter of the world's population in the Fourth World, GNP per capita is less than $300.

A very low GNP per capita suggests limited economic production by the society, but it does not reveal that resources are very unequally divided in most Third World states and that even the most basic goods are minimally available to many people. For example, more than 1 billion people live in chronic hunger, eating less than the daily subsistence level of calories; only one in two can read; and one in seven children dies before the age of 4 (World Bank 1983:142–145).

These stark statistics are more graphic illustrations of the life conditions represented by many states' relatively low scores on the "index of social progress" in Table 16.2. The most prosperous Third World states have index scores in the 60s and 50s, and the scores decline until Ethiopia, where the conditions are so appalling that the index is computed as −6. While the subindexes with particularly low scores vary among countries, the scores on welfare, health, political rights, and women's status, as well as economic development, are often among the lowest ones.

It is noteworthy to point out that there is some correlation between GNP per capita and index score, but it is far from perfect. The Middle Eastern oil states have particularly high GNP per capita in comparison to their social progress index. Efforts by the state or by private actors in some of the Latin American countries and China seem to have produced a higher quality of life than might be expected given their resource base.

For many Third World states, prosperity is an elusive (impossible?) dream as much as it is a goal on which steady improvements are presumed. These states attempt to prosper in a competitive global economy within which they are deeply disadvantaged. Any strategy for development in a less developed country depends on the seriousness of certain obstacles.

Obstacles to Prosperity

Dependence on a Few Export Commodities.   During the colonial period, the dependent Third World state was a source of inexpensive primary commodities and a market for the master state's own manufactured goods and skilled services. Thus reliance on basic commodities for export and the import of more advanced products and services were established as a structural feature of most of these states under colonialism.

Foreign exchange capital is essential if a state is to import food, oil, desired consumer goods, machinery, and other productive resources to expand and diversify its economy, and also to pay the interest on its debts. While there has been some diversification of exports, most Third World states still depend on primary commodities for the majority of their foreign exchange capital (Ruffin and Gregory 1986:434–436). Consider the source of foreign exchange capital in these recent examples:

Gambia: 97 percent from groundnuts
Zambia: 92 percent from copper
Ghana: 69 percent from cocoa
Uganda: 77 percent from coffee and cotton
Latin America as a whole: fully 80 percent is generated by the export of basic commodities.

TABLE 16.2. Prosperity Measures for Selected Third World States

State	GNP per Capita 1987	"Index of Social Progress" 1983
Kuwait	$14,610	n.a.
Singapore	7,940	59
Saudi Arabia	6,200	26
Libya	5,460	35
Venezuela	3,230	62
South Korea	2,690	53
Algeria	2,680	36
Argentina	2,390	62
Uruguay	2,190	66
Brazil	2,020	56
South Africa	1,890	41
Mexico	1,830	51
Costa Rica	1,610	63
Turkey	1,210	46
Cuba	950	61
Nicaragua	830	33
Egypt	680	39
Philippines	590	41
Zimbabwe	580	37
Ghana	390	14
Pakistan	350	17
Kenya	330	26
India	300	28
China	290	37
Tanzania	180	21
Laos	170	12
Bangladesh	160	16
Zaire	150	22
Ethiopia	130	−6

SOURCE: The World Bank 1989: Table 1 for GNP data and Estes 1988: Table A.1 for index of social progress data.

A strong, developed economy is diversified, producing a wide variety of goods for export. But Ghana's export economy can be devastated by drought or pestilence, as can Zambia's by a major drop in the price of copper. The central importance of primary commodities in many Third World countries' exports leaves their economies extremely vulnerable to uncontrollable fluctuations in international market prices and the forces of nature.

Inefficiency and Corruption.   The search for prosperity in many Third World states is also thwarted by high levels of inefficiency or corruption or both (see, e.g., Rosenblum and Williamson 1987). One source of organizational inefficiency is the absence of Weberian bureaucracies (as defined in Chapter 7) in most of these states. Actions are complicated or disrupted because predictable, rule-following behavior cannot be assumed from those in public and private organizations. And a major source of productive inefficiency is the limited availability and ineffective use of modern technologies. Many Third World states have been unable to establish and maintain either efficient infrastructure capabilities, such as transportation systems and communications systems, or sophisticated (and costly) technological equipment.

Corruption exists in every society; but these patterns tend to be especially widespread in public and private organizations in the Third World. Words like *baksheesh* (literally, "something given"), *chai* (literally, "tea") and *dash* are commonly used to signify the private payoffs that are usually necessary to induce organizational personnel to act. Minor personnel might view such payoffs as a necessary supplement to their inadequate wage. Members of the elite might exploit their power and position to extract resources from the productive system and divert them into their own private holdings. A few examples from 1977–1979 are illustrative.

> Only $122 million in revenue actually returned to Zaire from the Zairian coffee crop valued at $400 million.
> More than half of the earnings of the Cocoa Board in Ghana were reported "missing."
> One-third of the Tanzanian coffee crop was smuggled into neighboring Kenya rather than sold to the nationalized trading companies.

High Birth Rates.   Most Third World states have high birth rates and growing populations. The annual rate of population growth for the entire Third World is 2.4 percent, which will result in an overall increase of 80 percent in the Third World population between 1980 and 2000 (Long 1987:10). Populations in some countries, including Bangladesh, Kenya, and Mexico will more than double in this period.

Prosperity is typically measured as GNP or income per capita. These measures indicate the level of income and goods that are generated and available to each person in the society. Since most of these states are increasing population almost as fast as they are increasing production, there is little increase in per capita resources available. More food must be produced, more schools and housing built, and more health care provided just to maintain the existing, quite low standard of living. This leaves few or no surplus resources for economic expansion and increased welfare distribution.

Neocolonialism.   The colonial and postcolonial experience of the Belgian Congo/ Zaire, which was detailed in Box 13.1, exemplifies the continuing dependency of many Third World states long after they have gained their political independence. During colonialism, the master states did not train most Third World peoples to be self-sufficient or to have extensive organizational and technical capabilities. The dependency approach (Chapter 11) is a controversial analysis that claims that colonialism has now merely shifted to a more unofficial and indirect, but no less dominant, control of the economic resources of Third World states by First World states and institutions (Evans 1987; Wallerstein 1980; Weatherby 1987:28–30).

Whether or not the interactions are labelled neocolonialism, many firms in less developed states are linked to political, financial, and business elites of the developed countries. The developed countries are the major source of the financial capital, advanced technologies, organizational skills, and product distribution that a Third World firm needs to compete effectively in the international marketplace. Thus many public and private sector firms in developing countries establish economic arrangements with developed countries, international financial institutions, and multinational corporations (MNCs). These arrangements are described in the next section. Given a history of resource exploitation and current economic underdevelopment, it is debatable whether Third World countries have much choice about whether to enter such arrangements with the developed countries (Evans 1987).

Strategies for Prosperity

Industrialization.   Industrialization is the classic strategy that many Third World states emphasize in their attempt to increase economic development and hence prosperity. The aim is to use labor and capital to transform commodities into intermediate goods (e.g., steel, electricity) and then into more refined and valuable goods (e.g., radios, furniture, tractors). This requires a well-organized system of resource control, a trained and disciplined urban working class, effective technologies, and an efficient infrastructure for distributing goods. It can facilitate *import substitution*—the exchange of goods within the country to provide people's wants without relying on imports. Or it can encourage *export promotion*—the production of goods that can be sold to the rest of the world to earn foreign exchange capital.

Industrialization can be promoted in a market, mixed, or command economy (Chapter 8). Some Third World states rely heavily on the private market and profit-seeking entrepreneurs. A larger number of states have opted for greater state control of the political economy, assuming that economic dependency and underdevelopment can be overcome only by more centralized planning, control, and distribution of the society's productive resources. Regardless of type of political economy, industrial development requires the creation of surplus. As much surplus as possible should be reinvested in order to expand economic capacity. Minimal surplus should be spent on current consumption by, and welfare for, the population.

Many Third World industrialization strategies have emphasized import substitution, as a means to reduce dependency upon more refined goods from developed countries. As implemented in countries like Brazil and India, it has been moderately successful. These states have developed a solid industrial sector that produces a variety of goods for the domestic market. Because the firms are partially protected from the world market's pressures for efficiency, they can be somewhat inefficient. A more serious problem is that these firms are often dependent on foreign corporations, financial capital, and technology. Moreover, even in the Third World states that have been most successful, only a few sectors have industrialized effectively and thus national economic development is extremely uneven.

The strategy of export promotion has become more popular because of the success of the NICs. Even when the state allows private profit, there is extensive state control of the "free" market. The state facilitates the entry of foreign capital and corporations, imposes strong controls to insure a disciplined labor force, discourages domestic consumption, and explicitly directs production to the export market. This strategy has facilitated some industrial development in LDCs like Sri Lanka and Mexico. But it enables foreign actors to play a strong role in the economy (Ruffin and Gregory 1986:431–435).

A serious problem with a primary emphasis on industrialization has been the "dual poisoning" of both the rural and the urban sectors (Schumacher 1973). Many of the most capable and productive workers migrate to urban areas from the rural sector, which then has far-diminished capacity for food production. Those remaining in the rural sector revert toward subsistence agriculture, and cannot produce sufficient food for those in the cities. Thus, rather than exporting food for surplus capital, the state is required to import food. At the same time, the overpopulated urban sector is overwhelmed with people whose demands for good jobs, shelter, amenities, and even food cannot be handled by the political economy. Dissatisfaction grows among the urban population, increasing the likelihood of political decay and governmental crisis.

At its core, the strategy of industrialization depends upon the generation of surplus, which can be reinvested in further economic development. For reasons of cost or quality, domestic goods are often not competitive in the international market. Most Third World states remain net importers of capital, technology, manufactured goods, oil, even food. After purchasing such imports and providing a minimal level of welfare to the population, these states have little or no surplus left to reinvest in development. The LDC must borrow money to sustain the process, and even more to pay interest on foreign loans. Thus the process of industrialization actually increases economic dependency on external economic actors.

Agricultural Development.   Given the apparent problems with an emphasis on industrialization, the transition from subsistence farming to commercial agriculture might be the key to economic development. Minimally, Third World states need to feed their own populations. One billion of their citizens live in chronic hunger, and the level of death by starvation is tragic: 28 per minute, 1,600 per hour, 40,000 per day, 15 million per year (Alexander 1987:34). In recent years, there has actually been a substantial reduction in the amount of productive Third World farmland, due to deforestation and overgrazing caused by the need for more food (Brown 1985).

Commercial agriculture can produce considerably more food than the rural sector population consumes, providing extra food to support a (slowly) growing urban population. Equally important is the growth of food for export, since this generates capital that can be reinvested in either rural or urban economic development. The successful transition to commercial agriculture requires several elements: (1) techniques that increase crop yields and overcome such natural hardships as drought and pestilence, (2) stable and attractive prices within a reliable market, and (3) an efficient system of distribution. These elements might be enhanced by technology and by state control or private control of agricultural development.

New Technologies. Some Third World farms, especially the larger ones, have increased productivity by substituting farm machinery for labor. And the major initiative, since the 1960s, has been the "green revolution," using modern fertilizer and hybrid grains that provide higher yields and survive local conditions (e.g., drought, flood, insects, disease, temperature variance). Along with mechanization, new management techniques, and better irrigation systems, the green revolution increased average rice yields in Asia (especially Bangladesh, China, India, Indonesia, Japan, Myanmar, and the Philippines) by 40 percent and production by more than 60 percent between 1960 and 1980. Although population rose 55 percent during the same period, at least rice production increased a bit faster than the mouths needing feeding (Swaminanthan 1987). But production gains from the green revolution might be reaching their limits in many Third World states, because the costs of its components, especially fertilizer, are rising and yield increases are levelling (Brown 1984).

State Control. Some Third World states have political regimes that are committed to extensive state control of agriculture. Most productive land is owned by the state, which also establishes prices and distribution of all agricultural goods. There are large state/collective farms where technology is shared and where labor is grouped into production teams who are given quotas for certain crops as part of a state plan. This approach is especially evident in such command economies as China, Cuba, Kampuchea, and Tanzania. It has been only moderately successful, because most rural people resist social restructuring and are not as motivated to work hard for the general welfare as for their own personal profit. For these reasons, states like Tanzania have retreated from state farms, encouraging local collectives and more private production of cash crops (Sullivan and Martin 1987:114–116).

Private Control. Small privately owned farms are prevalent in some areas of the Third World where large land holdings were never widespread (e.g., Nigeria) or where states have implemented land reform policies that give local people the farmland that was previously controlled by a few large landholders (e.g., Kenya, Peru). Because of large rural population size and low market prices in most less developed countries, many small farms tend to produce little more than is necessary for subsistence (e.g., in Bangladesh, India, Indonesia, and Kenya).

To encourage entrepreneurial small farmers, some states control or subsidize the prices of farm products and organize an efficient system of distribution, markets, and export. Such state efforts to encourage private agriculture have been relatively successful in some countries, including the Ivory Coast and China (and it has worked well in the NICs of South Korea and Taiwan). Ironically, the most successful small farmers are those producing illegal cash crops such as coca and

BOX 16.2

Something Can Be Done!:
Agricultural Self-Help in Kenya

Many Third World states have implemented small-scale projects that have improved their agricultural productivity. One example is Kenya's efforts to conserve its eroding soil. In 1972, Kenya concluded that widespread soil erosion was its most crucial environmental problem. In 1974, the Kenyan Ministry of Agricultural promoted self-help projects by which small farmers could reduce soil erosion and also increase their productivity. The ministry gave farmers the materials and instructions to construct simple terraces that reduced water runoff. Farmers were also given seedling trees that would yield fruit, fuel, and fodder. Within 10 years, more than 100,000 small farmers were participating in these projects. Tens of thousands of miles of new terraces and hundreds of thousands of new trees are reducing soil erosion in Kenya, as well as capturing more moisture for crops, and increasing the farmers' incomes. With technical assistance and modest financial aid from Sweden and effective promotion by the ministry, Kenya's farmers have been able to increase their yields and to preserve their country's environment (based on Wolf, 1985).

opium rather than those producing legal crops, whose international prices tend to fluctuate greatly. Even with government assistance and domestic price supports, small private farms have been unable to support the transition to commercial agriculture in most of the less developed countries.

In many Third World states with market-oriented systems, less than 10 percent of the rural population owns half or more of the most productive agricultural land. Often, there are large farms ("plantations") owned by land barons or by national or multinational corporations. Some large landowners use approaches that result in low productivity—for example, many small farmers work the land as laborers or sharecroppers, with few incentives (Alexander 1987:46). Other large commercial farms are very efficient. But in many such cases, there is collusion between the political elite and private (national or foreign) elites. Thus the profits are primarily captured by the elites and are not used for national economic development or welfare (e.g., in Chile, El Salvador, the Philippines, and Zaire).

Results. Few Third World states have made large advances toward prosperity through a strategy emphasizing agricultural development. In some states, farming remains disorganized and inefficient, resulting in subsistence approaches and overuse of environmental resources. Some states have been so committed to shifting production to agricultural goods for export that production of basic foods for domestic need has deteriorated to the point where the state must import basic food. And in some states, the profits from commercial agriculture have often been captured by national and foreign elites, rather than being the engine for economic prosperity.

Even in the states where the green revolution has been most successful, increases in food production have barely outstripped population growth. And the limits of technological increases are now evident. The key puzzle seems to be how to encourage high levels of productivity in a manner that preserves the environment, feeds the domestic population, *and* produces surplus for export. An approach to agricultural development that achieves all three of these objectives will enable a Third World state to support its own population while also creating financial surplus for economic growth and welfare distribution. In most less developed countries, this puzzle remains unsolved.

Collaboration with Foreign Capital.   A third strategy in the search for prosperity is to embrace the foreign devils—to make explicit deals with First and Second World states. The developed countries (and their major national and multinational corporations) are the richest source of capital and technology for the less developed countries.

Foreign Aid. Many Third World states argue that the more developed countries "owe" them unconditional assistance. Decades or centuries of colonial exploitation have enormously benefitted the developed countries, while the Third World states have been left with depleted resources and severe underdevelopment in the international economic environment. Thus they demand a *New International Economic Order* (NIEO), with many forms of repayment to Third World states, including knowledge and technology transfer, cancellation of debts for previous loans, financial aid that has no conditions attached, and "reparations" for former resource use.

The developed countries do provide some unconditional aid and assistance to Third World countries, to assuage guilt, to gain international prestige for their philanthropy, and to curry ideological favor from Third World states. This assistance includes humanitarian aid, development aid, skilled personnel, and technology transfers to selected states for specific purposes. Both First and Second World states have financed and helped build such projects as hydroelectric dams and highways systems. First World states provide Third World states with about $35 billion per year in foreign aid (Ruffin and Gregory 1986:434). Such aid can increase prosperity.

There are many reasons why First and Second World states provide economic assistance. The most important motivations are usually based on an appraisal of their own national self-interest: political (to establish alliances or a political sphere of influence, to exclude ideological rivals), military (to deploy strategic military power), or economic (to obtain resources, to open markets for their own goods and services). But the more developed countries express little enthusiasm for an NIEO, which might result in a significant reallocation of wealth to the Third World.

Neocolonialism. Some Third World states decide that neocolonialism cannot be resisted, and so the most pragmatic approach is to negotiate the most favorable terms for obtaining capital and technology. States do not acknowledge that they have "sold out" to actors from more developed countries. But beneath the rhetoric of loans, trade agreements, and cooperative developments is the reality that the distribution of benefits from an agreement between a more developed country

BOX 16.3

Just Say No!: China

Some Third World states have refused to collaborate, insisting that their national self-interest is better served by preserving autonomy, rather than by accepting assistance from the more developed countries. A notable example of this is China during most of Mao Zedong's rule (1949–1976). Mao argued that to achieve political and economic self-sufficiency, China must not accept outside aid and, in the process, become dependent upon the aid givers. He was so committed to this policy of independence that during a catastrophic drought (1960–1962) the Chinese even declined humanitarian aid from the International Red Cross, while 20 million starved to death. But even Mao had periods of reliance on the Soviet Union, and the current Chinese leadership is energetically soliciting external involvement in China's economic development. Few Third World states have had the resource diversity and political will to attempt self-reliance. At most, they have temporarily resisted the demands of the developed countries regarding loan repayment to international lenders or more favorable treatment of multinational corporations with economic operations within their boundaries.

and a less developed country usually reflect the underlying inequalities in political and economic power.

Three styles of involvement illustrate the economic relationships that can emerge between the Third World state and external economic actors (i.e., more developed countries or transnational and multinational corporations):

1. *Elite cooperation.* The national elite agrees to allow external economic actors to pursue their interests under conditions very favorable to the external actors. In return, members of the Third World state's elite receive substantial rewards for their personal benefit (e.g., shares of the profit, military protection, bribes, etc.). An example is the long-standing relationship between the political elite in Honduras and the U.S.-based United Fruit Company.

2. *Profit sharing.* External economic actors are encouraged to enter the country under an explicit agreement that profits will be shared with the Third World state. In Guatemala, for example, the International Nickel Corporation was allowed to expand its mining operations as long as 75 percent of the profits were retained by the Guatemalan government (or, if one is less charitable, by its political-economic elite). Some of the oil states, including Saudi Arabia, the United Arab Emirates, and Venezuela, also develop forms of profit sharing with multinational corporations, although they require that local workers are trained to fill jobs at all levels.

3. *Open door.* External economic actors are given relatively free access to invest or to establish operations in the Third World state (e.g., Barbados, Sri Lanka). It is assumed that benefits will trickle down throughout the

internal economy (e.g., capital, jobs, taxes on profits, technological and organizational skills). Occasionally, a Third World state has expropriated some of the foreign actors' assets (e.g., Peru).

The effects of these strategies on the search for prosperity depend upon many factors, including the mix of strategies, the internal economic situation, the political economy of the state, the level of economic development, and the behavior of the external actors. The strategies can provide spillover benefits to the less developed country; but they also tend to sustain or even increase its economic dependency. None insures that the external economic actors, in pursuing their own interests, will act in ways that generate longer-term benefits for the less developed country, either in terms of increased economic development or of more extensive surplus.

Borrowing. Faced with the problem of insufficient surplus to finance economic development and welfare distribution, many states have implemented "quick fixes": Some states have merely printed more money. This enables the government to pay for welfare and to purchase products from abroad. The problem is that, in the absence of a strong economy to back this money, it becomes worth less and less externally and at home. This quickly produces a serious inflationary spiral unless the state can control virtually all domestic consumption.

The most common strategy has been to borrow funds from the international financial community, primarily composed of major First World banks (through the International Monetary Fund and the World Bank). Loans offer a short-run solution since they can be used to finance growth and welfare. But loans require repayment. The political economy soon finds itself saddled not only with this year's needs for surplus to support growth and welfare, but also with a large debt obligation from last year.

In the last two decades, many Third World states attempting to finance growth and welfare without a solid economic base have found themselves mired in the consequences of these "quick fix" strategies. As Table 16.3 indicates, inflation rates have generally been high, and sometimes staggering. The annual inflation rate has reached more than 1,000 percent for a year or more in several Latin American countries. In Argentina, inflation averaged about 300 percent per year for the entire eight-year period in the table. Obviously, it is impossible to maintain a coherent plan of economic development in the face of such inflation. With a few notable exceptions, most of the states in the table experienced very high inflation.

Many states are also now deeply indebted to First World financial institutions. Third World states now have an outstanding debt of more than $500 billion. Repayment of such debt can be a debilitating additional burden for a state facing the difficult challenge of generating economic surplus to finance current welfare and future growth. Table 16.3 reveals that many countries must expend more than 25 percent of their export capital (money generated by selling products abroad) to service their debts.

From 1981 to 1984, 40 percent of all export capital in Latin America was absorbed by debt payments to First World financial institutions. This resulted in a

TABLE 16.3. Economic Indicators for Selected Third World States

State	GNP per Capita Average Annual Growth Rate 1965–1987 (percent)	Inflation Average Annual Rate 1980–1987 (percent)	Debt Service As percent of Exports 1987
Argentina	0.0	299	52
Brazil	4.1	166	33
China	5.2	4	7
Costa Rica	1.5	29	14
Egypt	3.5	7	22
Ghana	− 1.6	48	20
India	1.8	8	24
Kenya	1.9	10	34
Malaysia	4.1	1	20
Mexico	2.5	69	38
Nicaragua	− 2.5	87	na
Philippines	1.7	17	26
Singapore	7.2	5	2
Turkey	2.6	21	34
Zaire	− 2.4	54	13

SOURCE: The World Bank 1989: Tables 1, 23.

net outflow of $106 billion from Latin America to the MDCs. When so much economic surplus is consumed merely to pay previous loans, something must be sacrificed. In Latin America, it was social welfare and the standard of living, which dropped 25 percent.

Table 16.3 reveals the variable success that Third World countries have had in their pursuit of prosperity:

> Singapore is an example of one of the few states that has enjoyed two decades of high economic growth with low inflation and almost no reliance on borrowing.
> The most common pattern, reflected by such states as India, Kenya, and Turkey, is a very limited level of economic growth tempered by double-digit inflation and major loan obligations.
> Argentina represents the bleak prospect of no economic growth coupled with rampant inflation and large debt repayments.
> Ghana, Nicaragua, and Zaire reveal the nightmare that, despite high inflation and substantial borrowing, the economy can substantially decline.

Prognosis

Most Third World states continue to vary their mix of the three broad strategies of industrialization, agricultural development, and foreign involvement as they search for a pattern the seems to correspond best to their own situation, both

BOX 16.4

Order and Progress
in Brazil: Sometimes

The motto on the Brazilian flag is "Order and Progress." The vision of order and progress has guided much of Brazilian policy since the founding of the republic in 1889, but the country's recent troubles have cast doubt on Brazil's ability to actualize its vision. In area, Brazil is the fifth largest country in the world, with a population of 138 million and vast natural resources. In many ways, Brazil is the promise of the Third World. But it is also a reflection of the Third World's troubles.

Progress

From the mid-1960s to the mid-1970s, the Brazilian state took the lead in guiding industrialization, emphasizing both import substitution and export promotion. The involvement of international capital and foreign corporations was encouraged. The results were impressive. Brazil's economic development was praised worldwide as a "miracle," with yearly growth averaging 10 percent. Brazil's economy is larger than that of all the rest of South America, and is now the eighth largest among the world's noncommunist systems. It is a Third World leader in the production of many goods, including such agricultural exports as coffee, sugar, and cocoa; such minerals as tin, gold, iron ore, and bauxite; and such industrial goods as textiles, cement, automobiles, and machinery.

Order

Politically, Brazil is a constitutional democracy. The government is a federal republic, with an elected president who has dominant power over the bicameral National Congress. It has a multiparty system, universal and compulsory voting, an independent judiciary, and a relatively free press. The large state bureaucracy has maintained social and political order, with minimal class-based conflict, and Brazil is often cited as one of the world's most successful multiracial societies. A strong military insures the security and sovereignty of Brazil.

Progress?

The economic miracle was built on a weak base. Industrial growth has essentially been debt-led, deeply dependent on external support for finance capital, technology, and markets. Much of the growth has been in the 600 state-owned companies, many of which are extremely inefficient and now technically bankrupt. The emphasis on industrial development has had many negative consequences: The agricultural sector has atrophied, resulting in 2 million landless peasants and the need to import basic foods; in urban areas, the upper and middle classes have received most of the benefits of uneven development, and there are large numbers of working poor and unemployed. The bottom 60 percent of the population receive only about 15 percent of personal income. In recent years, the economy has been in collapse. There is both high unemployment and hyperinflation, averaging 166 percent a year from 1980 to 1987 (Table 16.3). The country imports twice as much as it exports. Brazil's foreign debt is the largest in the Third World, reaching $113 billion by 1987. The government has oscillated between refusing to repay its massive debts (33 percent of exports in 1987) on schedule and imposing the austerity measures required by the International Monetary Fund's conditionality demands.

BOX 16.4 *continued*

Order?

However, when the current president assumed power in 1985, it marked the end of 21 years of authoritarian military rule. The military had taken power in a 1964 coup, supported by the middle class, against an elected government that was judged too sympathetic to the needs of the large numbers of rural and urban poor. The military government was repressive and ruthless, crushing leftist opposition, censoring the press, and compiling one of South America's worst records of human rights abuses. Since the return to civilian rule in 1985, the economic crisis has provoked a huge rise in social disorder: Crime rates have shot up; urban riots are frequent, especially in the huge shantytowns surrounding the cosmopolitan cities; and there is constant violence between peasants and landholders, who are disputing the government's announced but unfilled promises of land reform. In this situation, expectations grow that the discredited military will again intervene, replacing the discredited government and using its repressive approach to restore order. (Based on Goodwin 1990:59–64 and Henry 1987.)

political and economic. The encouraging evidence is that a few states have been quite successful in achieving economic development. The NICs seem to have found at least one strategy to transform into a developed country. Their formula is available to others: an open-door approach to foreign capital, agrarian reform to facilitate commercial agriculture by small farmers, the promotion of exports, and a steady transition to more complex manufacturing technologies (Chapter 11). Other Third World countries (especially those outside of East Asia) have attempted, but not yet been successful in importing this NIC strategy (Davis 1987; on an attempt in the Caribbean, see Conkling 1987).

The situation is not hopeless. There has been some economic growth in the Third World. Between 1965 and 1987, the middle-income (Third World) states have averaged a 2.5 percent annual growth in GNP per capita, while the low-income (Fourth World) states have averaged 3.1 percent (World Bank 1989). Some countries have experienced periods of strong growth in certain sectors of agriculture or industry (as in Brazil). But compared to growth in the developed countries, the Third World has barely stayed even and the Fourth World has lost ground since 1950. Although they are not widespread, there are pockets of material abundance in nearly every developing country. And, with the exception of those in some Fourth World states, the average individual's absolute conditions of life are improving: Health care is better, life expectancy is increasing, and more material goods are attainable. But in comparison with the developed countries, per capita GNP is less than one-eleventh as large, life expectancy is about 15 years shorter, and everyday existence far less comfortable (Ruffin and Gregory 1986:423–425).

Many Third World states are rich in human and natural resources. Yet apart from several oil-rich states, few have been able to sustain solid levels of economic development or to distribute a modest level of welfare to the population, let alone both. The general pattern remains economic underdevelopment in most countries and poverty for the great majority of people. The perplexing question for their leaders is how to convert these resources into prosperity, given their current underdevelopment in a harshly competitive international economic environment and given the internal challenges regarding security and stability.

GOAL: SECURITY

The states in the Third and Fourth worlds search for security in the face of pervasive insecurity. Their problems are grounded in low levels of political and economic development, which reduce their capacity to control their own population and resources. Such incapacity makes a state vulnerable to intervention by other states. Paradoxically, this relative weakness can also lead a state to be more aggressive in its interstate relations, both as a defensive reaction and to divert attention from internal problems. Virtually all wars since 1950 have been fought in the Third World (McLellan 1987). Unlike the states of the First and Second worlds, the very survival of many Third World states is uncertain. Thus our analysis of the search for security in the Third World focusses on interstate violence.

Interstate Violence

Much of the interstate violence in the Third World is between neighboring states. There are many reasons why such violence is so frequent.

1. Many of the geographic *boundaries* between these states do not correspond to those separating historically established nations, and thus conflict develops in an attempt to realign borders with nations.
2. States often look covetously at valuable *resources* in neighboring states and sometimes attempt to gain control of those resources by force or by conquest.
3. Differences in the *cultures* of two states, especially those orientations grounded in nationality, political ideology, or religious belief, can produce animosities so deep that violence erupts.
4. States with severe *internal problems* can use other states as scapegoats, redirecting internal frustration into violence against those states.

In the Third World, most between-state conflicts entail a combination of these reasons (see Box 16.5).

The Iran-Iraq war clearly exemplifies the interrelated themes of nationality, resources, ideology, and internal problems that are often at the core of interstate violence in the Third World (Cruikshanks 1987). Variations on these themes are evident in the recent struggles between Morocco and the former Spanish Sahara, Ethiopia and Somalia, Vietnam and Cambodia, and Syria and Israel. Sometimes the struggles explode into regional conflicts, such as that between South Africa and the neighboring states of Angola, Botswana, Lesotho, Mozambique, Nami-

BOX 16.5

Third World War: Iran versus Iraq

The brutal war between Iran and Iraq, which raged from 1980 to the 1988 cease-fire, is characteristic of the complex causes of interstate violence between Third World states. Iraq's effort to regain total control of the Shatt al-Arab was the manifest reason for the war that began officially when Iraq invaded Iran in September 1980. The Shatt al-Arab, a narrow strait between the two states, has strategic value to each as a trade outlet to the Persian Gulf. But the five factors listed below are also partial causes of the long-standing hostilities that resulted in war.

   1. There is a historical nation-based hostility between the Iranians, whose ethnicity is Persian, and the Iraqis, who are predominantly Arabic.
   2. There have been further disputes along the Iran-Iraq border, which was established after World War I, because of the attempts by the Kurdish nationality (whose region is along the border) to establish autonomy from the Iraqis and because of Iranian support for separatist political violence by the Kurds.
   3. The Kurdistan area has valuable oil resources that both Iraq and Iran want to control.
   4. The Iranian revolution (in January 1979) brought to power a fundamentalist Shi'ite Muslim regime under the Ayatollah Khomeini. The Shi'ites are deeply antagonistic to the religion of the Sunni Muslim minority who rule a Shi'ite majority in Iraq.
   5. Internal political difficulties in each country, and especially major economic problems in Iran after the revolution, provoked each state to redirect the frustrations of its population against the enemy across the border.

   Moreover, the actions and intentions of many other states in the First, Second, and Third worlds were also significant in the patterns of international relations that

BOX 16.5 *continued*

caused and sustained the Iran-Iraq War. For example, Egypt and other Arab states have supported Iraq's war effort due to their desire to prevent Islamic fundamentalism from spreading to their states. Syria, an Arab country that has long been in conflict with Iraq, has been a primary supporter of non-Arabic Iran. The United States, which had been the main supporter of Shah Reza Pahlavi's pro-American Iranian government, began to aid Iraq when the shah's government was replaced by a strongly anti-American Iran under Khomeini, who was deeply resentful of U.S. support for the shah. In turn, the Soviet Union limited its long-standing support for Iraq. And some arms-producing states like France sold large quantities of weapons to both Iran and Iraq.

The war has been devastating to the human and economic resources of both Iran and Iraq—there have been more than 1 million casualties. But the war is so embedded in a complex mixture of conflicts between Iran and Iraq (as well as other states) that neither side has been willing to relent. Few observers believe the cease-fire in August 1988 is a permanent solution to this conflict.

bia, Zambia, and Zimbabwe. Although such interstate violence is enormously costly, the frustrations and problems of many Third World states are so extensive and intense that war can become a distraction from the hopelessness.

There are few examples of direct conflicts between Third World states that share no border. In fact, many instances of interstate violence with nonadjoining states have their basis in a colonial or ideological struggle between a Third World state and a First or Second World state. (This is especially true if the conflicts between South Africa and its neighbors are interpreted in this manner.) In theory, and to some extent in practice, the Third World perceives of itself as a group of "nonaligned" countries, in relation to the competition between the First and Second worlds. But a First or Second World state can intervene with violence in a Third World state whose alignment is perceived as contrary to the interests of the First or Second World state. And agents of a Third World state can direct political violence against a First or Second World state that is perceived to be a source of oppression—as exemplified by Libya's reputed sponsorship of terrorist activities against Europeans and Americans (Walsh 1987).

Usually, interstate violence between a Third World state and a First or Second World state has not involved an official, declared war. Sometimes there is an intermittent exchange of violent acts, as those between Libya and the United States in 1984–1986. On other occasions, a more developed country intervenes with force to protect its strategic, economic, or ideological interests in an internal war, as the French did in Chad during 1983, as the United States did in Grenada in 1983, and as the Soviets did in (neighboring) Afghanistan in 1979. And, as discussed in Chapter 13, major powers also engage in "proxy wars" in the Third World to enable them to challenge each other without a direct confrontation.

Conflicts between a Third World state and a more developed country can escalate into direct interstate hostilities, as occurred between the United States and North Vietnam in the 1960s and between Great Britain and Argentina in 1982. The latter war was prompted by the Argentine desire to reclaim sovereignty over land off its coast, Las Islas Malvinas (the Falkland Islands), which had been occupied by Britain for 150 years. Argentinians were unhappy over their country's serious economic problems and also the governing junta's "dirty war" of state terrorism (1976–1981) against leftist elements of its own population. The Argentine military junta seems to have decided that a nationalist victory over imperialism would rally support for the government. This strategy worked briefly. But defeat by the British after a short, costly war resulted in the overthrow of the discredited military junta and a return to civilian government in Argentina.

Economic Security

The search for security is often extremely costly in economic terms. Many Third World states devote a very substantial amount of their limited resources to military expenditure. A few statistics provide some indication of the situation. Sixteen of the 19 countries spending more than 10 percent of their per capita GNP on military expenditures are in the Third World, as are 24 of the 35 countries spending between 5 and 10 percent (U.S. Arms Control and Disarmament Agency 1984:4). Between 1960 and 1982, the total armed forces in the less developed countries more than doubled, to 17.1 million. There are now 4 soldiers in their regular armed forces for every 10 workers in manufacturing industries, compared to a 1:10 ratio among the more developed countries (Sivard 1976:7). By 1982, less developed countries accounted for 82 percent of all arms purchases, and purchases are increasing at an annual rate of 8 percent (U.S. Arms Control and Disarmament Agency 1984:7). Thirty of the countries now produce many of their own military arms (Sivard 1982). Obviously, these huge expenditures on the military can enhance security and stability based on force, but they represent resources that are no longer available for economic development and social welfare. Aid from the developed countries increases the emphasis on military spending, since military assistance substantially exceeds economic assistance.

The fundamental fragility of the economic systems in many Third and all Fourth World states has been detailed in the previous section on the search for prosperity. Such economic weakness is a crucial element in the quest for security, because a state's goal of autonomy—of controlling its own destiny—depends in part on its capacity to resist external manipulation of its political economy. Most of these less developed countries must import agricultural products, energy resources, and manufactured goods, including both consumer goods and also the intermediate and advanced technological equipment necessary for economic development.

When Third World states receive economic assistance from other countries, those countries occasionally offer humanitarian aid in exchange for a smile and a friendly vote in the United Nations. But they usually expect more substantial benefits, such as advantageous joint ventures, favorable trade relations, termination of political relations with the benefactor's rivals, and rights to undertake strategic military activities within the state. Third World leaders usually decide that the loss of some control over the state's domestic and foreign policy is an acceptable cost, given the expected economic benefits (Evans 1987).

And the state can lose some control over its political economy. When the Third World owes more than $500 billion to First World financial institutions, intervention by the international financial community is inevitable. This control has come most explicitly through the International Monetary Fund (IMF), a consortium of First World financial institutions that sets economic policy and monitors the behavior of lenders and debtors. To grant additional loans or to reschedule payments on existing loans, the IMF requires "conditionality." This means that the debtor state must meet certain conditions imposed by the IMF. The common requirements are that the state devalue its currency, cut wages, and cut welfare distribution to its population. In some instances, as in Liberia, Haiti, and Zaire, the IMF has even required that First World bankers hold positions within the government. For example, there are periods when IMF personnel from Europe have staffed the Zairian Ministry of Finance Board, established Zaire's monetary and fiscal policy, and selected its treasurer.

Some Third World states, including Argentina, Brazil, and Mexico (as well as a few Second World states, such as Poland and Yugoslavia) have been close to defaulting on their loans. The repercussions of an actual default are unimaginable, both for the debtor state and also for the international monetary system. Does the IMF take over the country, the way a bank would take over a house on which the mortgage is in default? Who would cover the huge losses suffered by the First World financial institutions holding the loans? While there is much speculation about these potentially catastrophic circumstances, the Third World states and the First World financial community have thus far always managed to avoid such a default by agreeing to new conditions and by negotiating new terms for the outstanding loans.

A few states, such as Brazil and Peru, have resisted the strongest conditionality demands of the IMF; but most less developed countries lack the political and economic leverage to resist for long. The general dominance that First and Second World states enjoy over Third World states in the international economic system—due to their superior organization, technology, political and military power, and economic capacity—is even more strongly reinforced by this debtor status of most major Third World states.

Third World states with command political economies are somewhat more capable (than those with mixed or market economies) of resisting external manipulation of their economic systems. These states can control production, prices, wages, imports and exports, and surplus distribution. But every Third World state needs economic aid, goods, markets, and technology from the First or Second World.

This dilemma facing all Third World states was captured in a paradoxical comment by Kenya's President Daniel Arap Moi: "No country can maintain its independence without assistance from outside." In the contemporary political world, *no* state can survive as an independent entity. But the Third World states are particularly dependent upon outside assistance in many forms, especially economic and technological. Because they are susceptible to influence, manipulation, or even control by other states, few Third World states can escape this economic component of their insecurity.

GOAL: STABILITY

In contrast to most First and Second World states, many of the countries of the Third World find that achieving stability is as elusive as achieving prosperity and security. In their quest for social, economic, and political development, these states have not established structures that maintain social order and insure stable functioning of the political system through time.

Challenges to Political Institutionalization

Recall Kwame Nkrumah's credo: "Seek ye first the political kingdom and all else shall be added unto you." This perspective, shared generally by most Third World states, as well as Second World states, places primary importance on the political system as the crucial instrument for achieving the goals of prosperity, security, and stability. Whatever political framework a Third World state adopts, it typically faces a quite imposing set of challenges that seem to undermine the possibility of stability via political institutionalization.

In most states, the problems begin with some of the same features that threaten prosperity and security:

1. Third World states often must deal with problematical state boundaries that do not correspond to major regional, ethnic, religious, and linguistic groupings. Once the colonial "enemy" has gone, the citizens of the new multination state have little shared purpose or culture. Rather, historical nation-based cleavages become the basis for competition and conflict over the value allocations in the new state (Cruikshanks 1987).
2. Other actors in the international environment, particularly other states and major economic institutions (like multinational corporations), are usually motivated to use the Third World state to achieve their own goals. In most instances, their actions do not enhance the capacity of the state for economic development nor do they increase the sense of internal security of the state (Evans 1987).
3. Third World states usually lack sufficient economic capacity to achieve the levels of production that enable the state to distribute welfare to the population. The low level of final goods produced relative to population size (GNP per capita) is the distinguishing feature of Third World states. But the problem is even worse: In general, these states have the world's most unequal distributions of resources. Table 16.4 shows income inequalities in a few countries for which there are reliable data. In most Third World states, the disparity between rich and poor is huge and it is especially visible in urban areas. The economic elite, and often the political elite, enjoy a very high standard of living, an island of luxury in a sea of desperately poor people. This inequality always has the potential to be the basis of political frustration, conflict, and instability.

TABLE 16.4. Income Inequality in Selected Third World States

State	Ratio of Household Income, Highest to Lowest 20 percent of Households
Brazil	33:1
Kenya	23:1
Mexico	20:1
Costa Rica	17:1
Malaysia	16:1
Turkey	16:1
Argentina	12:1
Philippines	10:1
Egypt	8:1
India	7:1

SOURCE: The World Bank 1989:Table 30.

Other obstacles to the search for stability are more direct consequences of the political situation of most Third World states:

1. The political institutions in most Third World states (South American states are the general exception) have existed for less than 50 years. Modern political forms have been established, usually as a copy of the institutions of the former colonial master state, or as a hybrid between the colonial power's institutions and the traditional governing forms in the society. But these modern political institutions and the associated forms of modern political behavior usually have little historical precedent in the society. When subjected to the (inevitable) internal and external pressures, the institutions function ineffectively, if at all (Linz and Stepan 1978; Migdal 1987).

2. Most of these states lack a limited mandate—a regularized, nonviolent procedure for the transfer of authority and power from one person or group to another. The top political leader in most Third World states is more likely to leave the leadership position due to political violence, such as a coup or assassination, than due to an institutionalized procedure of succession, such as a genuine election. In one of the most extreme examples, as we have noted, Bolivia experienced 190 coups in the 156 years ending in 1982.

3. In most Third World states, there is minimal acceptance of the legitimacy and right of the current political structures and political leaders to allocate values for the society. This is, of course, the basic definition of political institutionalization—the infusion of value into political structures and roles, rather than in traditional or personalized bases of power. When demands remain unmet and problems become severe, there is a rapid loss of confidence in, support for, and obedience to the political system.

Political Decay

Initial Stages.   Samuel Huntington's (1968) model of political decay, described in Chapter 11, was "inspired" by the problems he identified in many Third World states. Many of the Third World case studies in this book include episodes of serious political decay: Brazil, Kampuchea, Pakistan, Uruguay, and Zaire (as well as Ghana and Lebanon; see Box 16.6). In such states, the combined effects of national independence, some modernization, some economic development, and increasing social mobilization generate high expectations among the population regarding increased welfare and a higher standard of living. Since the political system is usually unable to generate sufficient surplus to meet these expectations for welfare, the political leaders have several alternatives:

1.   Some request trust and patience, persuading the population that the system will eventually deliver the goods.
2.   Some attempt to substitute more symbolic rewards, such as greater political participation, for material benefits.
3.   Some impose repressive policies and force on a dissatisfied population to maintain order.

In most Third World states, the population has quickly lost patience with promises of "eventual" benefits. Starvation and death in the rural villages and the wretched conditions of life in urban shantytowns push people beyond tolerance and hope. The absence of violence and rebellion in many cases (where alternatives 2 and/or 3 are not implemented) is usually attributable to the impoverished citizens' preoccupation with sheer survival.

Increased political participation (alternative 2) can stimulate support for a while, since citizens might feel they have a genuine role in their state's political destiny. But this mobilization can be like unleashing a tiger. Participation primarily results in even more demands being placed on the political system. As Huntington suggests, frustration typically grows in such states, as citizens see that the system cannot deliver the goods. This leads to a rapid decline in the level of support for existing political institutions. In a situation of scarce resources (jobs, housing, health care, food, etc.), the underlying nationality animosities are exacerbated. The preconditions for political decay are abundant.

Some conflicts are resolved and some demands are met. But if public dissatisfaction grows, the Third World political leadership usually adopts a siege mentality associated with alternative 3. The political leadership, pressured by opposition groups and public criticism, restrains and then suppresses opinions and political actions that are unsupportive of the current governing group. Any critical media might be muffled, antigovernment demonstrations might be outlawed, opposition political leaders might be harassed or arrested, and opposition political parties might be banned. The political leadership increasingly relies upon repression and force to maintain itself in power.

In short, the major casualty is democratic processes (Huntington 1984; Linz and Stepan 1978). At this point, frustrated groups either acquiesce in the repressive policies of the political leadership, or they use political violence to oppose the political leadership. The manifestations of political decay—riots, terrorism, rebellion, revolution—appear. Where neither patience nor political participation can insure order, the state usually depends increasingly on repression. If repressive rule fails, it might be replaced by even more forceful leadership (often from the military) or the system can erupt into riots and rebellions, primordial violence, and separatist violence (Migdal 1987; von der Mehden 1973).

Military Regimes.   As in the example of Ghana (see Box 16.6), the military can be decisive in both the attempt to restore order and the transfer of political power. There are several reasons for its pivotal role. First, the military is normally the most powerful source of (human and material) force and violence in the state. Second, it is the societal structure that is most likely to have a relatively high level of institutionalization, given its members' professional norms, training, and acceptance of hierarchy. And third, a key norm within the military is a commitment to order and an abhorrence of social disorder. These norms induce its members to act when civilian (or even other military) leadership has failed to prevent political decay. At one point in the early 1980s, military regimes were in power in 15 of the 22 major Latin American states and in 20 of the 26 major black African states. In the late 1980s, there has been a substantial shift away from military regimes and towards elected leadership in Third World states, especially Latin America. But few analysts conclude that this is a permanent decline in military control of Third World political systems.

Revolutionary War.   When political decay becomes so extensive that even the military has difficulty maintaining order, civil war or revolutionary war becomes more likely. Chapter 12 noted that virtually all contemporary revolutionary wars are occurring in Third World states. Class conflict and nationality cleavages often underlie the struggle. Because most Third World states have failed to achieve their prosperity goals, their populations are susceptible to ideologies that promise a dramatic alteration (and improvement) in the economic system and in the distribution of values in the society. Variations of Marxism have particular appeal to frustrated groups within these states, who are persuaded that their situation fits Marx's revolutionary call that the people have nothing to lose but their chains.

Major internal violence in Third World states, whether a struggle for modification of the power distribution or for total revolution, is almost always supported by other First, Second, or Third World states who provide financial or military assistance to combatants. These other states intervene in an attempt to serve their own goals, such as weakening a rival state, defending a group with whom they share a national identity or an ideology, gaining greater control of key resources, or serving a global agenda.

Thus virtually every Third World civil war or revolutionary war mobilizes overt and covert support from other states: Syria and Israel invade Lebanon (see Box 16.6); Libya, France, and the United States assist factions in the civil war in Chad; the Soviet Union provides direct support (or indirect support via Cuba) for the "wars of liberation" in Angola, Ethiopia, Namibia, and Nicaragua; the United States and Pakistan aid the *mujahideen* in Afghanistan; South Africa provides military aid and troops to the UNITA "counterrevolutionaries" in Angola; the United States aids the *contras* in Nicaragua. Indeed, a key element in the pervasive insecurity *and* instability of Third/Fourth World states is the ease with which

BOX 16.6

Two Cases of Political Decay

Decay in Africa: Ghana

Historically, the Gold Coast of West Africa was dominated by the Kingdom of the Asante tribes and had trade linkages with many European powers. The British conquered the area only in 1901, giving Britain colonial control of the region. As the new nation-state of Ghana, it was the first colonial territory in sub-Saharan Africa to gain its independence, in 1957. Its early leader, Kwame Nkrumah, became an articulate spokesman for African freedom and independence in the postcolonial era.

In the decade before independence, an active multiparty system was created and there were quite democratic elections. Nkrumah and his Convention Peoples party (CPP) won the first postindependence election. But significant problems arose almost immediately, including serious economic shortfalls associated with a decline in world cocoa prices, with widespread corruption, and inefficiency within the CPP and the government bureaucracy.

Unfortunately, everyone lacked experience with the parliamentary style of government-versus-opposition. Other parties and groups vehemently criticized the failures of the CPP (''a party of incompetents'') and the extensive powers exercised by Nkrumah (''a dictator''). These criticisms embarrassed, threatened, and angered Nkrumah and the CPP. Thus the government passed laws restricting the activities in which the opposition could engage. Opponents protested these restrictions verbally and then physically. The government then introduced even more repressive measures, arguing that any opposition was unpatriotic.

The government became more and more autocratic. A 1960 election was obviously rigged, and a 1964 referendum of support for the government was a farce. By the 1965 election, legal opposition was virtually eliminated and all candidates of the CPP were declared elected. Both the economy and social order were in collapse and Nkrumah was behaving like a dictator. In 1966, the army intervened, overthrowing Nkrumah and installing a ''temporary'' military junta.

The history of Ghana since 1966 is one of alternation between civilian government and military coup. In 1972, 1978, 1979, and 1981, military officers took control of government in the face of civilian incompetence and corruption. A young air force officer, Flight Lieutenant Jerry Rawlings, led the last two coups. By 1981, Rawlings was convinced that his leadership and his answers were superior to those of civilian governments. Despite several assassination and coup attempts, he has ruled since 1981.

Whereas Nkrumah attempted to install a command economy in Ghana, Rawlings has used political power with equal purposefulness to install a market economy. He has denationalized most public corporations, collaborated with the World Bank to secure loans, and radically cut public services. Ghana's economic performance has somewhat improved under Rawlings, in the sense that, during his rule, GNP per capita has declined less rapidly to an average of about 1.5 percent per year (with some growth recently) and inflation has been ''held down'' to an average of about 50 percent per year (see Table 16.3).

Rawlings's initial commitment to democratic governance has completely disappeared, and he has become as authoritarian as Nkrumah, but without even the democratic trappings of elections. If Rawlings does build a strong economy, his epitaph as a ruler will be positive. To this point, however, his rule has not dramatically

BOX 16.6 *continued*

altered the motifs of politics in Ghana: High inflation and unemployment, corruption and mismanagement, dependency on external political and economic power, curfews, detention without trial, closed borders, dictatorial leadership, and political repression. Ghana, the state that was going to be a model for postindependence Africa, has provided a depressing model of political decay.

Decay in the Middle East: Lebanon

The example of Ghana is one common pattern of political decay in the Third World. However, even states with a longer postcolonial history, such as those in Latin America, or those with apparent political institutionalization, have experienced substantial political decay. Lebanon is a current example of the spread of political decay in a political system that seemed to be well institutionalized.

The economic and cosmopolitan center of the Middle East, Lebanon has literally been reduced to a shambles by the violent internal conflicts of the last twenty years. The mutually antagonistic groups include Maronite Christians, Sunni Muslims, Shi'ite Muslims, and the Druze (a Muslim group who follow the teachings of an Egyptian mystic). Even within these nationality groups, there are rival sects and family/clan groups whose conflicts span hundreds of years.

With the constitution of 1926, accommodation among the various groups in Lebanon was achieved by a subtle sharing of governmental power and economic resources. For example, the members of the legislature were elected by a careful formula that insured precise represention for the major subcommunities (six Christians to each five Muslims). By custom, the president would always be a Maronite Christian and the second leadership role taken by a Muslim. It also helped greatly that there was sufficient prosperity in Lebanon to satisfy all groups.

The possibility of maintaining social and political order became tenuous, and then impossible when other international political actors became more active. In particular, Lebanon became a base of operations and a refugee sanctuary for Palestinians. One group of Palestinians came to Lebanon after the 1948 Arab-Israeli War, and a larger, poorer, and less educated group arrived after the 1967 Six-Day War. Then in 1970, the militant Palestine Liberation Organization (PLO) was expelled from Jordan and moved its headquarters to Beirut. Now Israel began to retaliate extensively inside Lebanon for PLO actions. The presence of the Palestinians undermined the fragile equilibrium between Lebanese group, and civil violence broke out between Christian and Muslim extremists.

Things fell apart. There was a civil war in 1975–1976, resulting in a division of Lebanon into regions controlled by different factions. Then Syria invaded to enforce the cease-fire; Israel supported a Christian group taking control in one region; Israel invaded to drive the PLO out; a United Nations peacekeeping force (and U.S. marines) intervened; Israel invaded again and forced the Palestinians into areas controlled by Syria; and so on. Nothing has produced social peace. Now, there are a multitude of heavily armed, warring groups, each attempting to control areas within Lebanon. Street battles, assassinations, and other forms of violence are the norm. (This discussion is based on Spencer 1988: 86–90.)

other states can pursue their own policy goals within the context of internal political violence in these states.

Political Approaches

The fundamental question for Third World states that do attempt to first "seek the political kingdom" is, What political approach is appropriate? What approach will increase the likelihood of stability, security, and prosperity? Third World states pursue these goals within various political frameworks, which can be categorized in different ways. One useful method is to consider the political approach to two basic issues: resource equality and democratic participation.

The issue of *resource equality* concerns the extent to which the political system explicitly attempts to produce a more equal distribution of key economic and social values. The authoritative allocation of values by the political system can result in either greater equality or greater inequality in the distribution of such values as wealth, income, status, housing, health care, education, and jobs. While a command political economy can be most decisive in using public policy to enact its leaders' intentions regarding the distribution of values, any type of political economy can, at least in theory, implement public policies that are meant to increase or decrease equality.

The issue of *democratic participation* concerns the extent to which the people in the society are mobilized into active and meaningful involvement in the political process. As discussed in Chapter 6, a political system is more democratic to the extent that there is widespread participation in the selection of political leaders from among genuine alternatives, and to the extent there is freedom of discussion and participation in political issues. At one extreme, only one person has all political power and all others are prevented from any public manifestation of political belief or action. At the opposite extreme, every citizen has an equal role in political decision and action.

Obviously, no actual political systems are located precisely on the end of the continuum (for either resource equality or democratic participation). Figure 16.1 indicates four ideal-type political approaches that have different orientations toward a mix of equality and democracy: (1) conservative oligarchy, (2) modernizing oligarchy, (3) revolutionary socialism, and (4) constitutional democracy. The characteristic features of each are described below.

Conservative Oligarchy.   Conservative oligarchies have little or no commitment to resource equality. There is an effort to preserve the traditional socioeconomic order and culture. Certain groups enjoy great advantages in the distribution of economic and social power. The groups with power might be defined by lineage, ethnicity, class, religion, age, or some other trait. The socioeconomic elite, with support from the governmental apparatus, has great control over major sectors of the political economy. Usually, the same groups also exercise great political power and most people are allowed little or no role in the political process. Political repression of the mass can be based on traditional practices, especially religion, or on state actions, especially by such agents of the state as the police and the military.

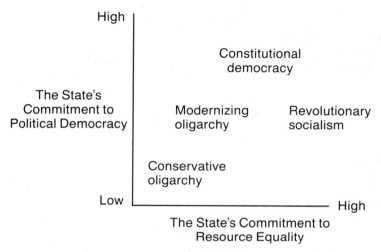

Figure 16.1. Ideal-Type Political Approaches

Higher levels of political stability tend to occur in conservative oligarchies where there are limited economic resources to distribute, where there is no ideology of egalitarianism, and where those groups who maintain order are well organized and loyal to the elite. As these conditions are less strong in the political system, the probability of instability increases. Contemporary examples of political systems where these conditions are most evident include Burundi, Paraguay, and Zaire. States like Saudi Arabia and Iran, despite support from traditional elites and fundamentalist religion, have more destabilizing features, especially due to the increasing societal wealth from petroleum resources and the associated pressures for modernization.

Modernizing Oligarchy.   Modernizing oligarchies differ from conservative oligarchies primarily in their willingness to allow minimal shifts in the directions of egalitarianism and democracy. Most such systems leave large parts of the political economy under private control. Substantial economic and social inequalities remain and there is no explicit attempt by the political system to reduce these. Rather, there is an assumption that economic development and modernization will have indirect, trickle-down effects by raising the absolute levels of economic and social power of the less advantaged.

These states claim to be evolving toward parliamentary democracies, and some political participation is allowed. However, there is a strong emphasis on stability, and considerable resources are allocated to create strong governmental capabilities for bureaucratic control and order maintenance. Only minimal levels of popular political participation are facilitated, and state policies regulate political behavior and restrain political opposition. Examples of modernizing oligarchies include Brazil, Kenya, Mexico, Singapore, and South Korea.

Revolutionary Socialism.   Revolutionary socialist regimes have a strong commitment to economic and social equality, but provide a very limited political role for the large majority of the population. The leadership contends that a small political elite is essential, since leaders must be decisive and unconstrained if they are to reduce the massive economic and social inequalities in the society. Thus the leadership acts on behalf of the population, asserting totalitarian control over the political economy and the society.

Revolutionary socialism emphasizes the massive political mobilization of the population, which is expected to support and implement the policies of the elite. There is an extensive and continuous program of political socialization through the educational system, social and occupational groups, culture, and media. The people are trained to understand virtually every action in terms of its political implications. The objective is to create a population who want to ''serve the people'' as a matter of value preference rather than due to fear of sanctions. In practice, most of these states do use repression and sanctions as well as positive socialization and peer pressure in the attempt to induce desirable mass behavior.

China, especially during the period under Mao Zedong, is a clear example of this political approach. Political mobilization has also been central to the approach in Cuba, Libya, and Tanzania. The Peruvian military junta in power between 1968 and 1976 was an example of revolutionary socialism in a noncommunist system. Examples where the political system has particularly emphasized sanctions and repression of the masses include Kampuchea under the Pol Pot regime (described in Box 5.4) and the current regime in Ethiopia.

Constitutional Democracy.   Constitutional democracies emphasize an open politics in which citizens are allowed considerable freedom to undertake many modes of political participation. In a constitutional system, political actors and political decisions are constrained by the rule of law, which guarantees the rights of the ruled and limits the powers of the rulers. And, in a democratic system, the political leaders are directly accountable to the citizens and receive a limited mandate by means of an electoral system with genuine alternatives. Open political opposition is allowed, the media are relatively free to discuss and criticize political actions, and public discussion of politics is encouraged.

In constitutional democracies, there is no major commitment to achieve economic equality by means of explicit public policy. A regulated but relatively free economic order is viewed as the best means to generate resources for the benefit of all. Thus the political system facilitates the operation of a mixed political economy, a substantial part of which is privately controlled. The state engages in some welfare distribution, particularly to those in greatest need. There also might be public policies to encourage greater social equality, but there is generally not a strong program to achieve this goal.

Colombia, India, Venezuela, and Costa Rica (see Box 16.7) are states that have generally maintained constitutional democracies in the postcolonial era, and many other Third World states alternate between periods as constitutional democracies and periods of nondemocratic rule. Constitutional democracies in the Third

BOX 16.7

A Third World Democracy That Works: Costa Rica

Costa Rica is one of the few Third World states that have implemented and sustained constitutional democracies. This Central American country of 2.8 million has a small (57-member) unicameral legislature and a president elected for one four-year term. Despite its proportionally representative electoral system, there is a stable party system dominated by two parties, which are generally pragmatic rather than ideological. There is an efficient (if large) public bureaucracy and a relatively independent judiciary. For most of the twentieth century, the state and the society have enjoyed high levels of political and social order. There is freedom of expression, a free press, and active political opposition. For those promoting constitutional democracy in the Third World, the obvious question is, How has Costa Rica done it?

Costa Rica has had a few intrinsic advantages. The great majority of the population shares ethnicity and language, and there is no large subservient class of nonwhite laborers. But Costa Rica seems to have many features in common with other Central and Latin American states that have not been able to sustain democratic politics:

It is small and hence a manageable size (but this has not helped neighbors Panama, Nicaragua, and El Salvador).

It has only limited natural resources and its export economy has been reliant on a few commodities such as coffee, bananas, and sugar.

It was part of the Spanish colonial empire, then was under the general hemispheric dominance of the United States after its independence in 1821.

It has a small, wealthy upper class that controls the large plantations, a substantial middle class, and significant numbers of poor and unskilled people who live primarily in rural areas.

Catholicism is the state religion.

Its population is about half urban, half rural (only highly urban Mexico is an exception to this pattern in Central America).

The success of Costa Rica as a constitutional democracy is based less on fortuitous conditions than on sensible policies and continuing commitment to democratic processes. The norms and the procedures of the political system encourage efforts to achieve political consensus within a framework of participatory government. Constitutional rules prohibit the president from serving a second term, balance the power of the executive and legislative branches, and encourage cooperation within a legislature that often does not have a single-party majority.

Consistent with the ideal-type constitutional democracy in Figure 16.1, the Costa Rican state does not have a strong commitment to use public policy to equalize resources within the society. The political economy is oriented toward the market system. The government has balanced some controls on the private economic sector and protection of workers' rights with policies that encourage and subsidize private farmers and business entrepreneurs. Economic and social inequalities remain.

However, there is a tradition of reformist policies that have gradually expanded social welfare and reduced inequalities. Public expenditure is allocated to subsidize extensive health services, public education, and financial support for the elderly (e.g., pensions, social security). Since the late 1880s, the state has provided free and

BOX 16.7 *continued*

compulsory education to all children. And, after a brief civil war in 1948, Costa Rica replaced its military with a small national police, allocating only 1 percent of central government expenditure on military support (compared to 7 percent in Honduras, 13 percent in Nicaragua, and 24 percent in El Salvador). (Goodwin 1988:24, 27, 33.)

Costa Rica has faced severe forces of destabilization in the last decade. While it still has one of the higher levels of per capita GNP in Latin America (ranking seventh among 27 states) (Gooden 1987, Table 6.1), it has not recovered from the world recession in the late 1970s and its fragile export economy is still reliant on a few agricultural commodities. There has been high unemployment, balance of payments problems, and the burden of an extremely large foreign debt. Moreover, the instability in neighboring Nicaragua and Panama has created many problems, including the entry of refugees equal to nearly 10 percent of Costa Rica's population. Yet its balanced policies have generated strong support for the legitimacy of the political system from all major groups within society. Costa Rica continues to provide hope, if not a model that can be duplicated, for other Third World states that aspire to political democracy. (This discussion relies on Goodwin 1988: 24–26 and Slann 1984: 388–415.)

World face substantial pressure during the inevitable periods when there are major problems in achieving the goals of prosperity, security, or stability. The political system must attempt to use democratic processes to satisfy groups on the left that demand policies of greater egalitarianism and groups on the right that demand greater economic freedom and a stronger government role in maintaining political and social order.

While the survival rate of constitutional regimes has been rather poor in previous decades, there are signs that more democratic systems might be gaining a broader and firmer base. The number of authoritarian regimes in the Third World dropped significantly during the 1980s, especially in Latin America and sub-Saharan Africa. Lucian Pye (1990), among others, accounts for these changes on the grounds that there is a "crisis of authoritarianism."

First, the apparent collapse of repressive regimes in Eastern Europe and the ideological retreat of the Soviet Union have undermined the belief among elite and mass publics that such systems can achieve prosperity and stability. Secondly, some authoritarian non-Communist regimes, especially the NICs, have allowed a more open politics to emerge as an outgrowth of their economic development.

And third, the new technologies of communications and production are also crucial factors. Citizens are exposed to global information, a global economy, and a universal technological culture, all of which reduce their tolerance for authoritarianism. These technologies have made it extremely difficult for most states to isolate their populations from the pressures of modernization and democratization or to operate without "the whole world watching."

If this analysis is correct, it reflects a renewed emphasis on the primacy of cultural and economic forces of modernization, relative to political ones (Chapter 11). Such a shift will not necessarily produce either greater social and economic justice or even fully realized democracies. But it should reduce the capabilities of most political systems to sustain strong authoritarianism.

Other evidence seems less sanguine. Many authoritarian systems in the Third World remain well entrenched. Certain forms of conservative culture, such as Islamic fundamentalism, reinforce authoritarianism. And few states have the economic resources to satisfy the material demands of a more modernized, mobilized citizenry. These factors, and the history of the last forty years, suggest that, despite "the outbreak of democracy," democratic political institutions in many Third World societies might again succumb to political decay.

Which Route?   Every state attempts to attain the broad goals of prosperity, security, and stability. But in terms of the dimensions depicted in Figure 16.1, there are fundamental choices about the approach by which these goals will be pursued. The rhetoric of political leaders in most, but not all, Third World countries implies a vision of their society that would place it in the upper right corner in Figure 16.1. Such a state would be characterized by both high levels of political democracy and considerable social and economic equality. (Conservative oligarchies are least likely to celebrate such a goal.) From a political perspective, the key question is how to determine the most effective route to reach that ideal.

The route taken by a state will be influenced by many factors that cannot be controlled in the short run. These factors relate to many of the themes in this book: a country's relations with other states, its political culture, its geopolitical situation, its nationality composition, its history of political institutions and leaders, and so on.

Given these kinds of constraints, political choices can be made regarding the route that will be attempted. One set of major choices centers in the structure of the political economy. Figure 16.1 reflects two other key choices. Modernizing oligarchy, revolutionary socialism, and constitutional democracy represent approaches that place different emphases on the balance between attempts to attain political democracy, on the one hand, and achievement of social and economic equality, on the other hand.

The most explicit trade-off between the two sets of objectives is evident in the differences between constitutional democracy and revolutionary socialism— between, on the one hand, greater individual and political freedom and, on the other hand, a strong interventionist state that promotes egalitarianism of social and material conditions rather than personal freedom. Modernizing oligarchies tend to move slowly (sometimes very slowly, and sometimes backwards) in both directions, and in most cases do not promote either democracy or egalitarianism aggressively.

When Third World states look for exemplary successes in reaching the ideal conditions represented by the upper right corner of Figure 16.1, there are few cases among developing countries that can serve as models. The assessment of an "enlightened" Third World leader who would like to achieve the ideal (and who has a pragmatic grasp of the recent histories of Third World states) might follow these lines:

> Revolutionary socialism is best justified if our economic conditions are desperate. The strong interventionist state can try to "bootstrap" development, by organizing the population and by installing a command economy that limits external economic control and makes the best use of societal resources. But few populations have sustained enthusiasm and support for this approach. Despite extensive efforts at political mobilization and socialization, stringent controls on personal freedom and repressive social policies are necessary to maintain stability. And the economic performance of command economies has usually been mediocre, leading to an equality of poverty.
>
> Constitutional democracies have the desirable feature of allowing greater personal freedom and stimulating more economic initiative. But they have also been characterized by very uneven economic development among regions, economic sectors, and population groups. There is usually an increase in inequality, between rich and poor, advantaged and disadvantaged. The economy is dependent on the support of developed countries, who enjoy most of the economic benefits from this neocolonial situation. These conditions, in conjunction with a commitment to democratic political processes, tend to produce considerable political and social instability. A government committed to democratic processes will not be able to prevent political decay, and there is a high probability that the government will face a military coup, civil war, internal revolutionary political violence, and/or direct foreign intervention.
>
> The modernizing oligarchy approach is a compromise with the least risks and the lowest potential gains regarding either goal. The NICs have used this approach to achieve prosperity and stability, although there is little evidence of much progress toward political democracy until recently. Material conditions improved marginally for most of the population, but there has been no substantial reduction in social and economic inequality. The most problematic factor, however, is that the NIC strategy has not been particularly successful when attempted in non-Asian cultures. In other cultures, this approach seems to produce short-run stability, but little progress toward either political democracy or social and economic equality.
>
> What should we do? And, more fundamentally, what can we do? The problems we face are not just management problems of choosing and implementing a strategy. We are not free and unconstrained. The problems created by forces of diversity and conflict within this country are substantial. And the problems caused by the actions of external actors, especially those from certain developed countries and some hostile states in this region, are enormous and sometimes overwhelming.

BOX 16.8

A Day in the Life: Third World

There are 3.4 billion stories in the Third World. This is one of them. . . .

Joseph Karuga wakes in the two-room flat that he shares with four others. Although the accommodations are very basic—four mattresses on the floor, some chairs and a table, a hot plate and a cold-water faucet—the rooms are clean, there are windows looking out towards an open area, and the rent is manageable. Joseph

BOX 16.8 *continued*

waits his turn for the toilet used by the several dozen people with rooms on his floor. He returns to the flat and jokes with two of the other men who are now dressing for their work. All of them have come to Nairobi, the capital city, from his region of central Kenya and they enjoy each others' company.

Without haste or enthusiasm, Joseph eats some dried food and drinks two cups of strong coffee. Two years earlier, when he was 16, he left his small village to come to Nairobi. The small farm owned by his father would eventually be shared by three of his older brothers. The four younger brothers, including Joseph, knew that there was no land for them, and that even the three older brothers would barely survive on the small farms they would inherit.

After he had finished his basic schooling in the village, he had travelled the 200 miles to Nairobi in hope of finding work. A Catholic priest at the parish church got him a job as a "shamba boy," taking care of the gardening and repairs at the house of a rich European businessman living in a suburb of Nairobi. A year later, a cousin helped him get his current job in a small factory manufacturing batteries for automobiles.

He walks to work in 15 minutes. Most of his nine-hour day, Joseph pulls a cart between the storeroom and the assembly floor, providing workers with the components to assemble the batteries. Joseph does not enjoy the work in the hot, dirty building, and the supervisor is constantly criticizing him for his slow work. But many men in Nairobi have no work, and so Joseph feels lucky to have this job, and he thinks he works hard for his modest wage.

After work, he joins other friends at a local park. In the cool shade, they drink beer and talk of life in their villages. Joseph hopes to earn enough money to return to his village, buy land for a small farm, marry, and have children. For him, life in this city of 1 million people is lonely and strange. The older men tease Joseph, making jokes about the hardships of farm life and telling him that he will never leave the city.

For now, however, Joseph misses his family and the close personal ties of village life. And he does not like the aggressive style of the Kikuyu, the largest tribal group in Nairobi, and the group whose members have most positions of power in the Kenyan government and bureaucracy. The owner of the battery factory and his supervisor are both Kikuyu, and Joseph fears that his job will be given to one of their relatives. He especially dislikes the owner, who seems mainly interested in driving his Mercedes-Benz around town. Joseph has been told that the factory was sold to this owner under the government's "Africanization" policy, which forced the factory's founder, an Englishman, to sell it to a Kikuyu.

As more beer is passed around, Joseph listens to the men joke about women, sports, and Kenyan politics. He has started to attend Saturday night dances, since the village girl he had hoped to marry was promised by her father to a prosperous farmer. He has no interest in politics, and believes that most politicians are clever criminals. Some of the men say that most Kenyans are poor because foreigners and foreign companies still control Kenya. Joseph doesn't know if this is true, but he does know that some people in Nairobi have unbelievable wealth. He is still as astounded by the wealth in Nairobi as he was when he first served as a shamba boy.

But as Joseph walks back to the crowded flat he shares, he sees only masses of men, women, and especially children who are poorer than the farmers in his village, but who have no communal life to compensate for their poverty. Back at the flat, he has one more beer and drifts off into a restless sleep, thinking of the small farm.

CONCLUDING OBSERVATIONS:
IT'S GOT TO GET BETTER?

In political forms, as in goals, there are no fundamental differences between the states of the Third World and those of the First and Second Worlds. The selection of a particular political approach in any Third World state is dependent upon many factors, especially the historical and geopolitical circumstances of the state. Similarly, some political economies are command economies, others are almost total market economies, and most implement a mixed system. There are constitutional democracies and there are totalitarian dictatorships. Economic underdevelopment is obviously the main distinguishing factor between the Third World and the developed countries. But the conditions of political underdevelopment are the pivotal problem, if the political system is to be the crucial instrument for social and economic change.

Regardless of the political approach selected, virtually all Third World states face difficult challenges in the attempt to use the political system as a means for achieving prosperity and security. Most have valuable natural resources and a population that is willing to apply its energies to achieve these goals. But their underdevelopment places them at an enormous disadvantage in the contemporary world, where political, military, and economic patterns have become globalized.

For many of these states, and especially the Fourth World states, it is possible that *no* political approach and *no* political economy can simultaneously achieve all these major goals. The leaders of any Third or Fourth World state must make very difficult decisions about how to gain partial success in meeting some of their goals. Some objectives will have to be sacrificed in the quest for others, and there is no assurance that any objective can be fully accomplished.

In the contemporary political world, the obstacles are pervasive, and determination of the best strategy is baffling. At every turn, the underlying political choices are fundamental: freedom versus security, economic development versus welfare, political equality versus economic equality, democracy versus efficiency, aid versus independence, market economy versus command economy, guns versus butter.

A poem by Robert Graves (1966:211) begins:*

> *Every choice is always the wrong choice,*
> *Every vote cast is always cast away—*
> *How can truth hover between alternatives?*

These lines must seem especially profound to political actors pursuing the goals of prosperity, security, and stability in Third and Fourth World states.

CHAPTER 17

The Last Chapter: Looking Backward, Looking Forward

It is not easy to understand the political world.

First, the scale of political phenomena is vast. There is an international political system, at least 160 national political systems, tens of thousands of local political systems, and then there are the political beliefs and actions of every individual in all those political systems. How would you estimate the number of politically relevant interactions on a single day? It is surely in the trillions.

Second, the range of political phenomena is immense. Politics affects every action and thought where the authoritative allocation of values and meanings is involved—in your life at school, in the workplace, at leisure, in your home.

Third, political phenomena are often complex, changeable, unpredictable, even paradoxical. The attempt to generalize about the political world is both fascinating and frustrating. Einstein's observation that politics is more difficult than physics in an apt characterization of the challenges facing those who attempt to understand the political world.

This book has provided you with some conceptual tools and some substantive information that are meant to improve your ability to understand the political world. A basic premise has been that it is possible to formulate some generalizations about politics. No political event is entirely unprecedented, no political system is entirely unique, and no one's political behavior is entirely random. To this point, the study of politics, as political *science,* has mainly provided descriptive taxonomies and only a modest level of explanation. But the application of more systematic methods and more rigorous thinking does seem to improve our insights about politics. Most of our reflections on the political world have related to four essential themes: political outputs, political structures, political processes, and political change. Let's review them briefly.

POLITICAL OUTPUTS

What is the domain of politics? One crucial task is to define the essence of politics and the range of phenomena that are political. This book has employed the widely used definition of the political system as that set of activities through which values are authoritatively allocated for the society. The crucial element in this definition is political outputs—those decisions and actions by the political system that determine the differential distribution of rewards and sanctions in the society.

The first central issue is, *What values will be allocated?* All societies are generally concerned with achieving prosperity, security, and stability. But, in the pursuit of these broad objectives, which value allocations are appropriately handled through the political process? In each society, it is politics that defines *res publica*—the things of the people. This sets the boundaries within which political action and decision are appropriate.

Some political systems assert extensive control over virtually every aspect of the lives of their citizens, while other political systems intervene only minimally into personal, social, and economic life. Thus different political systems reach dramatically different answers to political questions like these:

What (if any) religious instruction will occur in the schools?
Who will decide the value of a person's labor?
Who will pay for health care?
Who owns land and who can extract resources from it?
How will people be protected from physical harm by others?
What things is a person forbidden to say or to read or to do?

The second central issue is, *Who will benefit from and who will be burdened by* the particular configuration of value allocations? Most values are scarce and their very "value" is often subject to significant disagreement. Thus there are very few value allocations by the political system that are truly "Pareto optimal"—that is, value allocations that make someone(s) better off and no one worse off. Usually, a value allocation that produces a favorable outcome for some produces a negative outcome for others. In virtually all cases, the result of a particular allocation of values is that some receive greater benefits (or lower burdens) than others.

Politics tends to be personal for most individuals. That is, they are primarily concerned with the impacts that policies will have on their own lives. The essential question regarding any value allocation by the political system is, How does this decision affect me/my loved ones/my group? The individual wonders if she will pay higher taxes, receive increased health care benefits, be protected from cultural works perceived to be offensive, given access to a broader range of imported products.

But as a political analyst, you must also assess the broader effects of political decisions and actions on groups, on nation-states, and even on the international system. What groups or classes will experience a disproportionate share of the increased benefits or burdens from a public policy decision that revises taxation, that restricts imports of a product, that alters eligibility rules for a welfare service, that increases expenditure on nuclear weapons, that lowers the priority of prosecuting racial discrimination cases, or that implements collectivization of agriculture? Such concerns are at the core of the essential political question, Who gets what?

POLITICAL STRUCTURES

How do people organize themselves politically? In the late twentieth century, there are only a few societies that continue to operate without explicit, complex political structures. To understand the political world, one must have a clear knowledge of the structural arrangements through which political decisions are made and implemented.

At the *formal-legal* level, the study of political structures focusses on the nature of the state, the basic actor in international politics. The state exercises sovereign power over its people and its territory, and has primary responsibility for making and carrying out political decisions. Among other things, it formulates the basic laws, often embodied in a constitution, which define acceptable political behavior for individuals and groups, as well as for the state itself.

The *institutional* approach is explicitly concerned with the nature of political structures. This approach attempts to characterize different forms of executives, legislatures, judiciaries, bureaucracies, political parties and party systems, electoral systems, areal distributions of power, and so on. The key substantive interests of the institutional approach include explaining how political structures are organized, what responsibilities are associated with each role within a structure, and how the various roles and various structures interact.

Finally, the more *analytic* approach to political structures attempts to develop conceptual models based on abstractions that present the forms and relationships among those structures. The concept of a political system operating within an intrasocietal and extrasocietal environment has been the most widely used analytic framework for characterizing political structures.

POLITICAL PROCESSES

There are both micro- and macro-level dimensions to the study of political processes. The *micro-level political processes* concern how the individual understands the political world and how the individual acts politically. First, the political beliefs of a person can be characterized and the configuration of these beliefs can be summarized as her belief system. Similarly, the forms and frequency of political actions performed by individuals can be described. Second, these patterns of political beliefs and actions can be compared across individuals in the search for generalizations about micropolitical processes. And third, there are explanations of these processes—attempts to identify the factors that cause individuals to hold certain political beliefs and to act politically in some ways rather than others. This entails an analysis of the agents of political socialization, the cultural and political milieu within which the individual exists, and the individual's own physical and psychological characteristics.

Macro-level political processes are the politically relevant interactions among individuals and groups. The themes of power, authority, influence, bargaining, decision making, conflict, and conflict resolution are central. This is the "stuff" of politics for most of those who are interested in understanding the political world. There are many forms in which such processes emerge, as political groups form and then attempt to influence the selection of political actors and public policies, as political demands and supports are expressed, as value allocation decisions are made by the political system, as public policies are implemented, and as goods and services are produced and distributed in the political economy. When nation-states interact in the international environment, these processes include the patterns of cooperation, equilibrium, domination and dependence, and violence. The elite, class, and group approaches are three general forms of explaining the fundamental dynamics of macro-level political processes.

POLITICAL CHANGE

In the late twentieth century, more than ever in history, the political world is changing rapidly and constantly. New technologies of production, communications, transportation, and warfare have created an interdependent global village where every state is subjected to powerful forces of change. Among the key political questions about these potential transformations are the direction, rate, and controllability of change.

Direction

Chapter 11 explored the concept of modernization, emphasizing the changes that occur when social mobilization, economic development, urbanization, and political development interact. In most states, the exposure to increased organizational and technological knowledge results in increased specialization, rationalization, and predictability in the structures and processes of the political system, as well as other systems.

However, more than the "modernizing" transformations in the social, economic, and cultural systems, political development is susceptible to reversal into political decay. Political leaders can trample constitutional restraints, bureaucracies can be racked by inefficiency and corruption, party systems can collapse, political opposition groups can resort to political violence. The last 40 years provide ample evidence that the direction of political change is not necessarily toward greater order and rationality.

Rate

Even in the twentieth century, there are still a few groups, such as the Bushmen of the Kalahari Desert in southern Africa and the Masai in Kenya and Tanzania, whose social and political lives are almost unchanged over hundreds of years. And a few contemporary political system, like those of Britain and the United States, have changed only gradually over hundreds of years. But the rate of change in most current political systems is quite high. Sudden and fundamental (revolutionary) change has always been possible, and has become far more likely in the contemporary political world. Even in the absence of revolution, the dynamics of the modern world tend to transform most political systems at a very high rate. The impacts, structures, and processes of most political systems in the world have changed more during the past 40 years than in the preceding 400 years. The rate of political change is likely to continue to accelerate. Can you think of circumstances that would slow the rate of political change in a particular state?

Controllability

The leaders of every political system attempt to use governmental policies to control the changes that occur within the system and in its environment. Earlier chapters have provided dramatic examples of the capacity of strong political leadership to control the nature of changes in the society: Mao Zedong in China, Kemal Atatürk in Turkey, Pol Pot in Kampuchea, Ayatollah Khomeini in Iran. To achieve its goals, a political leadership needs some combination of political will, political skills, effective political structures, group support, relevant resources, and luck.

There are many reasons why the political system usually has only modest capacity to control change. First, there might be an insufficiency in such elements as will, skill, support, and resources. Second, in complex systems, powerful forces of inertia offer resistance to change. Third, unanticipated effects of action can be more significant than the intended changes. Fourth, attempts to control change can be undermined by the actions of the array of actors in the national and international environments as they pursue their own objectives. In short, despite the formidable powers that can be harnessed by political leaders, it is perhaps more remarkable that significant change can *ever* be controlled than that leaders often fail to achieve their objectives.

UNDERSTANDING AND ACTION

In thinking about the political world, fundamental questions are never far below the surface. Many of these questions entail the conflict between such desirable individual and group goals as freedom, material abundance, equality of conditions, and happiness. Each individual and each political system makes decisions about the importance attached to these values, and then attempts to create the political conditions under which those values are achieved.

The comparison of different political systems has highlighted variations in judgments about the relative importance attached to major political goals and, perhaps even more, about the relative success of various political systems in achieving their objectives. In some instances, the contrast is especially dramatic, as when two bordering states employ quite different approaches in pursuit of their preferred goals. The contrasts between North Korea and South Korea, between South Africa and Mozambique, and between the United States and Mexico are particularly stark.

There has never been such awareness of what is possible and such sensitivity about the gap between expectations and reality as in the contemporary political world. As more individuals, groups, and states increase their expectations and hence their demands, the possibility of satisfying everyone diminishes steadily. A widely quoted statistic is that the United States, with about 6 percent of the world's population, has been accustomed to using about 30 percent of the planet's resources. Obviously, as even a few countries approach the consumption levels of the United States, the total demand for resources will far outstrip the available supply and further accelerate the rate of serious environmental deterioration.

A recurrent theme in this book has been the efforts by political systems to control their own population and their environments, both internal and external. Political and economic development and contemporary technology have brought not only increased capacity for control but also for unparalleled violence and destruction. The increasing use of dangerous chemicals in agriculture and manufac-turing can poison the land, water, air, and ultimately people, as has been sug-gested by such environmental disasters as the chemical gas leak at Bhopal, India, in 1981. The dangers associated with concentrating enormous levels of energy in nuclear power plants and nuclear weapons have been intimated by the destruction at Hiroshima and Nagasaki in 1945, and by the widespread radioactive contamina-tion caused by the meltdown at the Soviet Union's Chernobyl nuclear power plant in 1986.

The reign of terror in Cambodia under Pol Pot (Chapter 5) is just one recent example of the use of political power to commit barbarous acts against a society's own people. And Chapter 12 emphasized the recurrent theme of the massive vio-lence that groups commit against each other in the name of self-interest or ideol-ogy. The total number of war deaths has been doubling each half-century for the past 200 years. And there has never been such potential for destruction as with the current technologies of violence. Five nations are known to have operational nuclear weapons (China, France, the Soviet Union, the United Kingdom, and the United States), three more are capable of producing such weapons (India, Israel, and South Africa), and eight more states are expected to have such weapons be-fore the year 2000 (Argentina, Brazil, Iraq, South Korea, North Korea, Libya, Pakistan, and Taiwan). In a nuclear war between the United States and the Soviet Union, a single American Poseidon submarine, with its 160 warheads, could kill 80 million people and destroy two-thirds of Soviet industry. Even scientists are uncertain about the longer-term effects of such radiation on the world. The vast expansion in technological capacity has occurred during a century in which hu-mans have killed far more of their race than at any time in history. Do you think that this is a coincidence?

Ultimately, it is a political question whether individuals, nation-states, and the international system will implement public policies that, collectively, provide a more protective approach to the earth's natural resources and utilize technolog-ies in safe and humane ways. As Benjamin Franklin observed at the American Constitutional Convention, "We must hang together, or, most assuredly, we shall all hang separately." Although Franklin was referring to the need for cooperation among the separate states of the emerging United States of the late eighteenth century, his insight applies with even greater force to the conditions on the entire planet in the late twentieth century. We live in an era when some people enjoy astonishing material abundance while one-fourth of the world's population lives on a subsistence diet and 15 million people die of hunger each year. Contemporary political systems spend more than $16,000 per year to support each of their sol-diers and less than $260 per year to educate each of their children. Political choices account for these circumstances.

A central objective of this book has been to increase your understanding of the political world. The discussions and many examples have been meant to help you, as proposed in Chapter 1, "to see more clearly than before" (Popper 1963:227). You should now have a more informed opinion about whether political *science* is feasible. And, even more importantly, you should have a clearer opin-ion about whether political analysis contributes to the pursuit of political good.

Voltaire observed, "If we believe absurdities, we shall commit atrocities." The political world is full of disagreement, hyperbole, and ruthless competition. Political science cannot necessarily make the world a better place. Its primary role is to increase our understanding about how politics works. But such understanding can be the basis of insights: about different conceptions of how politics should be organized; about the basis of any real political disagreements that require response; about mechanisms for conflict resolution; and about how to organize ourselves in the pursuit of specific (private, group, or national) interests within a framework of the common good.

As individuals, we often feel powerless in the face of the massive power mobilized in the political world. But every individual—even you!—can affect what happens. The democratic ideals that are widely celebrated in the political world are based on the assumption that people, individually and collectively, *can* make a difference. First, if you approach political questions with knowledge, insight, and sensitivity, you can better understand how to think and act in the political world. Second, you can communicate your own political demands and supports in order to influence the policies that are made by actors in the political system. Third, you can become a political activist, as a shaper of public opinion, a leader of a political group, or a public official. As American novelist F. Scott Fitzgerald observed, "One should be able to see that things are hopeless and yet be determined to make them otherwise." In the political world, things are not yet hopeless, unless people like you fail to think, to understand, and to act.

APPENDIX

Political Analysis

This book began with the claim that, in a democracy, men are more likely to vote than women. You were encouraged in Chapter 1 to read this appendix on political analysis as you considered this question about the relationship between sex and voting and as you assessed the data in Table 1.1. Chapter 1 defined *political analysis* as the attempt to describe and explain political phenomena. The following sections introduce you to some of the basic analytic tools for political analysis— that is, for conceptualizing, collecting, and analyzing data about actual political phenomena. After a brief discussion of the different types of data that are used in political analysis, we shall consider how to read data like those in Table 1.1 and how to draw a tentative inference based on those data. Most of the appendix describes four broad approaches used for political analysis: taxonomic analysis, formal analysis, constitutive analysis, and relational analysis.

DATA IN POLITICAL ANALYSIS

Many political analyses rely upon the assessment of data. Data is a general concept that can refer to virtually anything that provides a bit of information. The term *data* can be defined as any observations, facts, statistics, or other forms of information that attempt to measure or represent some aspect of reality. The data used in political analysis can be characterized on different dimensions. These include the style of measurement, the level of analysis, the composition, and the time dimension.

1. *Style of measurement*
   a. *Nominal data* measure by applying names to phenomena that have some common characteristic. Examples: male voters or female voters; Conservative, Labour, or Liberal parties in Britain; democratic, authoritarian, or totalitarian governments.

    b. *Ordinal data* rank phenomena in an order, such as from higher to lower, bigger to smaller, greater to lesser. Examples: more developed countries or less developed countries; voters who are older than 65, voters between ages 35 and 65, or voters younger than 35; political party systems that have one major party, two major parties, or many parties.

    c. *Interval data* are like ordinal data, but they also have a numerically equal distance between any two adjacent measures. In other words, the distance from 5 to 6 is the same as the distance from 81 to 82. For example, the Carter presidency of 1977–1981 (four years) was exactly half as long as the Reagan presidency of 1981–1989 (eight years).

    d. *Ratio data* are like interval data, but they also have a real zero point. Examples: a country's total expenditure on defense in a specific year; the number of citizens participating in antigovernment rallies; the percentage of seats in the legislature held by a particular political party.

2. *Level of analysis.* Political data can be measured at various levels of analysis. Examples: at the level of the individual, the strength of a particular individual's loyalty to a political party; at the group level, the percentage of Asian-Americans who vote; for a geographic area: the number of parliamentary seats in Wales.

3. *Composition.* Data can measure a *single* phenomenon, like a political leader's age or a country's yes or no vote on a specific issue at the United Nations; or they can be *aggregate* measures that combine phenomena, like the percentage of total votes cast for conservative political parties in an election, or a nation's average annual rate of population growth over 10 years.

4. *Time dimension.*

    a. *Cross-sectional data* measure a single point in time. Example: a person's vote for president in 1988.

    b. *Longitudinal data* measure several points through time. Example: a person's votes for president in 1980, 1984, and 1988.

    The example of voting in the 1976 presidential election in Chapter 1 uses data that are nominal (men versus women), ratio (percentages), aggregated (for many people) in a cross-sectional analysis (only one election). You might think of data as dry statistics; but the data in political analysis are rooted in real-world events. If properly analyzed, relevant data can increase our political knowledge on an endless list of questions. Examples: Are countries that spend the greatest amount on military preparedness more likely to avoid war? Is religion or social class a better predictor of whether a Frenchwoman will vote for the Socialist party? How much longer is average life expectancy in rich countries than in poor countries?

ON READING TABLES

Table A.1 (which is identical to Table 1.1 in Chapter 1) provides data from the 1976 presidential election in the United States. Does this table help you to clarify the relationship between gender and voting level in democracies? Since political

TABLE A.1. Participation of Eligible Voters in the U.S. Presidential Election by Gender

	1976	
	Men	**Women**
Voted	a 77%	b 67%
Did not vote	c 23%	d 33%

Yule's $Q = +.23$

	1988	
	Men	**Women**
Voted	a 56%	b 58%
Did not vote	c 44%	d 42%

Yule's $Q = -.04$

analysis often includes data presented in tables, it is useful to know the basic steps for reading tables. When you examine a table like Table A.1, the first thing is to establish precisely what the data are about. The title of the table and the names given to the variables (the key concepts measured in the table) indicate what the analyst who created the table thinks that it reveals. But the analyst can be misleading or mistaken. So it is worthwhile to assess whether the phenomena measured by the data correspond to the labels given to the variables, whether the data seem relevant to the analytic question, and whether the data seem accurate.

Next, you should examine the data in the table. What do the data measure? Table A.1 provides data on the percentage of men and women who did or did not vote in the election of the U.S. president in 1976 and 1988. How are such tabular data read? Are either of the two statements below supported by the 1976 data in the table?

1. Twenty-three percent of those who did not vote were men.
2. Thirty-three percent of the women did not vote.

It is useful, especially when there are percentages in a table, to examine how the columns (up and down) and the rows (across) are formed. In the case of percentages, find any direction(s) in which the data add to 100 percent. In this table, the columns add to 100 percent. Thus statement 2 is supported by the table and statement 1 is not. Can you see why this is so?

In many cases, the analyst uses more sophisticated techniques than tables in order to assess the relationships between variables. Later in this appendix, in the discussion of relational modes of analysis, the use of statistical techniques to examine these relationships will be considered. That section will explain the meaning of the Yule's Q statistics in Table A.1.

The use of statistics and other quantitative techniques can be helpful in political analysis. But the more demanding task for the analyst is to use careful judgment to decide whether the relationship identified by such techniques has *substantive* significance. The key question is, Do the tables, statistics, and so on provide useful insights about political processes or about how political phenomena are associated?

MODES OF POLITICAL ANALYSIS

Chapter 1 indicated that political science has little theory, in the strictest sense of the term; that is, it does not have a set of precise, systematically related generalizations. However, most contemporary political analysis does strive to make our understandings of politics more general, precise, and systematic. Such efforts at theory building involve primarily the ordering of empirical data, using one of the four modes of political analysis described below: taxonomic, formal, functional, or relational.

Taxonomic Analysis

Aristotle (384–322 B.C.), the father of political analysis, was interested in distinguishing different types of Greek city-states. He classified the city-states by using a concept derived from earlier work by Herodotus (c. 484–between 430 and 420 B.C.): the size of the ruling group. Aristotle defined three categories: The city-state might be ruled by one person, by a few people, or by many people.

This is an example of *taxonomic analysis*. Its objective is the orderly arrangement of some political phenomena by developing a set of distinct categories. Most political analysis begins with a taxonomy—a set of categories that classify data about politics into different types. The categories within a taxonomy establish the crucial concepts that define the analysis. The criteria for naming the types and for classifying phenomena into each type of arbitrary, in the sense that they are established by the analyst on the basis of her substantive concerns. But the categories ought to be exhaustive (all cases are classified), mutually exclusive (no case fits into more than one category), and comparable (all categories are distinguished by the same criteria). Relevant data might be of any type, although they are usually nominal or ordinal.

Aristotle's three categories of city-states are sufficient to create a taxonomy. But to enrich his analysis, Aristotle also employed a second concept: the group(s) whose interests are served by the ruler. Here, his two categories were (1) the ruler(s) could rule in the general interest; or (2) the ruler(s) could rule in her/their own self-interest. Thus Aristotle's taxonomy of governments had two central concepts, each based on nominal data, resulting in the six categories displayed in Table A.2. Aristotle then provided names for each category in the taxonomy. For

TABLE A.2. Aristotle's Taxonomy of Political Systems

How Many rule?	In Whose Interest?	
	General	Self
One	Monarchy	Tyranny
A few	Aristocracy	Oligarchy
Many	Polity	Democracy

example, Aristotle labelled as a *monarchy* any city-state where one person ruled in the general interest; if a few ruled in their own interest, the system was called an *oligarchy*. Notice that Aristotle labelled the most perverse case, where many attempt to rule in their own self-interest, a *democracy!*

Aristotle used his taxonomy for political analysis by placing each Greek city-state in one of the six categories. Athens, for example, was classified as an aristocracy. Notice that a taxonomy organizes data, but it does not answer the *how* and *why* questions. To explore such questions (e.g., Is a prosperous middle class more likely in an oligarchy? Under what conditions does a polity transform into a democracy?), the analyst must move beyond taxonomic analysis.

Formal Analysis

Suppose you want to travel around New York City on the subway. If you are unfamiliar with New York, you will probably use a subway map. The map indicates the spatial relationships among different subway stations and it also identifies the stations where one subway line connects with another one.

A subway map is an example of the product of formal analysis. A *formal analysis* specifies abstract forms that correspond to the reality in which the analyst is interested. The analyst attempts to "model" reality, in the sense that concepts are defined and interrelated so that the linkages among the concepts in the formal analysis reflect the dynamics and interactions among the actual phenomena. Some formal analyses have the same physical form as the actual phenomena being modelled, such as a miniaturized version of an automobile engine. But most formal analyses use symbol systems as abstract representations of the phenomena, such as a subway map or a schematic drawing of the circuitry in a radio or a mathematical formula for the trajectory of an object moving through space.

Most formal analyses of political phenomena are recent. Some political scientists have attempted to devise schematic diagrams that represent how some aspect of politics works. In one well-known example, David Easton (1965) developed an abstract diagram, composed of boxes and arrows, to reveal the flow of activities by which decision makers in the political system establish public policies. Their policy decisions are influenced by the resources available in the environment and the pressures they experience from various groups. This "political system model" is explained in detail in Chapter 5.

An array of formal analyses called *rational choice theory* has become an important approach in political science. Applications of rational choice theory can be quite complex, but these approaches share two basic features. First, these are attempts at representing political processes primarily by means of mathematical formulations or systems of symbolic notation. From the perspective of advancing a science of politics, such formal theories are given special prominence, because they aim to be general, systematic, abstract, and testable in actual settings.

Second, it is assumed that political actors (e.g., voters, legislators, political parties) behave purposefully. The approach does not assume that all political actors behave with complete rationality all the time, but it does assume that their behavior is goal-oriented and calculating. Both their preferences for various outcomes and also their calculation of the costs, benefits, and likely success of different strategies to achieve those outcomes can be formulated as quantified indicators or as systems of symbols.

To introduce the rational choice approach in a nontechnical manner, this book offers several simple examples grounded in the logic of the approach. In Box 3.1, the approach is employed to assess whether it is rational for an individual to vote in a U.S. presidential election. And in Box 13.2, expected utility theory is used to assess whether state B is deterred from using nuclear weapons against its antagonist, state A. The next paragraph describes another brief example (without the mathematics) of how the approach is applied.

Political scientist William Riker (1962) has posited the theory of the "minimum winning coalition." This is a mathematical representation of the well-known saying, "To the victors go the spoils." That is, it assumes that the benefits of any policy decision in a legislature will tend to be distributed among those who have voted in favor of the decision. However, Riker argues, as the size of the coalition voting for the policy becomes larger, the benefits must be distributed among more people (or the groups each person represents) and thus there is a smaller share of benefits available to each coalition member. In order to assure each coalition member of the largest possible share of benefits, there is a tendency to create a coalition that has just enough participants to insure victory—hence, the idea of a minimum winning coalition. This is developed as a formal theory by specifying mathematical equations that relate the size of the decision-making group, the size of the coalition, and the amount of resources available for distribution. (For an empirical analysis of national legislatures that challenges Riker's plausible theory, see Strom 1989.)

Functional Analysis

Suppose someone asks you how a car works. You are likely to discuss the key structural components of a car's power train, such as its carburetor, pistons, and driveshaft. You might then detail the processes of the internal combustion engine, noting how an ignited fuel expands in an enclosed area, pushing a series of mechanisms into directed motion. This style of description and explanation is the basis of functional analysis. *Functional analysis* describes the contributions of a certain element (process or structure) to the activities of the phenomenon under study.

In political science, one form of functional analysis identifies certain functions (i.e., processes) that occur within a political system, and it describes how and by what structures the functions are performed. Some scholars, like Gabriel Almond (1960), have defined certain functions, including political communication, rule adjudication, and interest articulation, that must be performed in every political system.

Applications of functional analysis are described in Chapters 5 and 11. As a brief example here, we can consider the interest articulation function. An individual might want her government to spend more on preschool care or to protect her right to own handguns. The processes by which she communicates these specific interests to others in the political world are called interest articulation. According to functional analysis, this communication of political needs and wants is a necessary function in every effective political system. Most functional analysts also describe and explain how structures perform such functions as interest articulation. Thus, interest groups emerge to amplify the shared interests of many individuals. For example, an organization like the National Rifle Association uses various strategies to promote many individuals' concerns about gun ownership to those who make and implement government policies on firearms.

Related to functional analysis is *constitutive analysis*. Constitutive analysis assumes that political functions can be explained primarily in terms of one fundamental concept. (Indeed, every scientific discipline strives to discover, eventually, *the* fundamental structure or process that accounts for more complex phenomena.) Among the concepts that have been proposed as the central one to explain politics are the interactions between groups, classes, or roles.

Constitutive theories are discussed in various chapters, especially in Chapter 10, where the elite, class, and group approaches to explaining politics are presented. As an illustrative example, Karl Marx's theory of politics pivots on one key concept: class. In every historical period, society is divided into a set of classes, based on the distribution of economic power. The structure of classes determines political and social relations, as well as economic relations. In political terms, the class structure determines who wields political power, for what purposes, and for whose benefit. The role of the state and the dynamics of political change are also explained in terms of class relations.

Relational Analysis

Chapter 1 began with the question of voting differences between men and women: Is there some relationship between an individual's gender and the likelihood that she or he votes? This is typical of the kinds of questions addressed by relational analysis.

The central goal of relational analysis is to discover and explicate the systematic connections between phenomena. Many interesting questions about politics can be addressed by relational analysis. The basic question is always, Are political phenomena linked? Examples: Are democratic countries more stable than undemocratic countries? Are older people more politically conservative than younger people? Are states dominated by the Islamic religion more warlike than states dominated by Hinduism? What conditions are associated with victory by revolutionary forces?

Both formal analysis and functional analysis also assume connections. But relational analysis tries merely to identify the connections between phenomena. It does not attempt to model or schematize the connections, like formal analysis. And it does not focus on crucial functions, like functional analysis. There are two levels of relational analysis: (1) correlational analysis and (2) causal analysis. To determine whether there is a systematic association between variables, most correlational and causal analyses use various statistical techniques. These statistics provide a mathematical appraisal of the extent to which change in one phenomenon is systematically related to changes in one or more other phenomena. Box A.1 provides further information about such statistics.

BOX A.1

Assessing Relations Between Phenomena

To interpret most quantitative analyses in political science (and most other social sciences), you need to understand a bit about the meaning of the most commonly used statistics (e.g., Pearson's r, regression analysis, factor analysis). Ideally, you will take some statistics coursework so that you understand the logic and assumptions of the statistics being employed.

The simplest relational statistics (e.g., Pearson's r, tau beta, Spearman's rho) usually range in value between $+ 1.00$, which indicates a perfect positive relationship between the variables, and $- 1.00$, which indicates a perfect negative relationship between the variables. Many of these simple statistics will also have a significance level—an indication of how likely it is that the observed relation between variables might have occurred by chance. This is normally measured in terms of this chance probability: .05, .01, .001. The smaller the probability of a chance relationship, the greater the analyst's confidence that the variables are actually associated.

In the case of two variables, a $+ 1.00$ correlation would look like graph A in Figure A.1—as one variable increases one unit in value, the other variable also increases at a corresponding rate. For example, you would find a $+ 1.00$ correlation if each \$100,000 spent on congressional political campaigns increased voter turnout by 1 percent. A $- 1.00$ correlation would look like graph B. There are rarely real-world phenomena in political science that come even close to a perfect positive or negative correlation.

A correlation statistic close to .00 means that there is virtually no linear relationship between the two variables, as in graph C. For example, you are likely to find that campaign expenditure levels have no consistent relationships with turnout rates. Political phenomena are often extremely complex and subject to many influences and thus they typically have little or no systematic relationship with other factors that you might consider. Thus in many political analyses, the statistical associations are low and/or are statistically insignificant. The strongest statistical relationships for interesting political data are usually at moderate levels of correlation, in the range of $\pm .10$ to $\pm .35$, as in graph D.

BOX A.1 *continued*

You can look at simple arrays of data, like those in Table A.1, and draw your own conclusions. Graphical representations (like the four scattergrams in Figure A.1) are another straightforward way to assess data. Each point in the figures represents one case, located at its appropriate value on each of the two variables in the analysis. This visual mapping of cases can provide useful insights about the nature of the relationship between two variables.

But as the data become more complex, statistics can help inform your judgment. Table A.1 indicates that the correlation between gender and voting in the 1976 election data is + .23, using a very simple correlation statistic for 2 × 2 tables called

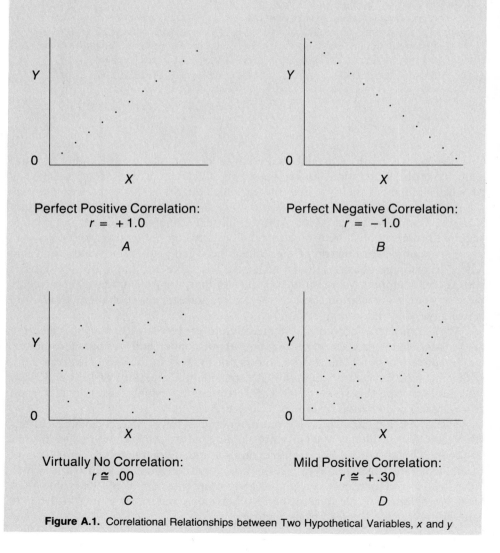

Perfect Positive Correlation:
$r = +1.0$

A

Perfect Negative Correlation:
$r = -1.0$

B

Virtually No Correlation:
$r \cong .00$

C

Mild Positive Correlation:
$r \cong +.30$

D

Figure A.1. Correlational Relationships between Two Hypothetical Variables, *x* and *y*

BOX A.1 *continued*

"Yule's *Q*." The correlation of + .23 suggests that there is a moderate, systematic relationship between male gender and higher probability of voting in these data. In the 1988 data, the relationship between gender and voting appears minimal, and this judgment is supported by the Yule's *Q* of − .04, which indicates that there is virtually no systematic relationship.

While most statistics of association require a calculator or a computer, you can calculate Yule's *Q* yourself for any 2 × 2 table: (1) multiply the values of the two cells on each diagonal: $a \times d$ and $b \times c$; (2) subtract the two products: $ad - bc$; (3) add the two products: $ad + bc$; (4) divide $ad - bc$ by $ad + bc$; (5) the result of this division should be a correlation score, ranging between + 1.0 and − 1.0. The formula for Yule's *Q* is thus: $(ad - bc)/(ad + bc)$.

Beyond simple statistics and graphs, political scientists have an array of sophisticated data analysis techniques to examine questions using quantitative data. But most of the techniques are elaborations on the basic idea of examining whether the values on phenomena seem to be systematically related to each other.

Correlational Analysis.   Correlational analysis determines whether there is a statistically probable relationship between two variables. It does not presume, as does causal analysis (below), that one variable actually is the agent which causes change to occur in another variable. It merely assesses the strength and direction of association between variables. Many empirical attempts to understand politics begin with the establishment of a correlation between political phenomena.

For example, evaluation of the linkage between gender and voting in Table A.1 is an example of correlational analysis. The table and the Yule's *Q* statistic both seem to support the tentative conclusion that, for 1976 at least, there seems to be a modest correlation (i.e., a systematic, statistically probable association) between gender and voting.

While this seems correct, there are obvious problems with using this election as the basis for a broader generalization about gender and voting. It examines only a single election. The relationship is not evident in the 1988 electoral data. In fact, women outvoted men in the U.S. presidential elections of 1984 and 1988. You might pursue this research on U.S. elections by asking: Is this a new trend or a temporary deviation from a 50 year pattern?

Moreover, a generalization about democracies might also consider elections other than the presidency and certainly should analyze other democracies in addition to the United States. For example, any generalization might take into account an analysis of British and West German national elections since 1970 in which there is no correlation between gender and voting rates (Walker 1988:Table 1). A further problem with the evident pattern between gender and voting in the 1976 data will be explored later in this section.

Causal Analysis.   Causal analysis goes beyond correlational analysis, because it explicitly identifies one phenomenon as the effective agent that brings about changes in another phenomenon. Much of the language in political analysis is loosely causal, implying that there is a cause-and-effect relationship between two variables. But causal analysis is the only approach that attempts an explicit empirical test of cause and effect. Causal analysis presents the "if X, then Y" mode of explanation described in Chapter 1. Here X is the *independent variable* that, given a certain value, actually causes Y, the *dependent variable,* to change in a particular way.

An example of causal analysis links the electoral system and the number of political parties. In his book *Political Parties* (1954), French political scientist Maurice Duverger contends that the type of electoral system *causes* the number of effective parties to increase or decrease. In particular, he hypothesizes that

1. Plurality electoral systems (where the candidate who receives the most votes wins) reduce the number of major political parties toward two.
2. Electoral systems with proportional representation (where candidates are elected to the legislature in proportion to their parties' share of the total vote) and with multimember districts (more than one legislator per district) allow more than two major parties.

Political analysts have tested Duverger's hypotheses using data from various electoral systems (e.g., Riker 1982; Taagepera and Shugart 1989, Chap. 13). Table A.3 presents data from 20 democratic countries for the period 1945–1965. Do you think that the data in Table A.3 support Duverger's hypothesis? Why?

TABLE A.3. Relationship between Number of Political Parties and Type of Voting System

Number of Parties[b]	Voting System[a]	
	Plurality	Other
Two	23	4
More than two	7	73

Yule's Q = + .97.

NOTE: Based on data from 20 Western democracies, in elections of legislative representatives, between 1945–1965.
[a]In plurality, or "first-past-the-post systems," the party/candidate with the largest number of votes wins a seat in the legislature, and all other parties/candidates gain no seats. In other systems, there is some form of proportional representation or vote transfer.
[b]Number of political parties with at least 5 percent of the seats in the legislature.
SOURCE: Rae 1971.

Drawing Conclusions from Empirical Analyses

The purpose of empirical analysis is to increase our knowledge about politics. It is especially important that the analyst draw appropriate conclusions. In political analysis, as in politics, things are often not what they seem. Let's consider some of the potential problems, using the causal analysis of electoral systems and party systems as an example. You probably concluded that the data in Table A.3 support Duverger's hypothesis. Do we now know that the electoral system causes different types of party systems? Yes, maybe . . .

YES: There is certainly some persuasive empirical evidence for such a conclusion. And, on logical grounds, it does seem reasonable that the electoral system might cause variations in the number of parties that survive over time.

MAYBE: However, the political analyst must always be cautious in drawing conclusions and making generalizations. Several questions should be considered.

1. Are the data and methods appropriate? Did the analysis use accurate, relevant data and the correct analytic techniques? Is the sample of nations or the time period examined typical? Does this generalization also hold for non-European nations? Were systems divided between "plurality" and "other than plurality" in a manner consistent with Duverger's hypothesis?

2. Are the analyst's inferences about cause and effect persuasive? Might the dependent variable (in this case, the number of political parties) actually have a significant effect on the presumed independent variable (the electoral system)? That is, since the parties in most legislatures have the power to establish the electoral system, certain parties might try to implement an electoral system that perpetuates their power via the existing party system.

3. Are there plausible rival hypotheses? That is, is there another independent variable, not considered in this analysis, that might better account for the pattern of values on the dependent variable? It is possible that both the number of parties and the electoral system are related primarily because each is correlated with the third variable? For example, the number of fundamental issues that divide the electorate might have the greatest effect in determining the number of major parties, if one party emerges for each pattern of positions on the fundamental issues (Taagepera and Shugart 1989).

When political scientists use the scientific method, any of these kinds of "problems" with a conclusion might be raised by other analysts. The data, or the methods, or the inferences might not stand up to such scrutiny. In our examination of Duverger's claims about the causal relationship between electoral systems and number of parties, none of the three problems just listed seems to undermine the analysis. Until one of these types of criticisms *is* supported persuasively, we can have some confidence that the generalization about the causal relationship is correct—that electoral systems do seem to cause certain types of party systems to evolve over time.

But the gender and voting analysis based on the 1976 election data in Table A.1 is an example of how an initial causal inference can be challenged. The three potential problems must be considered in assessing whether the data reveal that gender differences do cause different probability of voting.

1. The data and methods do seem appropriate. However, a generalization (even limited to the United States) would certainly require more than a single case.
2. The posited cause-and-effect relationship seems reasonable. This is the only possible direction of causality, since voting certainly cannot "cause" gender. And there are reasonable explanations for why men might vote at higher rates than women.
3. However, to make a compelling argument that the data reveal causality, it would be necessary to insure that there is no other causal agent (i.e., no plausible rival hypothesis) that better explains voting levels or that creates the apparent relationship between gender and voting. While the analyst can never disprove every competing hypothesis, it is important to examine and reject the most plausible ones.

Let's reexamine the 1976 turnout data. Can you propose another explanation of the incidence of voting in the United States that is as plausible as gender? Among those you might suggest are age, social class, occupation, interest in politics, identification with a political party, or education level. Table A.4 provides the relevant data on one of these—education level—for our analysis of voting in 1976. Do these data alter your judgment about the importance of gender?

One reasonable interpretation of Table A.4 is that the 1976 election revealed a considerable difference between men and women in the incidence of voting among those with minimal education, but that there is virtually no difference in the level of voting between men and women who have college education. In the absence of further analysis (and many further analyses could be attempted), these data about education seem to reduce the power of gender as an adequate causal explanation of voting. One might infer, at least on the basis of Table A.4, that both education and gender were important in 1976, but that education level was

TABLE A.4. Participation of Eligible Voters in the 1976 U.S. Presidential Election, by Sex and Education Level

Education Level	Percent Who Voted	
	Men	Women
Grade school	72	50
High school	69	64
College	86	84

a better predictor of the act of voting than gender. This should suggest to you that if you were developing a causal theory of voting turnout, you would need to consider many variables and diverse data.

This example reveals a common challenge for most of the interesting questions addressed by causal analyses of politics: There are almost always clusters of plausible explanatory factors that seem interrelated. Examples: What accounts for the decision to vote for the Socialist party in France: class, education, family experiences, union membership, wealth, beliefs about society, attitudes toward governmental leaders, or something else? What factors lead a group to undertake revolutionary violence: political oppression, poverty, corrupt government officials, charismatic leadership, unequal distribution of wealth, foreign domination, or something else?

KNOWLEDGE AND POLITICS REVISITED

Chapter 1 suggested a number of ways of knowing things about the political world. Your understandings about politics do not need to be grounded in the scientific method and in empirical analysis. Insight and understanding about politics might be based on the method of authority or the method of personal thought, or they might be derived from other sources such as literature, films, or art.

But in the attempt to develop precise and valid generalizations about politics, most contemporary political scientists use some form of the scientific method and some of the modes of political analysis described in preceding sections. Whatever types of data and modes of analysis they use, political scientists generally accept the notion that all aspects of their research should be subject to scrutiny and challenge by other analysts. And most agree that their hypotheses, inferences, generalizations, and theories must be subject to some empirical test of validity. Although various sources of knowledge can provide you with insights about politics, this book emphasizes the modes of political analysis described in this appendix as the best means for broad understanding of the political world.

References

Achebe, Chinua. (1959). *Things Fall Apart*. New York: Fawcett.

Adorno, T. W., Else Frenkel-Brunswick, Daniel Levinson, and R. Nevitt Sanford. (1950). *The Authoritarian Personality*. New York: Harper.

Agnew, John. (1987). *Place and Politics: The Geographical Mediation of State and Society*. London: Allen & Unwin.

Alexander, William. (1987). "People and Food in the Other World." In *The Other World*, edited by Joseph Weatherby, pp. 34–58. New York: Macmillan.

Allison, Graham. (1971). *The Essence of Decision*. Boston: Little, Brown.

Almond, Gabriel. (1960). "Introduction." In *The Politics of Developing Areas*, edited by Gabriel Almond and James Coleman, pp. 11–24. Princeton, NJ: Princeton University Press.

Almond, Gabriel. (1987). "The Development of Development." In *Understanding Political Development*, edited by Myron Weiner and Samuel Huntington, pp. 437–490. Boston: Little, Brown.

Almond, Gabriel, and G. Bingham Powell. (1966). *Comparative Politics*. Boston: Little Brown.

Almond, Gabriel, and Sidney Verba. (1963). *The Civic Culture*. Princeton, NJ: Princeton University Press.

Almond, Gabriel, and Sidney Verba, eds. (1980). *The Civic Culture Revisited*. Boston: Little, Brown.

Alt, James, and K. Alec Chrystal. (1983). *Political Economics*. Berkeley, CA: University of California Press.

Archer, Dane, and Rosemary Gartner. (1984). *Violence and Crime in a Cross-National Perspective*. New Haven, CT: Yale University Press.

Arendt, Hannah. (1963). *On Revolution*. New York: Viking.

Bachrach, Peter, and Morton Baratz. (1962). "The Two Faces of Power." *American Political Science Review* 56 (December): 947–952.

Banfield, Edward. (1974). *The Unheavenly City Revisited*. Boston: Little, Brown.

Banuazizi, Ali. (1987). "Social-Psychological Approaches to Political Development." In *Understanding Political Development*, edited by Myron Weiner and Samuel Huntington, pp. 281–316. Boston: Little, Brown.

Barber, James David. (1977). *Presidential Character*. 2d rev. ed. Englewood Cliffs, NJ: Prentice-Hall.

Barber, James David. (1988). "Barber on the Presidency." *Charlotte Observer,* July 3, pp. 4; 7.

Barnes, Samuel, and Max Kaase. (1979). *Political Action: Mass Participation in Five Western Democracies*. Beverly Hills, CA: Sage.

Baumol, William, and Alan Blinder. (1988). *Economics*. 4th ed. San Francisco: Harcourt Brace Jovanovich.

Bentley, Arthur. ([1908] 1967). *The Process of Government*. Reprint. Cambridge, MA: Harvard University Press.

Bill, James, and Robert Hardgrave. (1973). *Comparative Politics: Quest for Theory*. Columbus, OH: Merrill.

Bishop, George, Robert Oldenkick, Alfred Tuchfarber, and Stephen Bennett. (1978). "The Changing Structure of Mass Belief Systems: Fact or Artifact?" *Journal of Politics* 40: 781–787.

Bishop, Vaughn, and J. William Mezaros. (1980). *Comparing Nations*. Lexington, MA: Heath.

Black, Cyril. (1966). *The Dynamics of Modernization*. New York: Harper & Row.

Blondel, Jean. (1973). *Comparative Legislatures*. Englewood Cliffs, NJ: Prentice-Hall.

Bottomore, T. B. (1966). *Classes in Modern Society*. New York: Pantheon.

Brinton, Crane. (1957). *The Anatomy of Revolution*. Rev. ed. New York: Vintage.

Brown, Lester. (1984). *State of the World 1984*. New York: Norton.

Brown, Lester. (1985). "State of the Earth 1985." *Natural History* 94 (April): 51–88.

Brucan, Silviu. (1984). "The Global Crisis." *International Studies Quarterly* 28 (March): 97–109.

Bueno de Mesquita, Bruce. (1981). *The War Trap*. New Haven, CT: Yale University Press.

Bueno de Mesquita, Bruce. (1984). "Forecasting Policy Decisions: An Expected Utility Approach." *PS* 17 (Spring): 226–236.

Bueno de Mesquita, Bruce. (1985). "The War Trap Revisited: A Revised Expected Utility Model." *American Political Science Review* 79 (March): 156–173.

Burke, Edmund. (1855/1967). *The Works of Edmund Burke*. New York: Harper.

Cantril, Hadley. (1965). *The Pattern of Human Concerns*. New Brunswick, NJ: Rutgers University Press.

Cardoso, F. H., and E. Faletto. (1979). *Dependency and Development in Latin America*. Berkeley, CA: University of California Press.

Churchill, Winston. (1948). *The Second World War: The Gathering Storm*. Boston: Houghton Mifflin.

C.I.A. World Bookfact 1989. (1989). Washington, DC: Central Intelligence Agency.

Clausewitz, Karl von. (1833/1967). *On War*. Edited and translated by Michael Howard and Peter Paret. Princeton, NJ: Princeton University Press.

Conkling, Edgar. (1987). "Caribbean Basin Initiative." *Focus,* Summer, pp. 2–9.

Connor, Walker. (1987). "Ethnonationalism." In *Understanding Political Development,* edited by Myron Weiner and Samuel Huntington, pp. 196–220. Boston: Little, Brown.

Converse, Philip. (1964). "The Nature of Belief Systems in Mass Publics." In *Ideology and Discontent,* edited by David Apter, pp. 224–240. Glencoe, IL: Free Press.

Crozier, Michel, Samuel Huntington, and Joji Watanuki. (1975). *The Crisis of Democracy*. New York: New York University Press.

Cruikshanks, Randall. (1987). "Conflict Resolution in the Other World." In *The Other World,* edited by Joseph Weatherby, pp. 82–104. New York: Macmillan.

Cutright, Phillips. (1963). "National Political Development: Measurement and Analysis." *American Sociological Review*, April, pp. 253–264.

Cyert, Richard, and James March. (1963). *A Behavioral Theory of the Firm*. Englewood Cliffs, NJ: Prentice-Hall.

Dahl, Robert. (1961). *Who Governs?* New Haven, CT: Yale University Press.

Dahl, Robert. (1967). *Pluralist Democracy in the United States*. Chicago: Rand McNally.

Dahl, Robert. (1971). *Polyarchy: Participation and Opposition*. New Haven, CT: Yale University Press.

Dahl, Robert. (1984). *Modern Political Analysis*. 4th ed. Englewood Cliffs, NJ: Prentice-Hall.

Dahrendorf, Ralf. (1959). *Class and Class Conflict in Industrial Society*. Stanford, CA: Stanford University Press.

Dalton, Russell. (1987). "The Color Green." *Public Opinion*, January–February, pp. 55–57.

Dalton, Russell. (1988). *Citizen Politics in Western Democracies*. Chatham, NJ: Chatham House.

Davies, James C. (1971). "Toward a Theory of Revolution." In *When Men Revolt and Why*, edited by James C. Davies, pp. 134–147. New York: Free Press.

Davis, Winston. (1987). "Religion and Development: Weber and the East Asian Experience." In *Understanding Political Development*, edited by Myron Weiner and Samuel Huntington, pp. 221–280. Boston: Little, Brown.

Delury, George, ed. (1983). *World Encyclopedia of Political Systems and Parties*. New York: Facts on File.

Deutsch, Karl. (1961). "Social Mobilization and Political Development." *American Political Science Review* 55 (September): 493–511.

Donovan, John, Richard Morgan, and Christian Potholm. (1984). *People, Power and Politics*. New York: Random House.

Dunleavy, Patrick, and Christopher Husbands. (1985). *British Democracy at the Crossroads*. London: Allen & Unwin.

Duverger, Maurice. (1954). *Political Parties*. New York: Wiley.

Duverger, Maurice. (1980). "A New Political System Model: Semi-Presidential Government." *European Journal of Political Research* 8: 165–187.

Easton, David. (1953). *The Political System*. New York: Knopf.

Easton, David. (1965). *A Framework for Political Analysis*. Englewood Cliffs, NJ: Prentice-Hall.

Eckstein, Harry. (1960). *Pressure Group Politics*. London: Allen & Unwin.

Eckstein, Harry. (1966). *Division and Cohesion in Democracy: A Study of Norway*. Princeton, NJ: Princeton University Press.

Ehrman, Henry. *Politics in France*. 2d ed. Boston: Little, Brown.

Elms, Alan. (1976). *Personality and Politics*. New York: Harcourt Brace.

Engels, Friedrich. (1878/1978). "Anti-Duhring." In *The Marx-Engels Reader*. 2d ed. Edited by Robert Tucker, pp. 718–728. New York: Norton.

Erikson, Erik. (1950). *Childhood and Society*. New York: Norton.

Erikson, Erik. (1958). *Young Man Luther*. New York: Norton.

Erikson, Erik. (1969). *Gandhi's Truth*. New York: Norton.

Estes, Richard. (1988). *Trends in World Social Development*. New York: Praeger.

Eulau, Heinz. (1980). "The Columbia Studies of Personal Influence: Social Network Analysis." *Social Science History* 4 (Spring): 207–228.

Evans, Peter. (1979). *Dependent Development: The Alliance of Multinational, State and Local Capital in Brazil*. Princeton, NJ: Princeton University Press.

Evans, Peter. (1987). "Foreign Capital and the Third World State." In *Understanding Political Development,* edited by Myron Weiner and Samuel Huntington, pp. 319–352. Boston: Little, Brown.

Evans, Peter, Dietrich Rueschemeyer, and Theda Skocpol, eds. (1985). *Bringing the State Back In.* New York: Cambridge University Press.

Fagen, Richard. (1964). *Cuba: The Political Content of Adult Education.* Stanford, CA: Hoover Institute.

Feagin, Joe, and Harlan Hahn. (1973). *Ghetto Revolts.* New York: Macmillan.

Feierabend, Ivo, and Rosalind Feierabend. (1966). "Aggressive Behaviors within Polities, 1948–1962: A Cross National Study." *Journal of Conflict Resolution* 10 (September): 249–271.

Feuer, Lewis. (1969). *The Conflict of Generations.* New York: Basic Books.

Flanigan, William, and Nancy Zingale. (1983). *Political Behavior of the American Electorate.* 5th ed. Boston: Allyn & Bacon.

Foucault, Michel. (1979). *Discipline and Punish: The Birth of the Prison.* New York: Vintage.

Freud, Sigmund, and William C. Bullitt. (1967). *Thomas Woodrow Wilson: A Psychological Study.* Boston: Houghton Mifflin.

Fuller, R. Buckminster. (1970). *Operating Manual for Spaceship Earth.* New York: Pocket Books.

Garthoff, Raymond. (1985). *Detente and Confrontation: American-Soviet Relations from Nixon to Reagan.* Washington, DC: Brookings.

Gastil, Raymond, ed. (1988). *Freedom in the World. 1987–88.* New York: Freedom House.

George, Alexander, and Julliette George. (1956). *Woodrow Wilson and Colonel House.* New York: Dover.

Germani, Gino. (1978). *Authoritarianism, Fascism and National Populism.* New Brunswick, NJ: Transaction.

Gianos, Phillip. (1982). *Political Behavior.* Pacific Palisades, CA: Palisades Publishers.

Glasgow University Media Group. (1976). *Bad News.* London: Routledge & Kegan Paul.

Glasgow University Media Group. (1980). *More Bad News.* London: Routledge & Kegan Paul.

Glasgow University Media Group. (1984). *Really Bad News.* London: Routledge & Kegan Paul.

Goldman, Marshall I. (1987). *Gorbachev's Challenge: Economic Reform in the Age of High Technology.* New York: Norton.

Goldman, Minton F. (1988). *The Soviet Union and Eastern Europe.* 2d ed. Guilford, CT: Dushkin.

Gooden, Reginald. (1987). "Latin America." In *The Other World,* edited by Joseph Weatherby, pp. 105–144. New York: Macmillan.

Goodwin, Paul. (1986). *Latin America.* 2d ed. Guilford, CT: Dushkin.

Goodwin, Paul. (1988). *Latin America.* 3d ed. Guilford, CT: Dushkin.

Goodwin, Paul. (1990). *Latin America.* 4th ed. Guilford, CT: Dushkin.

Graves, Robert. (1966). "Whole Love." *Robert Graves: Poems Selected by Himself.* Middlesex, England: Penguin.

Greenstein, Fred. (1969). *Personality and Politics.* Chicago: Markham.

Gulick, Edward Vose. (1955). *Europe's Classical Balance of Power: A Case Study of the Theory and Practice of One of the Great Concepts of European Statecraft.* Ithaca, NY: Cornell University Press.

Gurr, Ted. (1970). *Why Men Rebel.* Princeton, NJ: Princeton University Press.

Habermas, Jurgen. (1975). *Legitimation Crisis.* Boston: Beacon.

Hagopian, Mark. (1984). *Regimes, Movements and Ideology*. White Plains, NY: Longman.

Hastie, Reid. (1986). "A Primer of Information-Processing Theory for the Political Scientist." In *Political Cognition*, edited by Richard R. Lau and David O. Sears. New York: Lawrence Erlbaum Associates.

Hayes, Edward. (1972). *Power Structure and Urban Policy*. New York: McGraw-Hill.

Hearst, Patricia. (1982). *Every Secret Thing*. Garden City, NY: Doubleday.

Henry, James. (1987). "Brazil Says: Nuts." *New Republic*, October 12, pp. 12–15.

Herlemann, Horst, ed. (1987). *Quality of Life in the Soviet Union*. Boulder, CO: Westview Press.

Heyne, Paul. (1973). *The Economic Way of Thinking*. Chicago: Science Research Associates.

Hobbes, Thomas. (1651/1958). *Leviathan*. Oxford, England: Clarendon.

Holsti, K. J. (1967). *International Politics*. Englewood Cliffs, NJ: Prentice-Hall.

Holsti, K. J. (1983). *International Politics: A Framework for Analysis*. Englewood Cliffs, NJ: Prentice-Hall.

Holsti, Ole, and James Rosenau. (1984). *American Leadership in World Affairs: Vietnam and the Breakdown of Consensus*. Boston: Allen & Unwin.

Horowitz, Donald. (1985). *Ethnic Groups in Conflict*. Berkeley, CA: University of California Press.

Hunter, Floyd. (1953). *Community Power Structure*. Chapel Hill, NC: University of North Carolina Press.

Huntington, Samuel. (1968). *Political Order in Changing Societies*. New Haven, CT: Yale University Press.

Huntington, Samuel. (1984). "Will More Countries Become Democratic?" *Political Science Quarterly* 99 (Summer): 193–218.

Huntington, Samuel. (1987). "The Goals of Development." In *Understanding Political Development*, edited by Myron Weiner and Samuel Huntington, pp. 3–32. Boston: Little, Brown.

Huxley, Aldous. (1932). *Brave New World*. London: Chatto & Windus.

Inglehart, Ron. (1977). *The Silent Revolution: Changing Values and Political Styles Among Western Publics*. Princeton, NJ: Princeton University Press.

Inglehart, Ron. (1989). *Culture Shift in Advanced Industrial Societies*. Princeton, NJ: Princeton University Press.

Inkeles, Alex, and David Smith. (1974). *Becoming Modern: Individual Change in Six Developing Countries*. Cambridge, MA: Harvard University Press.

Inkeles, Alex, and David Smith. (1983). *Exploring Individual Modernity*, New York: Columbia University Press.

Jennings, M. Kent, and Richard Niemi. (1981). *Generations and Politics*. Boston: Little, Brown.

Johnson, Chalmers. (1966). *Revolutionary Change*. Boston: Little, Brown.

Johnston, R. J. (1985). *The Geography of English Politics: The 1983 General Election*. London: Croom Helm.

Kaplan, Morton. (1957). *System and Process in International Politics*. New York: Wiley.

Kaslow, Amy. (1989). "Moscow Policies Burden East European Economies," *Christian Science Monitor*, December 12, pp. 1–2.

Keniston, Kenneth. (1973). *Radicals and Militants*. Lexington, MA: Heath.

Keohane, Robert, and Joseph S. Nye, eds. (1972). *Transnational Relations and World Politics*. Cambridge, MA: Harvard University Press.

Kerpelman, Larry. (1972). *Activists and Nonactivists: A Psychological Study of American College Students*. New York: Behavioral Pubs.

Kolosi, Tamas, and Edmund Wnuk-Lipinski, eds. (1983). *Equality and Inequality under Socialism: Poland and Hungary Compared.* Beverly Hills, CA: Sage.

Kranzdorf, Richard. (1987). "Africa." In *The Other World,* edited by Joseph Weatherby, pp. 145–183. New York: Macmillan.

Krasner, Stephen. (1978). *Defending the National Interest: Raw Materials Investments and U.S. Foreign Policy.* Princeton, NJ: Princeton University Press.

Kuhn, Thomas. (1970). *The Structure of Scientific Revolutions.* 2d ed. Chicago: University of Chicago Press.

Larsen, Stein, Bernt Hagtvet, and Jan-Peter Mykelbust, eds. (1976). *Who Were the Fascists? Social Roots of European Fascism.* Oslo: Universitetsforglaget.

Lasswell, Harold. (1936). *Politics: Who Gets What, When and How?* New York: McGraw-Hill.

Lasswell, Harold. (1960). *Psychopathology and Politics.* New York: Viking.

Latham, Earl. (1952). *The Group Basis of Politics.* Ithaca, NY: Cornell University Press.

Lenski, Gerhard. (1966). *Power and Privilege: A Theory of Social Stratification.* New York: McGraw-Hill.

Lerner, Daniel. (1958). *The Passing of Traditional Society: Modernizing the Middle East.* Glencoe, IL: Free Press.

Lijphart, Arend. (1978). *Democracy in Plural Societies.* New Haven, CT: Yale University Press.

Lindblom, Charles E. (1977). *Politics and Markets: The World's Political-Economic Systems.* New York: Basic Books.

Lineberry, Robert, George Edwards, and Martin Wattenberg. (forthcoming). *Government in America,* 5th ed. New York: Harper & Row.

Linz, Juan. (1978). *The Breakdown of Democratic Regimes: Crisis, Breakdown and Reequilibration.* Baltimore: Johns Hopkins Press.

Linz, Juan, and Alfred Stepan. (1978). *The Breakdown of Democratic Regimes.* Baltimore: Johns Hopkins Press.

Loewenberg, Gerhard, ed. (1971). *Modern Parliaments: Change or Decline?* Chicago: Aldine-Atherton.

Long, Dianne. (1987). "The Other World." In *The Other World,* edited by Joseph Weatherby, pp. 1–14. New York: Macmillan.

Lukes, Steven. (1974). *Power: A Radical View.* London: Macmillan.

Maccoby, Michael. (1967). "Mexico." In "National Character in the Perspective of the Social Sciences," *Annals of the American Academy of Political and Social Sciences,* March, pp. 64–73.

Macridis, Roy. (1986). *Modern Political Regimes.* Boston: Little, Brown.

Macridis, Roy. (1987). *Contemporary Political Ideologies.* 3d ed. Boston: Little, Brown.

Marx, Karl. (1867/1981). *Capital.* Translated by David Fernbach. New York: Vintage.

Marx, Karl, and Frederich Engels. (1848/1978). "The Communist Manifesto." In *The Marx-Engels Reader.* 2d ed. Edited by Robert Tucker, pp. 482–500. New York: Norton.

Maslow, Abraham. (1954). *Motivation and Personality.* New York: Harper & Row.

Maslow, Abraham. (1968). *Toward a Psychology of Being.* Princeton, NJ: Van Nostrand.

Mazlish, Bruce. (1973). *In Search of Nixon.* Baltimore: Penguin.

McClelland, David. (1961). *The Achieving Society.* Princeton, NJ: Van Nostrand.

McClosky, Herbert, and Dennis Chong. (1985). "Similarities and Differences between Left-Wing and Right-Wing Radicals." *British Journal of Political Science* 16:216–231.

McLellan, David S. (1987). "The International System: Unequal and Revolutionary." In

The Theory and Practice of International Relations, edited by William Olson, pp. 108–114. Englewood Cliffs, NJ: Prentice-Hall.

Mewes, Horst. (1987). "The Green Party Comes of Age." In *Comparative Politics 87/88,* edited by Christian Soe, pp. 110–118. Guilford, CT: Dushkin.

Middleton, Russell, and Snell Putney. (1963). "Student Rebellion Against Parental Beliefs." *Social Forces* 41 (4): 377–383.

Migdal, Joel. (1974). *Peasants, Politics and Revolution: Pressures toward Political and Social Change in the Third World.* Princeton, NJ: Princeton University Press.

Migdal, Joel. (1987). "Strong States, Weak States: Power and Accommodation." In *Understanding Political Development,* edited by Myron Weiner and Samuel Huntington, pp. 391–434. Boston: Little, Brown.

Milbrath, Lester. (1965). *Political Participation.* Chicago: Rand McNally.

Milbrath, Lester, and M. L. Goel. (1977). *Political Participation.* 2d ed. Chicago: Rand McNally.

Miliband, Ralph. (1969). *The State in Capitalist Society.* New York: Basic Books.

Mills, C. Wright. (1956). *The Power Elite.* New York: Oxford University Press.

Moore, Barrington. (1966). *The Social Origins of Dictatorship and Democracy.* Cambridge, MA: Harvard University Press.

Morawetz, David. (1977). *Twenty-five Years of Economic Development, 1950–75.* Washington, DC: World Bank.

Morgenthau, Hans. (1948). *Politics among Nations: The Struggle for Power and Peace.* New York: Knopf.

Morishima, Michio. (1982). *Why Has Japan "Succeeded"? Western Technology and Japanese Ethos.* Cambridge: Cambridge University Press.

Morris, Morris D. (1979). *Measuring the Conditions of the World's Poor.* New York: Pergamon.

Mosca, Gaetano. (1896/1939). *The Ruling Class.* Translated by Hannah Kahn. New York: McGraw-Hill.

Mouritzen, Poul Erik, and Kurt Nielsen. (1988). *Handbook of Comparative Urban Fiscal Data.* Odense, Denmark: Danish Data Archives.

Mueller, Carol, ed. (1986). *The Politics of the Gender Gap.* Beverly Hills, CA: Sage.

Musgrave, Richard. (1959). *The Theory of Public Finance.* New York: McGraw-Hill.

Nagel, Jack. (1975). *The Descriptive Analysis of Power.* New Haven, CT: Yale University Press.

Naylor, Thomas. (1988). *The Gorbachev Strategy.* Lexington, MA: Heath.

Nelson, Daniel, ed. (1984). *Soviet Allies: The Warsaw Pact and the Issue of Reliability.* Boulder, CO: Westview.

Nelson, Joan. (1987). "Political Participation." In *Understanding Political Development,* edited by Myron Weiner and Samuel Huntington, pp. 103–159. Boston: Little, Brown.

Nie, Norman, and Kristi Anderson. (1974). "Mass Belief Systems Revisited: Political Change and Attribute Structure." *Journal of Politics* 36: 540–587.

Niemi, Richard. (1974). *How Family Members Perceive Each Other.* New Haven, CT: Yale University Press.

Nixon, Richard M. (1982). *Leaders.* New York: Warner Books.

Nordlinger, Eric. (1987). "Taking the State Seriously." In *Understanding Political Development,* edited by Myron Weiner and Samuel Huntington, pp. 353–390. Boston: Little, Brown.

Norton, Philip. (1991). *The British Polity.* White Plains, NY: Longman.

O'Connor, James. (1972). *The Fiscal Crisis of the State.* New York: St. Martin's Press.

O'Connor, Robert. (1978). "Political Activism and Moral Reasoning: Political and Apolitical Students in Great Britain and France." *British Journal of Political Science* 4: 53–78.

O'Donnell, Guillermo. (1973). *Modernization and Bureaucratic Authoritarianism: Studies in South American Politics.* Berkeley, CA: Institute of International Studies.

Organski, A. F. K., and Jacek Kugler. (1980). *The War Ledger.* Chicago: University of Chicago Press.

Orwell, George. (1945/1964). *Animal Farm.* Middlesex, England: Penguin.

Orwell, George. 1949/1967). *1984.* Middlesex, England: Penguin.

Paige, Jeffery. (1975). *Agrarian Revolution: Social Movements and Export Agriculture in the Underdeveloped World.* New York: Free Press.

Parenti, Michael. (1988). *Democracy for the Few.* 5th ed. Boston: St. Martins.

Pateman, Carole. (1980). "The Civic Culture: A Philosophic Critique." In *The Civic Culture Revisited,* edited by Gabriel Almond and Sidney Verba, pp. 57–102. Boston: Little, Brown.

Pike, F. B., and T. Stritch, eds. (1974). *The New Corporatism.* South Bend, IN: University of Notre Dame Press.

Plano, Jack, Robert Riggs, and Helenan Robin. (1982). *The Dictionary of Political Analysis.* 2d ed. Santa Barbara, CA: ABC Clio.

Popper, Karl. (1963). *The Open Society and Its Enemies.* Vol. 2. New York: Harper & Row.

Pye, Lucian. (1962). *Politics, Personality and Nation-Building.* New Haven, CT: Yale University Press.

Pye, Lucian. (1990) "Political Science and the Crisis of Authoritarianism," *American Political Science Review* 84(1):3–19.

Rae, Douglas. (1971). *The Political Consequences of Electoral Laws.* Rev. ed. New Haven, CT: Yale University Press.

Ranney, Austin. (1982). *Governing: An Introduction to Political Science.* New York: Holt, Rinehart & Winston.

Reppy, Susan. (1984). "The Automobile Air Bag." In *Controversy,* 2d ed., edited by Dorothy Nelkin, pp. 161–174. Beverly Hills, CA: Sage.

Riker, William. (1962). *The Theory of Political Coalitions.* New Haven, CT: Yale University Press.

Riker, William. (1982). "The Two Party System and Duverger's Law." *American Political Science Review,* 76(4), 753–766.

Riker, William, and Peter Ordeshook. (1973). *An Introduction to Positive Political Theory.* Englewood Cliffs, NY: Prentice Hall.

Rokeach, Milton. (1960). *The Open and Closed Mind.* New York: Basic Books.

Rosenau, James, and Ole Holsti. (1986). "Consensus Lost, Consensus Regained?" *International Studies Quarterly,* pp. 375–409.

Rosenberg, Shawn. (1988). *Reason, Ideology and Politics,* Cambridge: Polity Press.

Rosenblum, Mort, and Doug Williamson. (1987). *Squandering Eden: Africa at the Edge.* San Diego, CA: Harcourt, Brace, Jovanovich.

Ruffin, Roy, and Paul Gregory. (1986). *Principles of Economics.* 2d ed. Glenview, IL: Scott, Foresman.

Rummel, R. J. (1986). "War Isn't This Century's Biggest Killer." *Wall Street Journal,* July 7.

Russett, Bruce. (1965). *Trends in World Politics.* New York: Macmillan.

Russett, Bruce. (1983). "International Interactions and Processes: The Internal versus External Debate Revisited." In *Political Science: The State of the Discipline,* edited by Ada Finifter, pp. 541–568. Washington, DC: American Political Science Association.

Russett, Bruce, and Harvey Starr. (1989). *World Politics: The Menu for Choice.* 3d ed. New York: W. H. Freeman.

Rustow, Dankwart. (1967). *A World of Nations: Problems of Political Modernization.* Washington, DC: Brookings.

Saikowski, Charlotte. (1988). "Strengthening the Social Fabric." *Christian Science Monitor,* November 15, pp. 16–17.

Sampson, Anthony. (1978). "Want to Start a War?" *Esquire,* March 1, pp. 58–69.

Sampson, Edward, ed. (1967). "Stirrings Out of Apathy." *Journal of Social Issues* 23 (3).

Schattschneider, E. E. (1960). *The Semisovereign People.* New York: Holt, Rinehart & Winston.

Schelling, Thomas. (1960). *The Strategy of Conflict.* Cambridge, MA: Harvard University Press.

Schmitter, Phillipe, and Gerhard Lembruch, eds. (1979). *Trends toward Corporatist Intermediation.* Beverly Hills, CA: Sage.

Schroeder, Gertrude. (1987). "Soviet Living Standards in Comparative Perspective." In *Quality of Life in the Soviet Union,* edited by Horst Herlemann, pp. 13–30. Boulder, CO: Westview Press.

Schumacher, E. E. (1973). *Small Is Beautiful.* New York: Harper & Row.

Schumpeter, Joseph. (1950). *Capitalism, Socialism and Democracy.* 3d ed. New York: Harper & Row.

Sears, David, and John McConahey. (1973). *The Politics of Violence.* Boston: Houghton Mifflin.

Silone, Ignazio. (1937). *Bread and Wine.* Trans. by Gwenda David. New York: Harper & Row.

Silver, Brian. (1985). "Language Policy and Practice in the Soviet Union." *Social Education,* February.

Sivard, Ruth Leger. (1976). *World Military and Social Expenditures 1976.* Leesburg, VA: WMSE Publications.

Sivard, Ruth Leger (1982). *World Military and Social Expenditures 1982.* Leesburg, VA: World Priorities.

Skinner. B. F. (1948). *Walden Two.* New York: Macmillan.

Skocpol, Theda. (1979). *States and Social Revolutions: A Comparative Analysis of France, Russia and China,* New York: Cambridge University Press.

Slann, Martin. (1984). *Eight Nations: An Introduction to Comparative Politics.* New York: Franklin Watts.

Small, Melvin, and J. David Singer. (1982). *Resort to Arms: International and Civil Wars, 1816–1980.* Beverly Hills, CA: Sage.

Smith, M. Brewster, Norma Haan, and Jeanne Block. (1970). "Social-Psychological Aspects of Student Activism." *Youth and Society* 1: 260–288.

Sniderman, Paul. (1975). *Personality and Democratic Politics.* Berkeley, CA: University of California Press.

Solzenitzyn, Alexander. (1963). *One Day in the Life of Ivan Denisovitch.* New York: Bantam.

Solzenitzyn, Alexander. (1973). *The Gulag Archipelago.* New York: Harper & Row.

Sophocles. (1967). *Antigone.* Trans. by E. F. Watling. Middlesex, England: Penguin.

Spencer, William. (1988). *The Middle East.* 2d ed. Guilford, CT: Dushkin.

Strauss, Leo. (1959). *What is Political Philosophy?* New York: Free Press.

Strom, Kaare. (1989). *Minority Government and Majority Rule*. New York: Cambridge University Press.

Sullivan, Jo, and Jane Martin. (1987). *Africa*. 2d ed. Guilford, CT: Dushkin.

Swaminanthan, Monkombu. (1987). "The Miracle of Rice." In *Global Issues 87/88,* edited by Robert Jackson, pp. 100–104. Guilford, CT: Dushkin.

Sylvan, David, Duncan Snidel, Bruce Russett, Steven Jackson, and Raymond Duval. (1983). "The Peripheral Economies: Penetration and Economic Distortion." In *Contending Approaches to World System Analysis,* edited by William Thompson. Beverly Hills, CA: Sage.

Taagepera, Rein, and Matthew S. Shugart. (1989). *Seats and Votes*. New Haven, CT: Yale University Press.

Taylor, Charles, and Michael Hudson. (1977). *World Handbook of Political and Social Indicators*. 3rd ed. New Haven, CT: Yale University Press.

Thompson, Leonard. (1966). *Politics in the Republic of South Africa*. Boston: Little, Brown.

Thoreau, Henry David. (1849/1966). *Walden and Other Writings,* edited by J. W. Krutch. New York: Bantam Books.

Tocqueville, Alexis de. (1835/1945). *Democracy in America*. New York: Knopf.

Todaro, Michael. (1989). *Economic Development in the Third World*. 4th ed. White Plains, NY: Longman.

Toma, Peter. (1988). *Socialist Authority: The Hungarian Experience*. New York: Praeger.

Treml, Vladimir. (1987). "Alcohol Abuse and the Quality of Life in the Soviet Union." In *Quality of Life in the Soviet Union,* edited by Horst Herlemann, pp. 151–162. Boulder, CO: Westview Press.

Truman, David. (1951). *The Governmental Process*. New York: Knopf.

U.S. Arms Control and Disarmament Agency. (1984). *World Military Expenditures and Arms Transfers 1972–1982*. Washington, DC: U.S. Government Printing Office.

U.S.S.R. *Facts and Figures Annual 13*. (1989). Edited by Allan Pollard. Gulf Breeze, FL: Academic International Press.

Verba, Sidney. (1980). "On Revisiting The Civic Culture." In *The Civic Culture Revisited,* edited by Gabriel Almond and Sidney Verba, pp. 394–410. Boston: Little, Brown.

Verba, Sidney, and Norman Nie. (1972). *Participation in America*. New York: Harper & Row.

Verba, Sidney, and Norman Nie. (1975). "Political Participation." In *Handbook of Political Science,* Vol. 4. edited by Fred Greenstein and Nelson Polsby. Reading, MA: Addison–Wesley.

Verba, Sidney, Norman Nie, and Jae-on Kim. (1971). *The Modes of Democratic Participation: A Cross-National Comparison*. Beverly Hills, CA: Sage.

Verba, Sidney, Norman Nie, and Jae-on Kim. (1978). *Participation and Political Equality: A Seven-Nation Comparison*. London: Cambridge University Press.

von der Mehden, Fred. (1973). *Comparative Political Violence*. Englewood Cliffs, NJ: Prentice-Hall.

Walker, Nancy. (1988). "What We Know about Women Voters in Britain, France and West Germany." *Public Opinion,* May–June, pp. 49–55.

Wallerstein, Immanuel. (1974). *The Modern World System*. New York: Academic Press.

Wallerstein, Immanuel. (1980). *The World System II*. New York: Academic Press.

Walsh, Charles. (1987). "The Other World's View of the Cold War." In *The Other World,* edited by Joseph Weatherby, pp. 59–104. New York: Macmillan.

Weatherby, Joseph. (1987). "The Old and the New: Colonialism, Neocolonialism and Nationalism.'' In *The Other World,* edited by Joseph Weatherby, pp. 15–33. New York: Macmillan.

Weber, Max. (1951). *The Religion of China: Confucianism and Taoism.* Edited by Hans H. Gerth. New York: Free Press

Weber, Max. (1958a). *From Max Weber: Essays in Sociology,* edited by H. H. Gerth and C. Wright Mills. New York: Oxford University Press.

Weber, Max. (1958b). *The Religion of India: The Sociology of Hinduism and Buddhism.* Translated by Hans Gerth and Don Martindale. New York: Free Press.

Wilber, Charles, ed. (1979). *The political Economy of Development and Underdevelopment.* 2d ed. New York: Random House.

Wilson, Edward O. (1978). *On Human Nature.* Cambridge, MA: Harvard University Press.

Wilson, William Julius. (1987). *The Truly Disadvantaged.* Chicago: University of Chicago Press.

Wolf, Edward. (1985). ''State of the Earth 1985.'' *Natural History* 94 (April): 51–88.

Wolf, Eric. (1969). *Peasant Wars of the Twentieth Century.* New York: Harper & Row.

Wolfenstein, E. Victor. (1967). *The Revolutionary Personality: Lenin, Trotsky, Gandhi.* Princeton, NJ: Princeton University Press.

Wolin, Sheldon. (1960). *Politics and Vision.* Boston: Little, Brown.

Wood, James L. (1974). *The Source of American Student Activism.* Lexington, MA: Heath.

World Bank. (1983). *World Tables.* Vols. 1 and 2. 3d ed. Oxford: Oxford University Press.

World Bank. (1989). *World Development Report 1989.* New York: Oxford University Press.

Zeigler, Harmon. (1990). *The Political Community.* White Plains, NY: Longman.

Index